THE BEETHOVEN ENCYCLOPEDIA

THE BEETHOVEN ENCYCLOPEDIA

by

PAUL NETTL

Professor of Musicology at Indiana University

A CITADEL PRESS BOOK
Published by Carol Publishing Group

WILMETTE PUBLIC LIBRARY

First Carol Publishing Group edition 1994

Copyright © 1956, 1994 by Philosophical Library, Inc.

A Citadel Press Book
Published by Carol Publishing Group
Citadel Press is a registered trademark of Carol Communications, Inc.
Editorial Offices: 600 Madison Avenue, New York, N.Y. 10022
Sales and Distribution Offices: 120 Enterprise Avenue, Secaucus, N.J. 07094
In Canada: Canadian Manda Group, P.O. Box 920, Station U, Toronto, Ontario M8Z 5P9
Queries regarding rights and permissions should be addressed to Carol Publishing Group, 600 Madison Avenue, New York, N.Y. 10022

Carol Publishing books are available at special discounts for bulk purchases, sales promotions, fund-raising, or educational purposes. Special editions can be created to specifications. For details, contact Special Sales Department, Carol Publishing Group, 120 Enterprise Avenue, Secaucus, N.J. 07094

Manufactured in the United States of America
10 9 8 7 6 5 4 3 2 1

Library of Congress Cataloging-in Publication Data

Nettl, Paul, 1889-1972.
The Beethoven encyclopedia / by Paul Nettl
p. cm.
"A Citadel Press book."
ISBN 0-8065-1539-2
1. Beethoven, Ludwig van, 1770-1827—Encyclopedias. I. Title.
ML410.B42N4 1994
780'.92—dc20
[B] 94-17636
CIP
MN

780.92
B393n

To my wife

MARGARET VON GUTFELD-NETTL

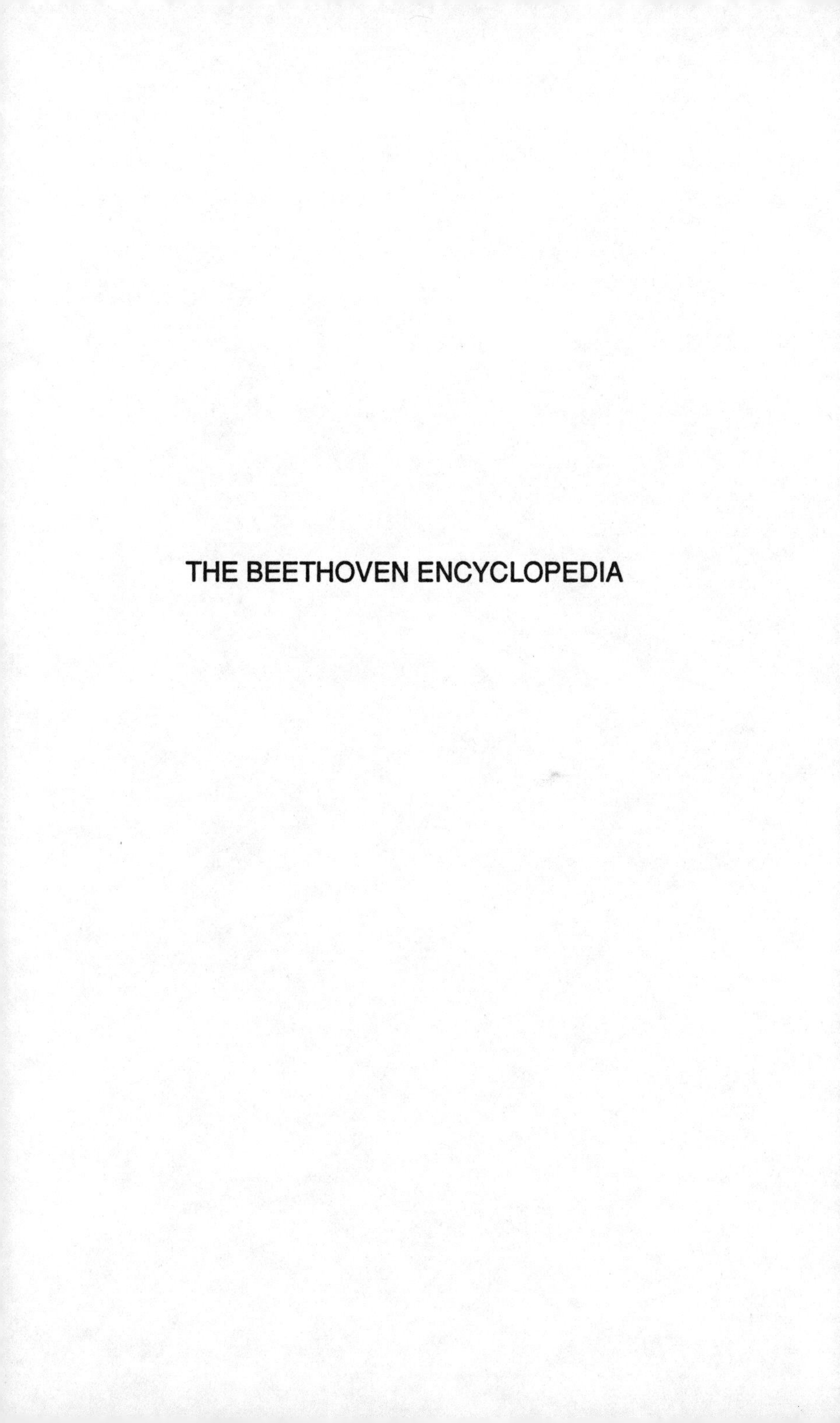

THE BEETHOVEN ENCYCLOPEDIA

A

A Schüsserl und a Reindl is all mei Kuch'lgeschirr

Austrian folksong, mentioned by Beethoven in a letter to Steiner, December 1816. Beethoven signed it "Generalissimus" and asked the publisher to send him the song. He used this song as the theme for variations on an "Air Autrichien" Op. 105: "Six Thèmes variés bien faciles à éxécuter pour le Piano-Forte seul ou avec accompagnement d'une Flûte ou d'un Violon (ad libitum) par Louis van Beethoven. Oeuvre 105." (cf. Th.-R. III, p. 628, and Tappert: *Wandernde Melodien,* p. 12).

Abendlied (Unter'm gestirnten Himmel)

Song by Beethoven on a text by H. Goeble, composed March 4, 1820, and first published in *Wiener Zeitschrift für Kunst* in the issue of March 28. It was dedicated to Dr. Anton Braunhofer. About later editions of the song see Nottebohm: *Thematisches Verzeichnis.* On April 19, 1820, Fanny del Rio noted in her diary: "Beethoven presented me with a gift of a new beautiful song, entitled 'Abendlied.' I enjoyed it tremendously." Nothing is known about the poet Heinrich Goeble. Wurzbach merely lists Karl Peter Goebel (sic), a painter who died 1823 in Vienna. The song is one of Beethoven's most outstanding compositions in this field. It is composed in highly elevated style and reminds one of his composition "Die Ehre Gottes in der Natur" (Gellert), and in many ways he anticipates Schumann's "Sonntag am Rhein" and "Mondnacht." (cf. Th.-R. IV, p. 239, and Friedländer: "Deutsche Dichtung in Beethovens Musik," JMP. 1912).

Adamberger, Antonie

b. Vienna 1790, d. 1867(?). According to Wurzbach, she was the daughter of the tenor Valentin Adamberger, whom the biographer called erroneously J. Adamberger. According to other sources the famous actress and singer was the daughter of Heinrich Adamberger. Antonie had inherited her dramatic talent from her mother, the famous actress Maria Anna Jacquet, while Collin, her teacher, introduced her to the German literature. In 1802 and 1804 she made a sensation in the Royal Theater in Schönbrunn. When Theodor Körner came to Vienna, he fell in love with her, and they became engaged; numerous poems of the poet dedicated to "Toni" prove his deep devotion to the lovely and gifted artist, in whom even Napoleon became interested in 1809.

In 1817 she married J. C. von Arneth, art historian. It was Toni Adamberger who first performed Beethoven's "Klärchen-Lieder." On May 11, 1813 she participated in a Beethoven concert. (cf. Alfred von Arneth: *Aus meinem Leben;* also von Jaden: *Theodor Körner und seine Braut,* and Entry: Körner.) There is a considerable confusion in the literature about names and dates referring to this artist.

Adelaïde

Famous song by Beethoven, composed during his studies with Albrechtsberger (1795-96). Many sketches of the song are preserved, some used by Nottebohm: *Beethoveniana* II. The title of the oldest edition, published February 1797, reads as follows: "Adelaïde von. Matthisson. Eine Kantate für eine Singstimme mit Begleitung des Clavier. In Musik gesetzt und dem Verfasser gewidmet von Ludwig van Beethoven. In Wien bey Artaria et Comp." L. A. Frankl, in his *Sonntagsblätter* 1845 told the story that when the singer Barth (possibly Jos. Joh. August, not Gustav, as called by Frankl) paid a visit to Beethoven, he found the Master about to burn the manuscript of the song. Barth tried the song from the manuscript and persuaded the Master to save the work. Frankl's story appears to be fictitious or at least incorrect, for Beethoven would hardly have burned a finished work. Matthisson's poem, written in 1788, was first published in 1789 in the *Vossische Musenalmanach.* It is based on a chanson by Jean François Marmontel (1723-1772); the first stanza runs as follows:

Adelaïde
Semble faite exprès pour charmer;
Et mieux que le galant Ovide,
Ses yieux enseignent l'art d'aimer
Ade'laï'de.

(For other compositions of the poem, see Entry: Matthisson).

It is interesting to compare Beethoven's and Schubert's setting of this poem with that of Philip Emanuel Pilz who, in his collection "Acht gefühlvolle Lieder," Leipzig 1794, presented a strophic composition of the poem, the banality of which can hardly be surpassed. On the other hand Schubert's setting, composed in 1814, approaches Matthisson's poem in a more romantic way. Beethoven's "Adelaïde," similar to Mozart's "Veilchen," shows the style of an instrumental composer. It is neither a cantata nor an aria, but a vocal composition sui generis. The song was frequently the subject of stories and poems, as in Landau's *Poetisches Beethovenalbum* (Ortlepp); also Saphir and Victor Hansgirg wrote poems with the name "Adelaïde." (cf. Friedländer: *Das deutsche Lied des 18. Jahrhunderts* II, p. 403; Böttcher: *Beethoven als Liederkomponist;* Th.-R. II, p. 112 and III, p. 488.)

"Ah, perfido"

Famous concert aria by Beethoven, composed in Prague 1796. The title page of a contemporary copy reads as follows: "Une grande Scène mise en musique par L. v. Beethoven à Prague 1796." One may assume that this aria was composed for Mme. Duschek, the famous Prague singer and friend of Mozart's, who first sang the aria November 21, 1796 in a concert in Leipzig; however the song was dedicated to the Countess Clari. The first page of the above-mentioned manuscript bears the following inscription:

"Recitativo e Aria composta e dedicata alla Signora Contessa Di Clari Da L. v. Beethoven." The work was published in 1805 by Hoffmeister and Kühnel (Bureau de Musique, Leipzig) as Op. 65. Countess Clari was a vocal amateur who married Count Christian Clam-Gallas in 1797. As a "picanterie" it might be mentioned that Count Clam-Gallas had previously been Mme. Duschek's lover and had given her the famous estate Bertramka, where Mozart's *Don Giovanni* was completed. We may visualize Mme. Duschek's emotions when she sang the aria, dedicated later to her rival. The aria was performed December 22, 1808, by Mme. Milder; however, Hauptmann, Milder's fiancé, had an argument with Beethoven and Hauptmann forbade Milder to sing the aria. The Master asked Mme. Campi to substitute, but she refused, being jealous of Milder, who had been asked first. With Schuppanzigh's assistance the singer Josephine Schulz-Killitschgy was hired, but at the concert, she was overcome by a terrific stage-fright, almost suffered a heart-attack, and the aria was a complete failure. The aria may be considered one of the most outstanding concert arias of the vocal repertory; it is full of verve, dramatic power and melodic beauty. Mozart's "Bella mia fiamma," also dedicated to Mme. Duschek, and arias by Salieri may have been its model. (cf. Th. -R. III, p. 83, Th. -R. II, p. 11, Nettl: *Mozart in Böhmen,* and Entry: Duschek.)

Akademie (Academy)

The name derives from Plato's favorite spot, the grove dedicated to the hero Akademos. Later the name was given to the scholarly group of Plato and his disciples. The term was adopted by the Renaissance to designate scholarly and artistic unions. In classical times "Akademie" did not mean an institution of higher musical culture (Academy of ancient music in London 1710-1792; "Académie de Musique" in Paris), but also a concert of greater significance. Compared with our concerts, an "Akademie" in Beethoven's time would last sometimes three or more hours and consist of a great variety of musical selections. Beethoven often presented academies consisting wholly of his own works. The most famous of these took place May 7, 1824 in the Kärntnerthor Theater with the first performance of the Ninth Symphony and excerpts of his *Missa Solemnis.* At that time Beethoven was almost deaf and directed the performance assisted by Michael Umlauf. A storm of applause broke loose, but Beethoven was not able to hear it. Only after Caroline Unger, the soloist, had turned the Master towards the enthusiastic public did he become aware of the tremendous success. Another academy took place December 22, 1808, in the Theater an der Wien, when the Fifth and Sixth Symphonies and the *Chor-Phantasie* were performed. This was Beethoven's last appearance as a pianist.

Albrechtsberger, Johann Georg

b. Klosterneuburg 1736, d. Vienna 1809. Famous theory teacher and composer. He was Beethoven's teacher in theory in 1794 and 1795, after Joseph Haydn had left Vienna for London. The friendly relations between Albrechtsberger and Beethoven continued as may be seen in three letters of Albrechtsberger's to the Master, written in 1796 and 1797. These letters were in the possession of Guido Adler. Dolezalek reported a derogatory remark of Albrechtsberger about Beethoven, which should not be taken too seriously. Albrechtsberger's instruction included the following subjects: strict and free counterpoint, imitation, fugue, fugued chorale, three categories of double counterpoint, double fugue, threefold counterpoint and fugue and finally, canon. As a textbook Albrechtsberger's *Anweisung zur Composition* in the edition of 1790 was mainly used. Nottebohm, who discussed Beethoven's course with Albrechtsberger thoroughly, called Albrechtsberger's way of teaching conscientious and accurate. (cf. D.T.O. XVI, Instrumental Works of Albrechtsberger, ed. by Oskar Kapp, Andreas Weissenbäck: *J. G. A. als Kirchenkomponist,* Wien 1927 and Nottebohm: *Beethoven Studien,* Leipzig 1873.)

Alexander I

Russian Emperor; b. 1777, d. 1825. He attended the Vienna Congress in which he played an important part. Razumovsky introduced Beethoven to the Emperor at the palace of Archduke Rudolph. In 1803 Beethoven dedicated to Alexander his three Violin Sonatas Op. 30, and when Prof. Wilhelm Würfel met the Czar in Warsaw (1825) they mentioned these works. A copy of Beethoven's *Missa Solemnis* was purchased by Alexander. (Cf. Entry: Razumovsky, Th.-R. V., p. 241.)

Alexiewna, Elisabeth

(Louise-Marie of Baden) Russian Empress and wife of Czar Alexander I. With her husband she attended the Vienna Congress (1814) where Beethoven was also introduced to her by Archduke Rudolph. He dedicated the Polonaise in C major, Op. 89 to her, which was published by Mechetti in March 1815. The piano score of the Seventh Symphony was also dedicated to the Empress, who rewarded the Master several times with considerable donations. (Cf. Entry: Alexander I, Kalischer: *Beethovens Frauenkreis* II, Th.-R. III, p. 465 ff.)

Amenda, Karl

b. Lippaiken, Courland, 1771, d. 1836. Theologian, close friend of Beethoven. He came to Vienna in 1798 as a reader to Prinz Lobkowitz. As a violinist he became acquainted with Beethoven and was one of the first to know about the Master's deafness. In 1799 Amenda returned to his native Courland, where he became a private teacher; in 1802, he became a preacher in Talsen, in 1820 provost, and in 1830 "Konsistorialrat." Amenda, who had studied theology in Jena, had the reputation of being an amiable and kindhearted man. On June 25, 1799, Beethoven sent him as a gift the first version of his F major Quartet, Op. 18 No. 1. The letter attached reads as follows: "Dear Amenda, accept this quartet as a small token of our friendship. Whenever you play it, remember the days we spent together and our mutual friendly feelings. . . ." Later Beethoven asked Amenda to keep the quartet for himself and not to show it to anybody, because he had made considerable changes. Amenda fulfilled the composer's wish. In 1894 the owner of the manuscript, Frau Pastor Anna Kawall, née Amenda, in Riga gave permission to publish part of the first movement (Vol. X of *Die Musik*). It was Amenda who told the story that Bee-

thoven described in the slow movement of this quartet the farewell of two lovers, referring to Shakespeare's *Romeo and Juliet.*
(Cf. Wedig: Beethovens Streichquartett Op. 18 Nr. 1 und seine erste Fassung, publ. by Beethoven Haus, Bonn 1922, Th.-R. II).

Andante favori

Piano composition in F major, Breitkopf and Härtel, Series 18, No. 10. According to Ries the piece originally belonged to Piano Sonata Op. 53 (Waldstein), but his friends persuaded Beethoven to remove the *andante* from the sonata, because of its length. Instead the Master added the introduction to the finale of the sonata. The *andante* appeared in fall 1805 in "Bureau des Arts et d'Industrie." An arrangement for string quartet was published by Hoffmeister. Riemann in his analysis of the Beethoven sonatas suggests that it might be possible to re-establish the original form of the sonata plus the introduction; however, the length of the *andante* and its *rondo* form (the finale is also a *rondo)* would be an obstacle.

An die ferne Geliebte

See Entries: Lieder; Jeitteles.

An die Hoffnung

See Entries: Lieder; Tiedge.

An Laura

Early song, text by Matthisson, composed 1790. The conception of the recitation is identical with the Bagatelle W o O. 112 No. 12. (Cf. Kinsky, *Allgem. Musikzeitung* 1913 and Entry: Bagatelles.)

An Minna

See Entry: Lieder.

Anschütz, Heinrich

b. Luckau 1785, d. Vienna 1865. Famous tragedian who came to Vienna in 1821 and met Beethoven there a year later. One day when Anschütz strolled in the neighborhood of Döbling, he met the Master, who was busily composing. According to Anschütz's memoirs (Heinrich Anschütz: *Erinnerungen aus dessen Leben und Wirken,* Leipzig Reclam 1866), he addressed Beethoven, who was impressed by the actor's clear articulation. Both met frequently after that and often discussed Beethoven's Macbeth project. It was Anschütz who gave the funeral oration, written by Grillparzer, at the Master's burial in front of the gate of the Währing Cemetery (Cf. Wurzbach, Grillparzer).

Appearance and Dress

The earliest evidence of Beethoven's appearance comes at about the age of 16 in the Fischer Manuscript. A silhouette of the same period reveals a rather long profile and a short neck; the prominent chin already exhibits the powerful appearance it would have in later life. The nose is round, the slightly receding forehead topped by black, curly hair. The complexion was dark and already marred by smallpox scars which testify to a grave illness. His was a short, stocky body with broad shoulders. By the time of his removal to Vienna Beethoven had become more slender, but was still rather homely with slightly protruding teeth that forced out his lips.

Beginning in 1800 the numerous portraits provide us with more evidence as to Beethoven's appearance. At this time his most prominent features were the sense of muscular power reflected in his

APPEARANCE

stocky body with very short legs, and the thick, black hair which seemed to defy the ministrations of comb or brush. The short fingers, which were so sensitive to the keyboard, were matched by broad, red hands. The square face was still dark but had taken on a heightened color and above the dark bushy eyebrows rose a forehead, broad and lofty, balanced by very powerful jaws. The nose was broad, the mouth strong and sensitive with a slightly protruding lower lip and a firm, straight upper lip; the cleft in his chin became more prominent as he grew older. Many writers have commented on the small, piercing eyes, possibly a result of his near-sightedness, for he wore glasses until about 1817.

By 1820 Beethoven's age was beginning to make itself manifest in the lines of his face which reflected the great suffering and mental anguish. About this time Sir John Russell reports the turbulent energy in his eyes and the mass of uncombed hair. His eyes retained their piercing look even when approaching death, but the hair had become almost completely gray.

In matters of dress he was as full of inconsistencies as in other factors of his personal life. Even as a child he was frequently scolded for the disarray and soiled appearance of his clothing. Undoubtedly his association with the von Breuning family exerted a good influence on him, for just after the move to Vienna there are entries in the diary which indicate that Beethoven made an effort to appear well-dressed; he bought a new coat, wig, shoes and black silk stockings. In a letter to Eleanor von Breuning in 1793 he asked that she send him a knitted waistcoat.

Contemporary reports give conflicting pictures of the Master, although we can assume that when he was working on a composition he was totally oblivious to the outer world and at such times was untidy in appearance. However, at other times he was undoubtedly more careful of his condition.

Grillparzer remarks on his elegance in 1804 or 1805 and yet two years later he found Beethoven untidy and frequently dirty. As he grew older Beethoven became more unconscious of his dress, although in 1816 Dr. Karl Von Bursy visited him and found him in gala dress.

Louis Schlösser met Beethoven during the period of the composition of the Ninth Symphony and was astonished to find the composer so elegantly dressed in a blue tailcoat with yellow buttons, impeccably white trousers and waistcoat and with a new beaver hat—as usual—worn on the back of his head. This seems to be the ensemble which the painter Klöber describes in 1816 although Klöber found his clothing *negligée.*

Nevertheless, at the first meeting with Weber in 1823 Beethoven received the composer of *Der Freischütz* in a shabby jacket with torn sleeves, and during the time he was working on the *Missa Solemnis* he was picked up and jailed as a beggar, because "Beethoven doesn't look like this."

Possibly the best description is the one based on Gerhard von Breuning's account from the last years of Beethoven's life. At this time he wore white stockings, light trousers and waistcoat, a white neckcloth and flowing, blue frockcoat, the pockets of which were over-laden with notebooks, ear trumpets, pencils, etc. The frockcoat was frequently covered with a green or blue walking coat. He wore a low top hat with a curling brim, which was always crammed on the back of his head. Lyser's sketch gives a very good representation of his hat and greatcoat. Gerhard von Breuning further mentions the frequent unbrushed appearance of his clothing, although his linen was always white and clean. This latter is in direct contradiction to Ludwig Cramolini's account of his mother upbraiding Beethoven for having received a Count Montecuccoli in dirty and torn linen which brought from Beethoven a request that she have a dozen shirts made for him.

All things considered, Beethoven appears to have been decidedly democratic in matters of dress; frequently, in moments of private relaxation or in the throes of composition somewhat careless about his appearance, although, upon occasion he could dress in the ruling fashion of the day.

Appleby, Samuel

One of Beethoven's English admirers who told Thayer a number of anecdotes about Cramer, Dragonetti, Bridgetower and others. Appleby owned some letters of Count Dietrichstein addressed to Bridgetower. Thomas Appleby, his father, was the authority on music for the Musical Society in Manchester (cf. Th.-R.II).

Arnim, Bettina

See Entry: Brentano.

Artaria

Publishing company, the founders of which were Cesare (1706-1785), Domenico (1715-1784), and Giovanni Casimiro (1725-1797). The three brothers came from Blevio on the Lake of Como, running a traveling art business. Giovanni with his nephews Carlo (son of Cesare), and Francesco (son of Domenico) established the firm of Giovanni Artaria and Co. in Mainz. The two nephews left the firm in 1766 and founded the firm Artaria and Co. in Vienna (1770). In 1776 the two firms were united under the name of Artaria and Co., Vienna and Mainz. After 1789 the Vienna firm was located at Kohlmarkt 9 (Zum Englischen Gruss). In 1793 Domenico took over the business in Mainz, moving it to Mannheim where it was merged with Mathias Fontaine (1819) as Artaria and Fontaine. In 1793 Tranquillo Mollo and Giovanni Cappi joined the Vienna firm. Mollo left the firm in 1796, establishing a business of his own. In 1803 the three associates of the firm separated. Carlo kept the old firm on the Kohlmarkt, Domenico joined Tranquillo Mollo, and Giovanni Cappi opened an art business on the Michaeler Platz. At the time of Beethoven, Carlo (1747-1808) son of Cesare, married to Maria Cappi, and Domenico (1775-1842), grandson of the founder Domenico, dominated the scene.

Artaria was Beethoven's first publisher. They printed his Piano Trios Op. 1 on a subscription basis. An argument about the Quintet Op. 29 became almost a serious incident. Originally Breitkopf and Härtel had published the work, but at the same time Artaria appeared upon the scene with copies of a "reprint" edition.

"Beethoven tried to placate Breitkopf and Härtel with a letter fulminating against Artaria. The Quintet had been bought by Count Moritz Fries for private use until a certain date, according to custom, after which the ownership, for publication, reverted to the author. The rogue Artaria, so said Beethoven, obtained the Count's private copy through oily misrepresentation, and promptly engraved it. All that Beethoven felt able to put upon Artaria was a restraint of delay, eased by the bribe of a new composition. He took the further dubious expedient of asking for the fifty copies which had come from the press of Artaria, for correction, and instructing Ries to make the corrections with such heavy pen strokes that they would be spoiled for sale. He further sought to protect the Leipzig firm by a public statement to the effect that the edition of 'Messrs. Artaria and Mollo' had no connection with him and was moreover 'faulty, incorrect, and utterly useless to players.' The result was legal action by Artaria, whom Beethoven had given a certain technical sanction by his corrections, and by Mollo, who had had no actual part in the affair, and so considered himself libeled. Beethoven countered that he had made only a partial revision—out of spite to Artaria. He had supposed that Artaria and Mollo were really one firm, describing them to Breitkopf and Härtel as a whole family of rascals. Spiteful half-revisions and false suppositions did not help him in the eyes of the law. The Polizei Oberdirection decided in favor of both firms, and Beethoven had to publish a retraction, exonerating Mollo." (Burk: *Life and Works of Beethoven.)*

The records of that law suit are extensively published by Th.-R. appendix II. For the second couplet of the *rondo* from the C Major Piano Concerto Op. 15 with the "Artaria-motif," see Entry: Concertos. (Cf. Th.-R., Dr. Ernest Gross: "Artaria u. Co.," *Neue Freie Presse,* Nov. 16, 1920.)

Aschaffenburg

City in Lower-Franconia, visited by Beethoven and a group of Bonn musicians (September 3, 1791) during his visit to Mergentheim. Aschaffenburg was the summer residence of the Electors of Mainz, and it was there that Sterkel admired Beethoven's piano playing. (Cf. Entries: Sterkel; Mergentheim; Schiedermair: *Der junge Beethoven.)*

Atterbohm, Peter Daniel Amadeus

b. Asbo (Östergötland) 1790, d. Upsala 1855. Famous Swedish poet and philosopher. Main representative of romanticism in Sweden. From 1817 to 1819 he traveled in Germany and Italy. Under the title *Minnen från Tyskland och Italien,* he speaks about Beethoven, whom he saw in a private concert. He described him as a short and stocky man with melancholic eyes, a powerful forehead and a face lacking every expression of joy of life. According to Thayer the above-mentioned concert took place January 17, 1819. The *Prometheus* Overture and the Seventh Symphony were on the program. In 1826 Atterbohm visited Vienna again and was introduced to Beethoven by Ignaz Jeitteles. The deaf Master lived at that time in the Schwarzspanierhaus and did not even notice the incoming visitors, who left him quietly in order not to disturb his composing. (Cf. Nielsson: *Svensk Romantik,* 1916 and Th.-R. IV, V.)

Augarten

Park with restaurant north of Vienna, originally in the possession of the Court. Joseph II donated it to the Vienna public in 1775. In Beethoven's time Ignaz Jahn was "Hof-Traiteur" (Caterer) of the Augarten hall, where the Master's first five symphonies were performed. (Cf. Entry: Jahn; Hanslick: *Geschichte des Conzertwesens in Wien.)*

Augsburg

City of southern Bavaria, visited by Beethoven on his return trip from Vienna to Bonn (1787). There Beethoven met the keyboard manufacturer Johann Andreas Stein and Stein's daughter Nanette, later married to Johann Andreas Streicher (cf. Th.-R. I, p. 211, and Entry: Streicher).

Autographs in America

See United States.

Averdonc, Johanna Helene

b. 1760, d. 1789. Contralto in Bonn and acquainted with Beethoven's family. She was godmother to one of Beethoven's brothers, born 1781. In 1778 she performed in the same concert in which young Beethoven played (cf. Th.-R. I, p. 65, 130; Schiedermair).

Averdonc, Severin Anton

b. 1768-(?). Possibly a relative of Johanna Helene Averdonc, author of the text to the Emperor Cantatas (Death of Joseph II, Enthronisation of Leopold II) (cf. Entry: Cantatas, Th.-R. I, p. 296, and Schiedermair).

B

Bach, Johann Baptist von

b. 1779, d. 1847. Lawyer in Vienna. He was Beethoven's consultant in many matters of law from 1816 on, particularly in the difficult matter of his nephew's tutelage. In 1827 (January 3rd), Beethoven handed him his will for final execution. (Cf. Frimmel: *Beethoven Handbuch* I, p. 26; Conversation-book 1820, May 1st-14th, where Bernard mentions Bach as a rich man; Schünemann: *Konversationshefte* Vol. II, p. 107.)

Bach, Johann Sebastian

Highly esteemed by Beethoven. According to Schindler, Beethoven owned among other works the *Well Tempered Clavier,* the Inventions and the Toccata in D minor. Hoffmeister in Leipzig intended to publish the works of Bach. Beethoven welcomed that project wholeheartedly. When the Silesian organist Carl Gottlieb Freudenberg visited Beethoven, the Master mentioned that Bach should not be called by his own name (brook), but "Meer" (Ocean). Philip Emanuel Bach was likewise esteemed by Beethoven and when Carl Czerny began to study with him, Beethoven suggested to Czerny's father Wenzel, that the boy bring along Philip Emanuel Bach's "Versuch über die wahre Art das Clavier zu spielen." The latter was also in high esteem with Neefe. The influence of Philip Emanuel Bach's Sonata in F minor on Beethoven's Sonata Op. 2 No. 1 speaks for itself.

Baden bei Wien

Beethoven visited this resort in 1817, 1821, 1822, 1824, and 1825.

Bagatelles

Short, lyrically conceived piano pieces by Beethoven. Among the seven Bagatelles Op. 33 Nos. 6 and 7 were composed in 1801 and 1802, the others before that time. The first edition of that collection was published in the Wiener Kunst-und Industrie-Comptoir. The original manuscript bears the inscription: "Des Bagatelles par Louis van Beethoven 1782." However, it is certain that not all of these five bagatelles were composed at that early date, if that date should be authentic at all. According to Nottebohm the manuscript belongs to a later period. Op. 119 contains 11 new bagatelles. The autograph of the first six bears the inscription "Kleinigkeiten—1822 November." The sketch of No. 5 (Risoluto) was written already in 1802,

Nos. 7-11 are found in the third section of F. Starke's "Wiener Pianoforte-Schule" under the title "Kleinigkeiten von Ludwig van Beethoven." Nos. 1-11 were published first in Paris by Schlesinger in 1823, then in May 1824 under the title "Nouvelles Bagatelles faciles et agréables pour le Pianoforte par Louis van Beethoven. Oeuvre 112 Vienne Publié par Sauer et Leidesdorf." No. 12 was added in 1828 by Diabelli. It was originally a song entitled "An Laura."

In 1825 Beethoven published 6 other bagatelles as Op. 126. The autograph bears the inscription "Kleinigkeiten von L. v. Btv." It was published under the title "Six Bagatelles pour le Piano-Forte composées par Louis van Beethoven. Oeuvre 126. Propriété des Editeurs. Mayence, chez B. Schott fils etc." In Nottebohm's *Zweite Beethoveniana* the short piece "Für Elise," written in 1810, is also called "Bagatelle."

Bathing

According to Schindler washing and bathing were among Beethoven's most indispensable habits. Like Richard Wagner he believed in the curative power of cold water (cf. Entries: Teplitz, Karlsbad and Franzensbad).

"Battle" Symphony

See Entry: Wellington's Victory.

Becking, Gustav

Musicologist, 1894-1945, wrote a dissertation "Studien zu Beethovens Personalstil: Das Scherzothema," Leipzig 1921.

Berlin

Beethoven spent several months in the Prussian capital in 1796. Ries mentions that Beethoven played several times at the court of King Friedrich Wilhelm II. Op. 5, the two Sonatas for Cello and Piano, dedicated to the King, were played by the first cellist Duport and himself. As a reward Beethoven received a golden box filled with louis d'or. Beethoven also played twice in the "Singakademie" the Director of which was Karl Fasch whose *Davidiana* gave impetus to an elaborate improvisation. Other connections made in Berlin were: Zelter, Prinz Radziwill, Himmel and Prinz Louis Ferdinand (cf. Kalischer: *Beethoven und Berlin*).

Bernadotte, Johann Baptiste Julius

b. 1764, d. 1844. Son of a jurist in Pau, France. Began his military career in 1780 and gained fame in Italy in 1797 under Bonaparte. After the peace of Campoformio, October 1797, he became French Ambassador in Vienna: he left the capital as a consequence of having raised the French tricolor on top of the Embassy. In 1806 he became Prince of Pontecorvo, won the battle of Wagram in 1809 and was adopted in 1818 by Charles XIII of Sweden and Norway with the purpose of becoming his successor. As a music lover he was attended in Vienna by Rodolphe Kreutzer. He became acquainted with Beethoven and was responsible for Beethoven's intention to write a heroic symphony on Bonaparte (Schindler's story on page 55 of the 1st edition of his Biography). In 1823 in a letter to Bernadotte, at that time already King of Sweden, Beethoven refers to the old times, thanks Bernadotte for having conferred on him membership in the Swedish Academy of Music and asks him to purchase a copy of the *Missa Solemnis* (cf. Masson: *Les*

Diplomates de la Révolution, Paris 1882). Needless to say Beethoven's relation to Bernadotte as given by Annemarie Selinko in her novel *Désirée* is pure fiction.

Bernard, Josef Karl

b. 1775, d. 1850. Writer and journalist. Born in Horatitz in Bohemia, studied in Saaz, Prague and Heidelberg. Came to Vienna in 1800 as a member of the "Hofkriegsrat." He was editor of the *Wiener Zeitschrift* in 1818, and in 1819 he was its editor-in-chief together with A. Demarteau. He was the founder of the Wiener Kunst und Industrie Comptoir, a publishing house. Bernard is already mentioned in 1815 in connection with Beethoven for whom he rewrote the text of the cantata *Der glorreiche Augenblick,* originally written by Weissenbach. He was also the author of the oratorio *Der Sieg des Kreuzes,* which Beethoven had projected for both Die Gesellschaft der Musikfreunde in Vienna and the Boston Handel and Haydn Society. Bernard's text, however, was not approved by Beethoven, who made numerous changes. In the version of Beethoven's corrections the text came to light in 1902. For many years Bernard was Beethoven's friend and knew more about the Master's daily life than anybody else, except for Schindler. In the Conversation-books Bernard appears frequently (cf. Schünemann), and is often consulted by Beethoven in many situations, as in matters concerning his nephew. He was a friend of Giannatasio del Rio, the owner of a private boarding school which Beethoven's nephew attended. Bernard visited also the Blöchinger private boarding school where Beethoven's nephew was a student several years later (cf. Frimmel: *Beethoven Handbuch*).

Bertolini, Dr. Andreas

He was Beethoven's medical adviser between 1806-1816. In 1814 Beethoven composed for him a four-part cantata *Un lieto brindisi,* text by Abbate Bondi, which was performed in honor of a festivity for Dr. Malfatti. Several years after Beethoven's death Bertolini suffered from cholera and destroyed the correspondence with Beethoven for fear of contamination. (cf. Th.-R.)

Beyer

Correctly Dr. Reger of Prague, whose name was read by mistake as Beyer.

Bigot, Marie

b. Colmar 1786, d. Paris 1820. Excellent pianist, née Kiene, married 1804 Razumovsky's librarian. 1806 she played from its damaged manuscript the "Appassionata" Sonata without mistakes (cf. Beethoven's letter to her in Th.-R. II, p. 551).

Bird song, Imitations of

From the time of Jannequin (Chant des oiseaux), composers have repeatedly introduced bird songs into music. Beethoven as an enthusiastic lover of nature was undoubtedly familiar with the different calls which he used in some of his works, i.e. "Mailied" (1792), "Wachtelschlag" (1804), the fourth song in "An die ferne Geliebte," and above all in his Sixth Symphony (Pastorale) scene at the brook (cf. B. Hoffmann: *Kunst und Vogelgesang*).

Birkenstock, Joh. Melchior, Edler von

b. May 11, 1738, d. Vienna, October 30, 1809. Viennese scholar, reformer of the

Austrian educational system, censor, art and music lover, collector. Beethoven appeared frequently in his house, where he met Bettina von Arnim in 1810. In 1798 Birkenstock's daughter Antonia married the Frankfurt merchant Franz Brentano. Beethoven probably also met Joseph von Sonnenfels, Birkenstock's brother-in-law, in the latter's house (cf. Wurzbach).

Birth

It is still unknown whether Beethoven was born on December 16 or 17, 1770, as only the day of his baptism is recorded. The house of his birth is not the "Hohe Haus" in the Rheingasse, but the house in the Bonngasse (cf. Entry: Bonn).

Blöchinger, Joseph, von Bannholz

b. Gobelingen, Switzerland, 1788, d. 1855. Director of a boarding school for boys in Vienna. Beethoven's nephew Karl entered this school on June 22, 1819, and remained there until August 1823. The boarding school was attended at that time by 32 students and was located in the Chotek Palace, 26, Strozzigrund, today 39, Josephstädter Strasse. In 1923 Frimmel found most of the rooms unchanged (cf. Th-R. IV).

Blumenstock

An old Viennese coffee house in Ballgassl, frequently visited by Beethoven. He lived in that house for a short time 1818-1820.

Boldrini, Carlo

Music publisher. In 1804 he was a clerk at the Artaria firm which he joined as a partner in 1810. About 1820 he was on close terms with Beethoven, whom he advised in financial matters. Beethoven jokingly called him Falstaff, as he did Schuppanzigh.

Böhm, Joseph

b. Pest 1795, d. Vienna 1876. Famous violinist, student of Rode from 1819 on. Professor at the Conservatory of the Gesellschaft der Musikfreunde in Vienna. After 1821 member of the "Hofkapelle." He was instrumental in introducing the later chamber works of Beethoven. While the performance of the String Quartet Op. 127 by Schuppanzigh on March 6, 1825, was a failure, its repetition by Böhm, whose playing showed Hungarian temperament, was a big success. (cf. Hevesy: *Les petites amies de Beethoven*, page 86.)

Bonn

Beethoven's birthplace. The residence of the Archbishops of Cologne. The city enjoyed a rich cultural, particularly musical, life. The "Musikkapelle" was founded in the 16th century and gained reputation through musicians like Jean Taisnier, Jacobus de Kerle, Massimiliano Neri, Johann Christoph Petz, dall' Abbacco, Anton Raaff, Joseph Touchemoulin, the Ries family (Johann, his son Franz Anton, who was the father of Ferdinand and Hubert), Johann Peter Salomon, Joseph Reicha and his nephew Anton, Bernhard und Andreas Romberg, Andrea Lucchesi, Christian Gottlob Neefe, and finally the young Beethoven, whose father and grandfather were also members of the Chapel. There is found the most important source of information on Beethoven's youth (cf. Th.-R.I.) in Bonn, namely the Fischer Manuscript.

Beethoven attended the public schools

in Bonn until his 14th year. His musical education was taken in hand in his fourth year by his father Johann, who taught him until 1779. His next instructors were Tobias Friedrich Pfeiffer, a music director and oboist, Heinrich van der Eden, the Court organist and the latter's successor, Neefe. In addition Beethoven received violin instruction from Franz Georg Rovantini, a cousin of Beethoven's mother and finally from the Franciscan Willibald Koch and the organist Zensen. A notable improviser on the piano, the young Beethoven composed in 1781-82 his first published compositions, three Piano Sonatas ("Electoral" Sonatas). In 1782, during Neefe's absence, Beethoven was his substitute at the organ, and in 1783 was appointed cembalist of the Opera orchestra. In 1784 Maximilian Franz, Austrian Archduke, succeeded Elector Clemens August and appointed Beethoven Assistant Organist at a salary of 150 guldens. He held this position until 1792. From 1788 Beethoven played the 2nd viola in the orchestra and in the Church while Reicha was the conductor. In 1787 Beethoven visited Vienna and paid a visit to Mozart (about this visit, see reports by Schindler, Ries, von Seyfried and Czerny). Authentic reports are lacking. Beethoven spent only two weeks, probably the first half of April, in Vienna, and was recalled to Bonn because of the serious illness of his mother, who died July 17. After the death of his mother, father Johann indulged more and more in drinking, a circumstance which affected the young Beethoven heavily as he had to take care of the whole family. When his father lost his job November 20, 1789, Ludwig received half of the paternal salary for the education of his younger brothers. On December 25, 1790, Haydn, on his return from London, arrived in Bonn where he met the young Beethoven. In September-October 1791 Beethoven traveled with some members of the Chapel to Mergentheim to the Chapter of the Teutonic Order. In Aschaffenburg he competed with the famous composer Franz Xaver Sterkel. Among the friends in Bonn the von Breuning family should be mentioned above all as most important. Also Count Waldstein and other friends gathered in the Gasthof Zehrgarten of the widow Koch. The circle included Carl August von Malchus, Private Secretary of the Austrian Ambassador in Bonn, the Court Surgeon Johan Heinrich Richter, J. M. Degenhard, canditatus iuris, who was presented a Duet for Flute *(allegro e minuetto)* on August 23, 1792 (reprinted in Th.-R. I), Joh. Joseph Eichhoff, the son of the Electoral cook, J. H. Crevelt, a physician, and a certain Klemmer. The members of the Zehrgarten Circle, including the widow Koch and Count Waldstein, dedicated to the departing Beethoven a "Stammbuch" which is preserved in the Bonn Beethoven Haus and which was published in facsimile in 1927 by Dr. Hans Gerstinger. Beethoven's general education in Bonn was climaxed by his matriculation into the University, which he entered 1789 simultaneously with his friends Anton Reicha and Karl Ferdinand von Kügelgen (1771-1832), the twin brother of Gerhard von Kügelgen, the painter whose son Wilhelm von Kügelgen (1802-1867) was in turn a painter and author and published his famous *Lebenserinnerungen eines alten Mannes*. Doubtless, during his university years Beethoven laid the foundation for his philosophical and literary knowledge, as he evidently studied with Van der Schüren Kant's "Logic, Metaphysics and Philosophy" and with Eulogius Schneider "Greek Literature" etc. His close connection with the Breuning family had a great influence on his education (cf. Entry: Breuning). Whether Beethoven's second journey to Vienna, which resulted in his permanent stay in that capital, was influenced by Haydn, Count Waldstein or other circumstances, is hard to determine. On November 2 or at the latest November 3, 1792 the young Beethoven boarded a coach bound for Vienna. At that time war with France already was raging in Germany and the "Kerl von einem Postillon" led the coach like a "devil" through the dangerous sections. Thus ended the first chapter of Beethoven's life (cf. Entry: Family). The following list gives the earliest works written according to Schiedermair's *Der junge Beethoven:*

1) "Variations pour le Clavecin sur une Marche de M. Dresler composées et dédiées à son Excellence Madame la Comtesse de Wolfmetternich née Baronne d'Assebourg par un jeune amateur Louis van Beethoven agé de dix ans";

2) Zweistimmige Fuge in D. "Verfertigt von Ludwig van Beethoven im alter von 11 Jahren";

3) "Schilderung eines Mädchens," Lied am Klavier "von Hrn. Ludwig van Beethoven alt eilf Jahr";

4) Rondo in C for piano;

5) "Drei Sonaten fürs Klavier dem Hochwurdigsten Erzbischofe und Kurfürsten zu Köln Maximilian Friedrich meinem gnädigsten Herrn gewidmet und verfertiget von Ludwig van Beethoven, alt eilf (13) Jahr";

6) "Un Concert [in Es] par le Clavecin ou Porte-piano Composé par Louis van Beethoven agé de douze ans";

7) "Rondo" in A for piano. "Del Sigre. van Beethoven";

8) "An einen Säugling," Song on the piano, "Von Herrn Beethoven."

Bossler, Heinrich Philipp

Publisher in Speyer. He published several early works of Beethoven, among them in 1783 the three "Electoral" Sonatas, and a Song and a Rondo in "Blumenlese für Liebhaber." The song "Schilderung eines Mädchens" bears the following note:

"Von Herrn Ludwig van Beethoven alt eilf Jahr." As a matter of fact Beethoven at that time was not 11 but 13 years old. Immediately after the song a Rondo in C major follows which was reprinted by Max Friedländer J.M.P. 1899, who considers the Rondo, which was published anonymously, a work by Beethoven.

Bouché, Alexandre

b. Paris 1778, d. there 1861. French violinist. Goethe recommended the artist to Beethoven, who received him April 29, 1822. At the occasion of that visit, Beethoven wrote for Bouché a short two-part piece, reproduced in Frimmel's *Beethoven Studien* II, p. 79, a study which informs us about Beethoven's relation to the great violinist. Bouché had a definite resemblance to Napoleon I. (Cf. Blaschke: "Napoleon I und die Musik" in *Neue Musikzeitung* 1907.) Kinsky W o O. 34.

Braun, Peter Freiherr von

b. 1758, d. Vienna 1819. Austrian government employee, later industrialist, who introduced silk industry in Austria. In 1792 he negotiated a loan for the Government, whereupon, in 1794, he was entrusted with the direction of the two Vienna Court Theatres and he received in 1795 the title of baron. He was extremely artminded. On his estate in Schönau he had a "Temple of the Night" built with inscriptions by Kotzebue and a monument for Alxinger. In his capacity as a Director of the theatres, Braun was instrumental in the performance of *Fidelio* in 1805. Because of the failure of the opera, Beethoven, in his somewhat brisk way, withdrew the score, and expressed a suspicion that Braun possibly had betrayed him financially (cf. Roeckl). In former times Beethoven had been on excellent terms with Braun, who arranged a concert in 1797 (Romberg'sche Akademie) in which Beethoven participated. Besides the Master dedicated the Piano Sonata Op. 14 and the Sonata for French Horn Op. 17 to Braun's wife. Wurzbach also lists some compositions of Braun "Leonore" (by Bürger) Vienna 1796, Sonata per il cembalo solo, Vienna 1800 and a Menuetto e Trio for the Pianoforte. (Cf. Frimmel, Th.-R., and Wurzbach, who lists other reference books.)

Braunhofer, Anton

Physician in Vienna who treated Beethoven 1820-25 for an intestinal disease. The "Abendlied unter'm gestirnten Himmel" (1820) was dedicated to the Doctor, who was Professor of General Natural History and Technology at the University of Vienna.

Breitkopf and Härtel

Famous Leipzig publishing company which was in close association with Beethoven from 1801 to 1815. During this period a number of Beethoven's works were published by the firm, among them the C major Quintet Op. 29, the Sextet Op. 71, the piano score of *Fidelio,* the Symphonies Nos. 5 and 6, the Sonata in A major for Cello and Piano Op. 69, the two Piano Trios Op. 70, and many other works. One of the firm's worthy ventures was its complete edition of Beethoven's compositions. (Cf. also "Der Bär" *Jahrbuch von Breitkopf und Härtel auf das Jahr 1927,* Beethoven Issue, which contains many relevant articles.) Beethoven's letters to the firm were first published by La Mara; others are printed in Th.-R. II, page 610.

Brentano, Clemens

b. Ehrenbreitstein 1778, d. Aschaffenburg, 1842. Celebrated poet, friendly with Beethoven, probably after 1811, in which year they met in Teplitz. A cantata on the death of Queen Louise by Brentano was supposed to be composed by the Master. (Cf. Max Unger: "Beethovens Badereisen 1811-1812" in *Neue Musikzeitung,* December 1917.)

Brentano, Elisabeth (Bettina)

b. Frankfurt a.M., 1785, d. Berlin, 1859. Daughter of Peter Anton Brentano and his wife Maximiliane, née Laroche. Orphaned early, she lacked a regular education and all her life was an unbalanced and somewhat queer person, whose character was a strange combination of high talent and mischievousness. By her wit and charm she attracted many personalities of high standing, including Goethe and Beethoven. A certain intrusiveness in dealing with people of high standing was frequently observed in her, e.g. by Goethe, with whom she was in correspondence. Many of Goethe's letters to her, published by herself, were falsified.

Beethoven met her in the house of Birkenstock in 1810 and was attracted by the "child." At that time she was engaged to Achim von Arnim whom she married on March 3, 1811. After Bettina's departure from Vienna, she wrote at least one letter to the composer, but published three. The other two letters are not authentic. Everything she wrote and said was only approximately true. Bettina possibly persuaded Beethoven to visit Bohemian resort places. It was also Bettina who called Goethe's attention in an exaggerated way to Beethoven. The legendary meeting of the Austrian Court with Goethe and Beethoven is another product of Bettina's imagination. Bettina was not only a poetess and talented sculptor, but also a composition pupil of Peter von Winter. She was never Beethoven's "Immortal Beloved" as was frequently stated. (Cf. Frimmel: "Beethovens Unsterbliche Geliebte" in *Bühne und Welt,* February, 1912 and Th.-R. III according to Register, Entry: Teplitz).

Brentano, Franz Dominik Maria Joseph

b. Frankfurt a. M., 1765, d. there 1844. Brother of Bettina, merchant and senator in Frankfurt. Husband of Antonia von Birkenstock, daughter of Melchior von Birkenstock. When father Birkenstock became sick in 1809 the Brentanos came to Vienna where they lived until 1812. Beethoven calls Franz Brentano one of his best friends in the world. The Master got frequent financial help from him without ever being reminded of his debts. Brentano also financed partly the publication of *Missa Solemnis* by Simrock. The Brentanos had a daughter Maximiliane (Maxe) b. 1802. To her Beethoven dedicated the "Trio in einem Satz" in B flat major and in 1821 the Piano Sonata Op. 109. Antonia played an important part when Beethoven planned to send his nephew to Sailer, a Catholic priest who was supposed to take over his education.

Breuning

Bonn family of greatest importance to the Master. The old "Hofrat Breuning," Joseph v. Breuning, had been fatally injured in 1777 when the Electoral castle burnt down. His widow Helene, née Kerich, continued to live in Bonn with her four children. Their names were: Christoph, b. 1773; Eleonore, b. 1771; Stephan (Steffen), b. 1774; Lorenz (Lenz) b. posthumously, 1777. Beethoven was introduced into the family by Franz G. Wegeler, when the Breunings were looking for a piano teacher for Eleonore and Lenz. Mother Breuning became a protectress (second mother) to Beethoven. Among the Breunings two became jurists: Christoph and Steffen. The latter took violin lessons from old Ries, simultaneously with Beethoven. Lenz became a physician. When Lenz and Steffen moved to Vienna in 1794 Lenz took lessons from Beethoven. An intimate friendship between the two developed until Lenz returned to Bonn in 1797 where he died in 1798. Steffen came to Vienna about 1800 and became a member of the Austrian Hofkriegsrat and was Hofrat in 1818. The relations between Beethoven and Steffen changed frequently, because of their similar temperaments. In 1815 a serious break occurred, the cause of which was Beethoven's brother Kaspar Karl. In 1815 they were reconciled permanently. Steffen married Julia von

Vering who died 1809. Beethoven had often played piano duets with her. Steffen's second wife was Konstanze Ruschowitz, who was on friendly terms with the Master. Their son was Gerhard, born August 28, 1813, who became a favorite of the sick Master. Beethoven called him Ariel (in memory of the character in Shakespeare's *Tempest*). Little Gerhard was known to be very dependent upon his father, consequently Beethoven liked to call him "Hosenknopf" (Pants Button). He visited Beethoven almost daily during his last year, when the Master lived in the Schwarzspanier Haus. Gerhard's reliable and accurate observations of Beethoven were published in Vienna in 1870 in his book entitled *Aus dem Schwarzspanier Haus,* one of the best biographical sources on Beethoven. Gerhard later became one of the best known physicians in Vienna. He died 1892. (Cf. Frimmel: *Beethoven Handbuch.)*

Bridgetower, George Polgreen

b. Biala, Poland, 1779, d. Peckham (England), 1860. Famous mulatto violinist, concertized 1789-90 in Paris and London where he became first violinist under George IV. On the occasion of a trip to Dresden, where his mother lived, he concertized there and later in Vienna. Prince Lichnowsky introduced him to Beethoven, who wrote for him his famous A minor Violin Sonata Op. 47, which was later dedicated to Rodolphe Kreutzer. According to Mr. Thirlwall (Th.-R. II, p. 397) Beethoven was jealous of Bridgetower, a very sturdy, handsome man, because of a young lady, and he broke with the mulatto. According to Ries the sonata was composed in a short time as Bridgetower left him little time on account of an imminent concert. One day Beethoven called Ries at 4:30 a.m. and ordered him to copy the sonata. At that time the piano part was only partly notated. The concert took place in the Augarten at 8 a.m. and Bridgetower had to play the Variations from the autograph. The last *allegro* in A major, however, was well copied because it had belonged originally to the first Sonata, Op. 30 in A major, dedicated to Czar Alexander. Czerny tells us that the first movement was composed within four days. Frimmel doubts that fact; an extensive sketch of that movement is preserved. However this fact does not contradict Czerny's report, as Beethoven probably used ideas for his sonata that had been conceived previously. (Cf. W. Hutschenruyter: *Programma van den Beethovencyclus,* 's Gravenhage 1911, with a description of Bridgetower's person, according to his passport, issued July 27, 1803.)

Broadwood, Thomas

Piano maker in London, whose firm was founded in 1732 by the Swiss Burkhard Tschudi. In Beethoven's time manufacturers of the most powerful pianos. In 1818 Beethoven received from them an excellent instrument as a gift (cf. Entry: Keyboard Instruments).

Brothers of Beethoven

Beethoven was the second of the seven children of Johann van Beethoven and his wife, Maria Magdalena Keverich.

His oldest brother was born and died in 1769. Franz Georg, born in 1771, died at the age of two. The remaining two brothers were Kaspar Anton Karl, born 1774, died in Vienna, November 15, 1815, and Nikolaus Johann, born 1776, died in Vienna, 1848.

Karl became a musician and was a music teacher in Bonn. He moved to Vienna in 1794. Some of his compositions are advertised January 11, 1801 in *Wiener Zeitung*. In 1800 he evidently changed his profession to clerk in the Department of Finances. In 1806 Karl married Johanna Reiss and they had a son Karl, the Master's ill-fated nephew (cf. Entries: Sisters-in-law and Nephew).

Nikolaus Johann was trained as a pharmacist. He went to Vienna in 1795 in order to finish his studies. He was a clerk in different pharmacies and became the owner of a pharmacy in Linz. In 1809 he furnished the Austrian Army with pharmaceutical supplies and became a wealthy man. In 1812 the Master visited his brother in Linz and mixed into Johann's family affairs. As a result of these quarrels Johann married his mistress, Therese Obermeyer. In 1819 Johann bought the large estate, Gneixendorf, near Krems. Johann's character is unfavorably described by Breuning and other contemporaries. He was a boaster and at the same time a miser. When Johann signed a letter to his brother as "Real Estate Owner," Ludwig replied "Brain Owner."

In several letters the composer refers to his brother as "unbrotherly" or as a scoundrel *(Schurke)*. However, he paid him a visit in Gneixendorf where he spent two months on Johann's estate "Wasserhof." On October 30, 1826, Beethoven entrusted his brother to hand the Quartet Op. 135 to Tendler and Mannstein in Vienna for the amount of 80 ducats.

Letters of Johann were published by Heinrich Rietsch in Sandberger's *Beethoven-Jahrbuch* I and III. Karl's son was the well-known nephew Karl (1806-1858) who married Karoline Naske in 1832. The couple had five children. Karoline, born 1833, married Franz Weidinger. Their children were: Marie Josephine, a painter, and Dr. Hermann Weidinger, lawyer in Vienna. Karl's second child was Marie, born 1835, who married Paul Weidinger, the brother of Franz. Karl's third child was Ludwig, born March 8, 1839, who married Marie Nitsche in 1865. Their son Karl Julius was born May 8, 1870. The fourth child was Gabriele, born 1844, married to Robert Heimler. All Karl's sons-in-law were bank clerks. Karl's youngest child was Hermine, born 1852, who became an established pianist. Marie and Franz Weidinger and Hermine van Beethoven had died in 1892, before their mother passed away. Ludwig was a "mauvais sujet" who had vanished with his family in 1889. He had pretended to be a grandson of the composer and used to call himself Baron von Beethoven. In 1872 he was jailed for four years for embezzlement after having misused the generosity of King Ludwig II of Bavaria. In 1927 another kinsman of Karl made his appearance in Vienna, whereas another one had probably emigrated to the U.S.A. (Cf. also Adolf Sandberger: "Beiträge zur Beethovenforschung" A.M.W. II, p. 398).

Browne, Johann Georg, Count

Russian Brigadier General, to whom Beethoven dedicated his String Trios Op. 9. The dedication calls him "Premier Mécène de sa Muse." According to Ries, Beethoven received from him a riding horse as a gift. At Beethoven's recommendation Ries was appointed as a piano player in the house of Count Browne where Beethoven's works were frequently performed. Once Ries improvised a march for which he gave credit to Beethoven. The Master discovered the friendly fraud, but did not take it seriously. As a result Count Browne commissioned Beethoven to write three marches for four hands, Op. 45, which later were dedicated to Princess Esterhazy. During the performance Count P. Palffy conversed so loud that Beethoven stopped playing and said: "Für solche Schweine spiele ich nicht." Beethoven's Variations A major No. 5 advertised April 29, 1797, in *Wiener Zeitung* were also dedicated to the Countess. (It was then that he received the riding horse.) Also the Sonata Op. 22 B flat major and the six Gellert Songs, Op. 48 were dedications to the Count; the Piano Sonata Op. 10 in C minor was dedicated to the Countess.

Brühl

Site, located on the Mödling River, frequently mentioned in Beethoven's writings. The Mödling Dances are frequently called "Brühler Tänze." Found by Hugo Riemann in 1907 in the Archives of the Thomas-Schule in Leipzig (cf. *Die Musik* VI, 24).

Brunsvik (also Brunswick)

Hungarian aristocratic family, the members of which were among Beethoven's most intimate friends; Count Franz as well as his sisters Therese (1775-1861) and Josephine (1779-1821) addressed Beethoven with "Du." There were two other sisters, the youngest, Julietta, born 1784.

Their mother was Countess Anna Elizabeth, née Baroness Seeberg, the widow of Count Anton Brunswick, who had died 1793, at the age of 47. Philipp von Seeberg (probably the brother of Countess Anna Elizabeth), friend and colleague of Nicolaus Zmeskall, was also acquainted with Beethoven and Frimmel speculates whether Beethoven's friendship with the Brunswick Seeberg families resulted from Beethoven's friendship with Zmeskall. A "Komtesse Brunsvik" appears among the subscribers of the Trios Op. 1, 1795. The subscriber was Countess Anna, whose children were highly musical. The Brunswicks lived at their castles Korompa and Martonvasar, in Hungary. Therese, a godchild of Maria Theresia, was a favorite of her father, whose enthusiasm for the independence of the United States of America was well known. In her Memoires we find phrases like the following: "America's fate was watched by my noble father with love and I grew up with the ideas of Washington and Benjamin Franklin." When Count Brunswick died, his daughters were brought to Vienna. The typical Hungarians could not adjust themselves to the social life of the Austrian capital. But there was one happy day in May 1799 when "Thesi" and "Pepi" paid a visit to the Olympian, who at that time was living on the "Peter's Platz." Therese's report on that visit reads as follows: "I carried my Beethoven Sonata for Violin and Cello under my arm (one of the Trios of Op. 1). The immortal dear Louis van Beethoven was very friendly and as polite as he could be. After some phrases 'de part et d'autre' he put me down at a piano (out of tune) and I began to play humming the violin and cello parts simultaneously. This charmed him so much that he promised to see us daily. We lived at that time at the Hotel Goldener Greif, which changed its name later to Erzherzog Karl. He did come daily at 12 noon and left at 4 or 5 in the afternoon. He did not get tired of keeping my fingers curved; I was used to holding them in flat position. We forgot even being hungry. Our good mother shared our starving; however, the innkeepers were mad at us when we took our lunch at 5 o'clock in the afternoon. From that time originated our deep and life-long friendship. (The Brunswicks at that time only remained for 16 days in Vienna.) Beethoven came to Budapest and to Martonvasar, accepted in our circle of excellent personalities." There follows a sentence which clearly indicates Therese's deep emotional devotion to Beethoven and she mentions that Beethoven never left her side. Beethoven dedicated to the sisters Brunswick, when they departed in May 1799, the song "Ich denke dein" with six Variations for four hands (Friedländer: Das deutsche Lied im 18. Jahrhundert, p. 202 reprints the title of an unknown edition of that song bearing the following title: "Musikalisches / Freundschafts-Opfer / dargebracht / den hochgeborenen Comtessen von / Brunswick / im Jahre 1799 / von / L. Van Beethoven / Andantino canto und Variationen / für das Piano-Forte zu vier Händen / Zum erstenmal gedruckt / Herausgegeben von Joh. Stika / Prag / Verlag von P. Bohmanns Erben." On the second page is found the following: "To the Stammbuch of two Comtesses of Brunswick. My sincerest wish is that you might recall sometimes, when playing and singing this little musical sacrifice, your Ludwig van Beethoven who venerates you most sincerely." Soon afterwards Countess Josephine married Count Deym, who under the name of Hofstatuarius Müller, owned the famous Kunstgallerie in Vienna. Beethoven wrote for this Kunstgallerie three short pieces to be performed by a mechanical instrument on which also "Ich denke dein" might have been played. Count Deym died in 1804, whereupon Josephine married Baron Christoph Stackelberg. Both Therese and Josephine Brunswick are considered the Immortal Beloved.

A cousin of the Brunswick girls was Giulietta Guicciardi, who was considered by Schindler and others to be the Immortal Beloved. Beethoven dedicated to different members of the Brunswick family a number of his works, i.e. the F sharp major Sonata, Op. 78, the so-called "Therese" sonata. He dedicated to Count Franz the *Appassionata* and the Piano Fantasy Op. 77. In 1811 Count Franz was supposed to accompany the Master to Teplitz. (Cf. La Mara: *Beethoven's "Unsterbliche Geliebte"* and Hevesy: *Les petites amies de Beethoven;* further, Romain Rolland: *Beethoven, Les grandes époques créatrices,* 1928; also Entries: Immortal Beloved and Müller, Hofstatuarius.)

C

Canons

Like many other composers of his time, Beethoven cultivated this form and used it for numerous purposes. Altogether Beethoven wrote more than 40 canons. Furthermore he used the canon form in *Fidelio* (Quartet *"Mir ist so wunderbar")*, and in the last movement of the Sonata Op. 28 (Sonnenfels sonata).

Cantatas

As a composer of cantatas Beethoven began auspiciously enough, but the medium itself did not seem to hold a great deal of interest for him. Each of the cantatas was written for a special occasion and perhaps for this reason they do not equal his output in other mediums.

The first two are the most ambitious and most successful of all the cantatas. They were written only a few days apart in 1790, the first to commemorate the death of the Emperor Joseph II, the second to celebrate the ascension to the throne of Leopold II. It was one or both of these which was shown to Haydn when he stopped in Bonn on his return from London in 1792 and possibly Haydn's reaction to these cantatas played an important part in influencing Beethoven to journey to Vienna for further study.

Of the two it is the Joseph II cantata which is the more satisfying, indeed it is the only one of all the cantatas which merits repeated hearings today. The poet of the text is not known with certainty, although Thayer suggests that it may have been written by Eulogius Schneider; Severin Anton Averdonc is also mentioned as the author. The work is in no sense revolutionary; the arias have their precedent in any number of 18th century operas. Nevertheless, the dramatic instinct and tonal representation are surprising in a young man of twenty. A phrase from the first soprano aria of this cantata was later used in *Fidelio*. The cantata has been recorded on the Vox label in a masterful performance by the Akademie Chorus and Vienna Symphony Orchestra with Clemens Krauss as conductor.

The Leopold II cantata is possibly not of the same high quality as the Joseph II cantata, although the massive final chorus is superb writing on a grand scale. Neither work contains an opus number and they were not published until they appeared in the Complete Works. There is no evidence that the works were performed in Beethoven's life. (Kinsky W o O. 87, 88)

In 1814 another major cantata was written for the Vienna Congress, a meeting which brought together all the crowned heads of Europe seeking to mend the political fences destroyed by Napoleon. Beethoven was honored several times during the congress and was commissioned to write the cantata *Der Glorreiche Augenblick* Op. 136, for the occasion. It was a setting for four solo voices, chorus and orchestra of a text by Dr. Aloys Weissenbach and was performed before all the royalty and nobility that had assembled for the meeting. Publication of the work was delayed until 1837, at which time it appeared with a different text under the title *"Preis der Tonkunst."* It has not proven to be a favorite of audiences who prefer the more inspired works from the Master's pen.

The above three cantatas are the only major works in the medium. A smaller work for four part chorus and orchestra, dating from 1815, is the setting of two Goethe poems *Meeresstille und Glückliche Fahrt.* Although some of the cantata seems to us uneven it nevertheless contains much of great beauty. The work was sent to Goethe for his opinion but Goethe failed to reply. The first performance occurred on December 25, 1815, but publication was delayed until 1822 when it appeared as Op. 112, dedicated to Goethe.

Still another work, the Birthday Cantata for Prince Lobkowitz is a cantata in name only. (Cf. Entry: Lobkowitz.)

F.T.W.

Cappi, Giovanni

b. about 1770, d. 1815. Art dealer in Vienna. First a clerk at Artaria. In 1802 he founded an independent firm. After his death the firm was managed by his widow Magdalena and after 1822 by his son Carl. By 1827 the business was run under the name Cappi and Czerny and the firm later changed to Joseph Czerny. Beethoven published a number of his works with Cappi, i.e. the Serenade Op. 25 for Flute, Violin and Viola, the Piano Sonatas Op. 26 and 27, the three Sonatas Op. 31. Pietro Cappi was a nephew of Giovanni. In 1793 he became a clerk together with Domenico Artaria in the firm of Artaria. In 1804 he became a partner of Artaria and founded in 1816 an independent publishing company by the name of Cappi and Diabelli. They published the Sonatas Op. 109, 110, 111 in a revised form, first published by Schlesinger in Berlin.

Carlsbad

Famous resort in Bohemia. Beethoven spent a short time there in 1812, coming from Teplitz. After his arrival in Carlsbad July 31 he concertized with the violin virtuoso Polledro for the benefit of the inhabitants of the city of Baden (near Vienna), which had been almost destroyed by a fire. Beethoven met Franz Brentano and his family in Carlsbad, where both were residing in the guest house "Auge Gottes." From Carlsbad the Master went for a short time to Franzensbad, returning hereafter to Carlsbad, where he met Goethe. On September 17 at the latest he was back in Teplitz.

Cartellieri, Casimir Anton

b. Danzig 1772, d. Liebhausen, Bohemia, 1807. Music Director of Prince Lobkowitz. Many of his compositions are preserved in the Lobkowitz castle in Raudnitz. He knew Beethoven well and many anecdotes about Beethoven and the cellist Kraft were told by Cartellieri.

Casentini, Maria

Famous dancer at the Vienna Opera about 1800. Beethoven saw her when she danced in Paul Wranitzky's ballet *Das Waldmädchen* (1796). He was evidently inspired by her to compose the Piano Variations on the Russian Dance from that ballet. Beethoven met her as well at rehearsals and performances of the ballet *Geschöpfe des Prometheus* which was given for the benefit of the dancer on March 28th, 1805.

Cassel

Capital of the Prussian province of Hessen-Nassau and for a short time the residence of King Jerôme of Westphalia. Beethoven was called to Cassel in 1808 as "Kapellmeister" with a salary of 600 ducats, but he rejected the job, because the Archduke Rudolph and the Princes Lobkowitz and Kinsky had granted him a yearly pension of 4000 gulden with the obligation to remain within the Austrian Empire.

Castelli, Ignaz Franz

b. Vienna 1781, d. Vienna 1862. Author, playwright and representative of the typical Viennese wit and humor. In his *Memoiren meines Lebens* 1861-1862, newly published by Bindtner (Georg Müller), Beethoven plays an important part. "Beethoven liked me very much," he says, "and whenever he saw me, he used to say 'Was gibt's wieder für kolossale Dummheiten?'" (Translation: What merry pranks do you have in mind now?) Castelli was the co-founder of the famous "Ludlamshöhle," an organization with a humorous ritual, the later "Schlaraffia." According to Lewald, Beethoven sometimes attended its meetings. Whenever something mischievous was planned, especially with the publisher Steiner, Beethoven wanted Castelli to join the party. Many anecdotes are told by Castelli about Beethoven (*Memoirs,* Müller Ed. II, p. 90).

Cello-Sonatas

(Cf. Entry: Violin Sonatas.)

Cherubini, Luigi

b. Florence, 1760, d. Paris, 1842. According to Grillparzer the two composers met in 1805 at a party in Sonnleithner's house. Cherubini came to Vienna in order to write an opera. He became acquainted with *Fidelio*, which he minimized. He also criticized Beethoven's piano playing. Beethoven on the other hand held Cherubini's opera in highest esteem and called him the best operatic composer of his time. Near the Josephstädter Theater there was an inn, frequently visited by Beethoven, where a mechanical clock played Cherubini's overture to *Medea.* According to Seyfried and Schindler, Beethoven enjoyed listening to this piece. In 1823 Beethoven asked Cherubini to put in a good word at the French Court on behalf of his *Missa Solemnis.* Though the draft of this letter became known through Schindler, Cherubini actually never received it, a fact which was regretted by the Italo-French composer in a conversation with Schindler in 1841. (Cf. Th.-R. IV, p. 369; also the Conversation-book, published in *Beethoven Jahrbuch* II p. 166, according to which the Paris publisher

Schlesinger speaks of Cherubini's great veneration for Beethoven in 1825.)

Choral Fantasia (Chor Phantasie)

Op. 80 for Pianoforte, Orchestra and Chorus, dedicated to Maximilian Joseph, King of Bavaria. First performed December 22, 1808; published in July 1811 by Breitkopf and Härtel. The piano introduction was added in 1809. The text *"Schmeichelnd, hold und lieblich"* stems, according to Czerny, from Kuffner, who wrote it together with the Master himself. The main theme appeared before in Beethoven's song "Seufzer eines Ungeliebten," text by G. A. Bürger, with a slight touch of Beethoven's "Lied an die Freude." The piano part was performed by Beethoven himself at that famous performance, when his Symphonies Nos. 5 and 6 were heard for the first time. It was the last striking appearance of Beethoven as a pianist, often described and commented on by Ries, Seyfried, Czerny, Moscheles, Dolezalek and others. Beethoven lost his temper at the dress rehearsal when he slapped the boy who held the candlestick. There was also a mishap during the performance and they had to start all over. (Cf. Nottebohm: *Beethoveniana* II, p. 255 and Th.-R. III, p. 109.)

Chronology

See appendix.

Clement, Franz

b. Vienna 1780, d. Vienna, 1842. Eminent violinist. He studied with his father and the violinist Kurzweil, Concertmaster of Prince Grassalkowitsch, and was able to perform successfully at the age of 9. He performed a Violin Duo by Deveaux together with another child prodigy, Bridgetower, in London in 1790. Participating in a concert, conducted by Haydn, he was asked to play in one of the concerts in honor of the doctoral graduation of Haydn in Oxford July 1791. After his return to Vienna in 1802 he became Orchestral Director at the Theater an der Wien and came immediately in touch with Beethoven. In April 1805 Beethoven's *Eroica* was performed for the benefit of Clement by the composer himself (the program calls it the Symphony in D sharp major). Beethoven was so much impressed by Clement's art, intonation and marvelous technique that he wrote for him the famous Violin Concerto Op. 61, which was first performed by the virtuoso December 23, 1806. In the year 1811 he toured in Russia where he met serious difficulties, being accused of espionage. When he arrived back in Vienna penniless in 1813, he was forced to accept an inferior orchestral position in Baden near Vienna. During the season 1813-14 Clement was Concertmaster in Prague. From 1818-24 he was conductor at the Theater an der Wien. Clement was a typical Bohemian who was never able to get established.

In 1827 he paid a visit to the Master, who was near death in his apartment in the Schwarzspanier Haus. Clement's album (Stammbuch) still exists in the National Library in Vienna and was recently described in an article by Robert Haas in *Musical Quarterly*. (Cf. also Hanslick, *Geschichte des Konzertwesens in Wien*, and Th.-R., V.)

Clementi, Muzio

b. 1746 in Rome, d. Evesham, Warwickshire, 1832. Composer and pianist who met Beethoven in 1807. As Ries reports, both musicians stayed in the Swan Inn in Vienna, sitting at different tables without noticing each other. According to Czerny, Beethoven had high esteem for Clementi, but refused to call on him first after Clementi came to Vienna. Clementi in turn recognized Beethoven's genius and his piano compositions, but did not think very much of him as a pianist. (Cf. Shedlock: *The Pianoforte Sonata* and Max Unger: *M. Clementis Leben* 1913.)

Coffee

See Entry: Eating and Drinking.

Collin, Heinrich Joseph von

b. Vienna 1771, d. Vienna in 1811. Poet. After the failure of *Fidelio* Beethoven intended to compose an opera on Macbeth with a possible text by Collin. Sketches are preserved. Other projects, in connection with Collin were an opera *Bradamante* and an oratorio *Die Befreiung Jerusalems.* Furthermore Beethoven wrote the overture for Collin's tragedy *Coriolan* in 1807. The sketch of a composition of Collin's *"Wehrmannslieder"* (they were completely composed by Kanka in Prague) is mentioned by Nottebohm (cf. numerous references in Caroline Pichler's *Denkwürdigkeiten,* published by Georg Müller 1914 and Laban: *F. H. I. Collin,* Vienna 1879. See also Entry: Macbeth).

Concertos

In contrast to Mozart, who wrote about 50 concertos, Beethoven did not complete more than seven. Supposedly there were two piano concertos written in Bonn, one in E flat major, composed about 1784, consisting of three movements of which only the piano part is preserved; the other in D major, described by Guido Adler in *Vierteljahrschrift für Musikwissenschaft* (1888), was proved by Prof. Hans Engel to be spurious and was identified as a work by Johann Josef Rösler, a Czech composer. This work was written in 1802 and published ca. 1826 (cf. Engel "Der angeblich Beethovensche Klavierkonzertsatz" in *Neues Beethoven Jahrbuch* II). The Bonn E flat major Concerto was performed in January 1949 in an arrangement by Willy Hess in New York by Thomas Scherman's Little Orchestra. The concerto fragment shows definite influence of Beethoven's teacher Neefe. Beethoven wrote also a violin concerto in Bonn which is preserved as a fragment. The fragment in C major, published by Schiedermair in *Der junge Beethoven,* shows influence of Joseph Reicha, anticipating the style of the Master's C major Symphony. Josef Hellmesberger and Juan de Manén completed the work, but in a very unsatisfactory way. A performance of the original was given in a "Collegium Musicum" at Indiana University (1950). All five of the famous piano concertos were composed in Vienna before 1808. The first one in C major, Op. 15, was dedicated to Princess Odescalchi and was published by Mollo. In spite of the low opus number of this concerto, it was composed later than Op. 19 in B flat major, dedicated to Carl Nikl, Nicklas von Nickelsberg. Beethoven in a letter of April 22, 1801, to Breitkopf and Härtel, confirms the earlier origin of Op. 19. The first two concertos may be considered as preliminary studies for the remaining three great concertos. They both breathe a friendly atmosphere reminiscent of older patterns in their clear transparent form, using frequently Alberti basses. The use of folk and popular tunes, a heritage from Mozart, makes the C major Concerto especially popular. There is a tradition, handed down in the Artaria family, that one of the "couplets" from the Rondo Op. 15 originated from Beethoven's habit of calling Artaria in the following way:

Der Artaría

Another "couplet" is nothing else but the old folk song, "Die Katze lässt das Mausen nicht," which first appeared as a Quodlibet in *Augsburger Tafelconfect* II, 1737 and was used by Mozart in his E flat major Divertimento, K. 252 and is still sung today as a German student song on Geibel's text, "Zwei lustige Musikanten marschierten einst am Nil." Both concertos are technically comparatively easy and could be played "a vista" as frequently done at that time. This is certainly not the case with the last three concertos in which Beethoven breaks with the old tradition, according to which the piano concerto is merely composed for the pleasure and entertainment of the listener. In these concertos Beethoven offers a synthesis of highest orchestral and pianistic art, based on his principle of poetic idea. The C minor Concerto Op. 37 is dedicated to Prince Louis Ferdinand of Prussia. It was published in 1804 "A Vienne au Bureau d'Arts et d'Industrie" although composed in 1800. The first performance probably took place in a concert in July 1804 with Ries as the pianist and Beethoven as the conductor. Ries mentioned that he never had a better orchestral accompaniment. This concerto forms the bridge between the first two and the last two. Beethoven's poetic idea about the "two principles" on which all his later works are based, is best expressed in that concerto. Tragic tones are held against gaiety, fighting mood against contemplation. Whereas in the early concertos the orchestra only plays an accompanying function, the C minor Concerto is a concerto in the true sense of the word. The orchestra is equivalent to the solo part; it inspires the soloist and confirms him. The grim, energetic *allegro* in C minor is contrasted to an emotional *largo* in E major, embedded in beautiful melismas. The spiteful *rondo* in C minor concludes this concerto, a milestone in Beethoven's oeuvre. The Fourth Piano Concerto in G major is dedicated to Archduke Rudolph. It was composed ca. 1805 and ready for print in February 1807. The oldest existing edition was published in August 1808 by the "Kunst und Industrie Comptoir." The first performance took place in a private concert at the house of Prince Lobkowitz. Beethoven had first in mind to dedicate it to his friend Gleichenstein. It was performed for the first time in public on December 2, 1808, and Beethoven himself played the piano part. Reichardt in his *Vertraute Briefe* described that concert in which the Choral Fantasy and the Sixth Symphony were also heard. He mentioned the tremendous difficulty of the concerto, which Beethoven handled beautifully in every respect. "The *adagio*, a masterwork of a beautiful *cantabile*, was sung on his instrument with deep melancholic emotion which found an echo in my own feelings." The G major Concerto is probably the most poetic composition of the concerto literature. According to an old tradition the poetic background of the concerto was the legend of Orpheus, who implores the powers of the Inferno. Indeed, it seems as if a gloomy god would oppose man's pleading, not in stormy fashion, but firm as a rock. This unison, staccato rhythm is reminiscent of the threatening phrases in Gluck's *Orfeo*. As in so many symphonies and sonatas of Beethoven's middle period, the finale portrays complete victory over fate. The Fifth Concerto in E flat major, Op. 73, dedicated to Archduke Rudolph is called in the Western world the "Emperor" Concerto. According to a tradition, a grenadier who heard the concerto in Paris long after all the wars were over, jumped to his feet and called out: "It's the Emperor." Another reason for that name is probably the fact that it was dedicated to the Archduke. There is no doubt that the grandeur of the composition justifies the popular title of the concerto, which according to some writers is a high stylization of the military concertos of that time. The heroic character of the themes, the predominance of war-like rhythms and a scarcity of lyrical sections shows Beethoven as the "Generalissimo," a name he used for himself. Who is not reminded of Beethoven's last dreams which transferred him to imaginary battle fields! Beethoven did not wish any cadenzas for this concerto, which was introduced to the public by Carl Czerny in 1812. Between the lyrical G major Concerto and its heroic counterpart, the E flat major Concerto, the Violin Concerto Op. 61. forms a bridge. It was published in 1809 by the "Bureau d'Arts et d'Industrie" and dedicated to Stephan von Breuning. The first public performance of the concerto was by Clement on December 23, 1806. Characteristically Beethoven wrote on the autograph, preserved in the National Library in Vienna, "Concerto par Clemenza pour Clement primo Violino e direttore al teatro di Vienna Dal L. V. Bthvn. 1806" (cf. Entry: Clement). The violin concerto belongs to the happiest and most joyful works of the Master. Whereas in the piano concertos the piano and the orchestra are equally presented ready to fight each other, the solo part in the violin concerto emerges almost casually from the orchestral introduction. The march-like rhythms are reminiscent of the "Emperor" Concerto, but they are by no means in contrast to the lyric scenes corresponding to the character of the violin. The last movement is a typical instrumental "chasse." Beethoven also arranged this concerto as a piano concerto. It was published in the complete works, Series 9^2, the tutti being arranged by Carl Reinecke. This piano concerto was dedicated to "Frau von Breuning" and was published originally by Haslinger. Finally the Triple Concerto Op. 56 in C major for piano, violin and cello should be mentioned. Written in 1804, it was published in 1807 "A Vienne au Bureau d'Arts et d'Industrie" and dedicated to Prince Lobkowitz. Originally Beethoven had assigned as soloists Anton Kraft (cello), Seidler (violin), and the Archduke (piano). It was the Archduke who was most responsible for the composition of this work, for Beethoven wanted to give him a chance to show his skill as a performer. As a result of these considerations, this work bears definite marks of an "occasional" composition. It is an outgrowth of the Baroque concerto grosso, and shows numerous, most interesting details, without having the sublime intuition of the last three piano concertos. The Rondo "Alla Polacca" is particularly remarkable with the splendid rhythms à la Weber. (Cf. Schering: *Geschichte des Instrumentalkonzerts,* Veinus: *The Concerto* and Th.-R.)

Conducting

From his years in Bonn, Beethoven had many opportunities to conduct from the keyboard instrument. Ignaz von Seyfried was an excellent witness for Beethoven's conducting. In his *Studien* he characterizes Beethoven as a conductor: "Our Master was by no means a model conductor and the orchestra had to be on the alert, in order not to get confused. He was only interested in his own composition and tried to achieve the desired effect through diverse gesticulations. He even would give a downbeat where an upbeat was expected. To indicate a *diminuendo,* he shrank and when the *pianissimo* came, he was almost invisible. To indicate a *crescendo,* he rose up from his desk. At the *fortissimo* he seemed like a giant, rowing with his two arms, trying to reach the skies. All the parts of his body were moving; the whole man appeared like a perpetuum mobile." With increasing deafness the situation deteriorated. Sometimes he marked the thesis, when the orchestra was already playing the arsis. He was more able to conduct movements in *piano* than those in *forte*. Sometimes his eyesight came to his help, as he watched the bowings of the strings. Ries tells that Beethoven was often very lenient during rehearsals and skipped necessary repeating. "It'll be all right, next time," the Master used to say. In contrast to that, he could be quite meticulous concerning expression, details of shading, *tempo rubato*. He was sometimes very accurate and discussed the questionable parts with the individual players. If he felt that the musicians followed his ideas with enthusiasm, his smiling face reflected satisfaction and he uttered a thunderous bravo.

When he conducted his Choral Fantasia he had to stop, and when the *Eroica* was performed in the Palace of Prince Lobkowitz the section of the first movement with the syncopation brought the whole orchestra into confusion. The changes of time in his *scherzos* were most disastrous. The observations of Seyfried and Ries are confirmed by reports from Spohr, Tomaschek, Atterbom, the violinist Joseph Böhm and Moscheles. When Beethoven's deafness increased, he had to be assisted by a second conductor; in such cases he only sat at the piano. In our times the concertgoer is spoiled by the meticulous performances, as introduced by Habeneck, Berlioz, Liszt, Hans von Bülow, Richard Wagner, Richard Strauss, Furtwängler, Toscanini and a host of others, and it is hard for us to realize that there was a time when the reproduction was considered less important than the work itself. (Cf. Schünemann: *Geschichte des Dirigierens,* Dorian: *History of Music in Performance,* Haas: *Aufführungspraxis.)*

Conversation-books Konversationshefte

Bound sheets, used by the deaf Beethoven as means of conversing with his visitors. Traces of such notes were found in a small note book, written before the years 1815 and 1816, seen by Frimmel in the possession of Countess Amadei. Many of such early notes are lost; slates, strips of paper and finally bound sheets were used. Breuning tells us that Beethoven in later years spoke in a loud voice and very vivaciously. On walks with Beethoven the person accompanying him frequently had to stop to write the answer to Beethoven's questions in the Conversation-book. Many contemporaries tell about such conversations, e.g. the organist Carl Gottlieb Freudenberg, the librarian D. Spiker, the Englishman John Russell, who speaks about the "Paperbook" (*A Tour in Germany,* Edinburgh 1825, II, p. 276), Grillparzer in his *Erinnerungen an Beethoven.* Others who conversed with the Master in the above-mentioned manner were Zuccalmaglio, the famous collector of folk songs, Ferdinand Hiller and above all his regular visitors: Schindler, Holz, etc.

After Beethoven's death Schindler quickly took possession of approximately 400 of these books which he used for his studies on Beethoven's biography. He numbered the pages and made comments in red pencil. In the spring of 1843 Schindler began his negotiations with the Royal Library in Berlin which led to the purchase of Schindler's Beethoven estate, which included 136 Conversation-books. Consequently 264 pieces were missing which Schindler had held back. The concealing of these missing copies was an act of deliberate and arbitrary intention. Thayer, Deiters, Riemann, Hans Volkmann, Kalischer, Nohl, and more recently Schünemann in his *Beethovens Konversationshefte,* 3 vols. Berlin 1941, used these Conversation-books abundantly. A complete edition of the Conversation-books still is pending and is eagerly anticipated by all Beethoven lovers.

Copyists

Because of Beethoven's illegible handwriting, he used copyists extensively, especially for copying parts. In Bonn, 1783 his copyist was Johann Baptist Paraquin, who was known to be an excellent double bass player and cellist in the Bonn Orchestra. He was also a fairly good bass singer. Wegeler calls him an excellent artist and a highly esteemed citizen. In a letter quoted by Wegeler and in Th.-R. I, p. 231, Paraquin is mentioned as a copyist. Beethoven was quite impatient with this category of musicians and sometimes they were honored with names like "Schurke," "Esel," etc. In about 1805 a musician, Gottfried Gebauer, was working for the Master.

Occasionally Beethoven was inclined to hire servants whom he could use as copyists, as shown by a letter written to Zmeskall in 1811. For about 30 years a certain Schlemmer together with his co-workers was employed by Beethoven. He was the most reliable of all copyists and his work was highly appreciated by Beethoven. This fact is proven by a letter of July 1823 showing that the copyist was entrusted with the revision of certain variations. He was the copyist of numerous works, including the *Missa Solemnis.* Schlemmer died in the summer of 1823. In a letter of December 17, 1824, Beethoven wrote to the publisher Schott. " . . . I am lacking an intelligent copyist. The one I had died 1½ years ago. I could rely on him." Most of the copyists had their own clerks and the office of a copyist might be compared to our modern typing services. Besides Schlemmer, Peter Gläser enjoyed Beethoven's confidence. This was not the case with Anton Wolanek, born about 1761, probably in Prague, a composer of ballets and dances. The author of this book found in the National Museum in Prague a manuscript volume containing contredances from Mozart's *Figaro* arranged by Kanka, and dances by Wolanek.

After having moved to Vienna Wolanek established a copying business, but he aroused the anger of the Olympian. In a letter of January 6, 1825, Beethoven wrote to Haslinger: "You can judge yourself what kind of a copyist I have. The guy is a stubborn Czech, a Pandur, he does not understand me . . ." However the "Pandur" addressed Beethoven in an ironic letter in which he referred to Beethoven's misbehavior against him. Even had Haydn and Mozart functioned as Beethoven's copyists, they might have suffered the same fate. Beethoven, emotional as he was, crossed out the whole letter and wrote the following words in big letters: "Stupid, conceited ass" and added on the margin: "Should I compliment a scoundrel who steals one's money? One better should pull his ass's ears!" Even the back of the letter was not spared the rage of the Master. "Schreibsudler, dummer Kerl!" he called him. "You had better correct your mistakes, made by ignorance and insolence."

Another of Beethoven's copyists of Czech extraction who did not meet his approval was Paul Maschek (1761-1826), known as a composer, brother of Vincenz Maschek, also a well-known composer. Paul Maschek was for a while the conductor of Graf Nostitz. A letter of Maschek to Beethoven concerning a copy is printed in Frimmel's *Beethoven-jahrbuch* II, p. 209. In a family chronicle of the Mascheks, Paul Maschek is mentioned as an intimate friend not only of Beethoven, but also of Archduke Rudolph, Weigl and others.

Coriolan Overture

Op. 62 C minor. Finished in April 1807 and dedicated to "Dem Hofsecretair H. J. R. Collin" (cf. Entry: Collin). First performed in December 1807. The Autograph, to be found today in the Beethoven Haus in Bonn, bears the inscription "Overtura, composta da L. v. Beethoven 1807." The first theatrical performance of Collin's drama took place on April 24, 1807. The concert performance in December was attended by Reichardt who was struck by the powerful beats at the beginning of the overture. Reichardt believes that Beethoven depicted himself rather than his hero in the overture. Bekker points out that this overture represents the philosophy of a destructive hero in sharp contrast to the first movement of the *Eroica*. Instead of the optimistic introductory harmonies, we hear dark threatening sounds. Wagner in his "Beethoven" erroneously links Beethoven's Overture to Shakespeare's *Coriolanus* and interprets Beethoven's music in a highly programmatic way. (Cf. Th.-R. III in contrast to Wagner and Hanslick's excellent, but purely formalistic interpretation in *Vom musikalisch Schönen.)*

Cramer, Johann Baptist

b. Mannheim 1771, d. London 1858. Son of Wilhelm Cramer, member of the Mannheim School, pupil of Clementi and

Abel. Excellent pianist and publisher. The following story was told by Mary DeFouche, daughter of the piano maker Tomkinson, to Thayer (cf. Th.-R. I, p. 405): "At a gathering of musicians Beethoven's Trios Op. 1 were played. Cramer, delighted, exclaimed: 'This is the man who will comfort us for the loss of Mozart.' " But Cramer did not always speak very kindly of Beethoven and in a letter to Ries Beethoven calls Cramer his "Contra-Subject" (opponent). Beethoven owned the first two books of Cramer's Etudes (cf. Shedlock: The Beethoven-Cramer studies, Schlesinger, J. B. C. Diss., 1925.)

Cressener, George

English envoy in Bonn. According to a story by the cellist Mäurer to be found in the Fischhoff Manuscript, Beethoven wrote a funeral cantata at the death of Cressener in 1781 (cf. Th.-R. I, p. 141).

Crevelt, J. H.

Physician, who wrote into the "Album" of 1792 a poem as an admirer and friend. He belongs to the circle of the widow Koch (cf. Th.-R. I, p. 502 and Gerstinger: *Ludwig van Beethovens Stammbuch,* 1927).

Czerny, Carl

b. Vienna 1791, d. Vienna 1857. Son of Wenzel Czerny, born in Nimburg (Bohemia) in 1750, who had settled in Vienna in 1775 as master of the keyboard. Many musicians gathered in Wenzel's house, Abbé Gelinek, Joseph Lipowski, Wanhall, Krumpholz and last but not least Beethoven. Krumpholz had introduced Carl Czerny as a child to the Master, who took over his music instruction. Beethoven gave him two lessons weekly based on Philip Emanuel Bach's *Versuch über die wahre Art das Klavier zu spielen.* These lessons were not given regularly. According to Czerny's *Erinnerungen aus meinem Leben* (published in C. F. Pohl's *Jahresbericht der Gesellschaft der Musikfreunde,* 1870) all scales had to be practiced in all the different keys. Hand positions, use of the thumb and *legato* playing were the main subjects of instruction. Recommended by Beethoven, Czerny became one of the most popular piano teachers in Vienna. Among his pupils were Queen Victoria, Liszt (1818-1821), Döhler, Rudolf von Vivenot, Caroline Belleville-Oury. Already in 1806, as a boy of 15, he had played Beethoven's Piano Concerto in C major in an Augarten concert and in 1812 the "Emperor" Concerto. In his home in Krugerstrasse house concerts took place, frequently with an all-Beethoven program. Many orchestra and chamber music compositions of Beethoven were arranged for piano, e.g., in Haslinger's *Wiener Musikalisches Pfennig Magazin* a "Romanze" (String Quartet Op. 59 No. 3, Second Movement), etc. He played all the piano sonatas of the Master, among them Op. 106, which he performed in 1820 for Wilhelm Christian Müller (cf. Ludwig Nohl: *Beethoven nach den Schilderungen seiner Zeitgenossen*). In his "Complete theoretical and practical Pianoforte School" he gave valuable hints to performers of Beethoven's piano works. Czerny handed down the way in which Beethoven played Bach's Well Tempered Clavier. For a while Czerny was the teacher of Beethoven's nephew Karl. In his autobiography he characterizes Beethoven's playing and contrasts its tremendous power and unheard-of bravura, velocity and expression to Hummel's gracefulness, tenderness and elegance. As a human being, Czerny was a typical musician of Slavic extraction. He was modest, friendly and diligent. He left in his estate two original manuscripts of Beethoven, the Violin Concerto and the score of the Overture Op. 115 which he willed to the Imperial Library. Czerny was also one of the torch-bearers at Beethoven's funeral. (Cf. Hellmuth Steger: *Beiträge zu C. Czernys Leben und Schaffen*. Munich Dissertation 1924.)

Czerny, Joseph

b. Horwitz, Bohemia, 1785, d. Vienna, 1842. Not related to Carl Czerny. Piano teacher and successor to Carl Czerny as piano teacher of Beethoven's nephew Karl. He also was the teacher of the piano virtuoso Leopoldine Blahetka. This fact is mentioned in one of Beethoven's Conversation-books. He became a partner of the publishing firm Cappi and Co., after 1826 Cappi and Czerny.

D

Dancing and Dance Music

About Beethoven's dance master in Vienna, see Entry: Lindner. Concerning his relationship to the dance music of his time and his own dances Schindler wrote the following: "What great importance Beethoven allotted to Austrian dance music is proved by facts. Prior to his arrival in Vienna in 1792, he had not, as he says himself, become acquainted with any folk music except the country folk songs from his Rhineland home, with their strange rhythms. The list of his works shows how much he busied himself with dance music, notwithstanding the fact that the musicians in Austria were unwilling to acknowledge his compositions of Austrian dance music as Austrian. His last attempt in this direction dates from the year 1819, the year of the creation of the *Missa Solemnis*. In the Zu den drei Raben inn at Mödling (a suburb of Vienna), there was a company of seven musicians from the country who played the unadulterated real music of his new home. The friendship between Beethoven and these native musicians grew apace and a number of dances, ländlers and others, were composed for their use. I was present when in the year mentioned above (1819), Beethoven handed his new opus to the leader of the band at Mödling. In a gay mood the Master mentioned he had so arranged the composition of these dances, that from time to time one or the other of the musicians could put down his instrument, take a rest, even go to sleep. After the leader, having accepted the gift, had left, Beethoven asked whether I had noticed how the village musicians often dropped off to sleep during their playing, and then again, as they woke suddenly, would chime in with a number of hearty loud notes, played at random, but for the most part in the right key, and so would alternate between napping and waking. In the Pastorale Symphony, said Beethoven, he had tried to imitate these poor fellows" . . . "If you, dear Reader, will look at the music on pages 106, 107, 108 and 109 (of the Breitkopf and Härtel edition) you will find the proof of it. You will see the stereotyped accompanying phrase of the two violins on page 105, you will see the sleepy second bassoon with the repeatedly abruptly dropped notes, while the bass, the cello and the viola have stopped altogether. Not until page 108 do we see the viola waking up, arousing in its turn the neighboring cello, then the second

DANCING AND DANCE MUSIC

horn begins, plays a few notes, but passes immediately. The last ones to be fully aroused to renewed activity are the bass and the two bassoons. The clarinet too has its time and space for a period of rest. Turn to page 110, and the *allegro* in 2/4 time shows in its form and character the essence of the ancient Austrian dance music. For dances existed in former times in which the duple rhythm changed suddenly to 3/4 time. I, myself, watching the dances in the woodland villages around the capital, have (in the decade from 1820-1830) seen such dances performed . . . "

The *Ländliche Tanz* of Beethoven's "Pastorale" does indeed seem to be a highly stylized ländler. As a matter of fact, we find that the ländlers played in Upper Austria and Styria have this transition from 3/4 time to 2/4 time. One of the best experts on this type of dance, Commenda, says in his book on ländlers what we may take to be a confirmation of Schindler's report: "Almost every fiddler or musician had his jealously guarded transcriptions of ländler tunes familiar to him often handed down for generations of musicians. To read these notes was possible only for a learned and accomplished musician, and for the actual dancing, the practice was not to play from the music but from memory. Most of the ländler transcriptions as well as those published from the old records are in 3/4 time. The same musician will sometimes play the melody in 3/4 time, sometimes in 2/4 time according to the pace observed by the dancers."

It might be recalled that the old "Grandfather dance" begins with a deliberate, slow 3/4 ländler, and changes, without transition, into 2/4 time. In the Austrian province around Salzburg, such dances still are being used.

Schindler continues in his report that Beethoven wrote a number of waltzes for the band in Mödling, copying the parts himself. To trace these lost dances seemed a vain task for Schindler, who simply said that the score was lost. It really seemed so for a long time, but in 1907 Hugo Riemann found the parts of these "Mödling Dances" in the archives of the Thomas Schule in Leipzig.

In all these waltzes, minuets and ländlers, the practice to which Schindler points, of the alternately sleeping and waking musicians, shows itself in the changing roles of the various instruments. They are highly stylized in spite of their relation to folk style, and Riemann points out that in their composition the creator had left behind him folklore of Austrian music, and was in truth writing real "Beethoven" dances.

We know that Beethoven was fond of dancing, though Ries tells us that he never really learned to keep in step. (Even Johann Strauss, the "Waltz King," did not know how to dance!) Perhaps this failing of the composer had some influence on the opinion of the Austrian dance composers of the time, who considered Beethoven's dance music unfit for dancing. While these severe critics of Beethoven repose unread in music archives, the dance rhythms of the Master still delight the world. Nevertheless, there are a great many Beethoven's dances which have not been re-edited or reprinted; as far as the musicians of today are concerned, they are non-existent. In the "Complete Works," Series II, there are twelve Minuets and twelve Deutsche Tänze (probably dating from 1795); in

Series XXV (Supplement), there are six ländlerische Tänze for 2 violins and bass, six Deutsche for piano and violin, six Deutsche Tänze for piano only, as well as six Ecossaises, and some other dances. In Series XVIII (Short Pieces for Pianoforte), there are six Minuets and thirteen ländlerische Tänze (of these No. 1-6, identical with those of Series II, No. 7-12, have been preserved only for the piano). However, we lack new practical editions; most of the Beethoven dances are written in a simple form and in this respect strongly resemble those of Mozart. Their structure shows a division into eight parts, they are based on few themes, and the harmonic plan is simple. Beethoven also liked to use themes from his earlier works; for example, in the "Mödling Dances" he used themes from his "Klavier Bagatellen" and he quoted the accessory theme from the *larghetto* of the Second Symphony in another dance of the same series. On the other hand, he used the seventh of his twelve Contredances for the *Eroica,* thus making it immortal. The most folk-like and popular of the dances are the germans and the ländlers, where we find a triadic melodic line, with Alpine strains most obvious in the trios. Like Mozart, Beethoven closes his Deutsche with a brilliantly developed long coda, returning to one of the motives of the last trio. The ländlerischen go so far in realism and primitive expression that they verge on caricature, as in the piano version of Dance No. 3, when the bagpipe accompaniment enunciates both tonic and dominant simultaneously and the impression resembles that made by the *Eroica* tonic-dominant combination. In Dance No. 7, the accentuation of the second beat often gives us a fine musical picture of the syncopated stepping of the peasants in the ländler.

Beethoven's contribution to ballet music also is considerable. In his youth he wrote a *Ritterballet* (Equestrian Ballet) which was performed on a carnival Sunday in 1791, in Bonn. Its "invention," that is, its arrangement, was by his patron Count Waldstein. The dancing master Habich from Aix la Chapelle helped to produce it, but the music's creator was not mentioned, apparently because it was intended that the whole should be credited to the Count. He may have contributed one or another to the tunes. A report found in Bonn tells us that this ballet dealt with the favorite pastimes of the ancestors; the hunt, the battle, carousing and love. It was a late descendant of the old ballet tournaments or perhaps a revival of one of those Renaissance "trionfi" of former centuries. The music is extremely popular in form, adapted to the requirements of the aristocratic society. There is a march, a Deutscher Gesang (faintly reminiscent of the melodies from Saint-Saëns' *Carnival des Animaux*), a hunting song, a romance, a battle song, a drinking song (resembling one of the German student songs), a Deutscher Tanz and a coda which harks back to previously used melodies. (Cf. Entries: *Prometheus* and Vigano.)

Degenhardt, J. M.

Candidatus juris, friend of Beethoven in Bonn to whom the young Master dedicated an Allegro and Minuet for two Flutes, published by Th.-R. I. He was one of the contributors to the Bonn Koch album of 1792. (Cf. Schiedermair: *Der junge Beethoven,* and Gerstinger: *Ludwig van Beethovens Stammbuch.*)

Deym, Count

See Entry: Brunsvik.

Diabelli, Antonio

b. Mattsee (near Salzburg) 1781, d. Vienna 1858. Studied with Michael Haydn in Salzburg; in 1800 entered the Raitenhasslach monastery in Upper Bavaria. Because of the secularization of the Bavarian monasteries in 1803 he had to give up his career as a priest. He moved to Vienna, where he was recommended by Michael Haydn to his brother Joseph. He taught clavier and guitar and joined the publisher Steiner as an editor. Beethoven called him "Generalprofoss und diabolus Diabelli." In 1818 he founded, together with Peter Cappi, the publishing firm of Cappi and Diabelli. In 1820 this firm incorporated the Johann Traeg publishing company; in 1824 he left the firm and founded an independent firm. C. H. Spina was active in this firm and later took over the firm as his own.

Diabelli composed numerous pieces for piano, guitar, and other instruments, sonatas, sonatinas, etc. Diabelli is known today not only for his sonatas for four hands, but also for his connection with Beethoven. In 1824 he had asked Beethoven to write for his firm a piano sonata for four hands. The project was not realized. Two years later Diabelli commissioned him to write a string quartet. Diabelli acquired the fragment from the estate and published it as "Beethoven's last musical thought" in two- and four-hand piano arrangements.

Diabelli became immortal through the famous Diabelli Variations Op. 120 by Beethoven. In 1821 the publisher had asked a number of Austrian composers each to write a variation on a waltz theme of his own. The work was published independently in 1823 and a year later as the first section of that famous collective work called *Vaterländischer Künstlerverein,* "Veränderungen für das Pianoforte über ein vorgelegtes Thema, componiert von den vorzüglichsten Tonsetzern und Virtuosen Wiens und der K. K. Osterreichischen Staaten. Erste Abteilung enthält: 33 Veränderungen von L. van Beethoven, 120.stes Werk. Preis 5 fl. 30 Kr. W. W. Zweyte Abteilung, enthält: 50 Veränderungen über dasselbe Thema von folgenden Tonsetzern als: . . . Coda von Carl Czerny. Pr. 10 fl. W. W. (Eigenthum der Verleger)."

The edition contains a long preface in which Beethoven is called the "Musical Jean Paul." It points out that it contains the first composition of a boy eleven years of age, Franz Liszt. Heinrich Rietsch, who analyzed the work in the 57th report of the *Lese-und Redehalle der deutschen Studenten in Prag* and in the first *Beethoven Jahrbuch* (publ. by Frimmel), discussed the autographs of the individual composers. Franz Schubert wrote the first and best variation. Other contributors were: J. Assmayer, C. M. v. Bocklet, E. Czapek, C. Czerny, J. Czerny, J. Count Dietrichstein, J. Drechsler, E. Förster, J. Freystädtler, J. Gänsbacher, Abbé Gelinek, A. Halm, J. Hoffmann, J. Horzalka, J. Huglmann, J. N. Hummel, A. Hüttenbrenner, F. Kalkbrenner, F. A. Kanne, J. Kerzhowski, C. Kreutzer, Baron E. Lannoy, M. J. Leidesdorf, F. Liszt, J. Mayseder, J. Moscheles, J. von Mosel, W. A. Mozart (fils), J. Panny, H. Payer, P. Pixis, W. Plachy, G. Rieger, P. Riotte,

F. Roser, J. Schenk, F. Schoberlechner, S. Sechter, Abbé Stadler, S.R.D. (Archduke Rudolph), J. de Szalay, W. Tomaschek, M. Umlauf, Dion. Weber, Fr. Weber, C. A. de Winkhler, F. Weiss, J. Wittassek and J. H. Worzischek.

Except for Schubert's variation (cf. Schubert's complete works, Series II, No. 8, page 134), most of these works are forgotten today. Mozart's and Rieger's variations are reprinted by Rietsch. Beethoven's Variations, originally dedicated to Antonia Brentano, are among Beethoven's greatest compositions. Hans von Bülow called them the "microcosmos of Beethoven's genius." All evolutions of musical thinking are compiled in that work; sublime profundity, audacious humor alternate in an infinite variety. Variation No. 22 is a typical practical joke of Beethoven's, with the quotation being Leporello's exclamation: *"Notte e giorno faticar"* (Mozart's *Don Giovanni*); it might have some autobiographical meaning (cf. Kahl's article on Diabelli in M. G. G.).

Dietrichstein, Count Moritz (Proskau-Leslie)

b. Vienna 1775, d., according to Wurzbach, Vienna 1864. About his military career, consult Wurzbach III 303 and XIV 423. After 1800 he dedicated himself to art and science. He was honorary chamberlain to the King of Denmark at the start of the Vienna Congress and somewhat later tutor to the Duke of Reichsstadt. From 1821-1826 he was "Hoftheaterdirektor" and from 1826 to 1845 Director of the Imperial Library. As "Hofmusikgraf" and Director of the Imperial Chapel he had great influence in all matters pertaining to music. To him Bridgetower owes most of the success of his concert in 1803. Dietrichstein was one of Beethoven's most sincere friends. When A. Tayber, court composer, died in November 1822, Count Moritz Lichnowsky and Dietrichstein suggested to Beethoven that he compose a mass which would enable Beethoven to obtain Tayber's position. Unfortunately this post was abolished. Beethoven dedicated his song "Merkenstein" (version in the Almanach Selam of 1816) to the Count, who himself became known as the composer of "XVI Lieder von Göthe dem Dichter gewidmet von Graf Moritz Dietrichstein." Friedländer's edition of the Goethe Lieder contains Dietrichstein's "Wonne der Wehmuth," a fairly well composed song.

Diseases (I)

Beethoven's hearing had started to deteriorate in his 28th year, or probably even earlier. First, the left ear was affected, soon afterwards the right ear. Continual humming and buzzing in the ears was especially distressing to him. It was inconceivable to him that he should lose his sense of hearing. After a long period of worrying and despair, he finally reached a state of quiet resignation and self-control. But at no period of his life, until the gray day of his death, did he give up the hope of being cured, the hope for a miracle.

Beethoven did not suffer from otosclerosis as is sometimes claimed, but from a disease of the inner ear, an affection of the acoustic nerve. The Master, as we know, first lost his capacity of hearing high notes—a characteristic sign of neuritis acoustica. At the post mortem examination, the acoustic nerve, especially that of the left ear, was found to be atrophied.

What was the cause of this atrophy of Beethoven's hearing nerves? Of all the possible causes, the most probable is a severe attack of typhoid fever in his youth. Infectious diseases often lastingly affect various nerves, and the acoustic nerve is highly sensitive to the toxins of such diseases.

The chronic stomach and intestinal troubles from which Beethoven suffered from his 30th year on, also find their explanation in the after effects of typhoid fever. They formed the basis for the fatal illness of which he eventually died, cirrhosis of the liver. It is easy to follow the successive stages of this sickness in Beethoven's life: jaundice, hemorrhages, dropsy. During his last years of life, the Master repeatedly had to be tapped on account of his dropsy. He suffered these operations with a good sense of humor. He told the tapping physician, Dr. Seibert: "Professor, you remind me of Moses striking the rock with his staff." He never lost his angelic patience.

Beethoven's financial circumstances and living conditions were irregular and unfavorable. Consequently he was not in a position to give his chronic stomach ailments the proper care and the necessary attention. Excessive alcoholism has been named a cause of Beethoven's liver complaints, but this is an unfounded invention. Beethoven was fond of an occasional glass of wine, and in his later years he preferred punch. But at no time of his life was he a drinker. Furthermore, we do not believe any more that abuse of alcohol is a proven provocation of cirrhosis of the liver. The chronic intestinal troubles such as Beethoven suffered from, give a valid explanation for the appearance of his liver complaints.

There is not the slightest evidence that Beethoven at any period of his life suffered from syphilis (as has been stated erroneously) or from any other venereal disease. Proof of this fact has been given in my book on Beethoven's diseases (1922) and in my study on Beethoven's physicians in the *Musical Quarterly*, 1945.

For years and years Beethoven underwent all kinds of treatments by doctors as well as by laymen and nature healers, and even tried the impossible to improve his hearing. He once said: "My whole life has been poisoned." These words show the deep depression of a chronic invalid, of a musician gradually but inevitably losing his most important sense. They show the profound despair from which originated the *Heiligenstadter Testament*, and which he always heroically conquered.

In fact there is hardly any progress in medical treatment of today which would have curative effects on Beethoven's deafness. However, a modern hearing aid might have proven infinitely more helpful to the master than the contrivances of his time which he tried to use for improving his hearing—to his permanent disappointment and dissatisfaction.

Beethoven died on March 26, 1827 after four consecutive tappings were necessary to give him relief. The next day, an autopsy was performed by Dr. Johannes Wagner in the presence of Beethoven's last physician, Dr. Andreas Wawruch, professor of special pathology and medical clinics in the surgical department of the Vienna hospital. Dr. Wagner gave a detailed report of the autopsy which makes the diagnosis cirrhosis of the liver obvious.

Dr. Wawruch's history of Beethoven's last illness and his entries into the Conversation-books show clearly that this excellent physician gave all his love and his efforts to the treatment of the revered Master; he even made three visits a day while Beethoven suffered from pneumonia shortly before his death. There cannot be any doubt about the kind of treatment, considering the fact that the autopsy had demonstrated an incurable disease of the liver. All that could be done, and was done, was to administer soothing and relieving remedies.

Beethoven's great genius made him a really great man in disease and the hour of death as well. His demon gave him the impulse to work and produce without any consideration for health and well-being. The will of a genius can eliminate and compensate for the effects of physical handicaps and defects.

W.S.

Diseases (II)

The literature about Beethoven's diseases is considerable. The following report of Beethoven's last physician, Dr. Wawruch, can be reprinted. It was given May 20, 1827.

"Ludwig van Beethoven declared that from earliest youth he had possessed a rugged, permanently good constitution, hardened by many privations, which even the most strenuous toil at his favorite occupation and continual profound study had been unable in the slightest degree to impair. The lonely nocturnal quiet always had shown itself most friendly to his glowing imagination. Hence he usually wrote after midnight until about three o'clock. A short sleep of from four to five hours was all he needed to refresh him. His breakfast eaten, he sat down at his writing desk again until two o'clock in the afternoon.

"When he entered his thirtieth year, however, he began to suffer from haemorrhoidal complaints and an annoying roaring and buzzing in both ears. Soon his hearing began to fail, and, for all he often would enjoy untroubled intervals lasting for months at a time, his disability finally ended in complete deafness. All the resources of the physician's art were useless. At about the same time Beethoven noticed that his digestion began to suffer; loss of appetite was followed by indigestion, an annoying belching, an alternate obstinate constipation and frequent diarrhoea.

"At no time accustomed to taking medical advice seriously, he began to develop a liking for spirituous beverages, in order to stimulate his decreasing appetite and to aid his stomachic weakness by excessive use of strong punch and iced drinks and long, tiring excursions on foot. It was this very alteration of his mode of life which, some seven years earlier, had led him to the brink of the grave. He contracted a severe inflammation of the intestines, which, though it yielded to treatment, later on often gave rise to intestinal pains and aching colics and which, in part, must have favored the eventual development of his mortal illness.

"In the late fall of the year just passed (1826) Beethoven felt an irresistible urge, in view of the uncertain state of his health, to go to the country to recuperate. Since owing to his incurable deafness he sedulously avoided society, he was thrown entirely upon his own resources under the most unfavorable circumstances for days and even weeks at a time. Often, with rare endurance, he worked at his compositions on a wooded hillside and his work done, still aglow with reflection, he would not infrequently run about for hours in the most inhospitable surroundings, defying every change of temperature, and often daring the heaviest snowfalls. His feet, always from time to time oedematous, would begin to swell and since (as he insisted) he had to do without every comfort of life, every solacing refreshment, his illness soon got the upper hand of him.

"Intimidated by the sad prospect, in the gloomy future, of finding himself helpless in the country should he fall sick, he longed to be back in Vienna, and, as he himself jovially said, used the devil's own most wretched conveyance, a milk-wagon, to carry him home.

"December was raw, wet, cold and frosty. Beethoven's clothing was anything but suited to the unkind season of the year, and yet he was driven on and away by an inner restlessness, a sinister presentiment of misfortune. He was obliged to stop overnight in a village inn, where in addition to the shelter afforded by its wretched roof he found only an unheated room without winter windows. Toward midnight he was seized with his first convulsive chills and fever, accompanied by violent thirst and pains in the side. When the fever heat began to break, he drank a couple of quarts of ice-cold water, and, in his helpless state, yearned for the first ray of dawn. Weak and ill, he had himself loaded on the open van and, finally, arrived in Vienna enervated and exhausted.

"I was not sent for until the third day. I found Beethoven with grave symptoms of inflammation of the lungs; his face glowed, he spit blood, when he breathed he threatened to choke, and the shooting pain in his side only allowed him to lie in a tormenting posture flat on his back. A strict anti-inflammatory mode of treatment soon brought the desired amelioration; nature conquered and a happy crisis freed him of the seemingly imminent danger of death, so that on the fifth day he was able to sit up and relate to me with deep emotion the story of the adversities he had suffered. On the seventh day he felt so passably well that he could rise, move about, read and write. Yet on the eighth day I was not a little alarmed. On my morning visit I found him quite upset; his entire body jaundiced; while a terrible fit of vomiting and diarrhoea during the preceding night had threatened to kill him. Violent anger, profound suffering because of ingratitude and an undeserved insult had motivated the tremendous explosion. Shaking and trembling, he writhed with the pain which raged in his liver and intestines; and his feet, hitherto only moderately puffed up, were now greatly swollen.

"From this time on his dropsy developed; his secretions decreased in quantity, his liver gave convincing evidence of the presence of hard knots, his jaundice grew worse. The affectionate remonstrance of his friends soon appeased the threatening excitement and Beethoven, easily conciliated, soon forgot every insult offered him. His illness, however, progressed with giant strides. Already, during the third week, nocturnal choking attacks set in, the tremendous volume of the water accumulated called for immediate relief; and I found myself compelled to advocate the abdominal puncture in order to preclude the danger of sudden bursting.

After a few moments of serious reflection Beethoven agreed to submit to the operation, the more so since the Ritter von Staudenheim, who had been called in as consulting physician, urgently recommended it as being imperatively necessary. The premier surgeon of the General Hospital, The Mag. Chir. Hr. Seibert, made the puncture with his habitual skill, so that Beethoven when he saw the stream of water cried out happily that the operation made him think of Moses, who struck the rock with his staff and made the water gush forth. The relief was almost immediate. The liquid amounted to 25 pounds in weight, yet the afterflow must have been five times that.

"Carelessness in undoing the bandage of the wound at night, probably in order quickly to remove all the water which had gathered, well nigh put an end to all rejoicing anent the improvement in Beethoven's condition. A violent erysipelatic inflammation set in and showed incipient signs of gangrene, but the greatest care exercised in keeping the inflamed surfaces dry soon checked the evil. Fortunately the three succeeding operations were carried out without the slightest difficulty.

"Beethoven knew but too well that the tappings were only palliatives and hence resigned himself to a further accumulation of water, the more so since the cold, rainy winter season favored the return of his dropsy, and could not help but strengthen the original cause of his illness, which had its existence in his chronic liver trouble as well as in organic deficiencies of the abdominal intestines.

"It is a curious fact that Beethoven, even after operations successfully performed, could not stand taking any medicine, if we except gentle laxatives. His appetite diminished from day to day, and his strength could not help but decrease noticeably in consequence of the repeated large loss of vital juices. Dr. Malfatti, who henceforth aided me with his advice, a friend of Beethoven's for many years and aware of the latter's inclination for spirituous beverages, therefore hit upon the idea of recommending iced punch. I must admit that this recipe worked admirably, for a few days at any rate. Beethoven felt so greatly refreshed by the iced spirits of wine that he slept through the whole of the first night, and began to sweat tremendously. He grew lively; often all sorts of witty ideas occurred to him; and he even dreamt of being able to complete the oratorio *Saul and David* which he had commenced.

"Yet, as was to have been foreseen, his joy was of short duration. He began to abuse his prescription, and partook freely of the punch. Soon the alcoholic beverage called forth a powerful rush of blood to the head; he grew soporose and there was a rattle when he breathed like that of a person deeply intoxicated; he wandered in his talk and to this, at various times, was added an inflammatory pain in the neck with consequent hoarseness and even total speechlessness. He grew more violent and now, since colic and diarrhoea had resulted from the chilling of the intestines, it was high time to deprive him of this valuable stimulant.

"It was under such conditions, together with a rapidly increasing loss of flesh and a noticeable falling off of his vital powers that January, February and March went by. Beethoven in gloomy hours of presentiment, foretold his approaching dissolution after his fourth tapping, nor was he mistaken. No consolation was able longer to revive him; and when I promised him that with the approaching spring weather his sufferings would decrease, he answered with a smile: 'My day's work is done; if a physician still can be of use in my case (and then he lapsed into English) his name shall be called wonderful.' This saddening reference to Handel's *Messiah* so profoundly moved me that in my inmost soul and with the deepest emotion I was obliged to confirm the truth of what he had said.

"And now the ill-fated day drew ever nearer. My noble and often burdensome professional duty as a physician bade me call my suffering friend's attention to the momentous day, so that he might comply with his civic and religious duties. With the most delicate consideration I set down the admonitory lines on a sheet of paper (for it was thus that we always had made ourselves mutually understood). Beethoven, slowly, meditatively and with incomparable self-control read what I had written, his face like that of one transfigured. Next he gave me his hand in a hearty, serious manner and said: 'Have them send for his reverence the pastor.' Then he grew quiet and reflective, and nodded me his: 'I shall soon see you again,' in friendly wise. Soon after Beethoven attended to his devotions with the pious resignation which looks forward with confidence to eternity.

"When a few hours had passed, he lost consciousness, began to grow comatose, and breathed with a rattle. The following morning all symptoms pointed to the approaching end. The 26th of March was stormy, and clouded. Toward six in the afternoon came a flurry of snow, with thunder and lightning—Beethoven died. Would not a Roman augur, in view of the accidental commotion of the elements, have taken his apotheosis for granted?"

Dolezalek, Johann Nepomuk Emanuel

b. Chotěboř 1780, d. Iglau, Moravia, 1858. Cellist, composer and teacher. He met Beethoven in 1800 and was an enthusiastic admirer of the composer. He related to Otto Jahn his recollections of Beethoven. They are found in Th.-R. II. The Czech musician was introduced to the Master by Krumpholz.He became especially popular in Vienna as a composer of Czech songs. According to Dlabacz's *Künstlerlexikon aus Böhmen* he visited Prague in 1804. Of special interest are Doležalek's reports about the enmity of many Viennese composers against the Master. When Doležalek played Beethoven's C minor Trio for Koželuch, the latter threw the music on the floor. Doležalek was also a witness of the scene in the tavern Zum Schwan, when Beethoven absent-mindedly wanted to pay the bill for food he had never eaten. When Beethoven was sick and near death Doležalek visited him and expressed his deepest sympathy.

Dragonetti, Domenico

b. Venice 1763, d. London 1846. Famous double bass player. Beethoven met him in 1799. According to Appleby, he played with Beethoven the Cello Sonata Op. 5 No. 2. Beethoven watched attentively the movements of the virtuoso on the double bass and emotionally embraced him at the end. In 1813 Dragonetti participated in the performance of the *Battle of Victoria* ("Battle" Symphony). (Cf. Pohl: *Haydn in London.* Th.-R. III, p. 73.)

Dresden

Capital of Saxony. Visited by Beethoven April 23, 1796, according to the correspondence of Schall (Chamberlain and music amateur in Bonn) with the Elector Maximilian Franz. Beethoven stayed in Dresden for a week, where he gave a successful concert. He also played privately for the Saxon Elector who gave him as a gift a golden snuff box. (Cf. Schiedermair: *Der junge Beethoven.)*

Dressler, Ernst Christoph

b. about 1720, d. 1780. Opera singer in Cassel. One of Beethoven's earliest compositions is connected with his name: Variations on a March by Dressler, ca. 1782. K., W o O. 63.

Duncker, Johann Friedrich

d. 1842. First "Kabinettsekretär" of the Prussian King Friedrich Wilhelm III and "Geheimer Oberregierungsrat." When Duncker came with his King to Vienna for the Vienna Congress he wrote the play *Eleonore Prohaska,* the tragedy of a maiden who participated in the Wars of Liberation disguised as a soldier. The same subject was treated by Piwald in the play *Das Mädchen von Potsdam,* performed on March 1, 1814, in the Leopoldstadt Theater. Fanny del Rio in her diary remarks that the Viennese censor prohibited the performance of Duncker's play. In all probability the Piwald play was the obstacle to the performance of Duncker's play, for which Beethoven had composed several pieces: Krieger Chor for four voices; Romanze for soprano with accompaniment of the harp; a Melodrama with accompaniment of the harmonica; the Funeral March, an orchestral arrangement in F sharp minor of the funeral march of the Piano Sonata Op. 26 in A flat major.

Beethoven's association with Duncker lasted at least until 1823 when R. H. Henning in a Conversation-book expresses Duncker's high esteem for the Master. Nottebohm in his *Zweite Beethoveniana* printed sketches of those compositions, which are to be found in Beethoven's Complete Works, Vol. 24, p. 238.

Duschek, Josepha

b. Prague 1743, d. Prague 1824. Neé Hambacher, celebrated singer, whose husband was the composer Franz Duschek (1736-1799). She belonged to the Prague circle around Mozart, with whom she had become acquainted in Salzburg, the birthplace of her mother. In Leipzig 1796 she sang Beethoven's aria "Ah Perfido," which, however, had not been composed for her, but probably for Countess Clari. In a concert given by Mme. Duschek on March 29, 1798, Beethoven played the accompaniment of a sonata, probably one of his three Violin Sonatas Op. 12. The violinist might have been Schuppanzigh. (Cf. Th. R. II and Nettl: *Mozart in Böhmen,* Entry: "Ah Perfido.")

E

Eating and Drinking

It may be assumed that Beethoven's ways of eating and drinking were rooted in the unstable household of his parents. At the same time it should be remembered that Beethoven's mother was a cook by profession, who liked to provide her children with excellent food, often prepared in the Electoral kitchens. Furthermore the young Ludwig learned to appreciate in early years the excellent Rhenish cuisine in the Breuning house.

Probably "Wittib" Koch (nomen est omen) in her Zehrgarten prepared excellent meals, certainly well liked by those people who were signers of the Koch album. There are reports from Schindler about Beethoven's eating habits in later years. "He had coffee for breakfast, prepared by himself in a glass coffee machine. (This is also confirmed in a report by the piano teacher Friedrich Starke, who visited the Master in 1812.) Coffee seemed to have been his indispensable nourishment and he prepared it in a scrupulous way, much as an Oriental does. 60 coffee beans were used for one cup and frequently counted, especially in the presence of friends. One of his favorite dishes was macaroni with Parmesan cheese. Foods had to be very badly prepared for him to dislike them. This frequently happened, as he took very irregular meals. He was inclined to criticize his housekeeper's cooking often unjustly. "The soup is bad;" there was no appeal against this verdict. Once after Schindler contradicted his statement about the soup, he received a letter after several days: "I disapprove of your opinion about the soup, it *is* rotten." Fish was his favorite dish. Consequently guests were usually invited on Fridays in order to be served a Danube fish speciality, Schwerer Schill, with potatoes. His suppers were negligible, a plate of soup and some remainder of the midday meal. His favorite beverage was clear brook water which he consumed in enormous quantities in the summer time. As to wine, he preferred an Ofener Gebirgswein (Ofen=suburb of Budapest). Unfortunately he liked best adulterated wine which was harmful to his weakened abdomen.

No warnings helped. Beethoven was certainly not a heavy drinker, as was claimed by his last physician, Wawruch. The Master also liked a glass of good beer in the evening, at the same time smoking his pipe and reading the paper. Wähner among other contemporaries confirms his predilection for Hungarian wine, a fact which is contradicted by Sporschill (cf. Volkmann: *Neues über Beethoven*), who reports that Beethoven liked venison and red Austrian claret, as Hungarian wine was not good for his health. In the last years of his life Beethoven frequently could be seen in wine-taverns at Selig's or in the Kameel. When Beethoven worked on his *Fidelio* Overture in E major in 1814, Treitschke found him in the morning fast asleep and next to his bedside a glass of wine filled with dipped zwieback. When Friedrich Kuhlau came to Vienna in 1825, he had lunch with Beethoven in Helenenthal near Baden. They were in high spirits and Schindler (unfortunately) removed some pages of the Conversation-book, as it contained frivolous jokes. "Sillery" (evidently Schiller, light Hungarian country wine) was consumed abundantly, and in the evening the drinking bouts were continued in Beethoven's apartment.

There Vöslau wine was in evidence, the result often being slight intoxication. Other favorite dishes were breadsoup, prepared with 10 eggs (Seyfried), roast veal and wild boar (Conversation-book of 1820). Furthermore, he liked to eat "Blutwurst mit Kartoffel" according to Franz Lachner (*Recollections* 1822) with whom he had lunch in Die Eiche. In the last years of his life his menu had to be fixed according to doctor's orders. The following menus are found in the Conversation-book: saftsuppe, meat and gravy, red cabbage with potatoes, wild duck or hazel hen, duck, water-hen. In another Conversation-book: "The sausages have to be sufficiently fried."

Oysters played an important part in his culinary life. They had to be sent from Trieste, but sometimes arrived "black," and Beethoven exclaimed emphatically: "I wish I could eat the oyster from the source," a desire which was closely associated with his lifelong desire to live in foreign countries.

Eder, Joseph

Art dealer and publisher. Firm (founded 1789) changed later to Jeremias Bermann. In 1798 Eder published Beethoven's Piano Sonatas Op. 10, dedicated to the Countess Browne and the Sonata Pathétique Op. 13, dedicated to Prince Carl Lichnowsky.

Eeden (Eden), Heinrich van der

b. about 1710, d. Bonn 1782. Court organist in Bonn and probably Beethoven's first teacher outside of the family. As he had died by 1782, his career as a teacher must have been of short duration (cf. Schiedermair: *Der junge Beethoven).*

Egmont

Goethe's famous tragedy completed in 1775. Beethoven was an ardent admirer of the work and composed the music for it (Op. 84) between 1809 and June 1810 by the order of the Court Theatre. According to Czerny, Beethoven wanted to compose Schiller's *Wilhelm Tell,* but the administration of the Theatre decided to give him the commission for *Egmont.* The creation of this composition coincided with the restless war year of 1809, which wrought grave disturbances in Beethoven's life. Very likely the work was completed in Baden in the spring of 1810. The manuscript of the overture bears the date 1810. On June 6 of that year Beethoven offered his work to Breitkopf and Härtel. The first performance took place June 15. Previously, on May 24, the drama had been performed without Beethoven's music (cf. Killan: *Allgem. Musikzeitung*. Jan. 21, 1921 L and K).

Some details of the performance were recorded by Toni Adamberger, the singer and bride of Theodor Körner, who sang the "Klärchen Lieder" (cf. Th.-R. III, p. 202). Beethoven had advised Goethe of the score in a letter and had urged the Leipzig firm to hurry the composition to the poet. On April 12, 1811, he wrote to Weimar: "You will receive in the near future the music for your magnificent *Egmont* . . . I wish to have your opinion, even your criticism will be helpful to me." Beethoven's friend Franz Oliva delivered the letter. Sulpice Boisserée, the art historian, was present when Oliva played a composition by Beethoven after dinner, supposedly a "Klärchen Lied" (cf. Firmenich-Richartz: *Sulpice and Melchior Boisserée als Kunstsammler*, 1916). The score, however, did not arrive in Weimar until 1812 and was played before Goethe by an amateur. Only gradually did Goethe learn to appreciate Beethoven's music.

Beethoven's *Egmont* music consists of the following parts: 1) Overture in F minor, one of the greatest instrumental works, representing Egmont's struggle against tyranny and the victory of freedom; 2) Klärchen Lied (Die Trommel gerühret) with phrases illustrating the sound of pipe and drum and expressing Klärchen's sympathy with the hero; 3) First Entre-Act Music (Andante-Allegro); 4) Second Entre-Act Music (Larghetto); 5) Klärchen Lied (Freudvoll und Leidvoll); 6) Third Entre-Act Music (Allegro in C major); 7) Fourth Entre-Act Music (Poco sostenuto e risoluto E flat major); 8) Klärchen's Death (Larghetto D minor); 9) Melodrama (Poco sostenuto E flat major, later D major); and finally 10) the "Victory Symphony" in F major relating to the final part of the Overture.

The music to *Egmont* is often performed in different sequences. Grillparzer wrote a connecting text which is frequently used for concert performance. Other poetical arrangements for the same purpose were written by Mosengeil and Bernays. (Cf. Th.-R. III and Bekker's evaluation of the music).

Eichhoff, Johann Joseph

Beethoven's friend in Bonn who contributed to widow Koch's album. He was the son of the Electoral Court cook August Eichhoff and his wife Eva, who was a singer and member of the Electoral Chapel. (Cf. Gerstinger: *Ludwig van Beethovens Stammbuch,* and Schiedermair: *Der junge Beethoven.*)

Eleonore Prohaska

See Entry: Duncker.

Eppinger, Emanuel

b. Vienna 1768, died there 1846. Of Jewish extraction. Administrator of the hotel Zum Römischen Kaiser in Vienna. Philanthropist who became acquainted with Beethoven. He was helpful on the occasion of the performance of Beethoven's oratorio *Christus am Ölberg* (cf. Frimmel: B. H. and Wurzbach).

Eppinger, Heinrich

Violinist of Jewish extraction. Musical amateur and composer. One of the first who played Beethoven's compositions. He played second violin at the chamber music performances in E. A. Förster's home, where Beethoven's String Quartets Op. 18 were frequently performed in 1800 (cf. Th.-R. II, 122, 185).

Equale

A composition for equal voices, particularly for equal instruments. A composition, especially written for trombones, to be played at a solemn occasion. Beethoven wrote three equales at the suggestion of Franz Xaver Glöggl in Linz (cf. Entry: Glöggl). Glöggl had asked him to write an equale for six trombones. Beethoven had heard an equale as played at funerals in Linz at that time and composed three such pieces for four trombones (1812). They were used at Beethoven's funeral on March 29, 1827, arranged for male chorus as "Miserere mei" (First Equale), "Amplius lava me" (Second Equale) in an arrangement by Ignatz Seyfried. The autograph of the Equales bears the inscription: "Linz den 2ten November 1812" (November 2nd being All Souls' Day, on which day the pieces were played in Linz).

Erdödy, Countess Anna-Marie

Née Niczky. b. 1779, d. 1837. Married Count Peter Erdödy (b. 1771, d. ?) June 6, 1796. Acquainted with Beethoven from about 1803. According to Schindler, the Countess was his intimate friend to whom he confided his unhappy love for Giulietta Guicciardi. He spent many days on her estate at Jedlersee. Once he disappeared and the Countess believed that he had returned to Vienna. After three days he was found in a remote corner of the Schlossgarten by the music teacher Brauchle. Reichardt in his *Vertraute Briefe* of 1808-09 reports that Beethoven lived at the house of the Countess, who invited Reichardt for a musical dinner. Reichardt acclaimed her highly and described her as a short but pretty and refined young woman, 25 years of age. (In fact she was 30 years old at that time.) She limped as a result of a disease contracted at the birth of her first child. Reichardt paid another visit to the Countess in December of the same year, when the two Trios Op. 70, dedicated to her, were played in her house. At those performances either Beethoven or the Countess played the piano part. Beethoven's quartets were performed at her house by Schuppanzigh and his group. Reichardt highly praised the congenial atmosphere of these gatherings and exclaimed: "Lucky artist who can rely on such listeners."

Beethoven used to improvise at the house concerts and Reichardt was moved to tears when listening to him. Reichardt was particularly enthusiastic about the E flat major Trio and calls the movement in A flat major (*allegro ma non troppo)* a heavenly cantabile, the loveliest and most graceful music ever heard.

According to Trémont, Beethoven showed a strong inclination towards the Countess (1809). In the same year, however, their relationship was severed by an unpleasant affair because of one of her servants. Beethoven left her house and their friendship was not renewed until 1815. As a result he dedicated his two Cello Sonatas Op. 102 to the Countess. Perhaps she was responsible for the agreement of the three aristocrats (Archduke Rudolph and the Princes Kinsky and Lobkowitz) to pay Beethoven a yearly pension for rejecting the post of "Kapellmeister" at the Court of King Jerôme of Westphalia. In May 1815 a beloved son of the Countess died (Fritzi). Letters to the Countess are preserved, showing Beethoven's deep sympathy for her. Later, at the end of 1819, when the Countess visited Vienna, he wrote on December 31 the Canon in F major *Glück, Glück' Glück zum neuen Jahr.* The relationship with the Countess lasted until she was exiled in 1820, an affair which was shrouded in mystery. The Conversation-books of that time tell of the arrest of the Countess, the teacher Brauchle, and Countess Mimi. Obviously there had been a family fight which resulted in the death of Count August, another son of the Countess. The exiled Countess died in 1837 in Munich. (Cf. Kalischer: *Beethovens Frauenkreis* and Th.-R.).

Erlkönig

Famous poem by Goethe from the Singspiel "Die Fischerin" written 1780 or 1782. Frequently set to music (by Corona Schröter, Reichardt, Zelter, Löwe, and above all, Schubert). There exists the sketch of a composition by Beethoven, owned by the Gesellschaft der Musikfreunde, partly published by Nottebohm (*Beethoveniana* I, p. 100) and Friedländer: *Gedichte von Goethe in Kompositionen seiner Zeitgenossen,* p. 143. A facsimile was published in Naumann's *Illustrierte Musikgeschichte.* Even a completion of that sketch by an arranger was published by J. Schuberth and Co. According to Nottebohm the sketch originated between 1800-1810, whereas Schubert's famous song was composed in 1815. There is hardly any connection between the two songs. However, it is highly interesting to compare the piano part of Beethoven's sketch (Postlude) to the beginning of Schubert's song "Der Wanderer" (1816). They are almost identical.

Ertmann, Dorothea von

b. Offenbach? 1781, d. Vienna 1849. Pianist and intelligent interpreter of Beethoven's works. Née Graumann, married May 1798 to Captain Stefan Ertmann, who was transferred to Milan in 1818. First a pupil of W. K. Rust in Vienna, she became Beethoven's pupil before the year 1804. Dates about her life differ in various sources. Frimmel (*Beethoven Handbuch)* had his information about her from a private source. Another source, Mathilde Marchesi: *Erinnerungen aus meinem Leben,* lists doubtful information. When Baroness Ertmann lost her son, Beethoven comforted her by playing a moving improvisation on the piano. In 1824 she played, with Schindler as the violinist, Beethoven's Trio in B flat major Op. 97. In one of his letters Beethoven calls her his "dear and worthy Dorothea Cäcilia." To her he dedicated his Piano Sonata Op. 101. When young Felix Mendelssohn passed through Milan in 1821, he paid a visit to the Ertmanns. He relates that he and the Countess alternately played compositions by Beethoven and that General Ertmann was familiar with many stories about Beethoven. Reichardt gives an exact description of Dorothea's piano playing which combined tender delicacy with imposing power. (Cf. Reichardt: *Vertraute Briefe,* ed. by Gugitz, and Frimmel: *Beethovenforschung.*)

Estate

In the archives of the "Landesgericht" in Vienna a portfolio is preserved containing the documents referring to Beethoven's estate. Frimmel in his *Beethoven Studien* II gave a survey of these documents. They refer to his will (the last one written March 23, 1827), his property and his relatives. Listed under the property are the French gold medal, sent by Louis XVIII, four string instruments, pistols (bought by his nephew, when he intended to commit suicide), a salt-shaker, different jewels, linen and clothes, music and books. Of great interest is one share of the Austrian National Bank. Inventory and evaluation of Beethoven's estate was made August 16, 1827, including a listing of Conversation-books, manuscripts, printed music and books. (Cf. Entry: Reading).

Eskeles

Viennese Jewish banking family. Partners in firm of Arnstein and Eskeles. Bernhard Eskeles, born in Vienna 1753, died there in 1839. He was the banker of Joseph II and Franz I of Austria. Eskeles was an art lover in whose house numerous writers, artists and composers found a congenial atmosphere. Beethoven made use of the banker's service in 1809 and considered a job for his nephew Karl with this bank. The daughter of Eskeles was Marie, later Countess von Wimpffen, an excellent pianist who preferred Beethoven's compositions, as his nephew Karl remarked in one of the Conversation-books. Beethoven dedicated a "Stammbuchblatt für Gesang und Klavier" with the text "Der edle Mensch sey hülfreich und gut," alluding to Goethe's poem *Das Göttliche* to her. Marie's mother was Cäcilie von Eskeles, née Itzig, a sister of Fanny von Arnstein. During Beethoven's last illness she sent him preserves (cf. Wurzbach and Kaznelson: *Beethovens Ferne u. Unsterbliche Geliebte,* Zürich 1954).

Esterhazy de Galanta

Celebrated Hungarian aristocratic family, members of which played an important part in 18th century music history. Nikolaus Joseph, b. 1765, d. 1833, well known for his associations with Haydn, was also one of Beethoven's patrons. He was not only one of the subscribers for the Trios Op. 1, but in 1806 commissioned Beethoven to write a mass. The Master began to work immediately. However, sickness and other obstacles, possibly a short trip to the Slovak resort Pistyan and sojourns in Baden and Heiligenstadt interrupted the production. On July 26, 1807 he promised Prince Esterhazy to have the composition finished by August 20. The Mass was rehearsed in Eisenstadt, the summer residence of the Prince, and first performed there on September 13. The performance proved unsatisfactory. According to Schindler, the Prince was said to have addressed the Master with the following words: "My dear Beethoven, what kind of a job is that?" These discouraging words were accompanied by the laughter of Kapellmeister Johann Nep. Hummel. Beethoven, badly hurt, left Eisenstadt the same day. Frimmel expressed the opinion that the rift with the Prince was due to the intrigues of the princely chaplain Abbé Gelinek, otherwise well known as a composer (cf. Entry: Gelinek).

Kretzschmar in his *Führer durch den Konzertsaal* II, 1, p. 160 pointed out that "Beethoven with his C major Mass entered a new era in the composition of masses, so different from the mass type of Haydn and Mozart." It was his guess that Beethoven's change of style, so different from the Viennese mass style, caused the acid criticism of the Prince. Beethoven did not forgive the Prince this remark and finally dedicated the Mass to Prince Ferdinand Kinsky. However, after Beethoven had completed his great Mass in D major *(Missa Solemnis)*, Esterhazy received an invitation to subscribe to a copy of the manuscript. Beethoven in a letter to Schindler on June 1, 1823, expressed his doubts that Esterhazy would comply with the request; in fact Esterhazy did fail to order a subscription. The three Marches Op. 45 for Piano Duet are dedicated to the Princess Marie Esterhazy, née Princess Lichtenstein. (Cf. Entry: Mass).

F

Family

The family of Beethoven can be traced as far back as the 17th century in Antwerp. A Peeter Beethoven was an apprentice of the painter Abraham Genoels in 1689 or 1690. Another Beethoven was a master sculptor in the artist's guild in 1712. Beethoven's great-grandfather was Henry Adelard, a tailor, who died in 1745. Henry's son was Louis van Beethoven, who moved from Antwerp to Louvain, and from there to Bonn. He was the first musician in the family, becoming Electoral Kapellmeister in 1733. He was Ludwig van Beethoven's grandfather (cf. L. de Burbure: *Biographie nationale publiée par l'Académie Royale des sciences, des lettres et des beaux arts de Belgique,* Tome II, p. 105 Bruxelles 1868).

Grandfather Louis was born December 23, 1712, and was a tenor in Louvain 1731. He married Maria Josepha Poll, who died in 1775. From this marriage he had three children, of whom Johann, the youngest, was Beethoven's father, born 1740(?) in Bonn, died there 1792. Grandfather Louis was a bass violinist in the electoral service, enjoying an excellent reputation in Bonn. His portrait came into the possession of the Master, who held it in high esteem (cf. Entry: Schwarzspanierhaus). Later his nephew Karl inherited it. Karl's daughter, married to Herr Paul Weidinger, owned it afterward. Grandfather Louis was a handsome man with an oval face, a broad forehead, a round nose, large eyes, red cheeks and a stern expression. As an additional support he was a wine dealer.

Unfortunately his wife was a drinker who caused him much trouble. This vice was inherited by Beethoven's father, Johann. The latter married Maria Magdalena Keverich, who was the widow of Johannes Leym, who had been in the service of the Archbishop of Trier. Their wedding took place in Bonn, November 12, 1767, at St. Remigins church. Her family had a fine reputation and prospered both in Koblenz and Ehrenbreitenstein. Maria's father was Inspector of the Electoral Kitchen; her mother, née Westorff, could name high ranking persons among her ancestors.

The drunkenness of Johann van Beethoven became increasingly serious, particularly after the death of his wife, July 17, 1787. Johann was otherwise quite popular, and the diplomats of Austria, France and England liked him as a voice teacher for their families. Unfortunately they often permitted him the free use of their wine cellars. According to recollections of Stephan von Breuning, young Ludwig once had to persuade the police to set his father free. As a result of Johann's behaviour, the Elector decided to transfer him from Bonn to a small Electoral town. Young Ludwig managed to keep this plan from being realized, and Johann remained in Bonn up to his death, December 18, 1792. Ludwig became from then on the sole supporter of his family, and the official owner of his father's apartment. About his brothers, see Entries: Brothers and Family-Tree.

Fandango

Spanish national dance, the melody of which was used by Gluck in his ballet *Don Juan* and in Mozart's *Le nozze di Figaro*. It appeared also in Vieth *Encyclopedie der Leibesübungen* (1794-1818) from which Beethoven evidently copied it in a sketch of 1810, published by Nottebohm II, p. 281. (Cf. Nettl: *Story of Dance Music*.)

"Fate Motif"

According to Schindler Beethoven compared the entrance motif of the first movement of the Fifth Symphony to knocking of Fate, using the words: "So pocht das Schicksal an die Pforte." Schindler suggested this motif be played somewhat slower than the rest of the symphony, an idea generally rejected today.

Fidelio

Beethoven's only opera. Rolland suggests that the "glittering illusion" of fortune which the theater offered may have stimulated the creation of *Fidelio*. There is doubtlessly some truth in this since Beethoven was never quite free of financial difficulties; however, there appears to be more than just this reason of necessity. Had Beethoven been interested solely in the glittering illusion of fortune, would he have rejected libretto after libretto? Many books came into the hands of Beethoven only to be forgotten after some enthusiastic but brief consideration.

Fidelio or "Leonore" as Beethoven would have preferred, may be looked upon as an expression of two ideals which the composer wished to convey to the world—the ideal of conjugal love and the ideal of justice for mankind. It is an account of a woman's heroism in a successful attempt to rescue her husband from the hands of his political enemy (only a theme such as this could merit Beethoven's attention). At the beginning of the opera we find that Florestan is imprisoned unjustly by Pizarro and that Leonore, assuming the name Fidelio and the disguise of a lad, enters the service of Rocco, the very jailer in charge of Florestan. In the course of the opera Pizarro appears for the expressed purpose of disposing of Florestan, so that the Prime Minister of Spain, Don Fernando, would not discover the injustice when he visits the prison. Since Don Fernando is expected to arrive at the prison shortly, Pizarro dispatches a trumpeter to signal the arrival of the governor. In the meantime, Rocco and Fidelio are sent to dig Florestan's grave in his cell. The conversation in this grave-digging scene indicates somewhat Beethoven's disdain for injustice:

Leonore: Er muss ein grosser Verbrecher sein.

Rocco: Oder er muss grosse Feinde haben, das kommt ungefähr auf eins heraus.

The grave dug, Pizarro comes to do the killing. Just as he is about to stab Florestan, Fidelio, now revealing her true identity, throws herself upon her husband exclaiming, "Tödt' erst sein Weib!" When Pizarro tries to remove Leonore, she draws a pistol and holds him at bay. Seconds later the trumpet call is heard announcing the arrival of the governor; thus justice is meted out to Pizarro and thus Florestan and Leonore are happily reunited. The opera closes with the stirring chorus, "Wer ein holdes Weib errungen, stimm' in unseren Jubel ein!"—words of Schiller used in both *Fidelio* and the Ninth Symphony (see Entry: Symphonies).

There is also a secondary plot of very little real importance: Marcelline, Rocco's daughter, is in love with Fidelio, not suspecting the latter's true identity. Fidelio sees the advantage of good relations with Rocco's family and "plays along" in the act, much to the disgust of Jaquino, the porter.

The Fidelio story itself dates back to the reign of terror of the French revolution. At that time, as we learn from the *Memoirs* of Jean Nicolas Bouilly (1763-1842), an incident similar to that which is related in the opera actually occurred. Bouilly was then administrator of a department near Tours. In 1798, Bouilly presented, together with the composer Pierre Gaveaux (1761-1825), this theme (with its secondary plot) in the opera *Léonore ou L'Amour Conjugal* at the Théâtre Feydeau in Paris. The success of this opera was immediate; for example, to cite the critique from the Journal de Paris, February 22, 1798: "On n'a vu depuis longtemps sur aucun théâtre un succès aussi complet et aussi universal, que celui de la première répresentation de *Léonore ou L'Amour Conjugal* . . ." Bouilly fortunately had the discretion to place the opera in a Spanish setting, since his audience could remember the Revolution only too well.

The Bouilly-Gaveaux work was shortly taken over in a work by the Italian, Ferdinando Paër (1771-1839), called *Leonora ossia L'Amore Coniugale.* The librettist in this case has not been conclusively identified but it is commonly assumed to have been a certain G. Cinti. This opera was first performed October 3, 1804, in Dresden. Paër's most important innovation was an increased emphasis on the love-triangle theme. Since this work was not performed in Vienna until 1806 and then only in a private performance for Prince Lobkowitz (and it is not likely that Beethoven heard this), it has been commonly assumed that Beethoven knew only the Gaveaux score when he wrote *Fidelio.* Engländer (*Neues Beethoven Jahrbuch,* 1924) suggests, however, that Beethoven may have become acquainted with the Paër work early in 1803, at which time Paër was present in Vienna for the performance of his oratorio *Il san sepolcro.* In any case, the scores of both Gaveaux and Paër were to be found among the items in Beethoven's estate.

One other setting of the Bouilly text should be noted: this setting is an opera by Johann Simon Mayr (1763-1845), the libretto of which was prepared by Gaetano Rossi. This was performed in Padua early in 1805.

As to the work of Beethoven, it is

quite certain that Beethoven began the sketches of *Fidelio* sometime in 1803, perhaps shortly after Paër's visit to Vienna and perhaps at the suggestion of Schikaneder, then manager of the Theater an der Wien. Nottebohm proposes that it was begun sometime between May, 1803 (at the earliest) and February, 1804 (at the latest). The work continued throughout 1804 and 1805 and throughout the making and breaking of agreements with the theater managers. Schikaneder had contracted with Beethoven for an opera—quite likely *Fidelio;* when Baron von Braun purchased the Theater an der Wien, Schikaneder was thrust out of his position as manager and the agreement with Beethoven was nullified. A new agreement was soon drawn up with Baron von Braun, though. Beethoven elected Joseph Sonnleithner (1766-1835) to adapt the Bouilly text to the German stage. In reality Sonnleithner did little more than to translate the French into "acceptable" verses; he did, however, make a few adjustments. The most notable of these was that he changed Bouilly's two acts into three and saved most of the dramatic action until the third act. This, to some critics, was a grave mistake.

Beethoven had completed most of the sketches by spring of 1805; the first performances took place November 20, 21, 22, 1805. These performances were, to be sure, hardly successful. The *Allgemeine Musikalische Zeitung* of January, 1806, reported, with special reference to the overture, that this work hardly compared with his earlier instrumental works. Even those of Beethoven's circle agreed that *Fidelio* should be revised (and this was shortly undertaken). Since the completion of Erich Prieger's reconstruction of the 1805 version, performed in concert in 1886 and on the stage in 1905, some widely varying reactions have been expressed. Schiedermair, for example, maintains that the first version could easily hold its own with the third; Bekker, on the other hand, doubts that the first version could pass muster before *any* audience. Those who tend to pass gentle judgment on the 1805 version quickly call to our attention the French occupation of Vienna shortly before the first performance of *Fidelio*—hence the audience was composed primarily of French officers.

In December of 1805 the revision was begun. Josef August Röckel has described the activities of one evening that December at the Lichnowsky palace: a number of Beethoven's friends assembled there for the purpose of persuading him to make certain improvements in his *Fidelio.* Stephan von Breuning had rewritten the libretto. The entire opera was read—there were two singers, piano, and violin—and piece by piece it was trimmed, slashed, and re-fitted. Beethoven violently opposed every proposed alteration of his score but finally agreed to everything; in its new form the opera was reduced from three to two acts. When the second version was presented on March 29, 1806, it "made a distinctly better impression" but was withdrawn after a quarrel with the theater manager.

It was not until the spring of 1814 that any further action was taken with *Fidelio.* Georg Friedrich Treitschke undertook the revision of the libretto. Beethoven was apparently pleased with Treitschke's work, for he wrote Treitschke: "I have read your revision of the opera with great satisfaction. It has persuaded me to rebuild the desolate ruins of an ancient fortress." The resulting third and final version naturally displays certain inconsistencies of style since it represents a span of a decade's creative activity, but it is quite generally considered to be the most satisfactory version. This was performed for the first time on May 23, 1814, according to most authorities, in Vienna; however, Weber's stage diary indicates May 27. It shortly found performance on other German stages, and by the 1840's the opera had found its way to most of the capitals of Europe as well as to New York.

Having now briefly traced the events leading to the final version of this opera, it may be well to compare it with the original 1805 version. In general, the "numbers" were shortened in the last version; two were omitted altogether; three were slightly lengthened; and four remained the same. The two-act arrangement of the 1806 opera was retained in the final version; today, however, it is usually produced in three acts—each of three scenes is simply treated as an act. The over-all results of the final revision were that the secondary plot retreated somewhat more into the background, and that the material preceding the main action was shortened a great deal.

Beethoven wrote a total of four overtures to *Fidelio*. The overture performed in 1805 with the first version of the opera is now known as "Leonore No. 2." The overture to the 1806 version is now called "Leonore No. 3" and is now played as an introduction to the second act in most cases. The next in chronological order of composition is the "Leonore No. 1," written for a performance in Prague (May, 1807) which did not take place. The final overture, today called the *Fidelio* Overture, was first performed on May 26, 1814; it was not ready in time for the first performance of the Treitschke version of the opera, though it was intended for that performance. Today it is used as the overture to the opera.

Beethoven was never completely satisfied with the outcome of his efforts. *Fidelio* remained a cup of bitterness to him for the remainder of his life. Though he had always desired to compose for the stage (he even went so far in 1806 as to offer himself to the management of the Hoftheater—then a board of directors including Prince Lobkowitz, Prince Schwarzenberg, and Prince Nikolaus Esterhazy—as "composer to the theater"), he could say bitterly, "This business of the opera is the most tedious in the world . . ." Cf. Carner, Mosco, "'Leonore' and 'Fidelio'," *Musical Times* XCII (1951); Engländer, Richard, "Paërs 'Leonora' und Beethovens 'Fidelio'," *Neues Beet.-Jb.* IV (1930); Prod'homme, J.-G., "Leonore ou l'amour conjugal, de Bouilly et Gaveaux," *SIMG* VII (1905-6); Schiedermair, Ludwig, "Uber Beethovens 'Leonore'," *SIMG* VIII (1907); Jos. Braunstein: *Beethovens Leonore Ouvertüren* Leipzig 1927, and Entry: Sporschill.

T.A.

Finta, Joseph von

Hungarian Colonel, later Major-General, 1734-1802, whose second wife Elizabeth, née Brunswick, was "Aunt Finta," the oldest sister of Count Anton Brunswick, the father of Therese and Josephine. The four youthful daughters of the Colonel belonged to the circle of the Brunswicks, both in Vienna and the Hungarian castles. (Cf. Hevesy: *Les petits amies de Beethoven,* and Kaznelson: *Beethovens Ferne und Unsterbliche Geliebte*).

Fish

See Entries: Eating and Drinking Habits.

Fischenich, Bartholomeus Ludwig

Jurist, later "Staatsrat," professor of law at the University of Bonn. Studied in Jena where he became acquainted with the poet Friedrich von Schiller. There exists a letter of Fischenich dated Jan. 26, 1793, addressed to Charlotte, Schiller's wife: "I am enclosing a composition of the poem *Feuerfarb'* (poem by Sophie Mereau-Brentano) and I would like to know your opinion about it. It is composed by a local young man whose musical talent is generally praised and who had been sent recently to Haydn in Vienna by the Elector. He will also compose Schiller's *Freude,* each stanza separately. I am expecting something perfect, as he is only interested in great and sublime matters. Haydn has written to Bonn that he wants to commission great operas to the young man and is afraid he will quit composing (because of the young Beethoven's talent). He (Beethoven) is otherwise not interested in such trifles as the enclosed music, which he only composed at the request of a young lady." Charlotte answered in a letter, dated February 11: "The composition of *Feuerfarb'* is very good; I am expecting a lot of the artist and I am looking forward to his composition of *Freude.*" Fischenich was one of the visitors of Widow Koch's Zehrgarten (cf. Schiedermair).

Fischer, Gottfried and Cäcilia

Gottfried b. 1780, his sister Cäcilia b. 1762. Children of the Bonn baker Theodor Fischer, who owned the house in the Rheingasse in Bonn where Beethoven's family spent many years. Gottfried began to write his recollections of Beethoven in 1838. They form an excellent source of knowledge of Beethoven's youth and were almost completely reprinted by Th.-R. I, p. 442.

Fischhoff, Joseph

b. Butschowitz (Moravia) 1804, d. Vienna 1857. Pianist. First studied medicine, later composition with J. v. Seyfried. Important for Beethoven's biography as the collector of biographical material, compiled by Hotschevar, the guardian of Beethoven's nephew Karl. The manuscript from Fischhoff's estate was bought by the Royal Library in Berlin and used as a source for research on Beethoven.

Folk Music

In the year of Beethoven's birth (1770) Klopstock, the German poet, wrote to a friend traveling in Scotland asking her if she could "get hold of a musician . . . who could set in our notation the melodies of those places in *Ossian* that are outstandingly lyrical?" Klopstock was referring to the forgeries, published by James Macpherson, which purported to be *Fragments of ancient poetry collected in the highlands of Scotland and translated from the Gaelic or Erse language* (1760). The *Ossian* forgeries, coupled with those of *Fingal* (1762) and *Timora* (1763), which followed shortly after, aroused an intense European interest in "folk poetry" and "folk song"—an interest which led such famous contemporaries of Beethoven as Herder, Goethe, von Arnim, and Brentano to collect and publish folk songs gathered from all over Europe.

That this characteristically romantic interest was shared by Beethoven is shown by a letter (August 8, 1809) addressed to Breitkopf and Härtel, asking for a complete edition of Goethe and Schiller, in which he says "these two poets (i.e. Goethe and Schiller) are my favorites; likewise, Ossian and Homer, (although) unfortunately I can read the latter only in translation."

At this time Beethoven was occupied, in a desultory fashion, with the setting of some Scotch, Irish, and Welsh folk songs for the Edinburgh collector and publisher, George Thomson (1757-1851). Thomson was not the first publisher in this field in the British Isles, and it was probably the earlier successes of publications by William Napier and William Whyte which led Thomson to enter this field in 1793. He first contacted Beethoven on October 5, 1803, and they actively corresponded until sometime in the summer of 1820.

Beethoven was by no means the first composer Thomson approached. He had already published several collections containing settings by Leopold Kozeluh (1752-1818), Ignace Pleyel (1757-1831), a pupil of Haydn's, as well as Haydn himself. Thomson sent Beethoven the unadorned "airs" without words, and Beethoven was expected to set them simply for either one or two voices, pianoforte, violin, and violoncello. Beethoven was unaware that in many cases words were being supplied independently of the music, and he frequently complained about their absence:

> "Once again, I beg you to send me the words of the songs, as they are very necessary if one is to give the proper expression." (Postscript to a letter, dated November 23, 1816).

On the other hand, Thomson frequently complained about Beethoven's settings being too difficult, and asked him to make alterations which Beethoven refused to do. The chief difficulty lay in the fact that Thomson's ideas of an aesthetic of music were absolutely opposed to Beethoven's. For example, in his introduction to the *Select Collection of Original Scottish Airs for the Voice With Introductory & Concluding Symphonies & Accompaniments for the Piano Forte, Violin and Violoncello* . . . (1804) Thomson says:

> "The accompaniments are admirably calculated to support the Voice, and to beautify the Airs, without any tendency to overpower the singer. Instead of a Thoroughbass denoted by *figures,* which very few can play with any propriety, the harmony is plainly expressed in musical Notes, which every young Lady may execute correctly.
>
> "There are many persons, who never having cultivated Music, have little relish for Accompaniments. The Editor well knows, that, when a Scottish Song is sung by a fine voice, the words distinctly and feelingly expressed, it gives very great pleasure without any Accompaniment—But everyone conversant with Music knows, that the voice needs the support and guidance of an Accompaniment, otherwise, that it insensibly falls from the pitch in which

it set out; and that the Italians, who have numberless charming airs equally simple with the Scottish, always set Accompaniments to them, not with the purpose of supporting the voice, but of giving variety and effect to the song."

All in all, Beethoven added "symphonies" or "ritornellos" to forty-one Scotch, fifty-nine Irish, and twenty-six Welsh airs published by Thomson from 1814-1841. His first contributions appeared in the two volumes of Irish airs published in 1814 and 1816, and in the third volume of Welsh airs published in 1817. In August of 1818, Beethoven made his first appearance as an arranger of Scottish airs, contributing twenty-five of the thirty songs contained in this collection, the remaining five being set by Haydn. The rest of the volume contained a setting of Robert Burns' *The Jolly Beggars* by Henry Bishop (1786-1855). (Concerning the special bibliographical problems raised by Thomson's publishing methods, see Hopkinson and Oldman, *Thomson's Collections of National Songs with Special Reference to the Contributions of Haydn and Beethoven,* Edinburgh Bibliographical Society, *Transactions,* II, 1940.)

In addition to these settings of Scotch, Irish, and Welsh songs, Beethoven also evidently planned a collection for Thomson to contain folk songs of various other nations, as well. Thus, in addition to the twelve *Folk Songs of Various Nations* found in the *Gesamtausgabe,* Beethoven also made twenty-four settings for a planned international collection found in manuscript, and first fully described by Wilhelm Lütge (*Bericht über ein neu aufgefundenes Manuskript, enthaltend 24 Lieder von Beethoven,* Der Bär, Leipzig, 1927). Some of the songs in this manuscript are dated 1816 in Beethoven's own hand, and are of further interest in that he obviously collected the tunes himself from various sources, and had the words before him when he set them. The manuscript contains three settings entitled *Air russe,* all taken from Ivan Pratsch's *Sammlung russischer Volkslieder* (1790), probably the same source from which he borrowed the two Russian themes found in the quartets written for Count Razumovsky, Op. 59, Nos. 1 and 2. Other tunes from this collection were probably taken from the pages of the *Allgemeine musikalische Zeitung,* a famous musical periodical of the day, and the text of one, the Swiss *An ä Bergli bin i gesässe* is found in von Arnim and Brentano's famous literary collection of folk songs, *Des Knaben Wunderhorn* (2nd ed., II, 502). One of the tunes, entitled *Air cossaque* by Beethoven, is still widely known under the text supplied by Christian Tiedge in 1808 (i.e., *Schöne Minka, ich muss scheiden*). Altogether, this manuscript contains one Danish, two German, five Tyrolian, two Polish, two Portuguese, four Russian (including the *Air cossaque*), one Swedish, one Swiss, two Spanish, one Hungarian, and two Venetian folk songs.

Three of the tunes in this manuscript are also found in either Op. 105 or 107. These two opus numbers, also undoubtedly written for Thomson although they were not published by him, contain sixteen sets of variations on various folk songs, written for either piano alone or with flute or violin obbligato. Of particular interest is Op. 105, No. 3, called *Air Autrichien* by Beethoven, but more familiar to us as the old German student song, *Gaudeamus Igitur,* used by Brahms in the *Academic Festival Overture.*

Various scholars have suggested that Beethoven used folk song material thematically in other, more serious, works. These suggestions, for the most part highly doubtful, are listed here for what they may be worth: (1) Piano Concerto, No. 1 in C major, Rondo (*Die Katze lässt das Mausen nicht*); (2) Septet, variations *(Sind wir geschieden);* (3) Piano Sonata Op. 110, Allegro molto (*Ich bin liederlich, du bist liederlich);* (4) Seventh Symphony, Finale (*Nora Corina,* Irish folk song); (5) Ninth Symphony, Second Movement, Presto (*Kamarinskaja,* Russian folk song).

Concerning other folk songs, used as themes for variations, see Entry: Variations; A Schüsserl. P.E.M.

Förster, Emanuel Aloys

b. Wiedersbein near Glatz (Silesia) 1748, d. Vienna 1823. For many years he worked in Vienna as a music teacher. His compositions resemble in style those of the young Beethoven. A selection of them (chamber music) was published in D. T. Oe., Vol. 67 by Karl Weigl. Wegeler in his *Biographische Notizen* reports that a quartet by Förster was performed at the house of Prince Lichnowsky. The cellist, who was unfamiliar with the brand-new work, probably one of the Op. 11, got completely lost and stopped playing. Beethoven kept on playing, singing the bass part at the same time. Chamber music was cultivated in Förster's house; Förster himself also composed for the piano and contributed to Starke's piano school. His *Anleitung zum Generalbass* was published in 1805. Beethoven recommended Förster as a teacher to Prince A. K. Razumovsky, according to a report of Förster's son to Thayer. Young Förster was Beethoven's student for a short period. The six-year-old boy, whose father lived on Peters Platz one flight above Beethoven, had to get up at 6 a.m. in order to take his lesson. Once he returned crying because the Master had hit his fingers with a steel knitting-needle. (Cf. Weigl: *Sammelbände der I. M. G.* VI, 2, Franz Ludwig: *Zschr. der I. M. G.* IX, 353 and Saltscheff: *E. A. F.* Munich dissertation 1914.) According to Wurzbach, Förster senior had an amiable and kind personality.

Forti, Anton

b. Vienna 1790, d. there in 1859. First a viola player at the Theater an der Wien, later baritone and chamber musician of Prince Esterhazy. After his success as "Sarastro," (*Magic Flute*) he was appointed to the Imperial Opera. When Count Gallenberg became Director of the Kärntnerthor Theater, Forti retired in 1834. His wife was the famous singer, Henriette Theimer. The couple were among Beethoven's personal acquaintances. Forti repeatedly sang the part of Pizarro in Beethoven's *Fidelio* (1818, 1822) and was selected again in 1824. His name also appears in Tomaschek's autobiography in the *Libussa Jahrbuch* (1845 ff.), when Forti sang in Meyerbeer's opera *Die beiden Kalifen* (cf. Th.-R. III, IV and V, and Wurzbach).

France, Beethoven and

Beethoven's music has enjoyed great popularity in France ever since the first quarter of the 19th century, the first two symphonies, the septet, some of the trios and quartets being known very early. The first performance of the *Eroica* in France was given at a Conservatoire concert in 1811, conducted by François Antoine Habeneck. Between 1814 and 1823 the Conservatoire concerts were suppressed by the government, but during these years the Concerts spirituels continued where the *Prometheus* Overture, the *Christ on the Mount of Olives* and portions of the Mass in C were performed.

The Société des Concerts du Conservatoire was reestablished in 1828 with Habeneck as conductor and musical director, and thenceforth Beethoven's music was heard regularly. The first concert of the new series presented Beethoven's *Eroica,* which was performed again two weeks later at a concert à la mémoire de Beethoven, together with the Benedictus from the Mass in C, the first movement of the Piano Concerto in C minor, the quartet from *Fidelio,* the Violin Concerto (played by Baillot), and the entire *Christ on the Mount of Olives.* Between 1828 and 1831 all of the symphonies were performed, and out of a total of 408 performances of symphonies by the Concerts du Conservatoire between 1828 and 1859, 280 were of those of Beethoven, an extraordinary evidence of his popularity.

The chamber music and other works also received some notable performances during these early years. In 1830 the last quartets and trios were played by the celebrated Frères Bohrer; in 1829 Ferdinand Hiller played the E flat Concerto at a concert conducted by Berlioz; at Chopin's first concert in the Salle Pleyel on January 26, 1832, the opening number was a Quintet by Beethoven, and in the same year Mendelssohn played the C minor Concerto at a Conservatoire concert; in 1834 Franz Liszt and Chrétien Urhan performed the "Kreutzer" Sonata; the last quartets received a fine performance in 1835; in 1836 Liszt played the Piano Sonata Op. 106, and later that same year the Trios in B flat, D, and E, at the Salle Erard with Urhan and Batta.

In 1858 the Société Armingaud, organized to give six chamber music concerts each season, played Beethoven's music more frequently than that of any other composer. In 1863 Lamoureux founded the Séances populaires de musique de chambre, and in 1864 another Société de musique de chambre was organized. These all did much to promote Beethoven's chamber music.

Though the piano sonatas were heard less frequently than the other works von Bülow, Clara Schumann, Liszt, Saint-Säens and Ritter all included them in their programs.

Founded in 1861, the Pasdeloup concerts did much to make Beethoven's music familiar to a wide public, as did the Concerts Colonne, established in 1863, and the Lamoureux Concerts in 1881, for all of them devoted a very large proportion of their repertoire to Beethoven. There have been some notable Beethoven cycles, such as that conducted by Weingartner in 1905, and by Walter Damrosch in 1924, and some famous performances such as the Ysaye Quartet's presentation of all the quartets, and Raoul Pugno's unforgettable concerts of all the pianoforte sonatas. There is no doubt that a statistical study would show that during the last hundred years the orchestral and instrumental music of Beethoven has been presented in France more often than that of any other musician.

French critical opinion about the music and the personality of Beethoven has had an interesting development during the century and a quarter following their introduction. The advent of the Romantic movement in France was delayed by the political and social events of the last quarter of the 18th century so that it was not until 1830 that romantic literature and romantic painting "officially" made their appearance. This date coincides almost exactly with the first performances in Paris of the works of Beethoven. The controversy as to the merits of classical versus romantic art was at fever pitch and the crusaders for the romantics, the Jeune France, Victor Hugo, Balzac, De Musset, and especially the music critics, Berlioz and Castil-Blaze, seized upon this new music and its composer as fulfilling all their romantic ideals, and Beethoven became for them a symbol of their own visions and poetic enthusiasms. The freedom-loving composer and revolutionary musician incarnated their own "liberté, égalité, fraternité," and they heard in the Third and Fifth Symphonies echoes of the idealistic enthusiasm of the great Revolution. Others found in his personality a religious quality; he was a great genius through whom suffering and despair could be alleviated—just as he conquered pain and suffering so could he help others to salvation. Hector Berlioz shared in the semi-deification of his personality, and was also fully aware of the merits of his music, going into ecstasies of admiration for "the music of the starry spheres."

With the passing of the militant stage of romanticism, after it had won acceptance in the plastic arts, in literature and in music, the Beethoven literature in France becomes soberer in tone, more scholarly and common-sense in its attitude and conclusions. The Beethoven cult died out, only to be revived again with renewed energy after the publication of Romain Rolland's heroic biography in 1903. In addition to being a great musicologist, Rolland was a great humanitarian under the influence of Tolstoi, and an intense internationalist and pacifist. He felt humanity had need of heroes to worship, not military men who were destructive, but heroes of suffering, of the soul. He wrote his famous *Vie de Beethoven* to present the epic figure of the genius who surmounts every obstacle to attain greatness. Rolland's work became extraordinarily popular and once again revived the cult of the musical genius as the symbol of the suffering, conquering soul of man.

Since 1920 Beethoven criticism in France has been almost exclusively confined to the investigation of the facts of his life and his music.

C. MacC.

Frankl, Ludwig August

b. Chrast (Bohemia) 1810, d. Vienna 1894. Writer of great importance during the pre-March period. His *Sonntagsblätter,* which he published from 1842 to 1848, contained many articles on music and literature pertaining to Beethoven. (cf. Stefan Hock: "Erinnerungen von L. A. Frankl," Vol. 29, Bibliothek Deutscher Schriftsteller aus Böhmen).

Franz I

b. Florence 1768, d. Vienna 1835. Austrian Emperor, son of Leopold II. Emperor at the time when Beethoven lived in Vienna (1792-1827). Like all the Habsburgs, Franz I was a great music lover. In 1791 he attended a concert where Haydn's *Seven Words,* a symphony by Eybler, and Beethoven's Quintet Op. 16 were played. Beethoven dedicated his Septet Op. 20 to Maria Theresia, the second wife of the Emperor. While Maria Theresia was favorably inclined toward Beethoven, Maria Ludovica, the Emperor's first wife, showed an indifferent attitude. Whether or not this might be explained by Beethoven's behaviour toward the Austrian Court in Teplitz (reported with a great deal of imagination by Bettina Brentano to Prince Pückler-Muskau) is a matter of opinion. Empress Maria Ludovica died in Verona 1816.

Little is known about the relationship of the Emperor and Beethoven. Baron de Trémont reports that Beethoven was considered an outspoken Republican at the Vienna Court (1809), and that the Court never favored him and never attended any performances of his works. Fournier published some secret police records from the Vienna Congress in which the name of Beethoven appeared. Many Republican quotations by Beethoven are known, as, for instance, a conversation with Grillparzer, who quoted "Freedom of Thought" in the U. S. A.

Freemasonry

Whether or not Beethoven was a Mason is uncertain. Th.-R. take it for granted (III, p. 197) that he was a Mason and state that he dropped his membership after he lost his hearing. This does not hold true, as Masonry was abolished after 1790. However, a membership in Bonn might have been possible. On May 2, 1810, Beethoven writes to Wegeler: "I was told that you are singing a song of mine in your Masonic Lodge, presumably in E major, which I don't possess. Send it to me, I am going to replace it and you won't be sorry." According to Wegeler it was Beethoven's *Opferlied* (by Matthisson), to the music of which Wegeler had written a Masonic text. Wegeler published two Masonic texts of his own in the appendix of the *Notizen:* (1) "Bei der Aufnahme eines Maurers" (music *Opferlied)* and (2) "Maurerfragen" (music of Beethoven's song: "Wer ist ein freier Mann?". Obviously Beethoven was well informed about the happenings in the Lodges on the Rhine, a fact which speaks for his possible membership. Beethoven's teacher Neefe was a very active member of a Masonic Lodge. Whether Schindler was a Mason is uncertain. When he met Beethoven for the first time they shook hands in a certain way, which indicated the possible membership of both. Besides Beethoven calls Schindler occasionally "Samotracier," an allusion to a mystic brotherhood.

Friedrich Wilhelm III

King of Prussia; ruled from 1797 to 1840. Beethoven had already visited Berlin by 1796 and he played for Friedrich Wilhelm II (1786-1797). Ries tells us that the Master performed several times before the King, to whom he dedicated two Cello Sonatas (Op. 5) probably written for Pierre Duport, first cellist of the King. As a reward he received a golden box filled with louis d'or. The King himself played the cello, a fact which perhaps explains Beethoven's dedication. No doubt the Crown Prince, later Friedrich Wilhelm III, became acquainted with Beethoven at that time. This acquaintance was revived at the time of the Vienna Congress. Beethoven very likely met the King at Razumovsky Palace through Archduke Rudolph. Another intermediary was Johann F. L. Duncker. (Cf. Entry: Duncker). Wilhelm von Humboldt, Prussian Ambassador, was living at that time in the hotel Römischer Kaiser where Beethoven was frequently seen. When Beethoven's cantata *Der glorreiche Augenblick* was performed in honor of the Vienna Congress, Beethoven received 20 ducats from the Prussian King, a fact which was commented on by Karl von Bursy as "mighty stingy" compared with the 200 ducats given him by the Russian Czar. For the copy of the *Missa Solemnis* Beethoven received 50 ducats. It is well known that Beethoven dedicated his Ninth Symphony to the King. Samuel Heinrich Spiker, Royal Prussian Librarian, was chosen to present a copy of the Symphony, with Beethoven's handwritten dedication, to the King. Spiker wrote in Beethoven's Conversation-book of 1826: "The King is very fond of you." It was Prince Hatzfeld (Franz Ludwig) who functioned as intermediary between Beethoven and his friends and the Prussian Court.

Fries

Aristocratic family of Swiss bourgeois descent. Moritz, 1777-1825, was a great art lover who owned an important library and picture gallery. One of the wealthiest men in Vienna and head of a banking company, Fries and Co., Count Fries was in close connection with leading Viennese musicians. To him Beethoven dedicated the Violin Sonatas Op. 23 and 24 ("Spring" Sonata), the String Quintet Op. 29 and the Symphony No. 7. The famous contest between Beethoven and Daniel Steibelt took place in the house of Fries. Count Moritz belonged to the first 50 Representatives of the newly founded Gesellschaft der Musikfreunde in 1812. After 1810 the decline of Fries and Co. began to be felt. This fact is mentioned in a letter of the Master to Archduke Rudolph, dated July 24th. The partner of the banking house, Mr. Parish, committed suicide by drowning himself in the Danube in 1826, whereupon the Count announced his bankruptcy. Fries's first wife was Princess Hohenlohe Waldenburg-Schillingsfürst; his second wife was Fanny Münzenberg, with whom he moved to Paris, where he died in 1825. (?) According to Holz, Beethoven received a regular subsidy from Count Moritz up to the latter's bankruptcy (Th.-R. quotes 1822). The banking firm also served as the receiver of money and manuscripts for Beethoven, ordered by George Thomson for Beethoven's arrangements of Irish, Welsh and Scottish songs.

Frimmel, Theodor von

b. Amstetten 1853, d. Vienna 1928. Art historian, writer on music and physician. Was appointed to the Imperial Art Museum in Vienna (1884). In 1893 he became Director of the Art Gallery of Count Schönborn-Wiesentheid. Frimmel was an ardent admirer of Beethoven and among his works are: *Beethoven und Goethe* (1883), *Beethoven Studien* I and II (1905/6), *Beethovens Wohnungen in Wien* (1894), and *Beethoven Jahrbuch* (1908/9), and *Beethoven Handbuch* in

2 Vols. (1926), which served as a model for this book.

Fuchs, Aloys

b. Raase (Austrian Silesia) 1799, d. Vienna 1853. Official in the Hofkriegsrat. Musical scholar and collector. We are indebted to him for much information about Mozart and Beethoven, which he handed to Otto Jahn, who in turn handed it over to Thayer. Some of his articles can be found in L. A. Frankl's *Sonntagsblätter* 1845-46 and in the *Wiener Allgemeine Musikzeitung* (cf. Th.-R. IV, p. 24). In his youth he was a soprano and met Beethoven while serving as a chorister in Troppau on the occasion of Beethoven's visit with Count Lichnowsky in Grätz.

Fugue; Fugato

Beethoven belonged to a period in which, generally speaking, the fugue was outdated. However, in his later years he frequently turned to contrapuntal writing and fugato sections are quite common in the last piano sonatas, quartets, etc. In that respect Beethoven might be compared with Mozart, who indulged during the later years of his life in "constructive" rather than homophonic music. In fact, Beethoven frequently introduced a fugato or a fugue as a climax, as in the Piano Sonata Op. 110 or in the String Quartet Op. 59, No. 3, etc. However, there exists one short two-part Organ Fugue in D major which can be considered an independent composition of its own, composed in 1783, Series 25, No. 309 of the Complete Works.

Friedrich Deutsch in his essay "Die Fugenarbeit in den Werken Beethovens" (Festschrift für die Beethoven Zentenarfeier 1927) gives a detailed analysis of Beethoven's work on the fugue. Beethoven himself studied fugal composing with Albrechtsberger. (Cf. Nottebohm: *Beethoven Studien* "Beethovens Unterricht bei J. Haydn, Albrechtsberger und Salieri".) Altogether Beethoven wrote about 25 fugues (fugati) and it is striking that the works of his master years contained many more strict fugues than during any other period; i.e., Piano Sonata Op. 101, the Cello Sonatas Op. 102, the Piano Sonata Op. 106 (2 Fugues), Piano Sonata Op. 110 (with an inversion of the theme), the Diabelli Variations for Piano (2 Fugatos), the *Missa Solemnis* (3 Fugatos), the Ninth Symphony and the String Quartets Op. 131, Op. 133 (*Grosse Fuge*) the Cantata *Der glorreiche Augenblick* and the Fugue in D major for two Violins, two Violas, Cello, Op. 137.

Most of the baroque devices of the fugue are used in Beethoven's works, as, for instance, the three-fold *stretta* in the Piano Sonata Op. 110. And yet, Beethoven used the fugue often loosely, not in a strict sense, according to the philosophy of the baroque. Nottebohm quotes in his *Beethoven Studien* 1873: "There is no doubt that Beethoven failed to receive a thorough training in the form of the fugue from Albrechtsberger." To Beethoven the form was only a tool, the fugue a medium of expression and not an art in itself.

Funeral

No sooner had his friends, with bleeding hearts, done him love's last services, than they came together to determine the solemn details of his funeral, which owing to the preparations necessary, was set for the afternoon of March 29th. Cards of invitation were at once printed and distributed in lavish quantity. The mild, beautiful spring day lured a countless number of the curious into the open, to the scarpment of the Alser suburb before the Schottentor, at the so-called Schwarzspanierhaus, in which Beethoven had lived. A crowd of some 20,000 persons of every class gathered and the gate finally had to be locked, since the spacious court where Beethoven's bier had been placed no longer could accommodate the densely packed multitude. At four-thirty the clerical dignitaries appeared, and the procession set out. Although the distance to the church, in a straight line, amounted to no more than 500 feet, it took more than an hour and a half to traverse in an extremely slow progress made through the swaying crowds, which could not have been kept in order without using violence. Eight singers of the Royal and Imperial Court Opera carried the coffin. Before they raised it to their shoulders, however, they intoned the chorale from B. A. Weber's opera *Wilhelm Tell.* Then all the mourners—artistic colleagues of the deceased, friends and admirers of his exalted genius, poets, actors, musicians etc., all in deepest mourning with black gloves, fluttering crape, bouquets of white lilies fastened to their left arms and torches with crape ribands—formed in order. After the crucifer, who led the procession, came four trombone players and sixteen of the best singers in Vienna, who alternately played and sang the Miserere mei Deus, whose melody had been composed by the deceased Master himself.

It was, in fact, in the late autumn of the year 1812, when he was staying with his brother in Linz, that choirmaster Glöggl of the local cathedral had asked him for some short trombone pieces for his "Tuners" (city musicians) to be used on All Saint's Day. Beethoven wrote a so-called Equale a quattro tromboni, true to the venerable ancient style, but stamped with the originality of his own bold harmonic structure. Out of this four-part composition for the brasses, choirmaster von Seyfried, quite in the spirit of the creator of these serious devotional mortuary hymns, then shaped a four-part vocal chorus to the words of the psalms mentioned, which, thus admirably sung and alternating with the hollowly reverberating chords of the trombones, made a tremendously moving impression. After the band of priests, all those in the funeral procession followed the splendidly ornamented bier, surrounded by the conductors and choirmasters Eybler, Hummel, Seyfried and Kreutzer, on the right, and Weigl, Gyrowetz, Gänsbacher and Würfel on the left, holding the long white ribbon-ends which hung down from above. They were accompanied on each side by the torch bearers, among them Castelli, Grillparzer, Bernard, Anschütz, Böhm, Czerny, Lablache, David, Pacini, Rodichi, Meric, Mayseder, Merk, Lannoy, Linke, Riotte, Schubert, Weidmann, Weiss, Schuppanzigh.

The pupils of the Vienna Konservatorium and Saint Anna Music School, as well as the most distinguished notables, such as Count Moritz von Dietrichstein, Court Counsellors von Mosel and Breuning (the latter the friend of Beethoven's youth and executor of his testament), brought up the rear of the ceremonial processional.

Upon reaching the church the blessing was given before the high altar, during which ceremony the sixteen-voice male chorus sang the hymn Libera me, Domine, de morte aeterna, which Seyfried had set in the "lofty style." When the splendid hearse, drawn by four horses, bore off the lifeless clay past the aligned crowd, it was escorted by more than two hundred equipages. At the cemetery gates Master Anschütz, with the most solemn pathos and emotion, spoke the incomparably beautiful funeral oration written by Grillparzer, whose profound feeling and masterly presentation drew tears from generous eyes in memory of the departed prince of music. Many hundreds of copies of the two poems by Castelli and Schlechta were distributed among those present, who, after the coffin together with its three laurel wreaths had been lowered into the grave, departed the sacred resting place, profoundly touched, as the twilight shadows began to fall.

From a contemporary report, reprinted by Kerst from Landau's "Beethoven Album" 1877. (*Beethoven, Impressions of Contemporaries,* G. Schirmer, Inc.).

"Für Elise"

Short piano composition, marked by Beethoven in his autograph as "Für Elise am 27, April zur Erinnerung von L. V. Bthvn." This little Bagatelle had caused some speculation concerning for whom it was written. Possibly for Therese Malfatti. (Cf. K., W o O. 59)

G

Galitzin, Prince Nikolaus Boris

b. 1795; d. 1866. Russian aristocrat and admirer of Beethoven, a cellist whose wife, née Princess Saltikoff, was an excellent pianist. He transcribed some of Beethoven's piano compositions for string quartet. It is doubtful if he ever met Beethoven in person. On November 9, 1822, he wrote in French to Beethoven from St. Petersburg: "Being as passionate an amateur as an admirer of your talent, I am taking the liberty of writing to you to ask you if you would be willing to compose one, two or three new quartets. I shall be delighted to pay you for the trouble whatever amount you would deem adequate." Beethoven agreed in a letter of January 25, 1823, and asked for 50 ducats per quartet. Galitzin acted as an intermediary in the sale of a copy of the *Missa Solemnis* to the Russian court. When the money arrived, Schindler wrote the following humorous letter on July 9th to Beethoven: "I have the pleasure to inform you of the arrival of 50 Armored Horsemen, as a Russian contingent which, at the order of the Czar of all Russians, will fight for the Fatherland under your flag. The leader of these picked troops is a Russian Hofrat (Russian Chargé d'affaires von Obreskow)." It was signed "Fidelissimo Papageno" (nickname for Schindler). A performance of the Mass took place on April 6, 1824, in St. Petersburg, its first performance. Galitzin can be credited with having arranged that performance. Beethoven received a down payment for the first quartet only. Nothing happened subsequently except that Galitzin acknowledged his debt of 125 ducats to Beethoven. Many of Galitzin's letters to Beethoven and some to the banker, Henikstein, on the same subject are vague, not clear, and show slips of memory. They are reprinted with the necessary comment as Appendix II in Vol. V of Th.-R. There is no doubt that the Prince was not eager to reimburse Beethoven, and consequently he received no money for his hard work. Even his heirs had a bad time collecting the missing money, and it took them until 1852 to settle the matter in a satisfactory way. Finally a payment of 150 ducats was made. Beethoven had dedicated the overture *Die Weihe des Hauses* Op. 124 to the Prince. The quartets in question, dedicated to the Prince, were Op. 127 in E flat major, Op. 130 in B flat major and Op. 132 in A minor.

Gallenberg, Wenzel Robert, Count

b. Vienna 1783, d. Rome 1839. Musician, trained in Vienna by Albrechtsberger. He wrote fifty ballets, among them *Alfred der Grosse* and *Margarethe Königin von Catanea* choreographed by Philip Taglioni. At the age of 20 he married Countess Giulietta Guicciardi, a year younger than himself; the couple went to Naples, where he became *Directeur des ballets de sa Majesté.* Some of Gallenberg's letters to contemporary composers are preserved, such as those to Cherubini. Possibly he may also have been in correspondence with Beethoven himself; the Master received a call to Naples which might have been suggested by Gallenberg. When the impresario, Barbaja, came with an opera ensemble to Vienna he brought the Gallenbergs along (1821). Barbaja headed the Kärntnerthor Theater, and Gallenberg became its librarian. In one of the Conversations-books (1823) a dialogue between Beethoven and Schindler is recorded, dealing with the score of *Fidelio,* which was scheduled to be performed in Dresden. This conversation reveals that Gallenberg at that time showed some animosity toward Beethoven. Gallenberg blames him for carelessness, as Beethoven had obviously lost the score which he required. Whether or not this animosity was a result of his rivalry with Beethoven, who was once a declared lover of the Countess, is uncertain. Shortly after Beethoven's death, Gallenberg in 1829 took over the direction of the Imperial Opera in Vienna, but he had to quit his post in 1830 because of his complete incapability. After that time he lived alternately in Italy and France. The few scores known to this writer show him to be an inventor of pleasant melodies, without any deeper knowledge of craftsmanship. He seemed influenced by Rossini and other Italian composers. (Cf. Wurzbach; Kalischer: *Beethovens Frauenkreis;* Entries: Guicciardi, and Immortal Beloved.)

Games

Beethoven as a child and a youth indulged in games, as told in the Fischer Manuscript. Arrow shooting is especially mentioned in a letter of Justizrat Krupp (cf. Th.-R. I, p. 134). Nothing is known about Beethoven playing card games. Supposedly he played chess at the time his nephew Karl was at Blöchinger's Institute; he might have played chess with Blöchinger. Beethoven, devoted entirely to his art, never needed a hobby.

Gebauer, Gottfried

See Entry: Copyists.

Gelinek, Joseph Abbé

b. Selc (Bohemia) 1758, d. Vienna 1825. Priest and composer of piano fantasies and variations, which he produced in innumerable quantities; nicknamed the Variation-smith. Many compositions of variations by other composers sailed under his flag. He participated in the compilation of both the Diabelli Variations and "*In questa tomba oscura*" together with Beethoven. Czerny tells us in his autobiography how Gelinek was defeated by Beethoven in a piano contest. Czerny admitted that he never had heard anybody improvise in as perfect a way as Beethoven. Gelinek added, when asked by Czerny's father about the mysterious artist: "He is a short, ugly, black and stubborn-looking young man who was brought to Vienna by Prince Lichnowsky several years ago, in order to study composition with Haydn, Albrechtsberger and Salieri. His name is Beethoven." Gelinek and Beethoven were on good terms in the beginning and it was the Abbé who introduced Beethoven to Schenk, who in turn taught Beethoven for a while, as Haydn's teaching did not work out at all. Beethoven's lessons with Schenk had to be kept secret as Schenk reports in his autobiographical sketch (cf. Entry: Schenk). It is known that the relations between Beethoven and Gelinek deteriorated.

However, the piano arrangement of Beethoven's First Symphony was made by Abbé Gelinek and the title page of the piano score bears the inscription "*Arrangé . . . par son ami l'Abbé Gelinek*" (cf. Entry: Esterhazy). Gelinek had been Esterhazy's house chaplain in Eisenstadt since 1795, and it was evidently he who intrigued against Beethoven at the performance of the C major Mass.

Gerardi (Gerhardi, Gherardi), Christine

Singer and enthusiastic admirer of Beethoven. Two letters of Beethoven addressed to the singer are preserved. They indicate that the young lady had sent a poem of devotion to Beethoven. According to Th.-R., Leopold Sonnleithner made the following statement: "She was the daughter of one of the Court Officials of Leopold II and came from Italy with her family to Vienna. Although only an amateur, Christine sang frequently in public concerts, particularly for benefit occasions. Prof. Peter Frank, famous director of the Vienna General Hospital was a great music lover and in his house private concerts with Beethoven and Gerardi were frequently arranged. His son, Joseph Frank, was an amateur composer, and his cantatas, corrected by Beethoven, were performed. Joseph married Christine Gerardi in 1798 and both left Vienna in 1804. Nothing is known about Beethoven's having taught the singer. Dr. Bertolini mentions her as one of those who might have been Beethoven's Beloved, but Beethoven's second letter, dealing with a certain portrait of himself, closes with the ominous words: "To hell with you!" (Cf. Kalischer: *Beethovens Frauenkreis;* Th.-R. II.)

Gesellschaft der Musikfreunde

In 1813 Joseph Sonnleithner founded this society, one of the most important musical institutions in Vienna. After the performance of Handel's cantata *Timotheus* on November 29, 1812, by more than 700 amateurs in the "Reitschule," a number of music enthusiasts—among them the piano manufacturer Streicher, Baroness Fanny Arnstein, Ignaz Mosel, the businessman Tost, and Prince Lobkowitz—decided to continue their musical activities in the form of an official organization. Archduke Rudolph extended his patronage. In Beethoven's time, Prince Joseph Lobkowitz (1813), Count Anton Apponyi (1814), Count Egon Fürstenberg (1817) and Count Peter von Goess (1825) were presidents; Count Moriz Dietrichstein (1815), Count Moriz von Fries (1815-1817), Prince Innocenz Odescalchi (1818-1821) and Raffael Georg Kiesewetter (1821-1843) were vice-presidents.

On January 7, 1816, Beethoven's Symphony No. 2 was performed with

Kiesewetter as the conductor. Another concert, on March 10, included Beethoven's *Egmont* Overture conducted by Hauschka, who also directed a concert on February 2, 1817, of Beethoven's Seventh Symphony, and one on March 1, 1818, with the *Coriolanus* Overture. Beethoven's Second Symphony was performed again on April 18, 1819, by Woržischek, and his *Prometheus* Overture on May 9 of the same year. Franz Pechaczek was the conductor of a concert on February 20, 1820, where the *Eroica* was performed, and the same conductor directed on April 9 the Fifth Symphony and the chorus of *Christus am Ölberg*. On November 19, 1820, Leopold Sonnleithner conducted the Fourth Symphony and on April 29, 1821, Hauschka conducted it again. The Seventh Symphony was revived on November 13 by Sonnleithner, who also conducted December 15, the First Symphony and *Meeresstille und glückliche Fahrt*. February 23, 1823, brought a performance of *Christus am Ölberg* by F. Kirchlehner. The same year, on December 14, J. B. Schmiedel conducted the Second Symphony and the *Egmont* Overture. On April 4, 1824, Beethoven's *Opferlied* was heard. Schmiedel also conducted on November 28, 1824 the Eighth Symphony and E. von Lannoy, on April 4, 1825, led the second finale from *Fidelio*. On November 27, Beethoven's *Eroica* was heard under the baton of Kirchlehner; Lannoy conducted on February 19, 1826, the Second Symphony and *Egmont* Overture. Schmiedel was the conductor of a concert on December 10 of the Seventh Symphony. Immediately after Beethoven's death, the First Symphony was played on April 1, 1827, and on November 4 of the same year the "Pastorale" Symphony; on December 16 of Beethoven's death year the first movement of the Ninth Symphony was performed.

These dates show that though Beethoven did not hold an office in this society, his works were preferred above all others. The Society commissioned Beethoven to write a heroic oratorio and the Master intended to compose Bernard's *Der Sieg des Kreuzes*, which, by the way, had been promised simultaneously to the Boston Handel and Haydn Society. (Cf. Entry: United States of America).

Gläser, Franz

b. Obergeorgenthal (Bohemia) 1798, d. Copenhagen 1861. Musician and composer of operettas. In 1822 he was conductor at the Theater in der Josephstadt, where he became acquainted with Beethoven. His father, Peter Gläser, was Beethoven's copyist (cf. Entry: Copyists).

Gleichenstein, Ignaz

b. Heiligenstadt (near Vienna) 1778, d. 1828. Belonged to a noble family from Breisgau (Germany). His name appears in a letter of Albrechtsberger's to Beethoven (Feb. 20, 1797). Ignaz, son of Joseph, might have taken lessons from Beethoven. He was one of the best friends of the Master, addressed by him with the familiar "Du." Th.-R. quotes a statement of Ernst Münch, the biographer of Julius Schneller, the writer, historian, and friend of Beethoven: "Gleichenstein was one of the kindest persons whom the writer of this biographical sketch ever met." His wife was Anna Malfatti, the sister of Therese (cf.

Entry: Malfatti). Much of the correspondence between Gleichenstein and Beethoven has been preserved. Some of these letters might be important for the future solution of the Immortal Beloved problem, as indicated by Kaznelson's *Beethovens Ferne und Unsterbliche Geliebte.* In one of the Master's letters to Gleichenstein (March 18, 1809) we read: "Now you can help me to look for a wife. If you should find a good-looking one there in Freiburg—one who occasionally spares a sigh for my harmonies (but she must not be another Elise Bürger) [Elise Hahn, third wife of the poet Gottfried August Bürger; they were divorced in 1792 on the grounds of her misconduct]—then approach her on my behalf in advance."

The Cello Sonata Op. 69 bears the dedication to Beethoven's noble friend, Gleichenstein.

Glöggl, Franz Xaver

b. Linz 1764, d. there 1839. His father was city music director and director of gymnastics. The son was trained by Benedict Kraus in voice and by Anton Hofmann in violin playing. After 1790 he was theatrical director in Linz, Salzburg and Passau. Later he became music director of the Cathedral in Linz and was the author of several books on theory and editor of several musical magazines. In 1812 after Beethoven visited the resorts of Bohemia, he traveled to Linz in order to straighten out the family affairs of his brother, Johann. Glöggl, anticipating an introduction, announced on October 5 in the *Linzer Musikzeitung* the arrival of "the Orpheus and greatest musical poet of our time." Glöggl's son, Franz (1797-1857), told Thayer about his recollections shortly before Beethoven's death. According to him, Beethoven saw Glöggl daily and dined with him occasionally. He tells the story of the equales (cf. Entry: Equales), the soirées at the house of Count Dönhoff, a great admirer of Beethoven. (Cf. Th.-R. III, p. 343; and Wurzbach; Entry: Improvisation.)

Gneixendorf

Village north of Krems, where Johann van Beethoven had bought the large estate, "Wasserhof," in 1819. A castle, vast acres, vineyards, and a magnificent view to the Danube were the main features of that estate. Shortly after the purchase, Johann had invited his brother for a visit. But Beethoven did not make his first visit until 1826. At that time the Master was already in poor health. Beethoven left Vienna on September 28, after days full of confusion, as shown in letters to different publishers. He was in the midst of composing his last quartet. His nephew Karl accompanied him. Several notations written during the trip are preserved. Beethoven enjoyed the beautiful scenery. Several excursion spots, Imbach and Göttweig were mentioned. There was no doubt that Beethoven did not enjoy his stay. He was still deeply affected by his nephew's attempt to commit suicide.

His Quartet Op. 130 was finished in Gneixendorf on Oct. 30, 1826. While composing it, he roamed in the fields, humming and beating time. A team of oxen ran away, frightened by the strange sounds. He lost his sketchbooks in the fields; they had to be hunted for hours by his servant Kren. He was eager to return to Vienna, but Johann and his wife hesitated to travel with him. Consequently Beethoven, accompanied by his nephew, rode back in the chilly fall weather in an open milk cart. Beethoven caught pneumonia and returned in miserable condition in December to the Schwarzspanierhaus.

Godesberg

Well-known resort near Bonn. In 1792 the Electoral orchestra gave a breakfast in honor of Haydn, who had stopped in Bonn on his trip from London to Vienna. Beethoven showed him one or two of his cantatas, probably the one on the death of Joseph II (cf. Schiedermair: *Der junge Beethoven*).

Goethe, Johann Wolfgang von

b. Frankfurt a.M. 1749, d. Weimar 1832. World-famous German poet with whom Beethoven became well acquainted. Even in Bonn Beethoven had set some Goethe poems to music. In 1809 and 1810 he published a number of songs with text by Goethe. Op. 75 contains *Mignon, Neue Liebe, neues Leben* and the *König von Thule* (Faust); Op. 83 *Wonne der Wehmut, Sehnsucht* and *Mit einem gemalten Bande;* in the same year (1810) the music to *Egmont* was composed. It was at this time that Bettina Brentano directed the poet's attention to Beethoven's art. In an exuberant way she praised Beethoven as an artist and as a man, and it was she who acted as a mediator between the two geniuses. Goethe until then was little acquainted with Beethoven's works. Instrumental music was neglected in Weimar and the development of the classical symphony and sonata found no response. To Goethe, whose aesthetic ideas about the German lied were rooted in the theories of the Berliner Liederschule (Christian Gottfried Krause) and whose musical advisors had been Christoph Kayser, Reichardt and Zelter, Beethoven must have been a complete mystery.

Zelter had met Beethoven in Berlin in 1796. Although he was deeply impressed by his piano playing and his art of improvising, he rejected his compositions as an outgrowth of Romanticism and the counterpart of the poetry of Arnim, Brentano, Öhlenschläger and others. In the spring of 1811 Goethe received a letter from Beethoven announcing to him the forthcoming composition of *Egmont*. It must be admitted that the composer had promised too much, as the publication of the music was considerably delayed. Beethoven being favorably introduced by Prince Lichnowsky and Prince Kinsky, Goethe even invited him to come to Weimar. Instead of going to Weimar, he went to Teplitz in July 1812, where the famous meeting took place. A number of anecdotes and legends, originating from a letter of Bettina's to Prince Pückler-Muskau, became popular (cf. Entry: Brentano. Elisabeth). On July 19, Goethe wrote to his wife: "Never before have I met an artist more concentrated, more energetic and more fervent. He played splendidly," Goethe reported on July 21. Between July 19 and 23 they met four times. On July 27 Beethoven had to leave, but they met in Karlsbad between September 8 and 11. It is not known if the famous event, so vividly described by Bettina, took place in the Teplitz park. It seemed to be echoed in a letter of Beethoven's, dated

August 9, to Breitkopf and Härtel: "Goethe likes the Court atmosphere more than seems decent for a poet. There is little to say about absurdities of virtuosi if poets who should be considered the first teachers of the nation prefer that glitter to anything else." Goethe wrote to Zelter, Sept. 2: "I made Beethoven's acquaintance at Teplitz and was astounded at his talent. But I am sorry to say that he is an untamed personality. He is not far wrong in finding the world detestable, but he does not, therefore, make it any the more enjoyable either for himself or for others. He must be excused, however, and is greatly to be pitied for the loss of his hearing, which loss probably is more detrimental to the social than to the musical part of his being. Since he is of a naturally laconic disposition, this defect will make him still more so."

The reason for the lack of understanding between the two geniuses may be explained by the diametrical contrast between the two characters and types. According to Schiller's terminology, Goethe (like Mozart) was "Naiv," Beethoven (like Schiller) "Sentimentalisch." They were facing a fundamentally disunited realm of entities. Goethe aspired in his ethics to come close to his ideals, and he found his way. Beethoven denied the gradual approach to perfection. Beethoven's will was to change the world fundamentally and this will is sensed in every rhythmic beat, which is charged with gravity, permeated with an almost compulsive determination. In the terminology of Rutz and Becking, Beethoven belongs to "type 2" (like Schiller), Goethe to "Type 1" (like Mozart). These contrasts are reflected even in details of daily life. Goethe hated smoking tobacco, Beethoven liked his pipe; Goethe disliked animals, Beethoven was fond of them. And music itself meant to Goethe something completely different than it did to Beethoven. In the field of vocal music it meant to Goethe only an adornment for the poem. The new independent music of Beethoven, with its almost devastating effect on poetry, must have been totally strange to Goethe. Only unwillingly did he acknowledge the grandeur of Beethoven's symphonies. However, when the young Mendelssohn played for Goethe the first movement of the Fifth Symphony, Goethe found it exciting, but erratic. Beethoven dedicated *Meeresstille und glückliche Fahrt,* composed in 1814-15 to Goethe. For his sketch to the *Erlkönig,* see Entry: *Erlkönig*. Around 1820, *Heidenröslein* was sketched. Beethoven often considered setting Goethe's *Faust* to music. The first part of Goethe's drama was published in 1808, although the *Faust* fragment had been published as early as 1790. Beethoven knew the first version, for he composed the famous "Flea Song" of Mephistopheles at a very early date as an accompanied solo song with choral refrain. Later, he published it together with five other songs as Op. 75, in 1810. A sketch for *Gretchen am Spinnrad,* originating in 1803, also shows that Beethoven was deeply interested in *Faust* as an operatic subject. We read in the *Cottasche Morgenblatt,* Stuttgart, October, 1808: "Our genius Beethoven has the idea of composing Goethe's *Faust* as soon as he finds someone who will adapt it as a libretto for him."

Also, Friedrich Rochlitz, asked by Beethoven to be his biographer, reported a conversation he had with Beethoven in 1822: "When the conversation turned to the composition of *Faust,* Beethoven cried out, excitedly waving his hand, 'That would be a piece for me. Then something would happen!'" As late as April 1822, the following notation is found in one of Beethoven's notebooks: "As soon as this period is over, I must finally write something which for me, and for art, will be of the greatest,—*Faust.*"

But, alas, *Faust* was never actually undertaken by Beethoven, although, if theories of Prof. Schering are to be believed, it was under the spell of *Faust* that Beethoven composed his last string quartets, Op. 131, 132, and 135. (Cf. Romain Rolland: *Goethe et Beethoven;* Bode: *Die Tonkunst in Goethes Leben;* Abert: *Goethe und die Musik;* Entry: Teplitz.)

Graz

Capital of Styria (Steiermark); a city with lively musical activities. While Schubert visited this city, Beethoven's connections with it were only indirect. Later through Prof. F. B. Schneller (see Entry: Gleichenstein) and Joseph von Varena, an acquaintance from Teplitz (1811), Beethoven made his first contact with the city, where a concert (Akademie) in honor of Schneller was given on July 25, 1811, with Beethoven's Symphony No. 6 as the main feature. On December 27 of the same year the Choral Symphony (Ninth) was performed with Marie Koschak as soloist (cf. Entry: Pachler). Other concerts in Graz are listed by F. Bischoff: *Beethoven und die Grazer musikalischen Kreise.* In 1821 Beethoven became an honorary member of the Steiermärkische Musikverein. His diploma bears the date January 1, 1822. (Cf. Entry: Varena.)

Griesinger, Georg August von

d. Leipzig 1828. Saxon chargé d'affaires in Vienna and author of a biography of Haydn (1810), on which the French biography of Framéry is based. In 1822 Griesinger suggested to Beethoven the composition of a certain opera subject. Beethoven answered him on June 20 and referred to Griesinger's Haydn biography. The latter was also the intermediary for the purchase of the *Missa Solemnis* by the Saxon Court. (Cf. Th.-R. II and IV; La Mara: *Klassisches und Romantisches;* Kinsky: "Ungedruckte Briefe Beethovens" *Zeitschrift für Musikwissenschaft* II.)

Grillparzer, Franz

b. Vienna 1791, d. there 1872. The famous neoclassicist in the field of dramatic poetry, one of the most important contemporaries and personal acquaintances of the Master. His best known dramas are: *Ahnfrau* (1817), *Sappho* (1818), *Das Goldene Vlies* (1822), *König Ottokars Glück und Ende* (1825). He was well versed musically since his mother had been an established musician, the sister of Joseph Sonnleithner, who had been co-owner of the music publishing company, Kunst und Industrie Comptoir. Grillparzer himself had composed in his youth. He knew how to improvise on the piano and the violin. Four-hand playing was cultivated by Caroline Pichler and the Fröhlich sisters (friends of Schubert's). They frequently played Beethoven's symphonies on their duet programs. It was probably at Sonnleithner's house that Grillparzer met the Master in 1805, simultaneously with Cherubini and Abbé Vogler. Somewhat later in 1807 or 1808 young Grillparzer lived with Beethoven in the same house in Heiligenstadt. Grillparzer remarks: "At that time Beethoven was still slim, dark, and in contrast to his later habits, most elegantly dressed. He wore glasses, a fact which I recall, as he did not wear them in his later years."

When *Fidelio* was revived in 1822, Beethoven had promised Wilhelmine Schroeder-Devrient to write an opera for her. Breitkopf and Härtel were interested in the project (cf. Entry: Griesinger). Grillparzer tells us that Count Moriz Dietrichstein had asked him to write a libretto for Beethoven; probably Prince Lichnowsky was also in favor of the project. In a Conversation-book of 1823 Beethoven mentions Grillparzer for the first time. He intended to see the poet, who had two projects in mind: *Melusina* and *Drahomira.* A third project was discarded. The title was *Des Lebens Schattenbild. Melusina* was originally planned as a children's ballet, but had to be reshaped into an opera. Several meetings between the two took place and many technicalities were discussed in several Conversation-books. Beethoven asked the poet for some changes and Grillparzer agreed. An oratorio with the text *Messiah* was discussed at the same time, but the poet was reluctant. Another project *Judith* was mentioned, the idea of *Drahomira* revived. Discussions took place about the censorship of Grillparzer's drama *König Ottokar* and the poet notates: "One has to go to North America in order to express one's ideas freely." According to Rellstab, the *Melusina* project was discarded by April 1825. The last meeting between the poet and the composer took place on April 8, 1826, but they still saw one another occasionally in the tavern, Zur Eiche, where Beethoven was a regular guest on Saturday evenings. There has been much speculation why the opera project with Grillparzer was never realized. The poet was a great admirer of Mozart. Though he showed much admiration for Beethoven's works, he did not love his music wholeheartedly. Another obstacle may have been Beethoven's strange behavior. As an example, herewith is quoted the following from Grillparzer's recollections: "In the course of the summer of 1823, I visited Beethoven in Hetzendorf, on his invitation, together with Mr. Schindler. I do not know whether or not Schindler told me while we were there, or whether someone else had remarked before then, that Beethoven had been prevented, by urgent work he had been commissioned to do, from undertaking the composition of the opera. Hence I avoided referring to the subject in conversation.

"We took a walk and conversed together, half talking, half writing, while walking. I still recall with emotion that Beethoven, when we sat down to the table, went into the adjoining room and himself brought in five bottles. One he set down by Schindler's plate, one before his own and the remaining three he stood up in a row before me, probably to tell me, in his naively savage, good-natured way that I was at liberty to drink as much as ever I wished. When I drove back to town without Schindler, who remained in Hetzendorf, Beethoven insisted upon accompanying me. He sat down with me in the open carriage, but instead of merely going to the outskirts of the village he drove all the way back to town with me and, getting out at the gates, started off on his long hour-and-a-half journey home alone, after heartily pressing my hand. As he got out of the carriage I saw a paper lying on the spot where he had been sitting. I thought he had forgotten it and beckoned him to return. But he shook his head and, laughing loudly, like one who thought he had been successful in playing a trick, ran off all the faster in the opposite direction. I unwrapped the paper, and it contained the exact amount of carriage-hire I had agreed to pay my driver. So thoroughly had Beethoven's manner of life estranged him from all the habits and customs of the world that it never occurred to him how insulting such a procedure would have been under any other circumstances. I took the thing, however, as it was meant, and laughingly paid the coachman with the gift money."

It is well known that Schindler had asked Grillparzer to write the funeral oration for Beethoven. The poet tells us about his emotional feelings at the news of Beethoven's death. He was so overwhelmed that he was not able to formulate the oration in the precise way he had started it. He confessed that he really had loved Beethoven, a fact which is best expressed in the funeral oration. It runs as follows:

"As we stand here at the grave of the departed, we are, so to say, the representatives of a whole nation, of the entire German people, mourning the passing of the great renowned half of what has remained to us of the past glory of native art and patriotic spirit. Still living—and may he live long—is the hero of songs in the German language and tongue; but the last master of the song of tones, the sweet tongue of the art of tones, the heir to Handel and Bach, to Haydn's and Mozart's undying fame, has passed away, and, weeping, we are standing before the broken strings of an instrument whose melody has now faded away.

"The melody has faded away—let me call it that. For he was an artist, and everything he was, he was through art alone. The thorns of life had deeply wounded him, and as the shipwrecked clings to the shore, so he fled into thine arms, O thou glorious sister of the good and true, consoler of grief, O, heaven-sent Art! Firmly he clung to thee, and even when the door through which thou hadst come to him and spoken to him, was closed, when he had become blind to thy traits because of his deaf ear, he ever carried thy image in his heart, and when he died it was still lying on his breast.

"He was an artist, and who is to stand beside him?

"As the Behemoth storms through the seas, so he flew beyond the limits of his art. From the cooing of the dove to the rolling of the thunder, from the most intricate web of artistic form to the terrible point where culture passes into the uncontrolled violence of battling forces of nature—all that he passed through and perceived. He who is to follow him, shall not continue; he will have to begin over again; for his predecessor stopped only where art stopped.

"Adelaide and Leonore! Celebration of the heroes of Vittoria and the humble song of the mass! Children of the three and four divided voices! Roaring symphony: "Freude, schöner Götterfunken!"—your swan song! Muse of song and strings! Stand around his grave and bestrew it with laurel!

"He was an artist and he was a man, a man in every and the highest sense. Because he withdrew from the world, they called him misanthropic, and, because he shunned sentimentality, they called him heartless. O, he who knows himself strong, does not flee. It is the finest point which is most easily dulled, bent or broken. An excess of feeling avoids expression of feeling.

"He fled from the world because in the whole realm of his loving heart he found no weapon to combat it. He withdrew from his fellowmen, since they were not willing to reach him, and he was not able to descend to them. He remained a solitary because he found no equal. But to the very end, he preserved a human heart for all, fatherly feelings for his dear ones. His life was a sacrifice to mankind.

"So he was, so he died, so will he live for all time.

"But you who have followed us here, subdue your grief. You have not lost him. You have won him. No living man ever steps into the halls of immortality. The body must first perish, then only does immortality open its doors. He for whom you are now mourning, is standing among the great of all time, unapproachable for ever. Return to your homes, saddened but comforted. And whenever again in life the power of his creations overwhelms you like a storm, whenever a stream of joy flows for a generation not yet born—then remember this hour and think: 'We were there, when they buried him; and when he died, we wept.'" (Cf. Glossy and Sauer: *Grillparzers Briefe und Tagebücher;* Orel: "Beethoven und Grillparzer" in *Euphorion,* Vol. 28, 2; Anna Charlotte Wutzky: *Grillparzer und die Musik;* Th.-R. IV and V; Entry: Anschütz.)

Grosheim, Georg Christoph

b. Cassel 1764, d. there 1841. Musician, composer, author of a collection of folk songs and two operas, and arranger of piano scores. Author of several books on music. He seemed to be a special admirer of the German poet, Johann Gottfried Seume, who died in Teplitz in 1810. In 1816 or 1817 Grosheim sent Beethoven Seume's poem, *Über Glückseligkeit und Ehre,* and dedicated to him his own 8th Book of Songs. In 1819 Grosheim wrote to Beethoven: "I understand that you confessed at Seume's grave in Teplitz that you belonged among his admirers. It is still my desire that you should tell the world about your union with that poet. I have in mind the C Sharp Minor Fantasy and Seume's *Die Beterin.*" This poem is completely reprinted by Th.-R. II, p. 256. It is hard to believe that there exists a connection between this sonata (the "Moonlight") and the poem. However, Schering in his book, *Beethoven in neuer Deutung,* links the poem to his own idea that this sonata represents feelings which Beethoven might have expressed after having read Shakespeare's *King Lear* (cf. Entry: Schering). Seume's Beterin Lina and Shakespeare's Cordelia had the same fate. Grosheim's allusion still remains a riddle. (Cf. George Heinrich: *Beiträge zur Geschichte der Musik in Kurhessen etc.;* by the same author: *Beethovens Beziehungen zu Cassel und G. Chr. Grosheim;* and G. C. Grosheim: *Selbstbiographie.)*

Guicciardi, Giulietta

b. Trieste 1784, d. Vienna 1856. Wurzbach mentions Count Diego Guicciardi, member of a famous aristocratic family, and connects him with the Austrian Guicciardi dynasty. According to Thayer, Giulietta's father was Franz Joseph, "Kämmerer, Gubernialrat und Kanzleidirektor in Triest," her mother Susanna, née Countess Brunswick. Beethoven met her in the Brunswick's circle about 1800 and gave her piano lessons. In 1803 she married Wenzel Robert, Count Gallenberg (cf. Entry: Gallenberg). Giulietta went with Gallenberg to Italy and returned with her husband to Vienna in 1821. After that time she evidently approached Beethoven anew, but was rejected by the Master.

Schindler believed Giulietta to be Beethoven's Immortal Beloved, after he found the famous three-part love letter. Schindler was seconded by Ludwig Nohl in his Beethoven biography, and by others. 1806 was considered by Schindler to be the date of the letters. He changed his opinion in the third edition of his biography, stating the letters were written in 1803, as Giulietta had married in that year and moved to Italy.

Thayer, in his biography, made it clear that the Immortal Beloved was not Giulietta, but Therese Brunswick. The correct date of the letters is considered today to be 1812, and it is believed that they were written in Teplitz. Kalischer, however, stood by Schindler's idea that Giulietta was the Immortal Beloved and the letters were already written in 1801. It is well known that Beethoven dedicated the Sonata Op. 27 No. 2, the "Moonlight" Sonata (1802), to the Countess. (Cf. Entries: Sonatas, Immortal Beloved; and Kalischer: *Beethovens Frauenkreis* I.)

Gyrowetz, Adalbert

b. Budweis (Bohemia) 1763, d. Vienna 1850. Composer of operas, ballets, masses, symphonies, string quartets, etc. His best known operas were *Agnes Sorel* and *Der Augenarzt,* performed in Vienna. The autobiography of Gyrowetz, published in 1848, inspired by Ludwig August Frankl, was reprinted by Alfred Einstein in *Lebensläufe deutscher Musiker von ihnen selbst erzählt.* It is an excellent source for music history of that time. Gyrowetz showed little understanding of Beethoven. When Dolezalek bought a copy of the three Razumovsky Quartets, Gyrowetz remarked: "Better save your money." In a letter to Treitschke in 1814, Beethoven makes an acid remark about the new opera by Gyrowetz; however, Gyrowetz was among the eight conductors who were pallbearers at Beethoven's funeral. Castelli in his memoirs makes some fun of Gyrowetz, quoting him as a member of the famous "Ludlamshöhle," where he had a pseudo-Czech nickname, "Notarsch Sakramensky."

H

Halm, Anton

b. Wies (Styria) 1789, d. Vienna 1872. Educated in Graz, Halm served in the Austrian army 1809-1811 and was discharged as a lieutenant. Later he became a pianist and piano teacher in Graz. From 1813 to 1815 he was a music tutor at the house of Baroness Ghika, whose companion, Fräulein Sebastiani, later became Halm's wife. Halm met Count Franz Brunswick at the house of the Baroness, and it was Count Franz who recommended Halm and his wife to Beethoven. The couple moved to Vienna in 1814 or 1815, where Halm became a famous teacher, numbering among his students Stephen Heller, Adolf Henselt, Joseph Fischhoff, Joseph Sachs, and Julius Epstein.

The word "Halm" means "blade," and Beethoven, who liked puns, frequently called the musician "Strohhalm," (blade of straw), alluding to the somewhat inferior quality of his compositions. These compositions include: variations for the piano, piano sonatas, piano trios, and etudes, all characterized by a certain pianistic bravura.

Johann Peter Pixis in his memoirs (cf. Batka: *Kranz gesammelter Blätter über Musik)* tells the story about the performance of the Choral Fantasy Op. 80, when Halm, playing the piano part, failed completely. Pixis, anxious to get a copy of the work, went to Steiner and Haslinger, a music shop in the Paternoster Gässchen, where he found Beethoven infuriated, designating Halm as "Saukerl." He wrote with his pencil on the title page of the copy Pixis had just purchased: "Not every blade produces spikes."

Thayer received a lot of information about Beethoven through Halm, who in spite of his reputation, always behaved modestly toward Beethoven. Halm's piano arrangements of the Great Fugue, Op. 133, did not satisfy the Master and was replaced by Beethoven himself (cf. Th.-R. V, p. 298). Mme. Halm had expressed the desire to own a lock of the master's hair. Karl Holz was approached, and the lady received the required souvenir. When Halm visited Beethoven some time later, the Master declared emphatically and gravely: "You were deceived, you own the lock of a goat," and he thereupon gave him some of his own hair. There are different versions of that story, including one reported by Schindler (4th Edition) according to which Beethoven himself had agreed to send some goat hair to Mme. Halm. It is of general opinion that Halm through some of his pupils handed down to posterity Beethoven's characteristic piano playing. (Fischhoff and Dachs).

Hammer-Purgstall, Joseph, Baron von

b. Graz 1774, d. Vienna 1856. Son of Joseph von Hammer, an official of the Austrian government, he was a student at the Oriental Academy in Vienna and traveled in the near East, making studies mostly in Constantinople. Hammer-Purgstall is considered the founder of modern oriental studies and was the author of innumerable books in the field of history, geography, literature, etc. In 1807 he settled in Vienna where he became court interpreter for oriental languages. In 1816 he married Karoline, the oldest daughter of Baron Joseph Henikstein. In 1835 he was made Baron Hammer-Purgstall, being the heir of Countess Purgstall, who had been his friend for many years. Three letters of Beethoven to the orientalist indicate that Hammer had sent a poem to Beethoven. Beethoven thanked him and asked if it were true that Hammer had written an operatic poem for him. In reply Hammer sent Beethoven two singspiele which were never set to music. Th.-R. indicates that the plays in question were *Memnons Dreiklang, nachgeklungen in Devajani, einem indischen Schäferspiele,* and *Anahib* (sic, misquoted by Th.-R. from Wurzbach, who spells it *Anahid) einem persischen Singspiel.* An oratorio *Die Sintflut* is mentioned in that same letter, text by Dobenz, later composed by Ferdinand Kauer. It is presumed that Beethoven was interested in Hammer's writings, as we find in his diaries references to oriental philosophy. (Cf. Leitzmann: *Ludwig v. B.* II, p. 370.)

Handel, Georg Friedrich

b. Halle 1685, d. London 1759. Highly admired by Beethoven. In a conversation with Stumpf (1824) he calls Handel the greatest composer who ever lived.

Handwriting

The most outstanding feature of Beethoven's handwriting, next to his self-styled spelling, is certainly its illegibility. It is not only illegible for today's researcher, but was so even for his contemporaries. "Yesterday," he writes to Zmeskall, "I took a letter to the post office and they asked me where the letter was to go. . . . I see therefore that my handwriting is misunderstood possibly as often as myself."

To ease the life of today's biographer, Max Unger described practically every letter of Beethoven's own alphabet. However, for personality research, it is important that it be observed in what respect Beethoven's characters differed from each other and what they had in common.

In his first letter when he was 17 years of age, to about his 28th year, the pen pressure that he exerted on the letters is on the downstroke; many words are in a line, and the distance between them is even and "normal," according to the school copy of the official so-called "Kanzlei" or office handwriting: roughly speaking, he is still healthy. He owned a horse and enjoyed his life at Lichnowsky's estate.

Simultaneously with his first almost neurotic fears and his shame of being discovered hard of hearing, the pressure on the downstrokes moves into the sidestrokes; the letters become bigger, the lines narrower at the end, and everything is written more rapidly. "Don't mention rest. I don't know of any other than sleep." The legibility is slightly decreased and everything points to growing nervousness, emotional anxieties and physical fear along with distrust and aversion against everything that is conventional.

From 1812 until approximately 1819, the period of his creative barrenness and fight for possession and love of his nephew, his handwriting becomes more and more illegible. From then on to his death, the period of complete deafness, the *Missa Solemnis* and the Ninth Symphony, his handwriting is extremely large, the Cyclopean handwriting, as it is called.

Here are a few points which all these handwritings have in common: There is the accuracy with which each i-dot is put in its place—a rare feat, indeed, in such a swift handwriting. This indicates the enormous amount of conscientiousness with which he executed the minutest detail as far as his music was concerned. There are the underscorings of important words, fast, distinct, almost commanding strokes to attract the reader's attention and to convince him of the importance of what he had to say. There are frequently oversized dashes—"strokes of thought," in German—which leave it to the reader to think for himself, not always making it clear what Beethoven was thinking about. There are the zig-zag lines at the end of his signature which fully reflect the mood in each individual letter: they are hasty when he was restless; big when he was angry; tiny when he felt inferior; and, there is both a small one and a big one in his letter to the Immortal Beloved, reflecting the ambiguity of this letter's contents.

The most important characteristic occurring in his handwriting is the artistic curve—a curved line with which he circumvents all obstacles represented by the angularity of the German script. It denotes his protest against pressure and convention, but it is a very artistic one. Only true artists are capable of writing such a curve, and only very few are able to write them in all directions the way he did it; his art takes over where reality seems to hurt him. "Do you believe that I think of your miserable fiddle when the Spirit dictates and I write it down?" he writes to Schuppanzigh.

And, finally, there is one more type of handwriting. In it this artistic curve is missing. When he wanted to write "beautifully," he regressed to the handwriting of his earliest childhood, possibly the only time when he was truly happy—when his father was not drunk, and his mother was still his "best girl friend." One can imagine how this handwriting looked from Ries' description of a letter Beethoven had asked him to forward for him to the King of England. "By the looks of it," he writes, "it was frightening; he had done it himself and thought it was written beautifully."

Many of his signatures under official letters or under pictures, or the dedications on scores, like for instance that on the 33 Variations, or the Ninth Symphony, are written in this script. He must really have enjoyed it; it was the finish of a work. Had he not written to the Immortal Beloved: "I always enjoy things when I have overcome them, luckily?" And at the same time he gave somebody something. The handwriting of his testament to his nephew, written in this script two days before his death, is very shaky, revealing thereby with all its angularity the tremendous will power that was still in this dying, frightfully weakened body. It is almost as if this writing wanted to speak for him: "Reality has taken over. This life I have finished, I enjoyed it as I always enjoy things when I have overcome them, luckily. And here I have something to give."

F. V.

Harp

Beethoven used the harp only in his music to *Prometheus.*

Harp Quartet (Harfen-Quartett)

A name frequently used for Beethoven's String Quartet Op. 74 in E Flat Major. Schindler mentioned that nobody could explain this surname; however, the numerous pizzicati in the first *allegro* movement give the effect of a harp. (Cf. Schering: *Beethoven in neuer Deutung,* p. 17.)

Haslinger, Tobias

b. Zell (Upper Austria) 1787, d. Vienna 1842. Composer and founder of a music publishing company, student of Glöggl in Linz. Came to Vienna in 1810 and joined the Steiner music publishing company, which he took over completely in 1826. Haslinger's son, Karl, expanded the business, which became one of the most important ones in Vienna. Haslinger as well as Steiner was called by Beethoven the "Pater-noster Gässlers." Haslinger himself was also a composer, but he specialized in popular hits with patriotic subjects; one entitled *Ideal einer Schlacht,* brought forth from Beethoven a homeric laughter. The writer of this owns such Haslinger works as *Deutschlands Triumpf oder Einzug der verbündeten Mächte zu Paris, Das neubeglückte Oesterreich, Der Courier oder Wiens Jubel bey dem Eintreffen der Sieges-Nachricht, Alexander I und Friedr. Wilhelm III in Wien* and others. A great number of humorous letters by Beethoven addressed to Haslinger are preserved. In conversations and correspondence with Steiner, Haslinger and later Diabelli, Beethoven called himself Generalissimus; Steiner was called Lieutenant-General and Haslinger was the adjutant; their music-shop was called the Foxhole. There exist two canons by Beethoven, directed to Haslinger: *O Tobias* and *Erster aller Tobiasse.* (Cf. Max Unger: *Ludwig van Beethoven und seine Verleger,* etc.; Frimmel: *Beethoven Forschung* 1925.)

Hauschka, Vincenz

b. Mies (Bohemia) 1766, d. Vienna 1840. A finance official at the Austrian Court; studied music with Laube, Zöger and Christ in Prague, became a cellist in the orchestra of Count Joseph Thun, toured as a cello virtuoso, concertizing in Carlsbad, Dresden and other German cities. He settled in Vienna where he became a cello teacher. In 1805 he took up the bariton, in which capacity he performed chamber music with Empress

Maria Theresia, the Emperor, Prince Metternich and other notables. He was one of the co-founders of the Gesellschaft der Musikfreunde (cf. Entry: Gesellschaft der Musikfreunde), and frequently conducted the orchestra of that organization. A large list of his compositions can be found in Pietznigg: *Mitteilungen aus Wien,* Vol. I, p. 196 and in Wurzbach. Beethoven and Hauschka were good friends, the Master dedicated to him *Ich bitt' dich, schreib' mir die Es-Skala auf,* a humorous canon. In 1818 Hauschka was asked by the Gesellschaft to negotiate with Beethoven about an oratorio to be performed by the Society. The text by Joseph Karl Bernard was chosen with the title: *Der Sieg des Kreuzes.* (Cf. Entry: United States of America.)

Haydn, Franz Joseph

b. Rohrau 1732, d. Vienna 1809. The young Master met him in Bonn in 1792 when Haydn, returning from England, made a stopover in that city. According to Wegeler the Electoral Orchestra gave a breakfast in honor of Haydn in Godesberg and Beethoven presented a cantata to the older master (cf. Entry: Cantatas) which was highly appreciated by Haydn. It is assumed that Haydn thereafter invited him to come to Vienna for study purposes. When Beethoven arrived in Vienna in the fall of 1792, he immediately paid a visit to Haydn because the Elector had sent him expressly to study with him. Some notes from Beethoven's hand are preserved, indicating several meetings between the two composers ("22 Pfennig für Haidn und mich chokolade" and another time "Kaffee 6 Pfennig für Haidn und mich"). Haydn obviously did not take the instruction too seriously, and when Johann Schenk (cf. Entries: Gelinek and Schenk) one day inspected Beethoven's workbook, he discovered inexcusable mistakes, neglected by Haydn. Schenk secretly took over Beethoven's lessons. Wegeler and Ries relate that Haydn had expressed the desire to be designated as Beethoven's teacher on title pages of the young Master's first works. Beethoven refused, because he felt that Haydn had taught him too little. It is well known that the flutist Drouet (who lived for some time in New York) handed down a statement of Haydn, according to which Haydn, after inspecting Beethoven's first Trios, declared: "This man won't have a future." This statement probably was made by Haydn, but indicates a certain jealousy in the old master. Ries told about the performance of Beethoven's Trio Op. 1 in Prince Lichnowsky's house, where Haydn was also present. Haydn advised Beethoven not to publish the Trio No. 3 in C Minor, which can be considered the most mature of the three. Although Beethoven suspected jealousy, he dedicated to Haydn his Piano Sonatas Op. 2. Aloys Fuchs in the *Wiener allgemeine Musikzeitung* 1846, No. 39, related that when Haydn congratulated Beethoven on his music to *Prometheus,* Beethoven answered: "Dear Papa, you are very kind, it is far from a *Creation.*" Whereupon Haydn answered: "I doubt that you will ever reach it." Haydn used to call the young and self-confident Master "Grossmogul."

There is no doubt that Beethoven was greatly indebted to Haydn. Haydn's influence on Beethoven in the field of composition was treated by Heinrich Jalowetz in an article on "Beethoven's Jugendwerke in ihren melodischen Beziehungen zu Mozart, Haydn und Ph. E. Bach" in *Sammelbände der Internationalen Musikgesellschaft* XII. Karl Nef in Volume XIII of the same journal treats melodic resemblances to Haydn, among them the *andante grazioso* of Beethoven's Piano Sonata Op. 31, No. 1, which reminds us strongly of Haydn's melody *Mit Würd' und Hoheit angetan* from his *Creation.* Haydn's G Major (Parisian) Symphony (Breitkopf No. 13) has a *largo* which returns five times in Beethoven's works. However, it should not be forgotten that the melodic vocabulary of Haydn and the young Beethoven are almost identical, and if Beethoven used phrases reminiscent of Haydn, they bear the mark of concentration and gravity, which distinguishes Beethoven's style from that of Mozart. Compare Haydn's Symphony (La reine) "Romance" and the corresponding theme in Beethoven's C Minor Piano Concerto. (Cf. Entry: Typology.)

Hearing

See Entry: Deafness.

Hearing Aids

Beethoven used a number of such devices after his deafness had become more acute. Mälzel and Streicher had made some efforts to help the Master. Big bellmouths were put on his piano. Several gadgets can be seen in the Beethoven Museum in Bonn, some others in the Gesellschaft der Musikfreunde in Vienna. (Cf. Catalogues of the Beethoven House; Entries: Mälzel, Streicher, Wolfssohn.)

Hebenstreit, Wilhelm

b. Eisleben 1774, d. Gmunden 1854. Influential writer in Vienna who inspired Beethoven to Germanize musical terms. Beethoven was evidently a reader of Hebenstreit's articles in the *Wiener Konversationsblatt. Die allgemeine musikalische Zeitung* carried several articles from his pen which advocated replacing Italian terms with German ones. In a letter to Tobias Haslinger, Hebenstreit is mentioned in defending the Germanization of the word pianoforte. Beethoven asked Steiner whether Hammer or Hammer-clavier or Hammer-Flügel would be adequate. Hebenstreit obviously belonged to that large group of Germanizers headed by Gottsched. The philological purism always found its echo amongst musicians; hence Beethoven's designation of Op. 106 as "Sonate für das Hammer-Klavier."

Heiligenkreuz

Famous monastery in Austria, west of Mödling, visited occasionally by Beethoven. Karl Holz, in his notes on Beethoven, tells, in connection with the *scherzo* of the *Pastorale* the story of a drunken bassoon player in Heiligenkreuz.

Heiligenstadt

Today a suburb west of Vienna; at Beethoven's time an independent village. According to Carl Friedrich Hirsch, a personal acquaintance of Beethoven, the Master lived there at Pfarrplatz and Grinzingerstr. No. 64. The *Heiligenstädter*

Testament, dated October 6, 1802, was probably written in the house at Probusgasse No. 6. Beethoven's physician, Dr. Schmidt, had advised him to avoid company and retire to the quiet Heiligenstadt, believing Beethoven's hearing might be improved. However, Beethoven fell into despair, a fact which resulted in his writing the famous document. After Beethoven's death the document was found among a pile of the Master's personal papers, and was bought by the older Artaria. It reads as follows:

"To my brothers Karl and [Johann] Beethoven:

"O, my fellowmen, you who have thought and called me inimical, stubborn and misanthropic, how you wronged me! You do not know the causes underlying these charges. My mind and my heart from childhood on were kindly disposed, and I longed to perform great deeds. But consider that, for the past six years, an unhappy lot, an incurable ailment, has befallen me, which has been worsened by ignorant physicians. Cheated of the hope of improvement from year to year, I was finally forced to accept the possibility of a lingering malady, which it might take years to cure, or worse still, which might prove to be incurable. Born with a fiery, vivacious temperament, and having a bent for social recreation, I was obliged, early in life, to retire from the world and to live a lonely life. When, at times, I tried to rise above this, how bitter, how sad was the experience, due to my poor hearing. And yet, I found it impossible to say to people: "Speak louder, shout, for I am deaf." How could I admit the weakness of a sense that, in me, should be keener than in most—a sense that at one time I possessed in full perfection—a perfection such as few in my profession have ever enjoyed. I could never do that. Therefore forgive me for withdrawing from you all, when I so gladly would have mingled with you. My misfortune is doubly hard to bear, because I know that I shall be misunderstood. For me there is to be no relaxation in human society, cultural conversation, exchange of views. Almost all alone, I can approach human society only as far as the barest necessities demand. I am condemned to live like one banished. Whenever I approach a social gathering, a hot dread fills me, lest my condition be noticed.

"And it was thus that I have spent these last six weeks in the country. Following the orders of my physician—orders which only too well met with my present disposition—I am as sparing as possible of my hearing, but, at times, a longing for social intercourse has driven me to disregard his instructions. But how humiliating, when someone standing beside me heard the playing of a flute from afar, and I heard nothing; or when a shepherd was heard singing, and I heard him not. Such experiences almost drove me to desperation and I was on the brink of taking my life.

"Art alone hindered me. It seemed inconceivable that I should leave this world, without having produced all that I felt I must. And so I go on, leading this miserable life, a truly miserable one, with a body so irritable that upon the slightest occasion a sudden change can throw me from the best condition into the worst one.

"Patience—that is the name of her who must be my guide, and I have made my choice. I hope my resolve to persevere will last until it pleases the relentless Parcae to break off the thread. Perhaps I shall succeed, perhaps not. I am resigned. To become a philosopher at the age of twenty-six is not so easy, and harder for the artist than for another.

"O God, Thou art looking down on me, Thou knowest, Thou canst see into my inmost being, Thou knowest that the love of humanity and the desire to do good ever actuate me. And, O, you human beings who read this, think how you have wronged me, and if there be among you one as unhappy as I am, let him console himself with the thought that he is not alone, that there is another like him, who, in spite of all natural obstacles, has striven to keep his place in the ranks of worthy artists and men.

"You, my brothers Karl and [Johann], if after my death Professor Schmidt should be still alive, please beg him, in my name, to give a description of my illness, and of the story of my malady, and, please, add these to the pages here, so that the world may become reconciled to me as much as possible. And at the same time I declare you both the heirs to my small fortune. Divide it justly, be friends, and help each other. What you may have done to hurt me has long since been forgiven, as you know. I thank you, my brother Karl, in particular, for the devotion shown me these latter days. I wish you a life better and less sorrowful than mine. Recommend virtue to your children: virtue alone, not money brings happiness. I am speaking from experience. It was virtue that uplifted me in my misery, and it is because of virtue and my art that I did not end my life by suicide. Farewell, and love one another.

"And I thank all my friends, in particular Prince Lichnowsky, and Professor Schmidt. I should like you (my brothers) to take charge of Lichnowsky's instruments. But let there be no quarrel among you because of them. As soon as they can serve a useful purpose, sell them. How happy it would make me, if even from my grave, I could be of use.

"And now it is done. I hasten toward death with joy. Should it come before I have had time enough to devote to the unfolding of all my powers, I might deem it too soon, despite my hard lot, and I might wish for it to come later. But even so—should not the thought of being free from infinite suffering be a cause for gratification? Therefore, Death, come when Thou wilt: I shall meet Thee with fortitude.

"Farewell, and do not forget me altogether after my death. I have earned this, for I have tried all my life to make you happy. So be it!

Heiligenstadt, October 6, 1802.

Ludwig van Beethoven"

It might be of interest that, according to Friedländer, some passages of the *Heiligenstädter Testament* are quoted from Goethe's *Werther*.

Held, Johann Theobald

b. Trebechovice (Hohenbruck) 1770, d. Prague 1851. Humanist and physician, professor and Dean of the Medical Faculty in Prague, famous specialist in internal diseases; in the field of music he was an eclectic. Wurzbach in his article on Held told a number of interesting stories showing how Held's remarkable musical ear helped him in his diagnosis by means of auscultation and percussion of the human body. As a composer he published arrangements of Czech folk songs, ballads and variations for piano, under the name of Orebski. An Italian aria by Held *"Se tu non vedi"* with guitar accompaniment, recorded by Supraphone in Prague in the collection *Anthologia Musicae Bohemicae,* shows a striking dependence on Mozart. In his autobiography, referred to in Th.-R. II, p. 388, Held reported how he accompanied Count Prichowsky during a visit in Vienna. They both met Beethoven on the street and the Master invited them to the house of Schuppanzigh, where several of his sonatas, transcribed for string quartet, were played. We may assume that among these arrangements the F Major string-quartet version of Sonata Op. 14 was heard. Held mentioned a number of musicians whom he met at Schuppanzigh's: Krumpholz, Schreiber, Kraft and Bridgetower.

Henickstein

Viennese Jewish banking firm. Joseph was the oldest son of Adam Adalbert von Henickstein and was highly musical. He belonged to the founders of the Gesellschaft der Musikfreunde. His name appears in a letter to Gleichenstein, who, together with Beethoven and Clementi, was invited by the Baron for dinner. The firm of Henickstein was also instrumental in providing the English piano for Beethoven in 1818. (Cf. Th.-R. IV and V.)

Hensler, Karl Friedrich

b. Schaffhausen 1761, d. Vienna 1825. Theatrical impresario and playwright in Cologne. He met Marinelli, the director of the Leopoldstadt Theater, which performed his play *Der Soldat von Cherson.* His influence stimulated the creation and performance of several famous plays, among them *Das Donauweibchen, Das Schlangenfest zu Sangora,* etc., many of them composed by Wenzel Müller, Ferdinand Kauer and others. After Marinelli's death (1803), Hensler took over the Leopoldstadt Theater, which he directed until 1813. In 1817 he took over the Theater an der Wien, and 1818 the theatres in Pressburg and Baden, where he met Beethoven, who evidently liked the popular playwright. When Hensler became director of the Josephstadt Theater he rebuilt the house and re-opened it with Beethoven's *Zur Weihe des Hauses,* a cantata (text by Carl Meisel), a new arrangement of the *Ruins of Athens.* According to a report in *Der Sammler,* dated October 17, 1822, the first performance was directed by Beethoven. When Hensler celebrated his feast day on November 3, Beethoven's *Gratulationsmenuet* and works by Gläser and Drechsler were played as a serenade. (Cf. Wurzbach; Bäuerle: *Allgemeine Theaterzeitung;* and Th.-R. IV, p. 310.)

Hering, Johann

See Entry: Neate.

Herzog, Anton

b. Wiener Neustadt ca. 1771, d. there 1850. Schoolteacher, organist and choirmaster. In 1791 teacher in the Patronats-Schule of Count Walsegg in Klamm (Lower Austria). There exist some notes by Herzog in the archives of the Wiener Neustädter Musikverein about Walsegg and Mozart's *Requiem*. (Walsegg had commissioned Mozart to write that *Requiem* which was supposed to be performed as a work of the Count.) Even within Beethoven's lifetime, the authorship of the *Requiem* was discussed and watched by the Master. Herzog was the man who saved Beethoven from jail in 1822 when a policeman of Wiener Neustadt arrested the Master, who had lost his way and gave the impression of a vagabond. This story was told by Beethoven to Fanny del Rio and noted in her diary.

Herzog

A couple supposed to have been servants in Beethoven's house in the fall of 1809, according to a letter of Beethoven to Zmeskall. (Cf. Th.-R. III, p. 157.)

Hetzendorf

Village, south of Vienna, not far from Schönbrunn. When Elector Max Franz of Cologne, the former employer of Beethoven, returned to Vienna, he took residence in the beautiful Schönbrunn Castle. In the summer of 1801 Beethoven lived in Hetzendorf. At that time, on July 26, Max Franz died and Beethoven might have attended his pompous funeral. The Master spent many summers in Hetzendorf, according to Schindler. In 1805 he worked on his *Fidelio* there and Schindler told the story that Beethoven loved to sit on the trunk of a stunted oak in the vicinity of the famous "Gloriette." Here he composed large parts of *Christus am Ölberg* and of the *Missa Solemnis*, and parts of the Ninth Symphony and the Diabelli Variations. Grillparzer, who resided at that time in the castle of Baron Sigismund von Pronay, the famous botanist, frequently saw Beethoven in these surroundings (cf. Wurzbach). Beethoven, accompanied by Schindler, evidently had some argument with Pronay, a conservative old gentleman, who demanded absolute quietness in his castle, a request with which Beethoven could not comply.

Hikes

It is well known that Beethoven liked extensive hikes. He needed them for his health, but we may assume that they also promoted his inspiration. In the appendix of Seyfried's *Studien*, Beethoven's walks are described. After lunch he took his usual promenades around the city of Vienna on the double-quick, disregarding rain, snow or hail, even if the thermometer showed -16^{0} C. Whether or not his "personal tempo" had something to do with his growing deafness is hard to say. It is well known that Beethoven strolled extensively in the suburbs and resorts near Vienna, as in Baden, Wiener Neustadt, Heiligenstadt, Mödling, etc. This habit he had already acquired in Bonn, and he kept it up as late as the fall of 1826. (Cf. Entry: Nature.)

Hiller, Ferdinand

b. Frankfurt a.M. 1811, d. Köln 1885. Composer, of Jewish extraction. He accompanied his teacher, Johann Nepomuk Hummel, and Hummel's wife, née Röckel, both on friendly terms with Beethoven, from Weimar to Vienna. At this occasion Hiller saw the Master in March 1827 during the last days of his life. Hiller describes this visit in his book: *Aus dem Tonleben unserer Zeit* (a publication partly reprinted by Leitzmann in *Ludwig van Beethoven,* Leipzig 1921). Hiller visited Beethoven three times, the last time on March 23. At that time Beethoven was already in agony and unable to speak; Hummel's wife had to dry the sweat on the Master's face. Three days later Beethoven was dead.

Himmel, Friedrich Heinrich

b. Treuenbritzen 1765, d. Berlin 1814. Composer, friend of Goethe and Zelter. After studying and traveling in Italy he became "Hofkapellmeister" in Berlin (1795), where he met Beethoven in 1796. According to a Berlin tradition he competed with the Master in improvising in the Jagorsche Kaffeehaus Unter den Linden. After Himmel had played a short time, Beethoven interrupted him with the following words: "When do you plan to start?" Himmel was an extremely successful composer and his opera, *Fanchon,* was the biggest hit next to the *Magic Flute.* Varnhagen von Ense called him a character tumbling from intellectual dryness to gay intoxication by champagne. Like Rossini, he was a gourmand and developed a considerable *embonpoint.* In indulging in cheap jokes, he once fooled Beethoven with a story that a lantern for blind people had been discovered. Beethoven accepted the story and asked for an explanation. Himmel answered in a way not fit for print. (Cf. Kalischer: *Beethoven und Berlin;* Bode: *Tonkunst in Goethes Leben.)*

Hirsch, Carl Friedrich

b. Vienna 1808, (?) d. Döbling 1881. Austrian official and composer of popular dance music (similar to Lanner and Strauss). For a short time he was a pupil of Beethoven. His wife Anna, was a daughter of Albrechtsberger. Beethoven and Hirsch met at the hotel, Römischer Kaiser, where the latter received his first instruction. (Cf. Frimmel: Carl Friedrich Hirsch in *Beethoven Studien.)*

Hoffmann, Ernst Theodor Amadeus

b. Königsberg 1776, d. Berlin 1822. Famous German poet and exponent of German literary romanticism; also a remarkable composer. His opera, *Undine,* was revived by Pfitzner, who published its piano score in 1906. Hoffmann showed great understanding of the Master's composition and wrote enthusiastic reviews about the Symphonies No. 5 and 6 in the *Allgemeine musikalische Zeitung,* 1810. Hoffmann's name can be found in a Conversation-book of 1820; a visitor remarked that in the poet's "Phantasiestücke in Callots Manier," Beethoven's name was frequently mentioned. On March 23 of the same year Beethoven wrote a friendly letter to Hoffmann, to whom he also dedicated a canon *Hoffmann sey kein Hofmann.* There is an extensive literature on Hoffmann as a poet and a musician, listed in all dictionaries of music and literature.

Hoffmeister, Franz Anton

b. Rotenburg am Neckar 1754, d. Vienna 1812. Musician and publisher with whom

Beethoven became acquainted as early as 1799. Hoffmeister founded, together with Ambrosius Kühnel, the firm of F. A. Hoffmeister and Kühnel, which published several of Beethoven's works between 1800 and 1803. A number of business letters from the Master to Hoffmeister are preserved, some of them addressed "Most beloved Brother." (Cf. Riehl: *Musikalische Charakterköpfe;* Th.-R. I and II.)

Holz, Karl

b. Vienna 1791, (?) d. there 1858. Musician and official in the Chancellery of the Niederoesterreichische Landstände. He played an important part in the history of the Vienna Concerts spirituels, the leadership of which he took over in 1829. In this capacity he cultivated Beethoven's works. He left a notebook with most valuable remarks on the musical conditions in Vienna; it contained many recollections of Beethoven, who was particularly fond of Holz, an excellent violinist, active in the quartets of Schuppanzigh and Böhm. Beethoven saw him for the first time as the second violinist in Schuppanzigh's quartet. Shortly afterwards Holz became one of the Master's copyists and subsequently an intimate friend. Schindler was somewhat jealous of the new factotum and gossiped that Holz had spread false rumours about Beethoven's excessive drinking. It is true that at the time of Beethoven's close relationship with Holz, he was indulging more in drinking than before. Beethoven was so fond of Holz that he planned to entrust him with writing his biography. A number of letters and slips addressed to Holz, as well as entries in the Conversation-books, are preserved, proving that Holz was a deeply devoted admirer of Beethoven and a great help to him. Holz, a master of jokes and puns, inspired the master frequently to call him "Dearest lignum crucis" (Holz=wood in German) or "Bestes Mahagoni Holz." When Holz got married (late in 1826) he withdrew somewhat from the Master. (Cf. Entry: Halm, where the story about the lock of goat hair is told.) Holz died of cholera. He left a great number of relics and letters of Beethoven, among them a violin, supposedly a gift from Beethoven. (Cf. Volkmann: *Neues über Beethoven;* Schünemann: *L.v.B. Konversationshefte,* with numerous references to Holz; also Th.-R.)

Honors

Beethoven was frequently honored. He always received honors after successful performances such as the famous "Akademie" on May 7, 1824, in the Kärntnerthor Theater, when the Ninth Symphony and parts of the *Missa Solemnis* were first performed. Beethoven, almost completely deaf at that time, could not hear the thunderous applause after each movement, until Caroline Unger, one of the soloists, had the splendid idea of having the Master face the public. This, says Schindler, was the signal for the outbreak of a tremendous and endless ovation, never heard before. One of his highest honors was his invitation to become first conductor for Jerôme Bonaparte of Westphalia in Cassel in 1808. Beethoven finally did not accept the post, and was given instead a yearly pension, paid by Archduke Rudolph and the Princes Lobkowitz and

Kinsky, as a reward for remaining in Austria.

In August 1809, Beethoven became correspondent of the Royal Institute of Literature and Fine Arts in Amsterdam (cf. Th.-R. III, p. 144). On Nov. 16, 1815, he became a citizen of Vienna (Th.-R. III, p. 524). In 1819 the Philharmonic Society in Laibach and the Kaufmännische Verein made him an honorary member. Three years later he received the same honor from the Musikverein in der Steiermark, and in 1823 from the Swedish Academy in Stockholm. Shortly afterward he became an honorary citizen of Vienna, and, in Oct. 1826, honorary member of the Gesellschaft der Musikfreunde in Wien, an honor which was given to him only reluctantly. He received a golden medal from the King of France (cf. his letter of September 7, 1826, to Wegeler). In 1824 he received a diploma on the recommendation of Count Moriz Lichnowsky, signed by aristocrats, musicians, writers and other dignitaries. The London Philharmonic Society commissioned Beethoven to write a new symphony in 1822/23 and sent him as a gift the first complete edition of Handel.

Hotschevar, Jakob

Relative of Johanna van Beethoven. Played a certain role in Beethoven's quarrels about the guardianship and education of his nephew, Karl. After Beethoven's death, March 26, 1827, and Stephan von Breuning's death, June 4, 1827, Hotschevar took over the guardianship of Karl.

Household

The Master was a very poor housekeeper. He lived a very irregular life and had little feeling for order and neatness. This tendency, which is typical of many artists, was greatly in evidence in Beethoven's household, growing worse as his deafness increased. During hours of creation and inspiration, he tolerated no disturbance and showed a remarkable stubbornness and opposition to servants and housekeepers. He did not hesitate to overturn a pail of water if the sight of the charwoman disturbed him. Contemporaries tell us that sometimes his apartment was a complete shambles. He changed his apartments innumerable times; he took his meals irregularly. However, a genius like Beethoven should not be blamed for such conduct, which was overemphasized in the wide field of biographic literature.

Huber, Franz Xaver

b. Bohemia, d. Vienna about 1809. According to Wurzbach and Nagl-Zeidler: *Deutsch-oesterreichische Literaturgeschichte,* two writers of the same name are known, one born in Bohemia, the other in Upper Austria. One of his best known plays was *Der Bettelstudent.* He also wrote the text of Abbé Vogler's *Samori,* and for Winter *Das unterbrochene Opferfest.* For Beethoven he wrote the libretto to the oratorio *Christus am Ölberg* Op. 85 (cf. Wurzbach and Th.-R. II).

Hummel, Johann Nepomuk

b. Pressburg (Bratislava) 1778, d. Weimar 1837. Pianist. In 1786, he came with his father, Johann Hummel, a musician, to Vienna, where he was instructed by Mozart. After a tour through Europe, father and son returned to Vienna. Young Hummel began his studies with Albrechtsberger, Salieri and Haydn. The latter recommended him for the position of conductor of the house orchestra of Prince Esterhazy in Eisenstadt. In 1816 he became Hofkapellmeister, first in Stuttgart, later in Weimar (1819).

Beethoven evidently met Hummel as early as 1787 in the circle around Mozart. A rift between Beethoven and the pianist took place when the Master's C major Mass was performed in Eisenstadt (cf. Entry: Esterhazy). After a derogatory remark of Prince Esterhazy's about the mass, Hummel was said to have laughed. However, when the Battle Symphony was performed on February 27, 1814, Beethoven asked Hummel in a letter to conduct "the drums and canonades," which he perhaps had done before. On the other hand, we have a report that Moscheles was chosen to arrange a piano score of *Fidelio,* because Beethoven was on bad terms with Hummel. Hummel and his wife Elisabeth, née Röckel, a famous singer, paid a visit to the Master during his last days. Beethoven had known the singer in her youth and had been quite fond of her. (Cf. K. Benyovsky: *J. N. Hummel,* Bratislawa 1934, containing numerous documents; Wurzbach; Bode: *Die Tonkunst in Goethes Leben.)*

Hüttenbrenner, Anselm

b. Graz 1794, d. Oberandritz (near Graz) 1868. Composer of operas, masses, instrumental music, cantatas, etc. Pupil of Salieri in Vienna, 1815. He became acquainted with Franz Schubert and was one of his best friends. In 1816 he met Beethoven, whom he deeply venerated. Introduced by a somewhat "eccentric" (Thayer) Jewish gentleman, Dr. Joseph Eppinger, Hüttenbrenner paid a visit to the Master, showing him some of his compositions. Beethoven exclaimed: "I am not worthy to be visited by you." Hüttenbrenner remarked to Thayer, to whom he had told the story: "If it was humbleness, it was divine; if it was irony, it was excusable." About eight days before Beethoven's death, Schubert, Schindler and Hüttenbrenner paid a visit to the Master. Schindler asked Beethoven which one he chose to see first, whereupon he remarked: "Schubert." On August 20, 1860, Hüttenbrenner wrote a letter to Thayer from Hallerschloss near Graz, his sons' estate, describing the last hours of the Master:

"Dear esteemed friend:

"Your esteemed letter of July 17th, from Vienna, gave me great pleasure. Although corresponding is not so easy for me as it was thirty years ago, and I do not like to look back on past sad events, in which I at one time took part, I will endeavor to grant your wish, to put down as much of Beethoven's last moments as my memory has retained. I have often desired to send an article on this subject to some review, but never got around to carrying out this resolution, because I like to get away from myself as much as possible and very reluctantly speak of myself and of my experience.

"When, on March 26th, 1827, at about three o'clock in the afternoon, I entered Beethoven's bedroom, I found with him Herr Hofrat Breuning, his son, and Frau van Beethoven, the wife of Johann van Beethoven, from Linz, and also my friend, Joseph Teltscher, portrait painter. I believe that Professor Schindler too was present. All these gentlemen left after a while, and they had but little hope of ever again seeing the dying tone poet.

"During the last moments of Beethoven's life, Frau van Beethoven and myself were the only ones present. Beethoven, from three o'clock until five, had been lying unconscious, in a struggle with death, when suddenly a stroke of lightning, accompanied by an immediate thunder clap, illuminated the room brightly. Snow was lying on the ground in front of Beethoven's door. After this unexpected phenomenon of nature, which struck me strangely, Beethoven opened his eyes, and with grim mien, and gazing fixedly upwards, he raised his right hand, tightly clenched, as though to say: 'I defy you, you hostile powers. Get you hence, God is with me.' It seemed as though—like a daring general—he wanted to call to his men: 'Courage, soldiers, onward! Trust me! Victory is surely ours!'

"When his raised hand fell back on the bed his eyes were half closed. My right hand was under his head, my left rested on his breast. No breath, no heart beat, any longer. The genius of the great master had flown from this world of appearances into the realm of truth . . .

"I closed the eyes of the departed, kissed them, then his forehead, mouth and hands. Frau van Beethoven, at my request, cut off a lock of his hair, and gave it to me, as a sacred remembrance of Beethoven's last hour.

"After that, deeply moved, I rushed to the city, and brought the news of Beethoven's death to Herr Tobias Haslinger; then some hours later, I returned to my home in the Steiermark.

"Beethoven's personality was more forbidding than attractive; yet the sublime spirit that breathes through his wondrous works has made a mighty, irresistible magic impression on all highly educated music lovers. We must esteem, love and admire Beethoven.

"It is not true that I asked Beethoven to take the last sacrament; but I did, upon request of Frau von Haslinger, persuade Frau van Beethoven in the tenderest manner, to urge him to gain strength by taking Holy Communion. It is pure invention that Beethoven said to me: 'Plaudite, amici, Comoedia finita est.' I was not even present on this occasion, March 24th, 1827. Nor do I believe that he made a remark so contrary to his straightforward nature to anyone else. But Frau van Beethoven did in truth tell me that her brother-in-law, after having received Holy Communion, said to the priest: 'Father, I thank you. You have brought me comfort.'

"I must give praise to Herr Johannes van Beethoven and his wife, as well as to Professor Schindler, for their very kind and obliging manner to me.

"Hoping, dear friend, to see you in Graz, before you return to America, and to embrace you, I remain with best regards

Your truly devoted friend
Anselm Hüttenbrenner

P.S. Will you now, honored friend, be content with what I related to you and only to you, about Beethoven's last hours in this letter? They are probably the last words I will ever write on musical matters."

I

Iken, Dr. Karl

Poet and writer in Bremen who was one of the first to interpret Beethoven's works in a programmatic way (1820). Iken's program notes of the Seventh Symphony were published by Schindler. Beethoven, who was sometimes in favor of such interpretations, protested in a letter, written in the fall of 1819, against Iken's poetic overflow. The letter, referred to by Schindler, is not preserved and Schering: *Beethoven und die Dichtung,* p. 570, suspects that Schindler, who himself favored such interpretations (if given by himself), was somewhat jealous of Iken and instigated Beethoven's protest, provided the whole story was true.

Immortal Beloved

The name refers to a passage in a three-part love letter of Beethoven to an unknown lady. It was found in Beethoven's estate. Consequently the letter may never have been mailed, or it may have been returned to the writer. The fact that the letter does not bear the year makes it difficult to identify the person. Schindler believed that the letter was addressed to Giulietta Guicciardi and expressed the opinion that it was written in a Hungarian spa. Thayer was in favor of Therese Brunswick. Kalischer backed Schindler's opinion, without being able to shed new light on the matter. Amalie Sebald was also included in the group by Thomas San Galli, the first to point out that the letter was definitely written in Teplitz (1812). Through Hevesy's book and the new publication by Kaznelson we have become more certain that Josephine Brunswick was probably the Immortal Beloved; however, Kaznelson's hypothesis that Minona von Stackelberg, Josephine's youngest child (born 1813), was Beethoven's daughter, is far-fetched and must be rejected. It seems apparent that Bettina Brentano, Magdalena Willmann and others must be excluded. The famous letter reads as follows:

[Teplitz] July 6, [1812]
in the morning.

"My angel, my all my ego!

Only a few words with a pencil (yours!). My apartment won't be ready until tomorrow. What a miserable waste of time!

"Why this deep grief when necessity speaks? Can our love subsist, except by sacrifices, by not asking for everything? Can you change the fact that you are

IMMORTAL BELOVED

not wholly mine—I not wholly yours? O, Lord, gaze at beautiful nature, and resign yourself to what must be. Love demands everything and rightly so; and thus it is for me with you, and for you with me. Only you so easily forget that I must live for both you and me. If we were wholly united, you would feel the pain as little as I do.

"My journey was terrible and I did not arrive before 4 o'clock yesterday morning. There were not horses enough and therefore, another route had to be taken, but what an awful road! At the station before the last, I was warned not to travel at night, I was warned of a forest we had to pass,—but that only tempted me the more. However, I was wrong. The coach broke down on a dirt road! Had it not been for the four postillions I had, I would have been left, lying on the way. Esterhazy, on his way here, had the same experience with eight horses that I had with four. But, on the other hand, I got pleasure even out of that, as is usual after I have overcome trouble.

Now quickly from the outer to the inner. We will probably see each other soon. I cannot, today, tell you about the observations I have made on my life these few days. Were our hearts ever united I would probably not have had to make them. My heart is overflowing with thoughts that I want to tell you. O, I think there are moments when language means nothing.

Be happy! Remain my true, my only love, as I am yours. As for the rest—what is to be for you and me—is in the hands of the Gods.

Your true
Ludwig.

Monday evening, July 6th.

You are suffering, dearest being—(only now do I realize that letters must be posted early in the morning, and that Thursday and Monday are the only days for mail to K.) You are suffering . . . Ah, where I am, you are with me; and in talking to you, I am talking to myself. Do what you can, so that I can live with you. What a life ! ! like this ! ! without you, annoyed by the kindness of people here and there, which I neither deserve nor want to deserve. Humility of man to man pains me. And when I consider myself in connection with the universe, what am I, and what is He, whom they call the Greatest? And yet it is herein that lies the divine in man. I weep when I realize that only on Saturday you will get first news of me. No matter how much you love me, I love you more . . . But never hide anything from me, don't . . .

Good night! As one of the patients here, I must go to bed. O God, so near! so far! Is it not an edifice of heaven, our love? And as firm too, as the fortress of heaven . . .

Good Morning, July 7th.

Even in bed, my thoughts rush to you, my immortal beloved; at times they are happy, then again sad, waiting for fate to fulfill our wishes. I can live, either altogether with you or not at all. Yes, I am determined to wander afar until I can fly into your arms, and make myself quite at home with you, and can send my soul, imbued with you, into the realms of spirits. Yes, thus it must be. You will be resigned, all the more so, since you know how true I am to you. Never will another possess my heart, never, never!

O, God, why must one leave what one loves so much? And yet my life in Vienna, as it now is, is but a poor one, and your love makes me the happiest as well as the most unhappy of men. At this period of my life I would need uniformity, a certain regularity; can this exist, our relations being what they are?

My angel, I hear that the post leaves every day; so I shall have to close, for you must get this letter at once. Be calm. Only by a calm revision of our being, can we attain our purpose to love together. Be calm! Love me!

Today, yesterday, what a tearful longing for you, you, you, my life, my all! ! Farewell. O! continue to love me! Never misunderstand the truest heart of your
beloved Ludwig."

Eternally yours.
Eternally mine.
Eternally we.

Improvisation

Ries in *Biographische Notizen,* p. 119, tells of Beethoven's art of improvisation, which was most extraordinary and original, particularly when he was in good spirits or emotionally moved. No artist ever surpassed him in this type of performance. His host of ideas, his whims, the variety of his performance, the complexity of his improvisations were unsurpassed. Ries continues: "After a lesson we discussed fugal themes. I started to play with the left hand the first fugal theme of Graun's *Tod Jesu.* Beethoven started to imitate it with his left hand, then adding his right hand, he improvised without interruption for almost half an hour. It is inconceivable to me how he stood this uncomfortable position that long. His enthusiasm made him forget the outside world."

The Fischer Manuscript tells about Beethoven's early improvisations in Bonn. At the age of 12 he improvised on the liturgical theme of a Credo, and was so successful that nobody stopped his playing. Even Mozart was amazed at his skill (1787), and Chaplain Karl Ludwig Junker raved about Beethoven's inexhaustible ideas when he heard him play in Mergentheim in 1791.

In 1798 Tomaschek heard him and was deeply moved. Beethoven's friend, Amenda, after having listened to such an improvisation, expressed his regret that such wonderful music went as fast as it came. His contests in improvising with Wölfl and Steibelt are well known. When Pleyel went from Paris to visit Vienna in 1805, he heard Beethoven play. Czerny reports that, after a private performance, the Parisian kissed his hands. In 1809, Beethoven repeatedly improvised for Baron de Trémont, who felt that these improvisations affected him emotionally more than anything else in his playing. (Cf. Michel Brenet in *Guide Musicale* 1892, and Chantavoine in *Mercur Musical* 1906.) In 1811 Varnhagen von Ense heard Beethoven play in Teplitz, where he performed also before Rahel Levin (Robert). This fact was recently exploited by Kaznelson in order to establish the famous Jewish woman romantic, later the wife of Varnhagen, as the Distant Beloved.

In 1812 Beethoven played for Goethe, who remarked in his diary: "He plays delightfully." In 1812 Friedrich Starke, military band leader and well-known editor of a piano manual, heard Beethoven improvise in 3 different styles:

in simple polyphonic style ("gebundener Stil"); in a fugato form; in chamber style. In the same year Beethoven visited his brother Johann in Linz, where he was invited by Count Dönhoff to a soirée. While the guests were at the dinner table, Beethoven played in a neighboring room for almost an hour. Gradually all the guests left the table and gathered around the Master. Then it dawned on him that he had not heard the call for dinner, and he rushed to the table, overturning all the china (cf. Gräflinger about Glöggl's "Recollections," *Linzer Tagespost* 1909). In later years, about 1818, Beethoven became more and more reluctant to improvise for people, as stated by Philip Cyprian Potter, English pianist. At that time Beethoven became more and more hard of hearing, a fact which had a harmful influence on his playing. But he enjoyed improvising at home for his own pleasure on the piano, the violin or the viola. Schindler relates that his improvisations on the strings, which he could not tune properly, were painful to the neighbors. His extemporizing on the piano was clear only occasionally. In the last years of his life the piano manufacturer, Konrad Graf, had constructed for him a special sounding-board which was to function as a hearing aid. This enabled him to hear individual tones more clearly, but the vibration of chords in a small room had a deafening effect on him. (Cf. Schindler, Edition of 1871, II, p. 191.)

Incidental Music

Beethoven created incidental music to three separate plays and part of a fourth. The first of these did not occur until well after his reputation as a composer was established, and strangely enough, the first attempt was the most successful.

When Goethe's tragedy, *Egmont*, was played at the Hofburg Theatre in Vienna on June 15, 1810, it was Beethoven's music which was performed. He had composed a total of ten numbers, including an overture, four entr'acts, two songs for Clärchen, Clärchen's death, Melodrama, and Song of Victory. The melodrama is the form which Beethoven used so effectively in the grave-digging scene in *Fidelio*. Attempts have since been made to perform the music as a concert work, with a commentary between numbers. These attempts have not met with success and it is only the overture which has found a place in the concert repertoire of today. The overture was published in 1810 and the other numbers in 1812, all as Op. 84.

When plans were made for the opening of the Josephstadt Theatre on October 3, 1822, the choice of a play for the opening performance fell on Kotzebue's drama, *Ruins of Athens*. This is the same drama for which Beethoven had composed incidental music in 1812. The title was changed to *The Consecration of the House* and the task of adapting the play for the Josephstadt Theatre was entrusted to Carl Meisl; Beethoven was to provide a new overture and one additional number, as well as revising some of the other music. The March with Chorus was rewritten and this version was published in 1826 as Op. 114. The Overture was published in 1825 as Op. 124. (For further information on the Incidental Music see Entries: Overtures and *Ruins of Athens*.) F.T.W.

In Questa Tomba Oscura

Arietta with piano accompaniment, text by Giuseppe Carpani. According to *Journal des Luxus und der Moden,* Nov. 1806, the Countess Alexandra Rosalia Rzewuska, at one of her musical gatherings, improvised an aria on the piano. The poet, Carpani, otherwise well-known as one of the first Haydn biographers, immediately improvised a text fitted to the music. He visualized a lover who had died from grief because his beloved did not respond to his feelings. The woman repents her cruelty, shedding tears on the grave of the deceased, whose shadow calls back: "Let me rest in peace in the darkness of my grave. . . ." The verses were sent to a number of music lovers and composers, among them Beethoven, and this symposium was published by Mollo in 1808. The title runs thus: "In questa tomba oscura /Arietta/ con accompagnamento di Piano-forte /composta in diverse maniere da molti Autori/ e dedicata a /S. U. U. Sig. Principe Giuseppe/ di Lobkowitz etc. etc./ Vienna presso T. Mollo." The title page contains in addition the picture of a tomb with a weeping nymph, with the same nymph reproduced at the end of the volume. The "Avvertimento" gave the history of the origin of the publication. Sixty three compositions followed. Beethoven's song was the last one of the group, but was followed by a minuet, in the style of Lully, by Jakob Heckel, set to the same text. Of course this minuet is meant as a parody. Besides the parodist Heckel, forty-six composers were introduced, among them: Danzi, Czerny, Eberl, Alois Förster, Gyrowetz, Kozeluch, Mozart's son, Paër, Righini, Salieri, Sterkel, Tomaschek, Dionys Weber, Weigl, Zelter, Zingarelli. The *Leipziger Allgemeine Musikzeitung* reviewed the work October 19, 1808, and designated the songs by Salieri and Sterkel the best. Beethoven's composition, No. 63, was called gloomy and melancholic. Altogether the reviewer, probably Rochlitz, was not enthusiastic. History reveals that only Beethoven's composition survived. A comparative stylistic analysis of the individual songs would be extremely useful. (cf. Schindler II, p. 23; Th.-R. III; Eugen Schmitz: "In questa tomba oscura," *Sandberger Festschrift,* Munich 1918).

Insanity

During Beethoven's lifetime, rumors were spread about the condition of his mind and many people intimated that Beethoven might be considered insane. This was especially the case about 1817, when the Master showed a high degree of excitability and his behaviour and appearance deteriorated. After Dr. Karl von Bursy visited him in 1816, the doctor alluded to these rumors in his diary, first published in the *Petersburger Zeitung,* 1854 (cf. Ludwig Nohl: *Psychiatrisches über Beethoven).* He described Beethoven's attitude, referring to the publisher Riedl, as "Künstler-Spleen." On December 30, 1816, the youngest of the Brunswick sisters, Charlotte (called Roxelane), made the following statement: "I learned yesterday that Beethoven had become insane. What a terrible loss if this holds true!" These rumors were possibly nourished by Beethoven's sister-in-law, Johanna, who was eager to eliminate Beethoven from the guardianship of her son Karl. Beethoven must have known about these rumours as proved in a letter of May 19, 1818, addressed to Nanette Streicher: "I don't invite you, everything is confused; however, they won't lock me up as yet in the madhouse." As Lombroso and many other psychiatrists confirm, the powers of a genius and insanity are close neighbors. Lombroso pointed out that the sudden change of emotion is proof of a certain type of mental degeneration: Beethoven represented a case in point. A certain "Ignaz" (Seyfried, Schuppanzigh) was addressed in a letter: "Don't come to see me any longer, you are a vicious dog, and they should be picked up by a knacker." The next day he wrote: "My sweet little Ignaz, you are an honest guy, and I was wrong." Outbreaks of rage were not unusual at all. He called friends and patrons by terrible names; for instance, Count Ferdinand Palffy was called a pig, because he disturbed the Master while playing duets with Ries. According to Doležalek, Beethoven owned a sword, which had to be taken away from him, because his friends considered it a dangerous weapon at times when Beethoven was suffering spells of rage. At taverns and inns waiters had to suffer frequently from Beethoven's bad moods. Rotten eggs and other food might be thrown out of the window. Grillparzer in a conversation with Dr. Herman Rollette (cf. Rollette: *Mein Lebensabriss,* edited by Paul Tausig 1908) said: "Beethoven, if irritated, acted like a wild animal." The veins on his forehead would swell and his face take on a ghastly expression. Waldmüller's portrait of 1823 gives an idea how the Master could look.

J

Janitschek

Couple frequently mentioned in Beethoven's Conversation-books about 1820. They belonged to the circle of Bernard and Peters, where there were somewhat superficial discussions pertaining to matrimony and sex. The couple was fond of pleasure and amusement.

Jaundice

See Entry: Diseases.

Jedlersee

A village not far from Floridsdorf. Countess Erdödy owned a house in the neighborhood where Beethoven was an occasional guest.

Jeitteles, Alois

b. Brünn 1794, d. there 1858. Son of Gottlieb, grandson of Jonas Jeitteles; member of a large Jewish family of physicians and writers. Graduated as a doctor in 1819. He belonged to the circle of Beethoven, Castelli, Deinhardstein, Grillparzer, Moscheles, Schneller and Veit. He was on the best of terms with the leading actors of the Burgtheater and translated a number of Spanish plays; he also published lyrical poems in the almanacs *Selam* and *Aglaia*. After traveling for scientific purposes, he settled in Brünn as a practitioner. In Berlin he became a friend of Tieck. When cholera broke out in Brünn in 1831 and 1836, he served as a volunteer in the general hospital. In the last years of his life, he was editor-in-chief of the *Brünner Zeitung*.

A large part of his output may be found in journals and almanacs, as for example in *Aglaia* (1817) the charming poems *Trutzständchen* and *Der Sanger und die Nachtigall*. However, better known is his parody of the Schicksalstragödie, called *Der Schicksalsstrumpf*, written in collaboration with Castelli. In 1827 he wrote *Beethoven's Funeral*, a poem of deep emotional feeling.

Jeitteles wrote his famous song cycle *An die ferne Geliebte* at the age of 21. It is not known whether or not Beethoven found the poems in one of the almanacs. (The writer of this book checked *Aglaia*, which does not contain the lyric cycle. Whether it is to be found in *Selam*, he could not determine.) Beethoven composed the beautiful cycle as Op. 98 in 1816 under the title *An die ferne Geliebte*, and dedicated it to Prince Lobkowitz. It should be mentioned that Beethoven's original manuscript bore the inscription: "An die entfernte Geliebte; 6 Lieder von A. Jeitteles in Musik gesetzt von L. v. Beethoven 1816 im Monath April." It has been generally conceded that this work is the first composition combining several poems into one musical work: a Song Cycle. Characteristic of this type of song composition is the composer's return in the last song to the theme of the first one, a procedure which was later used in other song cycles, such as Schumann's *Frauen Liebe und Leben.* Beethoven, as a typical composer of instrumental music, took the cyclic instrumental forms (sonata) as a model for vocal compositions. The last part in *An die ferne Geliebte* is in fact instrumentally conceived. Beethoven himself considered this work of his highly significant, as proven by his numerous revealing sketches. A theory was propounded by Siegmund Kaznelson (1954 Standard Buch-Verlag Zürich) that the Distant Beloved differed from the Immortal Beloved; the Distant Beloved is supposed to be Rahel Levin, married to Varnhagen von Ense, and the Immortal Beloved Josephine von Brunswick. However, this conjecture is very questionable in spite of his research and penetrating investigation. (Cf. Entry: Immortal Beloved; Wurzbach; Friedländer's Epilogue to his edition of the Song Cycle in *Insel Bücherei;* Boettcher: *Beethoven als Liederkomponist;* Don L. Earl: *The Solo Song Cycle in Germany,* unpublished dissertation, Indiana University 1952.)

Jeitteles, Ignaz

b. Prague 1783, d. Vienna 1843. Son of Benedict and grandson of Jonas Jeitteles, a cousin of Alois. Studied in Prague with A. G. Meissner, who taught aesthetics and classical literature. In Vienna Jeitteles became partner in a commercial firm; however, he devoted much of his time to the study of history and philosophy. He wrote numerous articles for the magazines *Morgenblatt, Elegante Zeitung, Dresdener Abendzeitung, Europa,* published by Lewald, etc. He never disavowed his Jewish past as did many other members of his family, who had assumed the title of Baron von Geitler. One of his most emotional poems is called *Gedanken an der Wiege eines Kindes jüdischer Eltern.*

August Lewald, in *Biographical Sketch,* tells about Jeitteles' great love for music. He not only met Carl Maria von Weber, but spent most of his evenings in the winters 1821 and 1822 in Beethoven's company. They usually met at the Zum Seitzerhof inn, where they had dinner together. Lewald was introduced to the Master by Jeitteles. Subjects of their conversation were operatic plots in which Beethoven was greatly interested. The Master at that time was working on an opera, *Bacchus.* It was Ignaz Jeitteles who introduced Peter Daniel Atterbohm, famous Swedish poet and philosopher, to Beethoven in 1826. Jeitteles led the poet into the Schwarzspanierhaus, but the deaf Master did not notice the visitors and after having watched the Master composing for a while, they left the room unnoticed. (Cf. Wurzbach; Th.-R.; Nohl: *Beethoven nach den Schilderungen seiner Zeitgenossen* 1877.)

Jenger, Johann Baptist

b. Kirchofen (Breisgau) 1792, d. Vienna 1856. Official of the Imperial army and musician; friend of Franz Schubert. Between 1819 and 1825 he lived in Graz, where he belonged to the circle of Pachler (see Entry: Pachler). He met Beethoven shortly before the Master's death. Before Beethoven's first operation on December 19, 1826, Jenger brought him two letters of Marie Pachler-Koschak which later came into Schindler's possession. Mrs. Pachler stated in this letter: "Herr Jenger is a close friend of our family and an ardent admirer of your Muse." There are letters of Jenger to Mme. Pachler which speak about Beethoven's state of health. Jenger was an important source of information about the Master's last days. (Cf. O. E. Deutsch: "Aus Beethovens letzten Tagen," *Oesterr. Rundschau* 1807; Th.-R. V.)

Jews

Schindler is responsible for having stamped Beethoven as an anti-Semite. After Wagner had published his ill-famed pamphlet *Das Judentum in der Musik* in Brendel's Leipzig *Neue Zeitschrift für Musik* (1850) under the pseudonym K. Freigedank, Schindler immediately fell in line with Wagner. He expressed himself against Moscheles (*Biographie* 1871, p. 173) thus: "There was a sky-high barrier between Moscheles and Beethoven which made it impossible for the Master to associate with him; it was Beethoven's hatred of the children of Israel in the field of Art, because they favored the new trend of making big business of music." If his prophecies had proved correct, Freigedank in the *Neue Zeitschrift für Musik* (1850) would have had Beethoven as his (Wagner's) predecessor. Schindler's hatred of Moscheles was the result of his jealousy of the Jewish pianist, who in his edition of the Beethoven sonatas (published by Hallberger, Stuttgart), claimed personal acquaintance with Beethoven between 1808 and 1820, when he, under the Master's supervision, worked on the piano score of *Fidelio*. Beethoven's occasional derogatory remarks about Jews should not be taken too seriously. There were many Jews with whom Beethoven was on friendly terms: the violinist Heinrich Eppinger; Dr. Joseph Eppinger, who introduced Hüttenbrenner to Beethoven; the bankers Alexander and Raymund Wetzlar von Plankenstern, the latter on good terms with Mozart because of the performance of the *Marriage of Figaro*. Other Jewish personalities closely associated with Beethoven were the banker and director of the Austrian National Bank, Josef Baron von Henickstein; the bankers Offenheimer and Herz, employers of Franz Oliva and Bernhard; Baron Eskeles; Heinrich von Pareira, son-in-law of Baron Nathan Arnstein; Marie Bernhardine Eskeles, later the Countess Wimpffen, and an ardent admirer of Beethoven; the family of the London banker Goldschmidt; the Berlin and Paris publishers Adolf Martin and Moritz Adolf Schlesinger; the Viennese bank clerk Leringer; the physician and poet, Alois Jeitteles of Brünn, and his cousin, the writer Ignaz Jeitteles of Prague; Giacomo Meyerbeer and Ferdinand Hiller, Adolf Bernhard Marx, Beethoven's biographer and editor of the *Berliner Allgem. Musikalische Zeitung* was praised by Beethoven in a letter to Schlesinger as particularly "witty," and last but not least Moscheles. There are some occasional anti-Semitic remarks to be found in

Conversation-books and letters. However, Beethoven was asked by the Israelitische Kultusgemeinde in Vienna in 1825 to write a cantata for the dedication of their new synagogue in the Seidenstättergasse, which is even now the main synagogue in Vienna. According to a conversation of the Master with his brother Johann, the Viennese Jews intended to open the synagogue with a choral cantata composed by Beethoven and they promised him ample remuneration. One of the Rothschild bankers was involved in the deal. The text of the cantata had already been handed to the Master but unfortunately he did not compose it; Kapellmeister Joseph Drechsler (1782-1825) did. Schilling in his Encyclopedia enumerated three cantatas by Drechsler, one for the dedication of the Viennese Synagogue. It is interesting that Beethoven's C sharp minor Quartet Op. 131 in its No. 6 *Adagio quasi un poco Andante,* measures 1-5, shows a striking similarity to the famous *Kol Nidre,* a fact already noticed by Emil Breslauer. There is a possibility that Beethoven, searching for original Hebrew melodies, came across that famous theme. (Cf. Volkmann: "Ein unausgeführt gebliebener Plan Beethovens", in Frimmel: *Beethoven Jahrbuch* I; Nettl: *Alte jüdische Spielleute und Musiker.*) Recently Kaznelson has claimed that Rahel Levin, married to Varnhagen von Ense, should be considered Beethoven's Distant Beloved (see Entries: Immortal Beloved; Moscheles and Wetzlar).

Junker, Karl Ludwig

b. Oehringen about 1741. Around 1797 Junker was chaplain for Prince Hohenlohe in Rupertshofen, whence he traveled to Mergentheim in order to hear the Bonn Musicians play. Junker wrote a glowing report for Bossler's *Musikalische Correspondenz.* This report was first published by Thayer in the *Atlantic Monthly,* May 1858, and later in his Beethoven biography (cf. Th.-R. I, p. 268). Junker's report is one of the best sources of information about the Bonn Kapelle. Beethoven (spelled Bethofen) is discussed; he called him one of the greatest clavierists. (Cf. Sandberger: *Beethoven Aufsätze;* Schiedermair: *Der junge Beethoven*).

K

Kalkbrenner, Friedrich Wilhelm

b. while his mother was traveling between Cassel and Berlin 1788, d. Enghien-les-Bains 1849.

Famous pianist and composer of piano works mostly in salon and virtuoso style. In 1824, Kalkbrenner gave a concert in Vienna. Schindler noted in the Conversation-book sarcastically: "Was Mr. Kalkbrenner gracious enough to honor you with a ticket for his concert?" Beethoven, already deaf at that time, did not attend the concert and nothing is known about any relations between him and Kalkbrenner.

Kameel (Camel)

Wine tavern located in the Bognergasse in Vienna. The Schwarze Kameel was one of the best known wine taverns in Vienna. Beethoven visited the place frequently, particularly around 1820. In a Conversation-book of 1824 Schindler wrote: "I am just occupied with the second movement of the Eighth Symphony—ta, ta, ta, ta—the canon on Mälzel. Wasn't it a gay night, when we sang that canon in the Kameel. Mälzel sang the bass, and I the soprano, I believe it was the end of December 1817" (Th.-R. III, p. 349). Doležalek reports: "He [Beethoven] drank claret in the Schwarze Kameel, and it is presumed that he enjoyed other wines as well. Sometimes he even used the tavern for entertaining and ordered Austrian white wine, sugar, coffee, etc." The place was owned after 1818 successively by Joseph Stiebitz, Joseph Söhnel and Ignatz Arlet. Stiebitz's wine tavern was frequently visited by Gustav Mahler, Johannes Brahms, and others. The writer of this book was taken there by his friend Guido Adler. (Cf. Frimmel: "Beethoven als Gasthausbesucher in Wien", Sandberger's *Beethoven Jahrbuch* I.)

Kanka, Johann

b. Prague 1772, d. Prague 1865. Lawyer and musician. His father, Johann Nepomuk, is mentioned in *Jahrbuch der Tonkunst von Wien und Prag* (1796) as a great music lover. Father Kanka played the cello, his son the clavier and the sister, Frl. Jeanette, the piano. Besides a number of scholarly books on Austrian law, Johann wrote a piano concerto (Leipzig 1804), 13 variations for piano, and published *Ländlerische Tanze* with Traeg in Vienna. He became famous as the composer of Collin's *Lieder Oesterreichischer Wehrmänner,* Prague 1809

(Gottlieb Haase). He also arranged Mozart *Figaro* melodies as German dances. Mozart refers to them in his famous letter to Jacquin in 1787.

Beethoven became acquainted with the Kanka family in Prague in 1796. In 1811 he met the family again in Carlsbad and Teplitz. After the deaths of the princes Kinsky and Lobkowitz, Kanka became the administrator of the estates of the two aristocrats, in which capacity he had dealings with Beethoven. It was through Kanka's influence that Beethoven received the full (not inflated) amount of the pension granted to him by the above-mentioned princes and Archduke Rudolph.

Kanka, as a composer, is an eclectic and his piano Concerto, recorded by Supraphone (*Musicae Bohemicae Anthologia*), shows definite influence of Mozart. (Cf. Max Unger in *Auftakt* III, 2; *Neue Musikzeitung 1923;* Nettl: *Mozart in Böhmen.*)

Kanne, August Friedrich

b. Delitzsch (Saxony) 1778, d. Vienna 1833. Poet, musician, critic and highly talented man with an extremely independent mind, a *Kraftgenie,* in many respects similar to Beethoven. He was on very good terms with the Master. Schindler II, p. 165, called him one of the oddest men, a man of fine education who had started out to study theology and medicine before he became a composer and writer on music. Twelve of his operas and singspiele were performed in Vienna. Wurzbach honored him with an extensive biography, enumerating many books and articles on the history of music, a poem *On the Death of Beethoven,* and the titles of his operas and singspiele.

Kanne came to Vienna in 1808. Beethoven might have met him in one of the taverns, probably the Schwarze Kameel where they were regular guests. When Kanne felt his death imminent, he dragged himself to the nearest tavern, drank half a pot of wine and went home to die. Schindler reported interesting discussions between Beethoven and Kanne about the characteristics of the different music keys. Beethoven believed in the specific, aesthetic character of each key, whereas Kanne stuck to purely acoustical principles. Heinrich Laube in his *Reisenovellen* Mannheim, 1847, characterized Kanne as follows: "Kanne and Beethoven belonged together. Kanne's hair looked even more shaggy and wild, his bony face even harsher, his stature even broader and clumsier than Beethoven's. He had the same large grey eyes as Beethoven. He was a living encyclopedia; he ran around in his dirty green cloth jacket. He wrote a manual on the aesthetics of music. He offered his first complete volumes to Steiner. Steiner felt that Kanne would not complete his work and refused an advance payment. Infuriated, Kanne ran home and destroyed the first volume. Beethoven consulted him frequently, as in 1825 about Bernard's oratorio text. Kanne was among the torchbearers at Beethoven's funeral. (Cf. Gräffer: *Kleine Weiner Memoiren,* München 1918; Castelli: *Memoirs;* Hitzig: "Briefe aus Beethovens Freundeskreis," *Der Bär,* Leipzig 1927.)

Karl van Beethoven

b. Vienna 1806, d. there 1858. Karl was

the son of Beethoven's brother, Kaspar Anton Karl, and Johanna Reiss, daughter of a paper hanger. The fact that Kaspar and Johanna were married only four months before the birth of their son did not please the Master, particularly since he felt Johanna's moral standards to be more than questionable. Beethoven was very fond of the child, and in Kaspar's last will (he died Nov. 15, 1815) Beethoven was appointed Karl's guardian. Unfortunately, Beethoven's other brother, Johann, was instrumental in having Johanna appointed as co-guardian, thereby causing a long series of troubles for the Master. Beethoven appealed to the Landrecht, which confirmed his exclusive guardianship, and for a while Beethoven took complete control over the boy, whom he loved like his own son.

Beethoven never forgave Johanna her pre-marital conception and always believed her a very immoral person, unfit to be a mother. Because of her moral habits Beethoven called her the Queen of the Night, for apparently even when Karl was living with her she frequently brought her lovers into the house or spent many nights away from home.

As soon as his guardianship was established, Beethoven removed Karl from his mother's influence and he was placed in an educational institution conducted by Cajetan Giannatasio del Rio. Thus began a period of great trial for Beethoven, culminating in Karl's attempted suicide. Beethoven never succeeded in winning Karl away from his mother's influence; he would escape from each institution and run to his mother, only to be found and brought back. Then began the arduous task of selecting a new school. The series of schools was a long one; from the del Rios he escaped to his mother, then lived with Beethoven for a while and attended the Gymnasium at the University. Again he escaped and then was returned to the del Rios.

At this time Johanna succeeded in disproving Beethoven's claim to nobility, and the lower courts reversed the decision. Johanna was awarded custody of the boy and again Beethoven instigated suit. The result of this was the naming of a co-guardian, a municipal clerk named Nussböck. Now (1819) Karl was sent to a boarding school run by Johann Kudlich, but Kudlich was no more successful than the rest and Karl escaped to his mother. Plans to send him to a school outside Vienna came to naught and Karl found himself a student at Joseph Blöchinger's institute. From there he escaped to his mother and was found by Haslinger, who returned him to Beethoven; there he lived for almost two years, attending the Institute of Technology in Vienna and spending much money in association with questionable companions.

There is little doubt that Beethoven's constant reproaches made life miserable for the young man, and, in August 1826 near the village of Rauhenstein, Karl took matters in his own hands and attempted suicide. In order to cover up the suicide attempt (a crime in Vienna), Karl was put into the army. Beethoven purchased a commission for the young man and he was sent as a cadet to Iglau in Moravia, and later, as a lieutenant, entered the Infantry Regiment Archduke Rudolph No. 8, commanded by Joseph Baron Stutterheim. In gratitude Beethoven dedicated the String Quartet

Op. 131, in C sharp minor, to Stutterheim. Apparently this was the turning point in Karl's life, for he became a good soldier, and, upon Beethoven's death, was his sole heir.

Contemporaries of Beethoven, among them Schindler, Neate, and Peters, relate that Karl was a handsome and gifted boy, but not industrious or persevering. His musical education began with Carl and Joseph Czerny; however because he was lazy, Beethoven insisted that Karl take his lessons at his home. Karl never revealed any scholarly capacities, most of his education being marked by a notable lack of success. Even in the army Karl did not distinguish himself. In 1832 he married Caroline Naske, daughter of Maximilian Naske, a lawyer of Iglau, and in the same year resigned his army commission and leased an estate near Niklowitz (Moravia). Again he was unsuccessful, and about 1846 moved to Vienna. He died there.

There can be little doubt that between the years 1815 and 1825 Karl acted as a detrimental influence on Beethoven, although Beethoven was no better for Karl. They were apparently two distinct types of personality that could not function together and Beethoven's constant reproaches and Karl's constant resentment could only lead to the almost inevitable climax it assumed. We can only regret that Beethoven was forced to expend so much of his energy during this period, energy which could have been used more profitably elsewhere. Posterity has been the loser. (Cf. Dr. Max Wancsa: *Beethovens Neffe;* Th.-R. III-V; Schünemann: *Ludwig van Beethovens Konversationshefte;* Hans Volkmann: *Neues über Beethoven;* Sterba: *Beethoven and his Nephew,* N. Y. Entries: Blöchinger, Kudlich, Rio.)

Keglewich, Anna Luise Barbara (Babette)

See Entry: Women.

Kerpen

Small village in the Prussian Rhenish province, where Beethoven spent some time with the Breuning family, according to Breuning: "Aus dem Schwarzspanierhaus." Beethoven played several times on the church organ in Kerpen.

Keyboard Instruments

Nothing is known about the instruments played by Beethoven in Bonn. In 1787 a young girl named Karth saw Count Waldstein in Beethoven's house; Beethoven was receiving a new instrument as a gift from the Count (cf. Schiedermair: *Der junge Beethoven* and Th.-R. I). In 1892 at the Exhibition of Music and Theatre in Vienna another instrument was shown, presumably given to Beethoven by Princess Lichnowsky. About 1800 Beethoven played instruments made by Walter, occasionally one made by Jakesch, and later exclusively those made by Streicher. In 1803 the Erard Brothers donated an instrument to Beethoven, as discovered by M. Bannelier from the business books of Erard in Paris. This instrument was given by Beethoven to his brother, Johann, in 1825. This piano can be seen at the Museum Francisco-Carolinum in Linz. In 1818 the London firm John Broadwood and Son presented a piano to the Master. Thomas Broadwood, who had visited Vienna shortly before 1818 and had made the acquaintance of the Master, was the donor proper. On Feb. 3, 1818, Beethoven sent a letter of gratitude to Thomas Broadwood which began: "Mon très cher ami Broadwood," a salutation indicating a personal acquaintance with the London piano maker. The instrument was shipped via Trieste to the Vienna customs house, from there to the piano depot of Streicher and, in the spring of 1818, to Beethoven's apartment in Mödling. After Beethoven's death it was acquired by the music dealer, Spina, whence it came into the possession of Franz Liszt in Weimar. Liszt willed it to Princess Caroline Sayn-Wittgenstein, whose daughter, Princess Marie Hohenlohe, presented it to the Budapest National Museum.

Another instrument used by Beethoven was loaned by Konrad Graf, a pianomaker (1823). This instrument may be seen today in the Beethoven Museum in Bonn. Other pianos played by Beethoven are mentioned in Frimmel's *Beethoven Studien* Vol. II "Der Klavierspieler Beethoven."

Keyboard playing

Keyboard instruction of the Beethoven child began very early. After some instruction by his father, Johann van Beethoven, Tobias Friedrich Pfeiffer became his teacher. Pfeiffer, who lived in the same house with the Beethoven family, left Bonn after one year. Van der Eden was the child's next teacher. It is known that the young Beethoven performed in an Akademie in Cologne in 1778.

Christian Gottlieb Neefe had a definite influence on the development of the young artist. Phil. Em. Bach's *Versuch über die wahre Art das Klavier zu spielen* and Marpurg's *Die Kunst das Klavier zu spielen* were used by Neefe, a great admirer of the Bach family. The *Well Tempered Clavier* was studied. This style of music, together with Bach's organ style forced Beethoven to cultivate the strict legato. Czerny reports that Beethoven's playing up to about 1800, was "masterly quiet, noble and beautiful, without any grimaces." Other contemporaries however, stress Beethoven's characteristic way of performing (cf. Entry: Improvisation).

When Beethoven arrived in Vienna in 1792, he was accepted by many aristocratic families. He played at the Lichnowsky's, at Baron Braun's and van Swieten's where Handel and both Bachs had been favored. It is known that Beethoven played the *Well Tempered Clavier* by memory. He performed for the first time publicly his own piano concerto, probably the B flat major, in 1795. Everyone who heard his performance was impressed by his skillful and sure art of transposing and score reading. Tomaschek calls him "the giant among the pianists" and the "lord of pianoplaying." Schönfeld's *Jahrbuch der Tonkunst in Wien und Prag* (1796) emphasized Beethoven's extraordinary velocity and his skill in overcoming technical difficulties. A characteristic account of Beethoven's playing is given in the *Allgemeine musikalische Zeitung* of April 11, 1799, which refers to the famous contest between the Master and Jos. Wölfl, which took place in Baron Raimund von Wetzlar's palace in Schönbrunn: "Beethoven's playing is extremely brilliant, however, less delicate [than Wölfl's] and has a tendency to blur. He gives his best when improvising freely." This shortcoming was emphasized by other contemporaries. Beethoven's playing was in contrast to Mozart's school, represented by Wölfl and Hummel, characterized by great clarity stressing mainly finger technique without much use of arms and body. Czerny indicated that Beethoven's playing was aimed at a broad reproduction, corresponding to the universal significance of his creations.

The climax of his performing power was possibly 1811-1812, when he played in Teplitz for Varnhagen von Ense, Rahel Levin and Goethe. In 1814 he played with Schuppanzigh his B flat major Trio and during the Vienna Congress 1815, he accompanied the singer Wild in "Adelaïde". Schindler noted that the elasticity of Beethoven's fingers vanished in proportion to the decrease in his hearing. More and more the Master asked for louder instruments. Sonority became more and more a main idea in his later piano compositions, which in many respects were influenced by his deafness and resultant imagination. Beethoven by that time was a creative musician, no longer a virtuoso. (Cf. Frimmel: "Der Klavierspieler Beethoven," *Beethoven Studien* II.)

Keyser, Elise

Singer, née Giannatasio del Rio, on friendly terms with Beethoven. There is a theory, propounded by E. Kastner, that Beethoven dedicated to her the piano piece *Für Elise*. (Cf. Entry: *Für Elise.)*

Kiesewetter, Raphael Georg, Edler von Wiesenbrunn

b. Holleschau (Moravia) 1773, d. Vienna 1850. Musicologist and nephew of the famous musicologist, A. W. Ambros. He studied counterpoint under Albrechtsberger in 1803 and later with Hartmann. Great admirer of Beethoven. He became an important official of the Gesellschaft der Musikfreunde and directed the meeting of the Gesellschaft on November 29, 1825, when Beethoven was elected an honorary member (cf. Entry: Gesellschaft der Musikfreunde).

Kinsky, Prince Ferdinand Johann Nepomuk Joseph Wchinitz und Tettau

b. Vienna 1781, d. Weltrusy (Bohemia) 1812. Son of Prince Joseph and Maria Rosa, Countess Harrach. His wife, whom he married in 1801, was Caroline Maria, Baroness von Kerpen (1782-1842). A well-known officer of the Austrian Army he advanced to the rank of colonel. An art-loving aristocrat and one of three donors of Beethoven's pension, granted to him by Prince Lobkowitz and Archduke Rudolph. Kinsky, with 1800 gulden was the top contributor to the pension of 4000 gulden. According to a letter of July 1809 to Breitkopf and Härtel, Beethoven was worried that Kinsky's share was missing, as the officer was busy with military affairs in Bohemia. Up till 1811 several instalments were paid irregularly. On February 20, 1811, the famous Finanzpatent was published, proclaiming a drastic devaluation of the Austrian currency. Kinsky's 1800 gulden (Banko-Zettel) were devaluated to 726 gulden W. W. The revaluation was granted by the Archduke and by Lobkowitz in 1812. When Beethoven traveled to Teplitz in the same year, he made a stopover in Prague in order to negotiate with Kinsky, who promised to follow the other two. However the Prince died in an accident on November 2, 1812. Beethoven was helpless and wanted to file a suit, instigated by his lawyer, Dr. Wolf, in Prague. Kinsky's estate was represented by Dr. Kanka, who functioned as a loyal mediator between Beethoven and Kinsky's heirs. He succeeded in straightening out the matter to Beethoven's benefit. (Cf. Entry: Kanka; V. Kratochvil: "Beethoven und Fürst Kinsky," Frimmel's *Beethoven Jahrbuch* II.)

Beethoven dedicated to Kinsky his Op. 86 (Mass in C major) and to Princess Kinsky Op. 75 (*Sechs Gesänge, Gedichte von Goethe*), Op. 83 *(Drei Gesänge, Gedichte von Goethe)* and Op. 94 *(An die Hoffnung aus Tiedge's "Urania")*. The dedications of the songs indicate that the Princess was interested in vocal music and poetry. (Cf. Max Reinitz: *Beethoven im Kampf mit dem Schicksal* Wien 1924).

Kirchlehner, Franz

Private person, deeply devoted to the Master. After Beethoven's death he was instrumental in providing the necessary funds for a tombstone at the Währing cemetery. (Cf. Seyfried: *Beethovens Studien im Generalbass* 1832.)

Klein, Franz

b. Vienna about 1778, d. Vienna 1840. Artist who created the famous bust of Beethoven in 1812 when, at the order of Streicher, he took a living mask of the Master. Klein did not succeed right away, as Beethoven felt he might choke. The mask later came into the possession of the sculptor, Dietrich, a routine artist, who manufactured many busts of Beethoven. From Dietrich's estate it was acquired by the Vienna Society of Sculptors, which handed it down to Prof. Kaspar Zumbusch, the creator of the famous Beethoven monument in Vienna. Klein's mask and consequently Zumbusch's bust are the most faithful, almost photographic, portraits of the Master. (Cf. Frimmel: "Beethovens äussere Erscheinung" *Beethoven Studien* I.)

Kleinheinz, Franz Xaver

b. Mindelheim (Swabia) 1772, d. Budapest about 1832. Musician who came to Vienna in 1802 where he studied with Albrechtsberger. He became music master in the house of Count Brunswick, later conductor at the Brünn Theater, and then piano teacher and conductor of the German Theater in Budapest. Composer of oratorios, operas, ballads, songs, etc. He arranged some of Beethoven's works for piano and dedicated a sonata to Countess Guicciardi. Sandberger wrote an extensive monograph on this less important musician, whose significance lies in his close connection to the Brunswicks. (Cf. Sandberger: *Ausgewählte Aufsatze zur Musikgeschichte* II.)

Klemmer

One of Beethoven's Bonn friends, who contributed to the Stammbuch. Horseman in the Electoral stables (?) (cf. Entry: Bonn).

Klippel, Michael

b. 1819 (?), d. 1907. Winegrower in Nussdorf, near Vienna. At the time of his death he was supposed to be the last living person who had seen Beethoven (cf. *Neues Wiener Tagblatt,* April 26/27, 1907). He pretended to have seen Beethoven when fishing on the Danube. However, his recollections have to be taken cautiously.

Klöber, August Karl Friedrich

b. Breslau 1793, d. Berlin 1864. Painter and from 1829, professor at the Berlin Art Academy. In 1818 he tried to make a portrait of Beethoven and the Master sat for him several times. However, the portrait got lost, and only Beethoven's head is preserved in two separate drawings. (Cf. Frimmel "Beethovens äussere Erscheinung," *Beethoven Studien* I.)

Klüpfeld (Klüpfell, Klüpfel)

Russian Imperial official and secretary to Prince Razumovsky. Beethoven used to visit with the Klüpfeld family about 1800. A certain Fräulein von Kissow lived with the Klüpfelds in about 1796. Ludwig Nohl in 1864 tried to get some information about Beethoven from the former Frl. von Kissow, now an old lady, married to a Herr Bernhard. She told Nohl that she frequently saw the "ugly Beethoven," who for a while used to send her some of his new compositions, accompanied by a humorous letter. (Cf. Nohl: *Beethoven nach den Schilderungen seiner Zeitgenossen,* 1867.)

Koch

In the literature about the young Beethoven the widow Koch and her daughters Barbara and Marianne play a certain part. The mother ran a high-class restaurant, the Zehrgarten, on the market place in Bonn. At about 1790, according to Wegeler, many famous personalities used to meet there, such as the two Rombergs, Anton Reicha, the Kügelgen twins, Dr. Crewelt, Prof. Velten, Staatsrat Fischenich, the later Bishop Wrede, the later Dutch Staatsrat von Kewerberg, Christoph von Breuning, and many others. The daughter Barbara was a recognized beauty, admired by Wegeler and, perhaps, also by Beethoven. She was an intimate friend of Eleonore von Breuning and later married a Count von Belderbusch, the nephew of the minister. Wegeler calls her the ideal of a perfect lady. In the album dedicated to Beethoven by the members of the Zehrgarten before he left for Vienna, Barbara's name is missing. In 1793 Beethoven wrote to Eleonore von Breuning: "Should you see B [Barbara] Koch, tell her please that I am waiting for her to answer my two letters." That seems to indicate that Beethoven was quite fond of her. (Cf. Wegeler: *Notizen;* Entry: Bonn.)

Körner, Karl Theodor

b. Dresden 1791, d. in action near Gadebusch in 1813. Poet and hero, he was also a musician and music lover. In the summer of 1811 he came to Vienna, where he wrote a number of plays and poems. There he met a group of people from literary and musical circles and became engaged to Toni Adamberger, the famous actress, who sang in 1810 the *Klärchen Lieder* at the first performance of Beethoven's *Egmont* music. Like many other playwrights, Körner also desired to write librettos for Beethoven. It is assumed that he sent him *Der Kampf mit dem Drachen* or *Odysseus.*

Beethoven did not return these texts for a while and answered Körner apologetically on April 21, 1812. He suggested a meeting at which the matter of the operas should be discussed. Beethoven indicated that he would prefer a different type of text. As late as 1813 Körner refers to *Ulysseus' Wiederkehr* as to be used by Beethoven. For Körner's stay in Vienna, refer to Caroline Pichler: *Denkwürdigkeiten* ed. by Blümml, München 1914; Castelli: *Memoirs;* Spohr: *Autobiography;* Entry: Adamberger.

Korompa

Village in Hungary, County Tyrnau. Today located in Slovakia. Around 1800 Beethoven spent some time there as a guest of the Brunswick family.

Kotzebue, August

b. Weimar 1761, assassinated in Mannheim 1819. Writer. In 1780 he was a lawyer in Weimar; a year later he went to Russia where he obtained a high position, a title of nobility, and made a fortune. After 1795 he lived on his estate, Friedenthal, near Reval until January 1798, when he went to Vienna, where he became director of the Burgtheater. Because of his unpleasant behavior towards the actors, he had to resign in December of the same year; however, he received a pension of 1000 gulden in anticipation of his further services as a playwright. On April 10, 1799, he left Vienna permanently in order to return to Russia. En route he was arrested and taken to Siberia accused of being politically unreliable. Czar Paul released him after a year and made him director of the German Theatre in Petersburg. After Czar Paul's death, he returned to Weimar, but there he was on bad terms with Goethe and subsequently went to Berlin, where he edited the magazine *Der Freimütige* with an outspoken tendency against Goethe and Romanticism. After many adventures in Russian service he was active as a Russian cultural attaché and political observer. In his *Literarisches Wochenblatt,* founded in 1818, he ridiculed the liberal ideas and the national enthusiasm of the German youth. Consequently he was looked upon as a Russian police spy and as such assassinated by a German student, K. L. Sand, in the midst of his own family. Kotzebue's magazine *Der Freimütige* contains a number of excellent remarks and observations about Beethoven. *Christus am Ölberg,* the Fourth Symphony, and the *Coriolan* Overture were reviewed by Kotzebue in the magazine. In 1808 the erection of a new theater in Budapest had been approved by Emperor Franz, but not until 1811 was the project finished; the house was to be opened October 11, the feast-day of the Emperor. Various circumstances prevented the opening which finally took place on February 9, 1812. Collin had been asked first to write a patriotic play, but because of lack of time, he refused. Kotzebue then delivered three texts: *Hungary's First Great Benefactor, Bela's Escape,* and *The Ruins of Athens. Bela's Escape* was eliminated, because the Emperor himself had twice found it necessary to flee before the advancing French forces within a two year period. The remaining texts were sent to Beethoven to be composed (cf. a letter of Varnhagen von Ense to Count von Bentheim, September

4, 1811). According to his letter, dated January 28, 1812, Beethoven considered Kotzebue "a dramatic genius." In this letter Beethoven expressed the desire to compose a libretto by the playwright, either romantic, serious, heroic-comical, or sentimental. He suggested a subject from the Dark Ages, i.e. Attila. Whether or not Kotzebue answered that letter, is unknown. (Cf. Entry: *Ruinen von Athen;* W. Von Kotzebue: *August von Kotzebue, Urteile der Zeitgenossen und der Gegenwart* 1884.)

Kozeluch, Leopold

b. Velvary (Bohemia) 1752 or 1753, d. Vienna 1818. Composer. Studied law in Prague; later he studied music. He composed a great number of ballets, pantomimes, and incidental music. In 1778 he went to Vienna where he became the music teacher of Archduchess Elisabeth. In 1781 he refused to take over Mozart's position as concertmaster of the Archbishop of Salzburg; however, in 1792 he took over Mozart's job as Imperial Chamber Composer. After 1785 Koželuch ran an extensive publishing business. (Cf. Alexander Weinmann: *Verzeichnis der Verlagswerke des Musikalischen Magazins in Wien 1784-1802; Leopold Koželuch,* Wien 1950). Koželuch was blamed by Jahn for having been an arch enemy of Mozart, an opinion which might not hold true in the future. In fact his relationship to Beethoven was not the best. When Doležalek played for Koželuch Beethoven's Trio in C minor, Koželuch threw the music on the floor.

When Beethoven wrote to the English publisher, Thomson, about the arrangements of Scotch and Irish songs, he mentioned that he believed himself much more able to handle this work than Koželuch. Beethoven referred to Thomson's collection of Irish and Scotch songs in arrangements by Pleyel, Koželuch, and Haydn, London 1803. (Cf. J. Srb (Debrnov): *Geschichte der Musik in Böhmen und Mähren;* A. Hnilička: *Portraite*; Wurzbach.)

Kraft (Krafft), Anton

b. Rokitzan (Bohemia) 1752, d. Vienna 1820. Father of Nikolaus, b. Esterhaz 1778, d. Stuttgart, 1853. Both cellists. Anton studied with the cellist Werner, later with Haydn in Vienna, and became first cellist of the orchestra of Prince Nikolaus Esterhazy. Later he served in the orchestra of Prince Grassalkowitsch and afterwards in that of Prince Lobkowitz. In 1792 he toured with his son, Nikolaus, in Germany. Haydn's D major Cello Concerto (1783) has been attributed to Kraft, but recent experts on Haydn (Jens Peter Larsen: *Die Haydn Uberlieferung* and Leopold Nowak: *Joseph Haydn*) do not question Haydn's authorship. Beethoven met Anton Kraft in Lobkowitz's house between 1795 and 1820, occasionally in Prince Lichnowsky's palace. Anton Kraft was the cello soloist in Beethoven's Triple Concerto (cf. Entry: Concertos). On March 5, 1809, Nikolaus Kraft gave a concert where the Cello Sonata Op. 69 was performed. In 1814 Nikolaus became a member of the Stuttgart orchestra while Anton remained in Vienna. In the summer of 1815 Beethoven asked Archduke Rudolph if Kraft might live in the palace because Prince Lobkowitz did not want to keep the aged cellist in his house any longer. In 1820 we read in a Conversation-book: "Old Kraft is sick. Consequently we could not play the Trio at Prince Lobkowitz'." (Cf. Pohl: *Haydn;* Wurzbach; Th.-R.)

Kreutzer, Konradin

b. Messkirch (Baden) 1780, d. Riga 1849. Composer. Studied law; became a musician after the death of his father. In 1804 he came to Vienna to study with Albrechtsberger. Maximilian Stoll, in his magazine, *Prometheus,* tells about a concert in honor of Haydn (1808), directed by Kreutzer. Beethoven, who was present at the concert, must have made Kreutzer's acquaintance on this occasion. In 1812 Kreutzer became Hofkapellmeister in Stuttgart and in 1817 Kapellmeister of Prince Fürstenberg in Donau-Eschingen; he returned to Vienna in 1822. On May 7, 1824, a famous concert took place when the Overture Op. 124 *Zur Weihe des Hauses* and the Ninth Symphony were on the program, Kreutzer directing from the piano. On February 2, 1827, Beethoven wrote to Schott in Mainz: "I have received your last letter through Kreutzer." We do not know too much about the relations between the two men. In Robert Hornstein's memoirs, partly quoted by Frimmel, *Beethovenjahrbuch* II, p. 369, we read this story, told by Schindler to Hornstein: Once Kreutzer paid a visit to Beethoven, who was attending a theatrical performance. Evidently Kreutzer talked to Beethoven in some intimate way objectionable to the Master. During Beethoven's last illness in 1827, Kreutzer tried to approach him again with the strong desire to be reconciled. He asked Schindler for permission to see Beethoven and was smuggled into the sickroom. When Beethoven saw him, he turned his back and remained in this negative position (cf. Th.-R. III and V).

Kreutzer, Rodolphe

b. Versailles 1766, d. Geneva 1831. Famous violinist of Silesian extraction, whose father, a musician, served in the French army. A student of Anton Stamitz, he was a professor at the Paris Conservatory and concertmaster at the Opera in Paris, besides being chamber virtuoso of Napoleon Bonaparte. In 1798, in the suite of General Bernadotte, he went with him to Vienna. In 1810 Kreutzer broke his left arm, as Spohr and Vieuxtemps did later, and dedicated himself from then on entirely to violin teaching. In Vienna Kreutzer became a friend of Beethoven. Beethoven praised his modesty and simplicity. As the Sonata Op. 47 is composed for a skilled violinist, the dedication to Kreutzer is more than justified. Evidently Kreutzer knew that the sonata was written originally for Bridgetower and therefore never played it himself. (Cf. Entries: Bridgetower, Bernadotte and Violin sonatas.)

Krumpholz, Wenzel

b. Moravia or Silesia ca. 1750, d. Vienna 1817. Brother of the famous harpist, Johann Baptist Krumpholz. Wenzel was an excellent violinist and virtuoso on the mandolin. He was one of Beethoven's oldest friends, having introduced Doležalek and Carl Czerny to the Master. According to Dlabacz, Krumpholz came to Vienna about 1795, and Ries told that Beethoven took violin lessons from the Bohemian musician, who also functioned as an adviser to the young composer. According to Glöggl (*Neue Wiener Musikzeitung,* 1857), Krumpholz was a frequent guest of Czerny's family. He belonged to that group of people (Schindler, Holz, Oliva) who were deeply devoted to Beethoven and believed in his genius. Beethoven called Krumpholz frequently his "fool." The death of this dear friend affected the Master deeply and while in this mood he composed the song of the monks from Schiller's Wilhelm Tell, *"Rasch tritt der Tod den Menschen an"*, for three male voices. The autograph bears Beethoven's inscription: "In memory of the sudden and unexpected death of our Krumpholz on May 3, 1817" (translated from the German). Krumpholz was an excellent mandolin player and evidently supervised Beethoven's compositions for that instrument (cf. Entry: Mandolin).

Kübeck, Karl Friedrich, Baron von

b. Iglau (Moravia) 1780, d. Hadersdorf (near Vienna) 1855. Austrian politician and statesman who was instrumental in the organization of Austrian railroads and telegraph. In his diaries, published 1909 by Gerold and Co., Vienna, Kübeck's recollections of Beethoven are mentioned. Kübeck, in his youth a mediocre amateur musician, was introduced by Beethoven to an aristocratic Italian family where he taught piano. Kübeck's description of Beethoven's personality is colorful and characteristic. (Cf. Frimmel: *Beethovenforschung,* July 1911).

Kudlich, Johann

Director of an educational institute in Vienna where Beethoven's nephew Karl was temporarily placed 1818-1819. At first Beethoven was enthusiastic about Karl's progress; later he became quite dissatisfied. From Kudlich Karl was transferred to Blöchinger's.

Kuegelgen, Gerhard von

b. Bachrach 1772, assassinated at Loschwitz (near Dresden) 1820. Famous painter. In his youth he became Beethoven's intimate friend in Bonn. He belonged to the group of intellectuals gathering in the widow Koch's Zehrgarten. His twin brother, Karl Ferdinand, who died in Reval in 1832, belonged to the same circle in Bonn. Both were daily guests of mother Breuning. Gerhard's son was Wilhelm, a painter and writer, whose memoirs were published in 1923 under the title *Jugenderinnerungen eines alten Mannes.* (Cf. Breuning: *Aus dem Schwarzspanierhaus;* Bücken: *Anton Reichas Leben und Kompositionen;* Schiedermair: *Der junge Beethoven;* Entry: Bonn.)

Kuffner, Christoph

b. Vienna 1780 (Wurzbach), died there 1846. Writer. He studied voice and violin with Anton Wranitzky and became acquainted with Haydn and Mozart. After 1808 Kuffner's name appeared in connection with Beethoven's circle. Czerny told that Beethoven and Kuffner together wrote the text of the Choral Fantasy. Nottebohm (*Beethoveniana* II, p. 503) denies the possibility because the text cannot be found in the 20 volume edition of Kuffner's complete works. In 1813 Beethoven composed the *Triumph-Marsch* in C major for Kuffner's tragedy,

Tarpeja. This tragedy is printed in Vol. II of Kuffner's works. It was performed with Beethoven's newly composed march on March 26, 1813. Beethoven thought that conversations with Kuffner in 1826 were extremely instructive, and Kuffner very witty. The Master was impressed by Kuffner's oratorio, *Saul,* and Kuffner promised to write the texts of a thousand oratorios for Beethoven. Kuffner's remarks on English and French playwrights, Rousseau and Voltaire, are worthwhile reading.

Kuhlau, Friedrich

b. Ülzen (Hanover) 1786, d. Lyngbye (near Copenhagen) 1832. Composer. In 1800 he came to Hamburg, where he studied with Chr. F. G. Schwencke. In 1810, he went to Copenhagen, where he became chamber musician in the Royal Danish Orchestra. In 1825 he went to Vienna as a Royal Danish Concertmaster. On an excursion to Baden, arranged by Haslinger, Kuhlau met Beethoven. Seyfried reported that the party, headed by Beethoven and consisting of the oboist, Joseph Sellner, Holz and Seyfried himself, went hiking; Beethoven, always ahead, was amused by the others' lack of skill in walking and running. There was a gay lunch in Helenenthal and a very gay party finally in Beethoven's apartment, where risqué jokes were told. Schindler deemed it necessary to remove these pages from the Conversation-book. Kuhlau improvised a canon on the name Bach and Beethoven dedicated a canon *Kühl, nicht lau* to Kuhlau. Beethoven made the following comment on his canon: "I must confess that yesterday's champagne affected me somewhat, and that my strength is more suppressed by alcohol than animated . . . Don't forget your ever devoted Beethoven," Baden, September 3, 1825. Beethoven seemed to have a liking for Kuhlau. (Cf. Th.-R. V, p. 240; Seyfried: *Studien.*)

Kunst und Industrie Comptoir

A publishing and printing company of importance between 1801 and 1814, frequently called Bureau des arts et d'industrie. All kinds of graphic art, including engraving of music, were produced. The company was later absorbed by Tobias Haslinger. Beethoven's Sonata Op. 28, the Fourth Symphony, the Piano Concertos Nos. 3 and 4, the Razumovsky Quartets, *Coriolan* Overture, the Romance for Violin Op. 50, the Bagatelles, Op. 33, and the *Andante favori* were printed by this publisher.

L

Lachner, Franz

b. Rain (Bavaria) 1803, d. Munich 1890. Famous composer. After 1823 he lived in Vienna, where he became an intimate friend of Franz Schubert, and got acquainted with Beethoven. He studied with Sechter and Abbé Stadler. In his recollections on Schubert and Beethoven, which he published himself in *Münchener Neueste Nachrichten* (1882), he related that he saw Beethoven every Saturday night in the Zur Eiche tavern, where the Master drank his Regensburger beer and smoked a pipe of tobacco.

Lachner had met Beethoven in the house of Streicher. Lachner as organist of the Protestant Church was admitted to that illustrious musical circle. One day while Nanette Streicher practiced Beethoven's Piano Trio Op. 97, the Master suddenly entered the room. With the help of a hearing aid he listened for a while, but did not seem satisfied by the performance of the theme of the last movement, which sounded somewhat timid. He played it for Nanette and left. Another time Lachner met Beethoven in Abbé Stadler's house. (Cf. Schindler; Ursprung: *Münchens musikalische Vergangenheit;* Moritz v. Schwind's famous *Lachnerrolle.)*

Laibach

City in Krain (Yugoslavia). In 1819 the Philharmonic Society of Laibach made Beethoven an honorary member.

Last Compositions

In 1838 Diabelli and Co., in Vienna, published a collection under the title *Wiener Lieblingsstücke der neuesten Zeit für das Pianoforte allein oder zu vier händen eingerichtet, von Anton Diabelli.* It contained Ludwig van Beethoven's "Letzter musikalischer Gedanke aus dem Original-Manuskript im November 1826 und Skizze des Quintetts, welches die Verlags-Handlung A. Diabelli u. Comp. bei Beethoven bestellt, und aus dessen Nachlass käuflich mit Eigenthumsrecht an sich gebracht hat." The *Allgemeine Musikalische Zeitung* (Leipzig 1828) referred to the composition, mentioning that only 30 to 40 bars of it were written down. As the original manuscript has not been preserved, it is hard to verify the statements of Diabelli. In 1840 Schlesinger (Berlin) published a short piano piece in B flat major under the title *Dernière pensée musicale.* However, Beethoven wrote this piece into an autograph book in August 1818, simultaneously with the last movement of the Sonata Op. 6. Another so-called "Last Thought" of two bars is found at the end of a small sketchbook in the Berlin State Library. This sketchbook contains motifs for the above-mentioned quintet ordered by Diabelli. The sketches for this quintet fill 12 pages. Following the quintet sketches, there are two bars which obviously have no connection with the quintet and Schindler remarked: "These are the last notes Beethoven ever wrote in my presence, about ten or twelve days before his death." Rulolf F. Kallir found a paper of one line of music, written by Beethoven's hand. In the right bottom corner were the following words in ink: "L. van Beethoven's own handwriting, written on his deathbed for me. J. A. Stumpf." Stumpf had given to Beethoven a magnificent 40 volume edition of Handel's works (Arnold Edition). In a letter of thanks to Stumpf, Beethoven asked if he could be of any service to him. Whereupon Stumpf answered: "I venture to request that only a few notes may be written by your dear hand to be as a souvenir, the supreme object of my desires." (Cf. Nottebohm: *Beethoveniana* II, p. 522; Kallir: "A Beethoven Relic," *The Music Review,* Vol. 9.)

Last hour

On April 12, 1827 Schindler wrote to Schott in Mainz: "I can't refrain from telling you about the last hours of Beethoven's consciousness, namely the morning of March 24 to one p.m. When I saw him on that morning I found his face distorted. He was so weak, that he could only utter two or three words. Soon thereafter Dr. Wawruch came and after a sharp look at the patient told me that the Master's troubles were coming to a quick end."

Leidesdorf, Max Josef

b. Vienna 1780, d. Florence 1839. Composer and publisher. He was one of the publishers who reprinted a number of Beethoven's compositions, the Piano Sonata Op. 111, the new Bagatelles Op. 119, and some songs, among them the *Abendlied.* Beethoven enjoyed making fun of Leidesdorf's name, addressing him once "Dorf des Leides" (village of suffering). He wrote: "Give the carrier of this letter some easy piano duet music for nothing. (Signed) Beethoven Minimus." Leidesdorf composed one of the variations on Diabelli's waltz for Diabelli's collection.

Leipzig

Supposedly Beethoven came to that city in 1796 from Dresden, but this fact is only indicated by letters, among them one written in Prague by Beethoven to his brother. He wrote: "I am planning to stay in Prague for several weeks and from here travel to Leipzig, Dresden and Berlin. . . ." Of greater importance are Beethoven's relations to Breitkopf and Härtel, the Leipzig publishing company. One of the most outstanding personalities in Leipzig was Ferdinand Rochlitz. He saw Beethoven in person in 1822 in Vienna, and referred to the Master's temporary visit in Leipzig. (Cf. Rochlitz: *Für Freunde der Tonkunst,* Vol. IV; Entries: Rochlitz, and Breitkopf and Härtel.)

Letters in America

See Entry: United States.

Lichnowsky

Aristocratic family of Polish extraction, who emigrated to Polish Silesia in the 14th century. According to an old family tradition the Lichnowskys originated either from the Granson family in Burgundy or from the Pilawa dynasty in Poland. During Beethoven's life the head of the family was Prince Karl Lichnowsky, 1756-1814, the son-in-law of Countess Wilhelmine Thun. She herself was a patron of Mozart, with whom Karl had studied. When Mozart traveled via Prague to Berlin in 1789, he was in the company of Prince Karl.

After Beethoven's arrival in Vienna, the young Master lived for a while in Prince Lichnowsky's palace, Alserstrasse. The Prince moved from there to Mölkerbastei, where the famous meeting about the rewriting of *Fidelio* took place (1805), in the presence of the singers, Meyer and Röckel, and his friends Breuning, Treitschke, and Collin. After these vehement discussions, Prince Karl would have a splendid supper served. Minor arguments and rifts with the Prince happened frequently. It is significant that Beethoven dedicated his Trios Op. 1 to the Prince, who purchased 27 copies. In 1800 Prince Karl granted the sum of 600 gulden to Beethoven. He also donated to him his valuable string instruments which were used whenever Beethoven's string quartets were performed. Among Beethoven's very few friends mentioned in the *Heiligenstädter Testament* the Prince holds first place, and in a letter of August 24, 1804, to Breitkopf and Härtel, Beethoven called him one of his most faithful friends and patrons.

Lichnowsky's wife, Marie Christine, treated Beethoven with the utmost sensitivity, but he frequently showed a kind of presumption and his behavior was occasionally criticized. In 1806, when the Master was guest of the Prince in Grätz near Troppau (Silesia), French officers were visiting at the same time. Lichnowsky asked Beethoven to play for them. Beethoven refused. When the Prince did not stop insisting in his unpleasant way, Beethoven immediately decided to return to Vienna. Seyfried has described this happening. The physician of the Lichnowsky family, Dr. Weiser in Troppau, provided Beethoven with the necessary passport for his return. Heavy showers on his way home were the reason for the manuscript of the "Appassionata" Sonata being completely soaked.

When Beethoven arrived in Vienna he destroyed the bust of the Prince. From then on Beethoven continued to live in the house of Lichnowsky, but he was not on speaking terms with him, a fact which is mentioned by Reichardt's *Vertraute Briefe,* November 1808. Beethoven stopped dedicating his works to Lichnowsky, although he had previously dedicated to him the Sonatas Op. 13 and 26, the Second Symphony Op. 36, and the Variations *"Quant' è piú bello!"* Later Beethoven frequently referred to the incident in Grätz in his letters and conversations. In 1811 Beethoven was again in Grätz as the guest of Lichnowsky.

Beethoven's C major Mass was performed in Troppau that year with Beethoven at the organ. He improvised for half an hour after the performance had ended. Lichnowsky proved to be the Master's most devoted friend. Frequently he paid him a visit, but the Master never interrupted his work and would not be bothered by any conversation. With a friendly adieu the Prince would leave. Sometimes Beethoven would lock his door in order not to be disturbed, a fact which the Prince did not seem to mind at all. Without grudge he would walk down the three flights, and leave.

Prince Karl's brother, Reichsgraf Count Moritz Lichnowsky, born 1771, died Vienna 1837, was likewise a friend of Beethoven's. Their friendship was on a more liberal basis, as seen in the canon dedicated to Moritz: *Bester Herr Graf, Sie sind ein Schaf* (Dear Mr. Count, you are a sheep). Schindler put this canon aside, in order not to aggravate the Count. In 1798 the Count could frequently be seen in the company of Bernadotte, who was on friendly terms with Beethoven. The Master dedicated his Piano Variations Op. 35 in E flat major, originally designated for Abbé Stadler, to Count Moritz. Later he dedicated to him the Piano Sonata Op. 90 in E minor. There was a rumor that this was because of Count Moritz's wife, the former singer Stummer. Beethoven was not always on easy terms with Count Moritz either, as can be illustrated by the following note to the Count: "I despise falsehood, don't see me anymore; the concert won't take place. —Beethoven." This slip referred to the concert actually given in 1824, when the overture *Weihe des Hauses* and the Ninth Symphony were performed. It is understood that Count Moritz was later on good terms again with the Master. Some of the ladies of the Lichnowsky family enjoyed Beethoven's friendship. After the death of Prince Karl, Princess Christina made a gift to the composer of a valuable clock from her husband's estate (see Entry: Women). Beethoven dedicated the Rondo Op. 51 No. 2 to Countess Henriette, sister of Prince Karl. The Clarinet Trio Op. 11 was dedicated to her mother, Countess Marie Wilhelmine (née Uhlefeld). (Cf. Wurzbach; Th.-R; Kalischer: *Beethovens Frauenkreis*.)

Liechtenstein, Princess Josephine

b.1775, d. 1848. Wife of General Joseph Johann Liechtenstein, née Countess Fürstenberg. Beethoven dedicated to her his Piano Sonata Op. 27 No. 1. Ries told the story that Beethoven once received a slap from a lady, presumably the Princess, in the house of Count Browne in Baden, because he had made a mistake in playing his D minor Sonata (cf. Kalischer: *Beethovens Frauenkreis*).

Lieder (Songs)

Beethoven completed 79 songs, some in French and Italian, including the complete song cycle, *An die ferne Geliebte.* Most of these songs are found in the complete works: others, some fragmentary, have come to light in more recent times, among them the song, *An Laura,* published by Kinsky (Katalog des musikhistorischen Museums von W. Heyer, Köln, Vol. 4). This song is in part identical with the Bagatelle No. 12 Op. 119. In Schiedermair: *Der junge Beethoven,* we find the *Punschlied,* composed in 1790, as well as the song, *An Laura.* In 1799 the fragment *Plaisir d'aimer besoin* was conceived. Some sketches, never completed by Beethoven, were published by Nottebohm in his *Beethoveniana* as *Gretchen am Spinnrad,* and

Erlkönig (Goethe), *Wunsch* (Matthisson), Collin's *Wehrmannslied* (otherwise composed by Kanka), *Gesang der Geister über den Wassern* (Goethe), *Zufriedenheit* (J. M. Miller), *Die drei Ritter* (Werner), *Badelied* (Matthisson), *Flüchtigkeit der Zeit* (Gleim), and *Heiderösslein* (Goethe). Goethe's *Rastlose Liebe* is found in *Revue d'histoire et de critique musicale* II, Paris 1902.

Beethoven's songs from his Bonn period show the influence of Neefe and Philip Emanuel Bach, but later he made himself independent. Though Beethoven composed just as many songs as Mendelssohn, the latter was always considered a typical song composer while Beethoven's lieder were negligible compared to his other works. Beethoven's song creations seem very uneven; songs of highest value, such as the cycle *An die ferne Geliebte,* alternate with less important ones. Beethoven supposedly said to Rochlitz in the summer of 1820: "I don't like to write songs." It is impossible to know whether or not Rochlitz's statement is true, but it is certain that Beethoven believed himself to be primarily an instrumental composer. The abstract musical form, as found in the cyclic treatment of the cycle *An die ferne Geliebte,* bears out this contention (cf. Jeitteles). Beethoven struggled just as much in composing a simple song as he did in shaping a movement of a great symphony.

Whereas Haydn and Mozart used many inferior texts, Beethoven was very text conscious. Goethe was one of his favorite poets and *Mignon, Sehnsucht* (1808), *Wonne der Wehmut, Mit einem gemalten Band,* and *Klärchen-Lieder* from *Egmont* belong to his best creations. Besides Goethe he used texts from the best known authors of his time frequently found in almanacs, magazines, and papers. Other poets used were Reissiger, Matthisson, Bürger, Pfeffel, Hölty, Claudius, Lessing, Gleim, Weisse, Tiedge, Stoll, Rupprecht, Weissenbach, Treitschke, Jeitteles, and lesser known ones. Beethoven also used Italian and French texts such as those by Metastasio, Carpani *(In questa tomba oscura)* and did not refrain from sketching the famous Air de trois notes *(Que le temps me dure)* of Rousseau's *Consolations des misères de ma vie,* 1793. Some of the best known songs are those from Gellert's *Geistliche Oden und Lieder,* all of which had been composed by Philip Emanuel Bach, although Beethoven composed only six of them, Op. 48, the best known being *Die Ehre Gottes aus der Natur.*

A statistical survey (Hans Böttcher) lists the songs in the order of the number of performances in the leading cities of Germany and Austria. *Die Ehre Gottes* Op. 48, 4 (77); the two *Egmontlieder,* Op. 84 (72); *Adelaïde* Op. 46 (39); *Wonne der Wehmut* Op. 83, 1 (38); *Zärtliche Liebe, Ah perfido* Op. 65 (36); *Busslied,* Op. 48, 6 (34); Liederkreis *An die ferne Geliebte* Op. 98 (28); *Bitten* Op. 48, 1 (27); *Der Kuss* Op. 128 (22); *Neue Liebe, Neues Leben* Op. 75, 2 (19); *In questa tomba oscura* (17); *An die Hoffnung* Op. 94 (14); *Gottes Macht und Vorsehung* Op. 48, 5 (11); *Die Liebe des Nächsten* Op. 48, 2 (10); *Andenken* (8); *Vom Tode* Op. 48, 3 (7); *Der Wachtelschlag* (6); *Mailied* Op. 52, 4 (5); *Mit einem gemalten Band* Op. 83, 3 (4); *Mignon* Op. 75, 1 (2); *Ruf vom Berge, Geheimnis, Resignation, An die Ge-*

liebte, Marmotte, Op. 52, 7 (1). (Cf. Böttcher: *Beethoven als Liederkomponist,* Augsburg 1928.)

Lind, Joseph

b. Mainz 1773, d. Vienna 1837. Renowned tailor in Vienna about 1820. Frimmel knew his grandson, Hofrat Dr. Karl Lind, in person. Beethoven was forced to write to the tailor the following letter "Dear Lind, stop sending me reminders. As soon as I shall be able to pay you, I'll do it." Lind had delivered to Beethoven's nephew a blue dress suit. In another letter to the tailor Beethoven mentioned a waistband. (Cf. Frimmel: *Beethoven Handbuch.*)

Lindner, Andreas

Dancing master in Vienna 1792. His name appears in Beethoven's oldest notebook. Beethoven may have made some attempts to study dancing with him. (See Entries: Dancing, and Dance Music.)

Linke, Joseph

b. Trachenberg (Silesia) 1783, d. Vienna 1837. Famous cellist. His father was in the service of Prince Hatzfeld. He taught his son, Joseph, to play clavier and violin. Later Linke came to Breslau, where he studied organ with Hanisch and cello with the first cellist of the Breslau Opera, Lose. At that time Carl Maria von Weber was the conductor of the Opera. Joseph Linke played in his orchestra. According to Wurzbach, Linke went to Vienna in 1808 where he was appointed to the orchestra of Prince Razumovsky. According to Thayer, the artist was already in Vienna in 1800. At that time the famous Razumovsky quartet was already organized. Linke frequently played in concerts when Beethoven's works were performed. When the Razumovsky palace burned down on New Year's Eve, 1815, the Prince's Quartet was disbanded, whereupon Linke became attached to the Erdödys, with whom he went to Croatia in 1815. From 1818 on he concertized again in Vienna and arranged a number of concerts at which some of Beethoven's works were performed. In 1823, when Schuppanzigh organized his quartet, another man named Linke became the cellist of this group. Joseph Linke was one of the few who best understood Beethoven's last string quartets. He was one of the torch-bearers at Beethoven's funeral. (Cf. Wurzbach; Th.-R.)

Linz

Capital of Upper Austria, where Beethoven stayed several times, once in 1787 on his journey from Bonn to Vienna, again in 1792 and 1796 on tour. In 1812 he visited his brother, a well-to-do pharmacist, there. Beethoven finished his Eighth Symphony in Linz. (See Entries: Glöggl, and Brothers.)

Lirveeld, Baroness Mathilde

She belonged to the circle of Caroline Unger and Henriette Sontag. In 1824 she paid a visit to Beethoven in the company of Karoline Unger, as reported in a Conversation-book of that time.

Liszt, Franz

b. Raiding 1811, d. Bayreuth 1886. Famous virtuoso and composer. He concertized in Vienna 1823, where he studied with Carl Czerny, who brought the child prodigy to Beethoven. The following reminiscences of Liszt were communicated in 1875 to his pupil Ilka Horowitz Barnay: "I was about eleven years of age when my venerated teacher Czerny, took me to Beethoven. He had told the latter about me a long time before, and had begged him to listen to me play sometime. Yet Beethoven had such a repugnance to infant prodigies that he had always violently objected to receiving me. Finally, however, he allowed himself to be persuaded by the indefatigable Czerny, and in the end cried impatiently: 'In God's name, then, bring me the young Turk!' It was ten o'clock in the morning when we entered the two small rooms in the Schwarzspanierhaus which Beethoven occupied; I somewhat shyly, Czerny amiably encouraging me. Beethoven was working at a long, narrow table by the window. He looked gloomily at us for a time, said a few brief words to Czerny and remained silent when my kind teacher beckoned me to the piano. I first played a short piece by Ries. When I had finished Beethoven asked me whether I could play a Bach fugue. I chose the C minor Fugue from the *Well Tempered* Clavichord. 'And could you also transpose the Fugue at once into another key?' Beethoven asked me. Fortunately I was able to do so. After my closing chord I glanced up. The great Master's darkly glowing gaze lay piercingly upon me. Yet suddenly a gentle smile passed over the gloomy features, and Beethoven came quite close to me, stooped down, put his hand on my head, and stroked my hair several times. 'A devil of a fellow,' he whispered, 'a regular young Turk!' Suddenly I felt quite brave. 'May I play something of yours now?' I boldly asked. Beethoven smiled and nodded. I played the first movement of the C major Concerto. When I had concluded Beethoven caught hold of me with both hands, kissed me on the forehead and said gently: 'Go! You are one of the fortunate ones! For you will give joy and happiness to many other people! There is nothing better or finer!," Liszt told the preceding in a tone of deepest emotion, with tears in his eyes, and a warm note of happiness sounded in the simple tale. For a brief space he was silent and then said: "This event in my life has remained my greatest pride the palladium of my whole career as an artist. I tell it but very seldom and—only to good friends!" (From Schirmer: *Beethoven: Impressions of Contemporaries).*

Lobkowitz, Prince Josef Max

b. 1772, d. Wittingau (Bohemia) 1816. Member of a widespread Bohemian aristocratic family. Son of Prince Ferdinand Philip Josef and his wife, Maria Gabriele von Savoyen-Carignan. The Lobkowitzes were previously Dukes of Sagan (Silesia). When in 1763 Silesia became part of Prussia, the Dukedom of Sagan had to be sold to the Duke of Courland. Emperor Joseph II made the Lobkowitz family Dukes of Raudnitz (Bohemia). In 1808 Lobkowitz formed his own "Jägerbatallion." The Duke is described as an outspoken personality who detested meetings and court festivals. He paid no attention to rank or aristocratic extraction, but favored only those whose company he enjoyed. He liked to receive visitors at night around 10 o'clock. Often he called in two violin players of his orchestra, with whom he liked to play till dawn. At 2 a.m. he would go to the Capucins to attend the Holy Mass. His charity was proverbial. In 1792 he was married to Carolina von Schwarzenberg, who bore him twelve children. He was a passionate admirer of Beethoven. In his palace in Vienna one can still see today the large hall and dining room where his private concerts took place. It is well known that he belonged to the group of aristocrats who prevented Beethoven from accepting a position as Kapellmeister for Jerôme of Westphalia by promising him a yearly pension. (See Entries: Cassel, Kanka, and Kinsky.)

When the depression came in 1811, Lobkowitz was unable to keep his promise. As a result, Beethoven complained about the Prince, whom he once called a princely scoundrel. Many of Beethoven's works were dedicated to the Prince: 6 Quartets Op. 18 (1801), the *Eroica* (1806), and the Triple Concerto Op. 56 (1807), the String Quartet Op. 74 (Harp Quartet 1810) and the song cycle *An die ferne Geliebte* (1816). The Fifth and Sixth Symphonies were dedicated to both Lobkowitz and Count Razumovsky. The Lobkowitz Cantata was written for Karl Peters, the tutor of the young Prince Lobkowitz. The young princes were supposed to sing it for their father's birthday December 7, 1816. However, their father was deathly sick at that time and died one week later.

Beethoven was certainly grateful to the Prince, who was occasionally absent-minded, a trait the Master disliked. In addition the prince did not have a real understanding of him. One day at a dress rehearsal, a third bassoon was missing. Lobkowitz, somewhat naïve, mentioned that two bassoons were plenty. Beethoven became angry and raged. Leaving the palace, he called through the door, "Lobkowitzischer Esel" (Jackass Lobkowitz) (cf. Th.-R. II p. 485). Beethoven alluded in a letter to Zmeskall (1809) to the absent-mindedness of the Prince: "Today at 10:30 or 10 the quartet will be rehearsed at Lobkowitz'. His Highness, who is mostly absent-minded anyway, is still out of town. Why don't you come?" Obviously in the absence of the Prince, who frequently spent weeks in Raudnitz, Eisenberg or Prague, music was performed at his home.

There were various associations between Lobkowitz and Beethoven. He appointed Castelli to the job of a house poet (1811) for the Kärntnerthor Theater which was solely under the subsidy of the Prince. Archduke Rudolph was a frequent performer at the Lobkowitz Palace. In 1798 Amenda became the reader for the Prince. An interesting account of Prince Lobkowitz was given by Countess Lulu Thürheim, sister-in-law of Prince Razumovsky. "This Prince was as kindhearted as a child and the most foolish music enthusiast. He played music from dusk to dawn and spent a fortune on musicians. Innumerable musicians gathered in his house, whom he treated regally." (Cf. Gräfin Thürheim: *Mein Leben 1788-1819*, München 1913; Wurzbach; Th.-R.; Entry: Gesellschaft der Musikfreunde.)

London

Beethoven frequently planned a trip to England and London, but his plans were never realized. However, he was in close contact and correspondence with prominent Londoners such as Ries, Neate, Stumpff, Broadwood, Cressener, Smart, the London Philharmonic Society, and Bridgetower. (Cf. Entries mentioned above.)

Louis Ferdinand, Prince Ludwig Ferdinand Christian of Prussia

b. Friedrichsfelde (near Berlin) 1772, killed in action in the battle near Saalfeld 1806. Highly gifted musician, nephew of Frederick the Great. He studied with J. L. Dussek, who edited several of his compositions. H. Kretzschmar, at the order of Emperor Wilhelm II, also edited a number of Louis Ferdinand's works.

The Prince was a great admirer of Beethoven, with whom he became very friendly when Beethoven visited Berlin in 1796. Ries tells that in Berlin Beethoven frequently met Himmel, whose piano playing was elegant and pleasant, but could not compete with that of Prince Louis Ferdinand; he said of the latter that his piano playing was not at all royal or princely, but that of an able pianist. When the Prince came to Vienna in 1804, he heard Beethoven's *Eroica* in the Lobkowitz palace. He enjoyed the performance so intensely that he asked for two repeat performances. There were many musical soirées given in honor of the Prince by different aristocratic families. After one of these soirées an aristocratic lady had a dinner party, but only aristocrats were admitted; Beethoven was excluded. The Master, enraged, made a few rough remarks, took his hat and left. Some days later Prince Louis Ferdinand gave a dinner to which that same Countess and Beethoven were invited. Each was seated beside the Prince, a privilege which Beethoven never forgot. Because of this, the composer dedicated to him his C minor Piano Concerto Op. 37. (Cf. Tschirch: *Hohenzollern Jahrbuch* 1916; Elisabeth Wintzer: *Louis Ferdinand als Mensch und Musiker,* 1916; Hans Wahl: *Prinz Louis Ferdinand von Preussen,* 1925; Kalischer: *Beethoven und Berlin* 1909.)

Löwe, Ludwig

b. Rinteln (Kurhessen) 1795, d. Vienna 1871. Famous actor, member of different theatres, mainly the Vienna Burgtheater. Beethoven met him in 1811 in Teplitz, where both were frequent guests at the Gasthaus zum Stern. Löwe was madly in love with Therese, the innkeeper's daughter. Usually he visited the inn in the evenings after all the guests had left, in order to be undisturbed. This was also the time when Beethoven used to show up. The girl's father objected to her love affair with Löwe and the latter kept away. One day Beethoven met Löwe in the Kurgarten (not Augarten as Th.-R. mentions). Löwe confided his troubles to him and Beethoven offered to act as "postillion d'amour." Shortly thereafter Löwe left for Prague for an appointment. Therese died some weeks later. (Cf. Th.-R. III p. 277; Hanslick: *Beethoven als Liebesbote*, Neue freie Presse 1870.)

Lucchesi, Andrea

b. Motta da Treviso 1741, d. Italy ca. 1800. Student of Paolucci (Padre), Seratelli, and Cocchi; composer of operas. He was Kapellmeister at the Bonn Theater from 1774 on, having come to Bonn with an Italian troupe three years before. Burney met him in Bonn in 1772. Between 1783 and 1784 Lucchesi was in Italy, and Neefe substituted for him in Bonn. The Italian maestro was favorably inclined towards Beethoven and, according to a story of Mäurer, Lucchesi performed a funeral cantata, written by Beethoven, on the occasion of the death of George Cressener, British Ambassador to Bonn (1781). Lucchesi's works are listed in Eitner: *Quellenlexikon*. (Cf. Entries: Cressener, Bonn.)

Lux, Joseph

Actor and basso cantante in Bonn. According to the Fischer Manuscript he used to sing for Beethoven's mother on her feast day. When the Court music was broken up in 1792, Lux went to Frankfurt, where he died in 1818 (cf. Th.-R. I; Schiedermair: *Der junge Beethoven*).

Lyser, Johann Peter Theodor

b. Flensburg 1803, d. Altona 1870. Writer, painter and musician. Lost his hearing at the age of 16. He became a scene painter and art teacher and worked from 1830 on in Hamburg as a writer and journalist. He was married to Karoline Leonhardt (later Pierson), a writer, who divorced him in 1842. Lyser wrote a number of short stories and novels in the style of E. T. A. Hoffman, among them *From the Sketchbook of a Deaf Painter*. He wrote about Beethoven in *Neue Zeitschrift für Musik* (1834), to which he contributed frequently. Lyser was never in Vienna during Beethoven's life time, and all his stories about the Master are fictitious. His famous drawing, showing Beethoven running through the streets, is highly imaginative, but is true to Beethoven's personality. (Cf. Friedrich Hirth: *J. P. Lyser, der Dichter, Maler und Musiker,* 1911.)

M

Macbeth

Tragedy by Shakespeare. Beethoven intended to use the subject for an opera and negotiated with H. J. von Collin about the matter. Collin finished the first act in 1808 which he published in *Wiener-Hof-Theater-Taschenbuch auf das Jahr 1809*. As Beethoven's sketches show, the Master was seriously involved in the project. In the complete works of Collin, Vienna 1814, Vol. 6, Matth. Collin, the brother of the poet, reported the following: "The text of *Macbeth* which my brother started to write, had to be stopped in the second act as the subject was too gloomy." Anyway, Collin died while working on the subject. (Cf. Nottebohm: *Beethoveniana* II p. 225; Entry: Collin.)

Maisch, Ludwig

Publisher in Vienna who edited: "6 Allemandes pour le Pianoforte avec accompagnement d'un Violon par Louis van Beethoven." Originated 1795 or 1796. Short popular pieces (cf. Nottebohm II and K. W o O. 42).

Malchus, Baron Karl August

b. about 1760, d. 1830. Visitor of the well-known Zehrgarten in Bonn. In a letter, dated November 2, 1793, from Vienna to Eleonore von Breuning, Beethoven mentioned that he had written three times to Malchus without receiving an answer (cf. Entry: Bonn).

Malfatti, von Montereggio, Johann

b. Lucca 1776, d. Hietzing (near Vienna) 1858. Physician. Studied with the famous Aloysio Galvani in Bologna. When Johann Peter Frank was called to Vienna (1795) to take over the direction of the general hospital, Malfatti followed him in order to complete his studies. He became an assistant to Frank, who left Vienna in 1804, whereupon Malfatti became a general practitioner. In this capacity he gained fame and treated many notables and members of the Court during the Vienna Congress. He was the founder of the Vienna Society of Physicians and its first president. Malfatti was one of the most famous physicians of his time and his writings, including *Entwurf einer Pathogenie* (1809), gained world-wide fame. Men like Franz Bader, Schelling, Hufeland, and Troxler were among his intimate friends. Malfatti's brother was a wealthy real estate owner.

Dr. Malfatti became Beethoven's physician after Prof. Johann Adam Schmidt died on February 19, 1808. Evidently Gleichenstein had introduced Beethoven to both Malfatti families, the physician and the real estate owner. The latter had two daughters, Anna (Nanette), who became Gleichenstein's wife in 1811, and Therese, who was very much liked by Beethoven. At that time Therese was about 21 years old, full of temperament and a Mediterranean charm. It is presumed that Beethoven proposed to her. Therese married Baron von Drosdick in 1817. It is well known that Beethoven had marriage plans of his own in 1810, as he asked Wegeler to furnish him with his certificate of baptism. Kaznelson tries to prove that the person whom Beethoven intended to marry was Josephine von Brunswick.

It is certain that Therese Malfatti was not Beethoven's Immortal Beloved (cf. Leitzmann: *Beethoven und Therese Malfatti,* Deutsche Rundschau 1911). There are preserved two letters written by Beethoven to Therese, in which he calls her flighty. A scrap of paper exists from the year 1817 or 1818; Schindler published it in facsimile with the following text: "Love alone is able to provide you with a happier life. Oh God, let me finally find the one who gives me virtue and whom I am entitled to own. Dated Baden, July 27, when M. passed and seemed to look at me." One may assume that this M. stands for Malfatti. Through a misunderstanding Beethoven had with Dr. Malfatti—Beethoven had doubts about his way of treating him—the good relationship with the family was broken up.

Dr. Malfatti's successor was Dr. Staudenheimer. When Beethoven was sick in 1826, Schindler urged Dr. Malfatti to look up his old friend. But Malfatti only assisted Dr. Wawruch in the treatment. A temporary improvement occurred, when Malfatti ordered an alcoholic sherbet, and one can read in one of Beethoven's last notes: "What a miracle, the wise doctors are defeated, and I shall live by Malfatti's skill." (Cf. Th.-R.; Frimmel: *Beethoven Jahrbuch* I p. 123.)

Mälzel, Johann Nepomuk

b. Regensburg 1772, d. 1838. Famous mechanic, expert on acoustics. His father, a mechanic and organ builder, trained him in the trade and made him study music. In 1792 young Mälzel came to Vienna, where he concentrated on music mechanics. He invented the panharmonicon, a mechanical orchestra consisting of trumpet, clarinet, viola and cello. The instrument had a powerful sonority and was able to reproduce all nuances of piano and forte. It caused a great sensation in Vienna together with another of his inventions, an automatic trumpeter that blew an Austrian military march. Mälzel's fame grew rapidly; he was even received by Napoleon in Schönbrunn. The instrument was sold in Paris, and Cherubini composed a special work for it, *The Echo.* In 1808 Mälzel was back in Vienna, where he constructed a new automatic trumpeter. No biography of Mälzel makes a clear distinction between him and his younger brother, Leonhard. Leonhard constructed several mechanical instruments, among them one called the "Orpheus Harmonie." Beethoven who evidently had known both brothers for some time, expressed himself favorably about the Orpheus Harmonie. It might possibly have been Leonhard who constructed a hearing tube for Beethoven. However, it was the older Mälzel who completed the metronome. Its original inventor was the mechanic Winkel in Amsterdam. Mälzel had his invention patented in France without mentioning Winkel's name. In the course of an extensive law suit the Dutch Academy recognized Winkel as the inventor. Schindler recorded that in 1812 Mälzel had promised Beethoven to construct several hearing aids for him. In order to spur this work, Beethoven composed for the panharmonicon a piece, *Schlachtsinfonie* (Beethoven's own name). The piece was so successful that Beethoven, at Mälzel's suggestion, orchestrated it. Mälzel kept his promise and constructed four hearing aids for Beethoven. At the time the two were on good terms, and the Master dedicated to him the canon *Ta, ta, ta, lieber, lieber, Mälzel* (later the *allegretto* of the Eighth Symphony). As late as 1814 Beethoven saw Mälzel frequently and both discussed models for a metronome; the Battle Music was also discussed. After the performance of the latter (December 12, 1813) a long copyright suit started, which was finally settled in 1817 by Beethoven's lawyer Carl von Adlersburg. In 1817 the metronome was completed and advertised in the *Wiener Allgemeine Musikalische Zeitung* (February 18) as having "recommendations by Beethoven and Salieri."

Mälzel toured all Europe. On December 20, 1825, he embarked with his different inventions for America and landed in New York on February 7, 1826. In that year he visited Boston and Philadelphia, in 1827 Baltimore, in 1828 Philadelphia and Boston, and returned to Europe by the end of that year. In 1829 he traveled to New York again. Between 1830 and 1833 he lived in New York, Philadelphia, and Boston; in 1834, in Richmond and Charleston. In 1835 he was in Washington; in 1836 in Richmond, Washington, Philadelphia, Pittsburgh, Cincinnati and New Orleans. At the end of 1836 he paid his first visit to Havana, and this visit was repeated the next year. On July 21, 1838, he was found dead in bed on board the ship from Laguayra to Philadelphia. He left a considerable fortune, estimated at half a million dollars. Among the inventions of Leonhard Mälzel was an orchestrion which imitated 50 instruments. About both Mälzels, see Wurzbach; Th.-R.; Nettl: "Musical Notes on Prince Bernhard's Trip to America, 1825", *American-German Review*, February 1944; Max Reinitz: *Beethoven im Kampf mit dem Schicksal*, Wien 1924.

Mandolin

The most recent instrument of the lute family. Guitars and mandolins were extremely popular in Beethoven's time. Anton Diabelli was originally a guitarist, and composed more than 200 works for this instrument. Another guitarist was Gottfried Heinrich Mylich (1773-1843), who came to Vienna in 1798 and belonged to the circle of Amenda and Beethoven. The Master's friend Wenzel Krumpholz was a virtuoso on the mandolin. Josef Zuth in his book *Simon Molitor und die Wiener Gitarristik* mentioned a number of guitarists of that time, and it may be assumed that some of them were acquainted with Beethoven. The Master wrote several pieces for mandolin. Two, a Sonatina and an Adagio, with the accompaniment of cembalo, are published in the Complete Works, Series 25 (Suppl.). Nottebohm places these works in the year 1805. There is another Sonatina for mandolin, found by Dr. Arthur Chitz in the Palace Clam-Gallas in Prague, possibly written for Countess Clari (married to Count Clam-Gallas).

Mannheim School

A German school of the mid-18th century, located at Mannheim and connected with the orchestra of Karl Theodor, Elector of the Palatinate (1743-1799). Most important members of that school were: Johann Stamitz (1717-1757), Franz Xaver Richter (1709-1789), Ignaz Holzbauer (1711-1783), Anton Filtz (ca. 1730-1760), Christian Cannabich (1731-1798) and Anton Stamitz (1754-1809). Hugo Riemann somewhat overemphasized this school's importance. He attributed to the Mannheim School a very strong influence on Beethoven. Features of that school were: melodic prominence of the violins, homophonic style, abandonment of imitation and fugal style (with the possible exception of Richter), extended crescendos, the "Mannheim rockets" and some other mannerisms which can also be found in contemporary literature. It is true that ascending triads, as in Beethoven's Piano Sonata Op. 2, No. 1, or Mannheim crescendos, as in the Sonata Pathétique Op. 13 (also found in one of the Electoral Sonatas), reflect a strong influence of the Mannheim School. Some other characteristics, like the "Mannheim sighs" (Beethoven Op. 14 No. 2, Op. 31 No. 3), belong to the general vocabulary of the 18th century. (Cf. Riemann: *Denkmäler der Tonkunst in Bayern,* Vol. III, VII and VIII; Riemann: *L. van Beethovens sämtliche Klavier Solosonaten,* 3 Vol. Berlin 1920; Th.-R.)

Manuscripts

". . . for the present we must see that the copy (as my manuscript does not appear to be legible enough) be quite correct, and above all to take it as a model." Beethoven wrote thus to his publisher Schlesinger in Berlin in July 1821 in regard to the Sonata Op. 109 in E major. Even if Beethoven's letter is accepted as a concession about the legibility of his handwriting, one should nevertheless be cautious in jumping to conclusions. When speaking of handwriting we refer to the writing of musical manuscripts, not the letters, which can be read only with great difficulty. Further, in discussing Beethoven's writing of music it is necessary to eliminate the sketches; because most of the sketches were written in a great hurry, often under difficult circumstances during outdoor walks, and because they were only for his own use, he frequently employed a kind of shorthand. However, such concessions cannot be made in regard to finished scores to be sent to the publisher or copyist. An inspection of those manuscripts which are available reveals that the general idea about Beethoven's "atrocious" handwriting is not quite justified. One has only to look at the fair copies of the Sonata Op. 78, or Op. 111, both reproduced in facsimile prints, to see how carefully each note is placed; there can be no question about the exact meaning. The poor legibility which Beethoven admits in the letter quoted above arises from a quite different cause; the trouble is caused not by a manner of writing, but rather by a manner of working. Beethoven made numerous corrections even in the fair copy, crossing out measures, whole lines, or even half a page, then rewriting above or below the crossed sections. This procedure naturally affects the appearance of the page and often causes alarming and disheartening impressions at first sight. The difficulty consists not in reading the notes but in finding the right ones. Beethoven's writing is actually very precise and characteristically sharp and thin. Where any doubts arise as to which notes are intended, Beethoven very often supplies letters for clarification.

Because of the nature of Beethoven's manuscripts, their study has a twofold purpose. In addition to being a source for producing editions in accord with the intention of the composer, they allow a glimpse into Beethoven's workshop. Changes made during the working out, or even in the last minute, reveal as much about Beethoven's way of composing as do the sketches. The double potentiality of the manuscripts makes it highly important that the original be preserved and made available at least in reproductions. It was Heinrich Schenker who inspired one of his students, Anthony van Hoboken, to furnish the means for founding an Archive of Photogramms at the National Library of Vienna. This enterprise helped to develop greater and deeper interest in the meaning and importance of musical manuscripts. Since only a few scores of Beethoven's works were available in facsimile print publications—Op. 26; Op. 27, No. 2; Op. 57; Op. 78; Op. 111, and the Fifth and Ninth Symphonies—the preserving of scores in photostats and microfilms made the loss of some of the originals less severe, a fact which was strongly felt during and after the last war. Many important scores in Germany which have disappeared, among them the Beethoven Symphonies No. 5, 9, and probably 7, are still available on microfilm.

Many of the manuscripts belonging to the former Preussische Staatsbibliothek in Berlin are now safe in the Western Sector in the libraries of Marburg and Tübingen. The Berlin collection of Beethoven manuscripts was by far the largest in the world and it would be impossible to enumerate those treasures here. Next to the Berlin collection, the most important is found at the Beethovenhaus in Bonn. Here we find such scores as the Pastorale Symphony, the Piano Sonatas Op. 27 No. 2, Op. 28, the first clean copy of the first movement of Op. 111, the string quartet Op. 59 No. 3, and the Mass in C major Op. 86. Of greatest importance is a collection of photostats of as many Beethoven manuscripts as were accessible. In Vienna at the National Library, where the Photogramarchiv is located, the score of the Violin Concerto Op. 61 can be found. This manuscript is of special interest because it shows the struggle Beethoven went through in working out the solo part for the violin, and in addition shows some indication for the piano arrangement which Beethoven wrote later. Further, the collection contains the Sonata in F major Op. 24 and the String Quartet in F minor Op. 95. In the library of the Gesellschaft der Musikfreunde in Vienna we find the revised copy of the *Eroica*, the preservation of which is made extremely important because the original manuscript of this symphony, as well as those of the first two symphonies, has been lost. Another treasure of this collection is the manuscript of the Piano Sonata in E flat major Op. 81a. As for other public libraries in Europe, the British Museum in London has the Violin Sonata Op. 30 No. 3 in G major and numerous sketchbooks (see Entry: Sketchbooks). The most important manuscript in the Librairie de Conservatoire in Paris is the Sonata Apassionata Op. 57. (Cf. Max Unger in *Neues Beethoven-Jahrbuch* 1935). Especially rich in Beethoven manuscripts are some private collections; first is the Bodmer collection in Switzerland, which contains one of the largest collections of Beethoven's letters as well as a number of important works such as the Piano Sonata Op. 78, Bagatelles Op. 33 and Op. 126, Fantasie Op. 77, Violin Sonata Op. 30 No. 2 in C minor, Piano Sonata Op. 53 in C major, and a manuscript of the third and fourth movement of the Sonata Op. 110 (cf. Max Unger, "Eine Schweizer Beethovensammlung" catalogue, Zürich 1939). The important Louis Koch Collection of Musical Autographs, formerly located in Frankfurt a.M. but now in Switzerland, includes the Piano Sonata Op. 101, Diabelli Variations Op. 121, Klärchen's Song "Freudvoll und Leidvoll," and numerous sketches and letters. The catalogue of this collection has been described and annotated by Dr. Georg Kinsky, Stuttgart 1953.

The last years have brought some changes in the ownership of manuscripts. Some of them have been brought to the United States, of which the most notable item is the Sonata Op. 109 in E major now in the Library of Congress (originally in the Wittgenstein collection in Vienna) and the Piano Trio Op. 70 No. 1 in D major.

O. J

Marches

There is a world of difference between the military marches by Beethoven, composed for practical purposes, and the metaphysically conceived funeral march of the *Eroica* and the one from the Sonata Op. 26. In both funeral marches the life of a hero is depicted; in Op. 26 a real march is presented, the image of a majestic procession with ghastly drums and sounding fanfares. The march of the *Eroica* unfolds the heroic struggle of a hero, possibly identifiable with Beethoven, and his surrender to fate. Op. 26 was orchestrated and transposed to B minor by Beethoven himself for Duncker's drama *Leonore Prohaska.*

Another march with refreshing rhythms is found in *Fidelio,* in B flat major, No. 6 in the score, (originally it was No. 7). *Tarpeja,* text by Kuffner, has a triumphal march, and Op. 113, the *Ruins of Athens* has under No. 6 a march with chorus which appeared also as Op. 114 in a different version. The same dramatic work contains also the famous *Marcia alla Turca.*

There are three Marches for four hands Op. 45, dedicated to Princess Esterhazy, which have a humorous background. Ries told the story that an old countess (Countess Thun?) heard him play a march which he had just improvised (1802). The lady, a strong admirer of Beethoven—Beethoven in turn was not too fond of her—asked Ries if this march was a new brilliant composition of the Master. Ries, who liked to make fun, answered in the affirmative. Next day Beethoven happened to meet the old lady at Count Browne's and she immediately started to talk about his wonderful new march. Ries had to explain the situation, which was taken humorously by Beethoven. This comical situation resulted in Beethoven's composing the three above-mentioned marches for Princess Esterhazy. Th.-R. questioned their value. However, there is no doubt that this amusing story is reflected in the gabbling rhythms of these marches, which make fun of military music.

The *Ritter Ballet* (1790) is introduced by a march. Furthermore there are two military marches: one in D major, *Marsch zur grossen Wachtparade* (June 4, 1816), published posthumously in 1827 in an arrangement for two hands by Cappi and Czerny, and the other one in F major *Für die böhmische Landwehr.* The latter was published with another one under the title "2 Märsche für Militair-Musik verfasst zum Carroussel an dem glorreichen Namensfest I.K.K. Maj. Maria Ludovika in dem K.K. Schlossgarten zu Luxenburg, von L. van Beethoven." The D major March has the characteristic orchestration: 2 Flauti, Piccoli, Oboi, Clarinetto in F, 2 Clarinetti in C, Corni in B. basso, 2 Corni in D, 3 Trombe in D, Tromba in B and G, Triangolo e Cinelli, Tamburo militare e gran Tamburo, Fagotti, Contra fagotto, Tromboni, Tenore e Basso, Serpente.

Maria Ludovica

Empress of Austria: b. Monza 1787, d. Verona 1816. Third wife of Emperor Franz, daughter of Archduke Ferdinand (the son of Empress Maria Theresia). Goethe, who had met her in Teplitz, felt greatly attracted to her. For a Carrousel of the Empress, Beethoven wrote two marches, which were performed on August 25, 1810. We know that the Empress assisted Beethoven financially. (Cf. Wertheimer: *Die drei ersten Frauen des Kaisers Franz,* 1893.)

Maria Theresia

Second wife of Emperor Franz I (1772-1807). She was musically inclined. Thayer believes she might have influenced the commission of Beethoven's *Prometheus* music. The Septet Op. 20 was dedicated to her. When *Fidelio* was performed in 1805 she straightened out difficulties with the censor.

Marschner, Heinrich

b. Zittau (Saxony) 1795, d. Hannover 1861. Famous composer whose operas *Hans Heiling, Vampir,* and *Templer und Jüdin* belonged to the standard repertoire of the nineteenth century. At the age of 21 Marschner visited Beethoven, who did not receive the young man in a very friendly way. According to Frimmel (*Beethoven Handbuch*) Marschner became acquainted in 1815 with the Hungarian Baron Amade de Varkony. The latter and the Thomas Cantor J. G. Schicht recommended Marschner to Beethoven. As Marschner moved to Pressburg, where he became the music teacher of Johann Nep. Zichy, he might have met Beethoven in Vienna.

In 1826 Marschner wrote to Hoffmeister in Leipzig that one of his sonatas was liked by Beethoven. (Cf. Max E. Wittmann: *Marschner;* G. Münzer: *Heinrich Marschner.*)

Martonvasar

Village in Hungary where the family of Count Brunswick owned a castle. Beethoven was there as a guest in about 1800 (cf. Entry: Brunswick).

Maschek, Paul

See Entry: Copyists.

Masses

A solemn service of the Roman Catholic rite, representing the commemoration and mystical repetition of the sacrifice of Christ on the Cross. It must be taken for granted that Beethoven, at the time of his youth in Bonn, was familiar with many contemporary masses, and that, as an organist, he frequently had to accompany the church service. It is also certain that he received some instruction in that field from Haydn, Schenk, and Albrechtsberger. This is shown by a piece of music written by Beethoven about 1794, containing a fugue for a Dona nobis pacem with an annotation probably by Albrechtsberger.

In 1806 Beethoven was commissioned to write a mass for Prince Esterhazy. It was completed in the summer of 1807 and performed on September 13 of the same year (cf. Entry: Esterhazy). As Bekker points out, this work is not an early work but a mature composition. Otto Ursprung refers mainly to the *Deum de Deo,* which shows that Beethoven, while composing that mass, was deeply taken by mysticism. This work is completely different from the rationalistic masses of Haydn, a fact responsible for Esterhazy's derogatory remark. This mysticism is also referred to in Beethoven's well-known letter to Breitkopf and Härtel, stating that he treated the text of the Mass in a completely new and unheard-of way. As Ursprung indicates, this mass foreshadows the masses of the Romantic period with their specific representation of a personal experience. Immediately after the completion of the C major Mass, Beethoven is supposed to have started working on a second mass, as reported in the *Journal des Luxus und der Moden* (January 1808). In 1823 Count Dietrichstein suggested to Beethoven that he write a mass in order to please the Imperial Court. Neither project was realized. The *Missa Solemnis,* however, became Beethoven's masterwork. (Cf. Th.-R. III, Ursprung: *Die Katholische Kirchenmusik* (Potsdam Athenaion), and Entry: *Missa Solemnis.*)

Matthisson, Friedrich von

b. Hohendodeleben 1761, d. Wörlitz (near Dessau) 1831. Lyric poet whose *Adelaide* and *Opferlied* were set to music by Beethoven. On August 4, 1800, the Master sent a copy of his *Adelaide* to the poet with an accompanying letter. Whether or not this letter was answered by the poet is unknown. However, in Matthisson's edition of his poems (1815), he makes the following remark, referring to *Adelaide*: "Several poets have this little lyrical poem to music, but it is my sincerest opinion that no composer so overshadowed the text as Beethoven." Mathisson obviously referred to such composers as Bernhard Wessely, Pilz, Reichardt, Zelter, Zumsteeg, Jensen, Bornhardt, and Righini.

Schubert's setting of the famous *Adelaide* was composed in 1814 and published only after his death in 1848. (Cf. Th.-R. II, p. 26; Friedländer: *Das deutsche Lied* II, p. 404; O. E. Deutsch: *Schubert Thematic Catalogue,* p. 95; Entry: *Adelaïde.)*

Mattioli, Cajetan

b. Venice 1750. Violinist and concertmaster in Bonn between 1774 and 1784. According to the Fischer manuscript he was a friend of Beethoven's father. Neefe, in Cramer's *Magazin der Musik,* praised his excellent qualities as an orchestral director. Neefe in his autobiography indicates that Mattioli, who was succeeded by J. Reicha, moved to Italy. (Cf. Schiedermair: *Der junge Beethoven.)*

Mäurer, Bernhardt

Cellist in Bonn. He was well acquainted with the young Beethoven. His reminiscences on Beethoven are found in the Fischhof papers (cf. Entry: Cressener).

Maximilian Franz

b. Vienna 1756, d. Hetzendorf (near Vienna) 1801. Austrian Archduke. The youngest of the five sons of Empress Maria Theresia; after 1769 Hoch- und Deutschmeister, 1780 Hochmeister des Deutschen Ordens, 1784 Elector of Cologne, and in that capacity of greatest importance to Beethoven. All contemporaries emphasize his kind-hearted character, his cheerfulness and his motto was *laisser vivre,* in accord with his own way of living. His enormous appetite affected his embonpoint to such a degree that he needed a special curved table in order to be able to reach his food. It is amusing to read the letters from his mother, Maria Theresia, giving him intelligent advice about his health.

Beethoven's travels to Vienna (1787 and 1792) and his visit to Mergentheim (1791) were made at the expense of the Elector. When the French invaded Bonn in 1794, the Archduke went to his bishopric in Münster; later to Mergentheim, Ellingen, and finally to Vienna, where he resided in the Sailern Castle in Hetzendorf. The Archduke was the founder of Bonn University (1786), which Beethoven attended. The Archduke always acted in a very lenient and gracious way toward Beethoven. Schiedermair quotes a letter to the Archduke from Schal (May 6, 1796) referring to Beethoven's arrival in Dresden, proving that the Elector was still interested in Beethoven. (Cf. Schiedermair: *Der junge Beethoven; Briefe der Kaiserin Maria Theresia,* ed. by W. Fred, München 1914; Breuning: *Aus dem Schwarzspanierhaus;* Th.-R. I.)

Maximilian Friedrich, Count von Königseck-Aulendorf

b. Cologne 1708, d. there 1784. Elector of Cologne in Bonn 1761. His predecessor, Clemens August, was a spendthrift under whose reign the finances of the Electorate had deteriorated considerably. Maximilian's new finance minister, Belderbusch, restored the economy and cut all expenses. Beethoven's family was comparatively little affected thereby because of their friendly relations with the minister. Ludwig van Beethoven, the Master's grandfather, had also little trouble acquiring the position of Kapellmeister (1761). Beethoven was born under the reign of Maximilian Friedrich. At that time the musical life of Bonn had improved, particularly by the foundation of the National Theater. During this period Neefe was appointed to Bonn. (Cf. Th.-R. I; Schiedermair: *Der junge Beethoven.)*

Mayer (also Meyer and Meier), Sebastian

b. 1773, d. Vienna 1835. Singer and actor, second husband of Mozart's sister-in-law, Josephina Hofer. Castelli characterized him as a mediocre singer but a good actor and stage director. He had been a member of the Imperial Opera since 1815 and retired in 1827. Mayer was on friendly terms with Beethoven and originated the role of Pizarro in *Fidelio*. Schindler tells how Mayer failed in the famous Revenge aria *(Fidelio)* and caused considerable laughter, whereupon Mayer remarked: "Never would my brother-in-law have composed such nonsense." Mayer also took part in the discussion held about *Fidelio* at the house of Lichnowsky. There are two letters by Beethoven, addressed to Mayer, referring to the performance of *Fidelio;* they show that the friendly relations between the two were continued. This is proven by the fact that at Mayer's benefit concert on April 11, 1808, the *Eroica* was performed. Mayer arranged in another benefit concert the performance of the Second Symphony and *Christus am Ölberg.* (Cf. Castelli: *Memoiren meines Lebens;* Th.-R. II.)

Mayseder, Josef

b. Vienna 1789, died there 1863. Excellent violinist. Probably introduced to Beethoven by Schuppanzigh. In a letter by Beethoven to Mayseder (1814), the Master invited him to participate in a performance. Frequently his name appears in Conversation-books and letters (cf. Wurzbach; Th.-R. V).

Mechetti, Carlo and Pietro

Owners of an art and music publishing company. Carlo owned the firm about 1800 and had taken his nephew, Pietro, into the business in 1798. Carlo died 1811, whereupon the firm changed the name to Pietro Mechetti quondam Carlo. Pietro died in 1850, and hereafter the firm ran under the name Mechetti & Diabelli. The C major Polonaise Op. 89 for Piano was published by Mechetti. There is preserved a letter by Beethoven to Mechetti (cf. Wurzbach).

Meisl, Karl

b. Laibach 1775, d. Vienna 1853. Popular playwright. In 1802 he wrote his first play *Carolo Caroline,* in 1844 his last play *Die blonden Locken,* in which Nestroy participated (cf. Wurzbach for an extensive list of his plays). Meisl wrote the text to *Die Weihe des Hauses,* for which the Master had written the overture in 1822. The dramatic play was written in honor of the opening of the Josephstädter Theater. The overture was published as Op. 124 and was dedicated to Prince Nikolaus von Galitzin. (Cf. Entry: Overtures.)

Meissner, August Gottlieb

b. Bautzen 1753, d. Fulda 1807. Writer, professor of literature and aesthetics at the University of Prague. His grandson, Alfred Meissner (b. Teplitz 1822, d. Bregenz 1885), belonged to the group of utraquistic Bohemian writers; his *Rococo Bilder* contained recollections of his grandfather, who knew Mozart and Beethoven. In a letter of Beethoven's dated November 2, 1803, to the painter Alexander Macco (b. Ansbach 1770, d. 1835) in Prague, the Master alludes to the text of an oratorio to be written by Meissner. Alfred Meissner refers to that fact; the contents were supposed to deal with the Christians at the time of Nero. Macco, likewise, was acquainted with Beethoven and may have painted a portrait of the Master. The authenticity of Alfred Meissner's stories is questioned. (Cf. R. Fürst: *August Gottlieb Meissner;* Nettl: *Mozart in Böhmen;* Th.-R. II.)

Melodic Recurrences

It is well known that Handel, Bach, and other composers used their own melodies in different compositions. Mozart quoted himself comparatively seldom, and if so, mostly with a certain purpose: i.e., in *Don Giovanni,* where a *Figaro* melody is introduced in Don Giovanni's table music. Beethoven quotes his own music more often. In the C major Piano Quartet (1785) there are three themes which are used later in his Piano Sonatas Op. 2, F minor and C major. (Cf. Riemann: *Analyse von Beethovens Klaviersonaten*; Schiedermair: *Der junge Beethoven.)* The second finale of *Fidelio* is based on Beethoven's cantata on the death of Joseph II. It is well known that Beethoven used a contredanse for his *Prometheus* music, the Variations Op. 35, and the last movement of the *Eroica* (cf. Entry: Prometheus). The minuet of the G major Sonata Op. 49 No. 2 is identical with the *tempo di minuetto* in his Septet Op. 20. A theme in the cantata *Seufzer eines Ungeliebten* appears in the Choral Fantasy. The Electoral Sonata in F minor is thematically and architecturally closely related to the Sonata Pathétique. The Variation theme Op. 76, a Russian theme, appears as *Alla Turca* in the *Ruins of Athens.* These are only a few examples. It is interesting to see how Beethoven used his melodies differently in different periods, such as the above-mentioned contredanse melody. In that case the deep philosophical connection with the *Prometheus* idea and the heroic idea of the Third Symphony should not be overlooked.

Mergentheim

City in Würtemberg (Germany) with famous spas. Between 1527 and 1809 it was the most important seat (Ballei) of the Knights of the Teutonic Order and for centuries the site of the Grand Master. In 1791 a meeting of the chapter took place and, to entertain the members of this chapter, Archduke Maximilian Franz hired the Häusslers, a theatrical troupe which had played mostly in Nürnberg and Eichstädt, and a troupe of actors from Bonn. A number of Bonn musicians joined the troupe, among them Beethoven. Sandberger in an article entitled "Zur Reise nach Mergentheim und Aschaffenburg" (*Ausgewählte Aufsätze zur Musikgeschichte* II, p. 131) gives the list of the participating artists and describes the festivities. The description was found in a diary written for Landkomtur von Roll, who had to miss the festivities. Count Waldstein participated in the meetings and Georg Josef von Breuning, the uncle of Stephan, was Geheimer Referendarius. In

Mergentheim Beethoven became acquainted with Karl Ludwig Junker, who wrote a favorable report on Beethoven in Bossler's *Musikalische Korrespondenz* (November 23, 1791). (Cf. Th.-R. I; Schiedermair: *Der junge Beethoven;* Entry: Junker.)

Meyerbeer, Giacomo

b. Berlin 1791, d. Paris 1864. Famous operatic composer, student of Franz Lauska, Clementi, Zelter, D. A. Weber and Abbé Vogler. He was on friendly terms with Carl Maria von Weber, who had been his fellow-pupil at Abbé Vogler's. His acquaintance with Beethoven dated from the Vienna Congress, and Meyerbeer's participation in the "Battle" Symphony (December 18, 1813.) Tomaschek tells in his autobiography about a conversation with Beethoven, at which time he had asked Beethoven if he had met the young man who had just arrived in Vienna. Beethoven, who evidently had not attended a piano recital which Meyerbeer had given, made the following remark: "I did meet him at the performance of the *Schlacht (Battle of Victoria),* at which occasion several of the local composers played some instruments. The big drum was assigned to that young man. Ha ha ha. And I was not at all satisfied with him. He did not strike it correctly, and always came in too late so that I had to give him a good calling down. Ha ha ha. That angered him. There is nothing to him. He hasn't the courage to strike at the right time." Meyerbeer himself composed a cantata *The Genius of Music* at Beethoven's grave. (Cf. Tomaschek in *Libussa,* 1845 ff.)

Milder-Hauptmann, Anna Pauline

b. Constantinople 1785, d. Berlin 1838. Famous singer. Her father, of Salzburg extraction, was a pastry baker in the service of the Turkish ambassador in Constantinople. When Anna was five years old, her father moved to Bucharest. In 1795 the little girl came with her family to Vienna where she studied voice with S. Neukomm, who had been Haydn's favorite student. When the latter heard her sing, he said: "My dear child, you have a voice like a house." Kalischer, in his article on the singer (*Beethovens Frauenkreis*), reports that, according to the memoirs of Gustav Parthey (1871), when it was decided that Anna should join the Theater an der Wien, she wept all day long, but never thereafter. She made her debut April 9, 1803, as Juno in *Spiegel von Arkadien* by Süssmayer. Beethoven wrote for her the role of *Fidelio* in the years 1803-1805 (cf. Entry: Fidelio). When the opera was remodeled in 1814, Milder insisted upon eliminating the aria in E major. This fact was told by the singer herself to Schindler. When Milder was supposed to sing the aria *Ah perfido* in a concert (December 22, 1808) Beethoven had an argument with her fiancé Hauptmann, and her appearance had to be canceled. At the rehearsal Beethoven had called Hauptmann "stupid ass" and Schuppanzigh's sister-in-law, Josephine Killitschgy, had to substitute for Milder. At that time Milder's fame was world-wide. Characteristic is the judgment of Reichardt, who, in the season of 1808-09 repeatedly heard the singer: "Her voice is one of the most wonderful and voluminous ones I ever heard; her way of expres-

MISSA SOLEMNIS

sion extremely intelligent and beautiful. She is of noble appearance, her gestures expressive and great."

At the time Milder was in vogue in Vienna, another singer, Imperatrice Sessi, was also popular and the competition between them was a favorite topic. In 1809 Anna sang seven times for Napoleon in Schönbrunn. He was so thrilled by her that he planned to engage her for the opera in Paris. Ledebur in his *Berliner Tonkünstler-Lexikon* quotes a statement by Napoleon: "Voila une voix; depuis longtemps je n'ai pas entendu une telle voix." In 1810 Milder's marriage to Peter Hauptmann, a jeweler, took place, and after this she began to tour extensively. Rellstab, the famous Berlin music critic, praises her especially in the role of Pamina *(Magic Flute)*. The year of 1814 was of great importance for Beethoven. Not only the remodeling of *Fidelio* took place, but also a concert was arranged, featuring Milder, for which Beethoven had been asked to contribute a composition. He remodeled a Trio for Soprano, Tenor and Bass with the accompaniment of an orchestra *Tremate empj tremate* (Text by Bettoni). Milder not only sang the third version of *Fidelio,* but was also instrumental in the performance of the cantata *Der glorreiche Augenblick.* After Milder had moved to Berlin (1815), she continued there her successful performance of *Fidelio.* A letter of Beethoven of January 6, 1816, to her is preserved: "My highly esteemed, unique Milder, my dear friend. How much would I like to join the enthusiasm of the Berlin public." He continues: "I kiss you. I press you to my heart." This sentence is written in music and signed in the same way, making a pun on her husband's name. Beethoven may already have known that her marriage was unhappy (a divorce was soon to follow). (Cf. Kalischer: *Beethovens Frauenkreis.)*

Missa Solemnis

Op. 123 in D major. Eleven years after the composition of the C major Mass, Beethoven wrote his great *Missa Solemnis.* His sponsor and pupil, Archduke Rudolph of Austria, had been elected Archbishop of Olmütz (Moravia) and his solemn enthronisation was scheduled for March 9, 1820. A note in Beethoven's diary says: "Installation of the Archduke of Olmütz on March 9 of next year." In spite of the Master's troubles with his nephew, he set to work in the winter of 1818. Schindler believes that the Credo was begun in 1819, which testimony cannot be doubted as he was very close to the Master at that time. He saw Beethoven in Mödling and met him in the midst of the composition of the fugue of the Credo, an activity full of the highest excitement, as the creation of the mass not only "elevated the Master to the stars" (Schindler), but was at the same time a very strenuous task. Beethoven realized that the work would not be ready on time, and consequently the Archbishop had to be enthroned without it. It took over three years to complete the mass, which was finished in the summer of 1822, and Beethoven mailed the score to Peters in Leipzig by the end of July. We know that no other work of Beethoven was written with so much care. The beautiful handwritten copy of the work was given to the Archbishop on March 19, 1823. He began his composition with the following self-

MISSA SOLEMNIS

admonition: "Once again sacrifice all trifles of social life to your art, and God above all." To the Kyrie he added: "Von Herzen. Möge es wieder zu Herzen gehn." Beethoven had planned to put the quintessence of all his artistic will power into this work. Schindler tells about the Master's rage and fury during the composition of the mass. Almost obsessed, he beat out the time with his hands and feet before putting the music down on paper. This activity made the landlord give him notice to leave the apartment. This was during the time when people believed that Beethoven was insane. One night he returned home bareheaded, his grey hair soaked by a rain shower; he had not even been aware of the thunderstorm and the fact that he had lost his hat.

The original title of the Mass was "Missa composta a Ludovico van Beethoven, Op. 123." The name *Missa Solemnis* was used soon hereafter. Beethoven wrote to Cherubini: "I have just completed a solemn mass and called it my biggest and most perfect achievement." In a letter to Zelter, dated February 8, 1823, we read "I wrote a great Mass; I did not want to publish it in the usual way, but sent it to the foremost Royal Courts (in handwritten copies). The honorarium is 50 ducats. Besides these copies no others will ever be published, but there would have had to be quite a number of them if it were to be worthwhile to the composer. Because I have been ailing for some years and not in the best of health, I chose this procedure. I have written much, but accumulated almost zero. My eyes directed to Heaven—man is forced to look down, for his own sake and that of others. But such is man's destiny." The score of the mass was offered by Beethoven to a number of royal persons, musicians and musical societies. King Louis XVIII of France called it "L'œuvre le plus accompli" and sent Beethoven a heavy gold medal with the inscription: "Donné par le Roi à Monsieur Beethoven." In a special letter Beethoven had asked Cherubini to put a good word in for him, but Cherubini did not answer. Neither did Goethe, whom Beethoven had asked to intervene at Weimar on behalf of the mass. Even the Swedish King, the former Bernadotte, did not react to Beethoven's request. Only six Royal Courts accepted Beethoven's offer, the Spanish, Russian, Royal Saxon, French, Darmstadt and Tuscany. The first performance of the complete work took place in Petersburg on March 26, 1824; Prince Galitzin had been instrumental in bringing about the performance.

It is well known that Vienna never had a complete performance of the mass during Beethoven's lifetime. In a concert on May 7, 1824, the Ninth Symphony and three items of the mass (Kyrie, Credo and Agnus Dei) were heard. In a repeat concert on May 23 only the Kyrie remained on the program. Because of the difficult solo parts, the singers Caroline Unger-Sabatier and Henriette Sontag protested against the performance. In Vienna it was not given in its complete form until 1845. The first complete *Missa Solemnis* in Austria was in 1830 in the little town of Warnsdorf (Bohemia), under the direction of Johann Vincenz Richter.

There has been much discussion about whether Beethoven's work should be considered liturgical or not. It is interesting that such representatives of church music as Otto Ursprung and Hermann Müller (Paderborn) are inclined to recognize the work as liturgical. The latter states that the mass was in complete accordance with the *Motu proprio* of Pius X, which, 80 years after the completion of the Mass, regulated the principles of ecclesiastical music. It must be admitted that the Pope expressed the wish that the size of the mass not exceed the liturgical action. This is definitely the case with Beethoven's *Missa;* the importance of music is so overwhelming that it places the liturgy in the background. The text of the *Missa,* as treated by Beethoven, is not strictly liturgical. The Master was a deist, and looked upon God as an architect and creator of the world. He attributed to God heroic qualities and we may say that the *Missa Solemnis* expresses ideas similar to the Eroica Symphony exalted to metaphysical magnitude. It represents a reasoning with his God which is best understood by the grandiose columns of the Kyrie, the representation of God's deeds as illustrated in the Credo, the mysticism of transubstantiation, the exalted jubilation of the Gloria, the mournful melody of the Passion and in the humble prayer for peace. Beethoven inscribed the "Dona nobis pacem" with the words: "Bitte um inneren und äusseren Frieden." These words alone show the subjectiveness of Beethoven's work. The entire mass is a unique human document. One has only to compare a mass by Palestrina with Beethoven's work to understand the metaphysical approach of a 19th century genius to the problem of God, men, and the world. Beethoven had made extensive studies not only of church music, but also of the Latin text. In a diary from Schindler's estate, now in Berlin, we find such excerpts from a Latin dictionary as: "Virgo die noch bey Keiner Mannsperson geschlafen—venio veni ventum, passio imperfectum ventum ist man ist gekommen. . . ."

There are a number of sketches treated in the second volume of Nottebohm; they show that Beethoven occasionally changed the concept. A march was to precede the Agnus Dei and while he was sketching, he added remarks about his own life to his jotting, for example: "Stärke der Gesinnungen des inneren Friedens über alles . . . Sieg." The literature on the *Missa Solemnis* is inexhaustible. (Cf. the ingenious remarks of Paul Bekker in his *Beethoven;* the articles of Johannes Wolf and Hermann Müller (Paderborn) in the report of the Vienna Beethoven Zentenarfeier 1927; Sternfeld: *Zur Einührung in Beethovens "Missa Solemnis;"* Lucie Dikenmann-Balmer: *Beethovens "Missa Solemnis,"* Zürich, 1952.)

Mittag, August

b. Kreischa (near Dresden) 1795, d. Vienna 1867. Military conductor in Dresden. From 1820 on bassoonist at the Hoftheater. He appears many times in Conversation-books, discussing improvement of bassoons. Beethoven seemed to have a great liking for the man (cf. Volkmann: *Neues über Beethoven,* p. 46 ff).

Mödling

Today a suburb of Vienna. In Beethoven's time a resort which was visited by the composer as early as 1799. He stayed there for a longer stretch of time in 1818-19-20 (cf. an extensive study in Frimmel: *Handbuch;* Th.-R. II, IV and V).

Mollo, Tranquillo

Music publisher in Vienna; first a clerk with Artaria and Co.; in 1793 a partner of the firm. In 1798 he founded his own firm, which was later joined by Domenico Artaria as his partner, but in 1804 the two separated. Mollo published the following compositions by Beethoven: Piano Trio Op. 11 and the Variations of Mozart's theme *Bei Männern welche Liebe fühlen* for Cello and Piano (1802). The title page of that book bears the inscription: "Variations pour le Clavecin sur le Thème . . ." which might suggest that the work was written for keyboard alone; however, the cello part goes with it.

Molt, Theo

Musician from Quebec, Canada. (Cf. United States.)

Moscheles, Ignaz

b. Prague 1794, d. Leipzig 1870. Famous composer and pianist; studied with F. D. Weber, who was quite opposed to Beethoven. After a successful concert (1806) Moscheles, at the age of 14, came to Vienna to study with Salieri and Albrechtsberger. There are doubts about Moscheles' relations with Beethoven. In his editions of the Beethoven Sonatas, published by Hallberger, Moscheles emphasizes his close personal connection with the Master to justify the authenticity of his edition. This aroused Schindler's fury, and in his Beethoven biography II, p. 138, he goes so far as to state that Beethoven never had any relationship whatsoever with Moscheles. This is in sharp contrast to another statement by Schindler where he stressed the fact that Beethoven received Moscheles most cordially when the latter handed him his Sonata in E. Moscheles should remember, said Schindler, how patiently and leniently Beethoven corrected the *Fidelio* piano score, commissioned to Moscheles by Artaria (1814). After the completion of the score, Moscheles noted at the bottom of it: "Fine, mit Gottes Hülfe" (finished, with God's help). Moscheles left the score for Beethoven to review, and when the score was returned, he found underneath his own remark the following one by Beethoven: "O Mensch, hilf dir selbst." Many facts prove that Schindler was prejudiced against Moscheles because of a certain jealousy and anti-Semitism (cf. Entry: Jews). In spite of this attitude Moscheles from the very beginning of his career was certainly a Beethoven enthusiast. It may be assumed that for a short time he was under the spell of the anti-Beethoven clique (Salieri, Eibler, Albrechtsberger, Spohr, etc.).

In 1816 Moscheles, who had been named choral director at the Kärntnerthor Theater in 1809, went on a concert tour which took him to Munich, Dresden, Leipzig, Paris and London. He concertized sensationally and settled in London in 1821. It is hard to say how much he was interested in Beethoven during that period. His success in Munich is reflected in one of the Conversation-books from the spring of 1820. Previously Moscheles had concertized in Vienna, as is revealed in a Conversation-book of December 1819. Oliva wrote on December 14 the following: "Yesterday Moscheles gave a concert. At the end of the concert the Jew started improvising." (Answer by Beethoven unrecorded.) Oliva continued: "What would he know about improvising?" One might assume that in the course of that conversation the Jewish issue was touched, and Oliva continued telling Beethoven that the Archduke had last week baptized a Jewish family of six members. When Moscheles returned to Vienna for concerts (1823), he borrowed Beethoven's Broadwood piano. Details about this are extensively discussed by Schindler, again revealing his definite animosity against Moscheles. In Schindler's Biography II, p. 139, a letter of Beethoven to Moscheles is published (Feb. 22, 1827) in which he asked Moscheles to intervene on his behalf in arranging a benefit concert in London. There is no doubt that Moscheles intervened in London many times in Beethoven's favor, the last time shortly before the Master's death. (Cf. *Aus Moscheles Leben nach Briefen und Tagebüchern von seiner Frau,* Leipzig 1827; Schünemann: *Ludwig van Beethoven Konversationshefte,* 3 vol. Berlin 1941.)

Mosel, Ignatz Franz, Edler von

b. Vienna 1772, d. there 1844. Musician and writer on music. He studied violin with Joseph Fischer and attended the Academy of Fine Arts as a pupil of Joseph Christian Brandt. He set to music Goethe's *Claudine von Villabella,* ordered by Schikaneder, but the performance was thwarted. Mosel won fame through his transcriptions of Mozart's *Cosi fan tutte* and *Clemenza di Tito,* and Cherubini's *Water Carrier* and *Medea.* Furthermore he transcribed Haydn's *Creation* for two pianos at the request of the blind pianist Therese von Paradis. When Count Moriz Dietrichstein took over the direction of both Imperial Theatres, Mosel became vice-director, and in 1829 he became the first Custos of the library.

Mosel was well acquainted with Beethoven, who did not care too much for him. When Mosel was elevated to the nobility for his musical merits, Beethoven remarked: "The Moselle flows muddy into the Rhine." Mosel, who wrote a biography of Salieri, was mostly on the side of Beethoven's opponents because of his close connection with the Italian maestro Salieri. It should not be held against him that he could not understand Beethoven's last string quartets. On the other hand Mosel is among those who signed an honorary address to Beethoven in February 1824. (Cf. Wurzbach: *Bibliography;* Batka: *Moseliana.)*

Mozart, Wolfgang Amadeus

b. Salzburg 1756, d. Vienna 1791. Beethoven met Mozart when visiting Vienna in 1787. It is assumed that Mozart gave Beethoven instruction in composition, but we do not have any details due to lack of documents. Schindler, like Wegeler, has not too much to tell about that trip but says the following: "Mozart, the source of all light in the region of harmony, encountered Beethoven on his first trip to Vienna in the winter of 1786-87." When Mozart heard Beethoven extemporize upon a theme that was given him, he exclaimed to those present: "This youth will some day make a noise in the world!" These words have been quoted many times in different variations, but it is uncertain when or where they were first said. Some people believed it happened in the presence of Emperor Joseph II, to whom Beethoven had a letter of recommendation from the Elector in Bonn. Beethoven himself was very reticent about all happenings in his youth and often confused and not sure of himself; he never mentioned anything about his meeting with Mozart. It may be assumed that Beethoven heard Mozart play since in Beethoven's opinion Bach, Handel and Mozart ranked highest. According to Thayer (IV, p. 211), Beethoven one day visited the widow of Major Baumgarten (1820), who took paying guests for meals. The Master's conversation with Baroness Born, Mrs. Baumgarten's sister, has been reported to have included the subject of Mozart. The Baroness asked Beethoven which opera of Mozart ranked highest in his opinion. Folding his hands and looking to Heaven, he exclaimed: *"The Magic Flute,* oh Mozart." Baroness Born was either the widow of Ignaz von Born, the leader of Viennese Masons in Mozart's time, or a close relative of that scientist, who was supposed, according to many contemporaries, to be the model of Sarastro. Beethoven liked Mozart's *Don Giovanni* much less, on account of the frivolous text. This is not the place to analyze the many influences of Mozart on Beethoven: however, in Beethoven's early Bonn works we find numerous Mozart reminiscences. Mozart's Violin Sonata in G major (Köchel 379) has been considered the model for Beethoven's E flat major Piano Quartet; Schiedermair, in *Der junge Beethoven,* Hans Gal, in his essay: " Die Stileigentümlichkeiten des jungen Beethoven" (*Studien zur Musikwissenschaft* IV) and Heinrich Jalowetz in his essay: "Beethovens Jugendwerke in ihren melodischen Beziehungen zu Mozart, Haydn and Ph. E. Bach" *(Sammelbände der internationalen Musikgesellschaft* XII) collected a great amount of material pertaining to this fact. Further Beethoven's early melodies are based on the suspension, a style characteristic of Mozart and the 18th century. This style of Mozart's melodics was used by Beethoven in several of his earlier works, but gradually he developed his own style by eliminating the suspension and chromaticism. Beethoven's sketch of the slow movement of his Fifth Symphony might be contrasted with its final version, which shows the transition from the "Mozart melody" to the characteristic "Beethoven melody" with its emphasis on the first beat.

Müller

b. Neuschloss near Arnau (Bohemia) 1750, d. Prague 1804. (See Entries: Brunswick, and Deym.) Hofstatuarius. His name was Joseph Deym Count von Stritetz. He entered a military career, but after a duel he fled across the Dutch border. In Holland he developed the art of moulding wax figures and quickly gained a reputation in this field. In Naples he was favored by Queen Caroline, who permitted him to copy in wax the most famous ancient statues and busts. When he came to Vienna in 1796 he made a sensation with his statues. He even received an imperial permission to build a gallery in the Rote Turmtor. His artistry won the acclaim of Emperor Franz, who was proud to own many famous statues in wax copies.

Müller's gallery was well known in Vienna at the time of Mozart, and the latter wrote a number of compositions for a mechanical organ designed for Müller's gallery. These pieces by Mozart were played in the "Bedroom of the Graves." Mozart's compositions for Müller's gallery included Köchel 608 and 616. (The original Köchel 608 is in this author's possession.)

After Mozart's death, Müller ordered Beethoven to compose for mechanical instruments. In an Autograph-convolut of Beethoven at the former State Library (Berlin), we find four variations of *Ich denke dein* for piano duet, an Adagio in F major (notated in four staffs), a Scherzo in G major (notated in two staffs) and an Allegro in G major. These are supposed to be the compositions ordered by Müller. It is well known that the variations were dedicated to the Countesses Therese and Josephine Brunswick. Josephine later became the wife of Müller-Deym. Their marriage was extremely unhappy, due not only to the difference in age, but also to the Count's unfortunate disposition, according to Therese Brunswick's diary. This diary has been used by Hevesy, Romain Rolland, and extensively by Kaznelson. The latter tried to prove that Josephine was later Beethoven's Immortal Beloved. After the Count's death Josephine kept her husband's gallery running. Müller had reassumed his title of nobility after his marriage to Josephine. In consequence of his luxurious life, he had wasted not only his own fortune but also that of his wife, and he became bankrupt. The couple had four children. Josephine's second husband was Christoph Baron Stackelberg. (Cf. Entries: Immortal Beloved, and Brunswick.)

Musical Education

See Entries: Bonn, Eeden, Pfeifer, Koch, Neefe, Albrechtsberger, Schenk, Salieri.

N

Nägeli, Hans Georg

b. Wetzikon (near Zürich) 1773, d. Zurich 1836. Composer, writer on music, and publisher. The composition of the well-known German song *Freut euch des Lebens* is attributed to him. Nägeli had organized music in Swiss schools and founded and directed the Schweizer Bund für Musikkultur. Beethoven's Piano Sonatas Op. 31a and b were published by Nägeli without an opus number in the fifth book of *Répertoire des Clavecinistes* (1803). The Sonata Op. 31c was published by Nägeli in the eleventh book of the *Répertoire* (1804). Ries was present when Beethoven read the proofs, and the Master asked him to play them. When he noticed the many printing mistakes he became impatient but he started raging when he became aware that Nägeli had made some additions of his own. Ries was ordered by the Master to list all the mistakes and mail the sonatas to Simrock, who should reprint them under the subtitle "Très correct."

Beethoven could never forget his unpleasant experience with Nägeli. Nevertheless the publisher reprinted a great number of Beethoven's works. He must have written several times to the Master, but only two answers of this correspondence are preserved. In one of these Nägeli asked Beethoven to help him in promoting his own collection of poems, and added his poem dedicated to the Master. In 1825 he published a book entitled *Vorlesungen über Musik mit besonderer Berücksichtigung der Dilettanten.* In this book he criticized Mozart, but praised Beethoven. Nägeli had in mind to approach Archduke Rudolph, to whom he had dedicated the above-mentioned book. (Cf. Frimmel: *Beethoven Studien* II; Nettl: "Goethe and Mozart," *Goethe Bicentennial Studies* 1950.)

Name

The name "Beethoven" originates from the Flemish. The word "Beete" appears in lower Saxony and is derived from the Latin *beta* which means beet. Consequently the word Beethoven means beetyard. The composer's name has the accent on the first syllable; in Vienna compound words frequently have the accent on the last syllable. The Viennese, for example, say Schönbrúnn instead of Schönbrunn, Beethóven instead of Béethoven. The Rhenish name van Béethoven was changed in Vienna to von Beethóven. Even poets like Lenau and

Ludwig August Frankl gave the wrong accent. A musical sketch of thanks by Archduke Rudolph to Beethoven, is accented: "Lieber Beet-hóven ich dan-ke.") In contrast to the German "von" which designates an aristocratic title, "van" (Dutch, Flemish) represents only part of the name. (Cf. Kluge: *Ethymologisches Wörterbuch der deutschen Sprache;* Nettl: "Erinnerungen an Erzherzog Rudolph," *Zschr. f. Musikwissenschaft* IV.) We find many different spellings for the name Beethoven, e.g. Pethoven, Pethofen, etc. The question of "von" or "van" played an important part in the composer's struggle for the guardianship of his nephew (cf. Entry: Nephew).

Napoléon Buonaparte

b. Ajaccio 1769, d. Longwood, St. Helena 1821. French dictator and Emperor. Beethoven, as Napoleon's contemporary, was naturally affected by the political events in Europe caused by the French foreign policy. An early reference to Napoleon is found in a letter of Beethoven to Hoffmeister (April 1802), after the publisher had asked the Master to compose a revolutionary sonata. This proposition was rejected. It is well known that Napoleon as Consul was highly admired by Beethoven. According to the most reliable sources Beethoven's *Eroica* was originally written with Napoleon in mind. Ries told the story that he saw the beautifully written score of the symphony on Beethoven's table. On the top of the title page it bore the inscription "Buonaparte." Ries was the first to bring Beethoven the news that Napoleon had proclaimed himself Emperor, whereupon Beethoven exclaimed infuriated: "Is he also nothing but a human being? He will sweep aside all human rights and live only for his own vanity and ambition. He will elevate himself above all other people and he will become a tyrant." Beethoven took the title-page of the score, tore it up and threw it on the floor. The first page was written anew and the title of the symphony changed to *Symphonia Eroica*. Schindler related that it was General Bernadotte who gave Beethoven the idea of writing this symphony and one may assume that Bernadotte, who later became the Swedish king, had suggested that Beethoven write a heroic symphony dedicated to Consul Buonaparte.

During the French invasion of Austria, Beethoven had to endure many hardships. When *Fidelio* had its first performance in 1805 the theater was empty because of Napoleon's invasion and Trémont related that during the invasion of 1809 a mine exploded in front of Beethoven's house. It is natural that Trémont, a Frenchman, emphasized the Master's deep admiration for Napoleon. When Trémont had invited the Master to Paris, Beethoven asked him if one could force him to see Napoleon. Truthfully he wished to see Napoleon, but did not want to show his feelings.

Stumpf compared Beethoven's build with that of Napoleon and there certainly were similarities in their character.

In 1824 when Czerny visited Beethoven in Baden the conversation turned to Napoleon, whose biography by Walter Scott just had been published. The Master said to Czerny: "Formerly I disliked him, but I changed my mind." Beethoven, who jokingly called himself "Generalissimus," had developed a sort of dictatorial attitude and saw in Napoleon some kind of an idol. This psychological phenomenon was stressed in Emil Ludwig's Beethoven biography.

Nature (love for Nature)

It is well known that Beethoven was an enthusiastic nature-lover who took every opportunity to leave the city. Döbling, Heiligenstadt, Baden, Mödling, and Nussdorf were his favorite spots, and he enjoyed the beauty of the Wiener Wald more than any other place.

Love for nature was a general phenomenon of that period which was a result of Rousseau's teaching "back to Nature." This warm feeling towards Nature was hardly apparent before Albrecht von Haller had published his poem *Die Alpen.* Goethe placed his experience of Nature in the very center of his poetic creations. In Mozart's letters from Italy there is no interest in the beauty of the Alpine scenery; Leopold Mozart called Bolzano a "sad place" and Wolfgang designates it a "Sauloch." Mozart's approach to Nature is that of a rationalist; even his musical representations of events of nature (*Idomeneo*) do not exceed those of Vivaldi and Rameau.

Beethoven was quite different from Mozart in his love of nature. Schindler dedicated a whole chapter in his biography to Beethoven's wanderlust and love for nature; he quotes a passage from C. H. Sturm's *Betrachtungen der Werke Gottes im Reiche der Natur* which Beethoven had pencil-marked: "One can rightly call Nature a school for the heart, because it teaches us our duties towards God and our fellow-men." Schindler says that in his youth Beethoven had learned to read in the great book of Nature. The biographer confessed that Beethoven taught him more about Nature than about music. Charles Neate told Thayer about his strolls with Beethoven across the fields, and remarked that he never met a man more enthusiastic about Nature, flowers, and clouds. The violinist Joseph Joachim owned a slip of paper handwritten by Beethoven with the following text: "On top of the Kahlenberg Sept. 1815. 'Oh God, I am happy in the woods, each tree echoes thy name . . . ' "

Many more documents prove Beethoven's unusual love for nature; the most notable is the Pastoral Symphony, in which the Master approaches the subject as a human being who felt himself identical with Nature.

Neate, Charles

b. London 1784, d. Brighton 1877. Musician, pianist. Neate received his early musical education from William Sharp and John Field, with whom he formed a close friendship (Grove). He studied composition under Wölfl. In 1813 he was one of the original members of the Philharmonic Society, of which he was for many years a director, performer and, occasionally, conductor. His admiration for Beethoven induced him in 1815 to visit Vienna, where he remained for eight months. He was introduced to Beethoven by Johann Hering, a Viennese merchant who excelled as a musician and directed the Liebhaber Konzerte.

Beethoven could not accept Neate as his pupil and recommended him to Förster; however, he supervised Neate's musical studies when strolling with him in Baden during the summer. Neate left Vienna on January 24, 1816, and the

Master dedicated to him two canons (*Rede, rede* and *lerne schweigen*), adding: "My dear English countryman. Don't forget your sincere friend Beethoven, whether you are silent or not." Neate had promised to publicize Beethoven's works in London. Because of the efforts of Ries, George Smart, and Neate, Beethoven became almost more famous in London than in Vienna. Neate acted as an intermediary between the London Philharmonic Society and Beethoven (1824), and there exists a large correspondence pertaining to the symphonies, quartets, and *Fidelio* to be performed in London. The Master was supposed to visit England at the expense of the Society and to compose for it a symphony and a concerto, but he refused the offer. (Cf. Grove: *Dictionary of Music and Musicians;* Th.-R. III, IV, V.)

Neberich

Wine dealer acquainted with Beethoven; he acted as an intermediary in delivering a letter from Beethoven to E. T. A. Hoffmann. In a letter to the Master from Franz von Brentano (1816), Neberich is introduced to him as one of the "fine artists of Europe" (cf. Th.-R. III p. 542).

Neefe, Christian Gottlob

b. Chemnitz 1748, d. Dessau 1798. Composer. Studied law in Leipzig and music with J. A. Hiller; received a law degree, but finally became a professional musician. Through Hiller's intervention he became musical director of the Seiler Theatrical Troupe (1776) in Dresden. They toured later in Frankfurt, Mainz, Cologne, Hanau, Mannheim and Heidelberg. In 1779 Neefe joined the Grossman-Hellmuth troupe in Bonn. There, though he was a Lutheran, he became court organist. In the summer of that year Neefe toured with Grossmann in Pyrmont and Cassel, returning to Bonn, where he remained till June 1782. In his autobiography Neefe mentioned casually: "During my absence, my post was filled by some 'vicar'." This was no one else but Beethoven. One might assume that Beethoven met Neefe shortly after the latter arrived in Bonn October 17, 1779. Probably Neefe started out as Beethoven's teacher soon after that date. The significance of Neefe's influence on the young Beethoven cannot be overemphasized. Though Neefe was not ranked among the top keyboard players, he was an excellent clavierist and pianist. Only gradually did he begin to appreciate the qualities of the pianoforte. The main sources for his teaching were Philipp Emanuel Bach's keyboard works, Joh. Sebastian's *Well Tempered Clavier* and some North and South German keyboard music of that period. Among the theory works, the manuals of Sorge, Marpurg, Kirnberger, and Philipp Emanuel Bach should be mentioned. For a long time, Neefe's influence on Beethoven was somewhat underrated because of Wegeler's statement that Neefe played a minor part in Beethoven's education. In this respect Beethoven's own words to Neefe (1793) should be quoted: "May I thank you for the advice you gave me so frequently, and which was instrumental in the development of my divine art." Neefe himself expressed his opinion about Beethoven in an article for Cramer's *Magazin der Musik:* "Louis van Beethoven plays with great dexterity and power, is a good sight-reader, in other words, he mostly plays Bach's *Well Tempered Clavier*, handed him by Mr. Neefe.

Everybody who knows this collection of preludes and fugues through all keys, which might be called the *non plus ultra,* will know what that means. This young genius deserves every subsidy. He should be allowed to travel. He certainly might become another Wolfgang Amadeus Mozart, if he will continue the way he started out." Neefe's autobiography was finished September 30, 1782. His widow continued the autobiography of her husband in the *Leipziger Allgemeine Musikalische Zeitung,* 1798-1799. She stated that in 1784, after the Electoral Kapellmeister, Andreas Lucchesi, had left that city, Neefe received a position as director of all church music in Bonn. However, just after Max Franz succeeded Max Friedrich as Elector on Aug. 15, 1784, Neefe lost a good deal of his income, and he was forced to give private lessons. It is typical of Neefe that when he settled in Bonn he bought a house and planted a garden with trees and flowers. Shortly thereafter he assumed his old position, which he held until the war with France began and the theater was dissolved. Frau Neefe gives a very sad picture of the life they led for the next two years. In 1794 Neefe assumed a position in the troupe of the impresario Hunnius, who played in Holland. There Neefe and his daughter (playing the role of Constanza) performed in Mozart's *Entführung aus dem Serail.* When Hunnius and his troupe went to Düsseldorf, Neefe and his daughter returned to Bonn. After the French invaded Bonn and forced the Elector to flee, Neefe was compelled by the invaders to do non-musical administrative work as a registrar. Shortly thereafter, Neefe and his family left for Leipzig, where, on his arrival, he found his dismissal from Bonn. On December 1, 1796, the Neefe family went to Dessau, where Neefe died on January 26, 1798, from a heart ailment which had lasted two years. Two daughters and a son survived him.

Neefe was a highly educated and gifted man who had influenced the Master in other than musical fields. Neefe's style of composing might be termed a gallant style, inasmuch as he abandoned polyphonic writing. He composed a great number of operettas, singspiele, songs, piano compositions, sonatas for piano and violin in the style of Christian Bach and Schubert. Mozart's style definitely influenced him. (Cf. Schiedermair: *Der junge Beethoven;* Irmgard Leux: *Christian Gottlob Neefe,* Leipzig 1925; Nettl: *Forgotten Musicians,* with the translation of Neefe's Autobiography, New York 1951.)

Nephew

See Entry: Karl van Beethoven.

Nürnberg

German city in Lower Bavaria. According to a letter of Stephan von Breuning to his mother, dated January 17, 1796, Stephan and Christian von Breuning traveled with Beethoven from Nürnberg to Vienna and aroused the attention of the police.

Nussdorf

Suburb of Vienna, located in picturesque surroundings near Kahlenberg and Leopoldsberg. Beethoven spent the summer of 1817 in Nussdorf, where he met Kuffner several times. Beethoven liked this village especially, because he enjoyed its fishing facilities. In 1822 he wrote to his brother Johann: "Good-bye, hope to see you this afternoon. Let's go to Nussdorf."

O

Obermayer

Baker in Vienna, brother-in-law of Johann von Beethoven, the brother of Therese Obermayer, whom Johann von Beethoven had married in Linz (1812). In 1822 Beethoven lived at the Obermayer's in the same house with Johann von Beethoven and his family.

Odescalchi, Princess Babette

née Comtesse Keglevich. See Entry: Keglevich.

Oliva, Franz

d. St. Petersburg (Russia) 1848. Bookkeeper of the banking firm Offenheimer and Herz in Vienna. Close friend of Beethoven. Thayer mentioned that the personal relations between the two are shrouded in darkness, although Oliva belonged to a musician's family.

A man by the name of Joseph Oliva, a hornplayer in Prague, was appointed by Dittersdorf to the chapel of the Bishop of Pressburg (1764). He later became a member of Prince Esterhazy's chapel under the direction of Haydn. In a Viennese address directory of 1801 a Joseph Oliva is listed as a violinist. It might be suspected that there is a relationship between the two Olivas. Evidently Franz was of Czech extraction.

Beethoven dedicated to Oliva the Piano Variations Op. 76 on an Exotic Theme, later used in the *Ruins of Athens.* In 1820 Schindler mentioned in a Conversation-book that the canon *Ta, ta, ta, lieber Mälzel,* which became the theme of the second movement of the Eighth Symphony, was sung in the Kameel tavern, where Mälzel sang the bass, Schindler the soprano, and Oliva the second bass. Schindler called Oliva a philologist; evidently he was highly interested in German literature. His connection with Varnhagen von Ense and his future wife Rahel Levin are of special interest as they play an important part in Kaznelson's conjectures about the Distant Beloved of Beethoven.

In April 1811 Oliva took a trip to Germany, and Beethoven had entrusted him to hand a letter to Goethe in which he informed him that the arrival of his *Egmont* music was imminent. Oliva saw the poet on May 2, in Weimar, at the same time that Sulpice Boisserée was visiting Goethe. Boisserée wrote in one of his letters to his brother Melchior, May 3-4, that he saw in Goethe's antechamber a tiny bent gentleman, dressed in

OPERA PROJECTS

black, wearing silk stockings. On May 4 Boisserée stated that there was piano playing after dinner. The performer was the same tiny polite man, Baron Oliva, supposedly a conductor from Vienna. In Goethe's music room there were symbolic paintings by the Romantic painter Philip Otto Runge, and Goethe remarked: "Aren't they beautiful and extravagant?" Boisserée answered: "Just like the music of Beethoven which this man is playing and the time in which we are living." Some time later Oliva met Beethoven in Teplitz; from where the Master wrote to Breitkopf and Härtel: "Oliva is here and will write you." Oliva had negotiated with Breitkopf about the B flat major Trio Op. 97. On his trip Oliva passed Reichenberg where Beethoven had planned to meet him. Beethoven had to inquire of the firm of Offenheimer and Herz in Vienna about the location of that Bohemian city.

In Teplitz Oliva was the intermediary between Beethoven and the Varnhagens (Rahel Levin). From the correspondence of the couple we learn that Beethoven and Oliva had a violent dispute, and the two men returned to Vienna separately, Beethoven via Grätz and Troppau. The rift with Oliva is reflected in a letter of Beethoven to Pasqualati: "The Lumpenkerl [scoundrel] Oliva, he is no noble scoundrel, will arrive in Hungary, don't bother too much with him; I am glad that this relationship, caused by an emergency, is completely over." From a letter, dated June 3, 1812, to Varnhagen, written by Oliva, we learn that Oliva changed his position from Offenheimer and Herz, who had treated him badly, to the firm of Mayer and Landauer.

In the following years Beethoven renewed his friendship with Oliva. In the Conversation-books of 1818-1820 his name appeared continuously. At that time he taught piano in Vienna. In 1820 he went to Russia illegally and married in St. Petersburg. There he died in 1848. (Cf. Th.-R. III-V, Kaznelson: *Beethovens ferne und unsterbliche Geliebte;* Varnhagen von Ense: *Denkwürdigkeiten des eigenen Lebens,* Leipzig 1843.)

Opera projects

Despite his miraculous *Fidelio,* Beethoven remained outside the field of opera, perhaps because of the terrific difficulties which the composer encountered during the creation of this unique work.

"The whole business with the opera is the most tiresome thing in the world," he said, "for I am dissatisfied with everything. There is almost no piece which would really and sincerely satisfy me."

In Beethoven's quartets, sonatas, and symphonies are found dramatic elements, lying within his programmatic material. As Arnold Schering has pointed out, according to Schindler, Beethoven's friend and first biographer, many of these compositions are "hidden operas."

His *Ritterballet,* written in his early youth in Bonn, was only a modest dramatic attempt. In all probability he was a ghost writer for Count Waldstein, who resided in Bonn at that time. Even as an eighteen to twenty-year-old youth Beethoven thought of operatic creation. In Bonn, he was inspired by the plays of Schiller, particularly by his *Fiesko,* but he did not breathe the atmosphere of the theater until 1803 in Vienna, where Schikaneder recognized the universal character of Beethoven's genius and tried to make him a theatrical composer.

In an article in the *Zeitung für die elegante Welt,* datelined Vienna, June 29, 1803, it is noted that Beethoven is writing an opera for Schikaneder. Nottebohm found sketches for a finale and duet of an opera which evidently belonged to that period, together with an overture which was begun, but never finished. The opera was based on a subject drawn from Roman history. The dramatis personae included: Porus (bass), Volivia, his daughter (soprano), Sartagones, lover of Volivia, and another person, undesignated, who would have been the rival of Sartagones. It is seen immediately that the sketches for the trio, *Nie war ich so froh wie Heute,* are identical with the beginning of the first version of the duet, *O namenlose Freude,* from *Fidelio.* The plot is evidently based on the story of Alexander the Great's generosity toward the defeated Indian king, Porus, a subject treated as early as 1693 in an opera by Johann Sigismund Kusser, based on a text by the Hamburg librettist, Bressand. Later Metastasio fashioned a libretto on the same subject, *Allessandro nell' Indie.* This libretto was set to music by many composers. (Cf. Entry: *Vestas Feuer.*)

One of the best poets in Beethoven's circle was Heinrich von Collin (1771-1811). Beethoven approached him as late as 1808 for an adaptation of Shakespeare's *Macbeth.* Collin wrote only the first part, publishing it in the *Wiener-Hof-Theater-Taschenbuch auf das Jahr 1809.* Nottebohm also published some sketches for the *Witches' Chorus.* It is a well-known fact that Beethoven frequently worked on two or more compositions simultaneously, and the above sketches appear on the same sheet which contains sketches for the *Largo* of the D major Trio Op. 70, No. 1. The *Largo* of the Trio is in the same key and atmosphere as the *Macbeth* sketches, suggesting the probability that Beethoven's preoccupation with *Macbeth* had a decisive influence on its origin and development. Here, as in other cases, it is seen that Beethoven started with an operatic idea, and ended with an instrumental work. Beethoven also worked on an overture to *Macbeth,* heading it with the notation, "Overture *Macbeth,*" which leads immediately into the *Chorus of Witches.*

Three years later, in 1822, Beethoven begged for a libretto from Kotzebue. He wrote to him on Jan. 28, proposing an opera based on the life of Attila, but adding, "However, I shall be grateful for any subject."

On July 11, 1811, he wrote to Count Ferdinand Palffy, "It is so difficult to find a good text for an opera," and in the same letter he mentioned that he was writing some music for a melodrama, *Les Ruines de Babylone,* but that he had little confidence in the subject as a melodrama (spoken drama, accompanied by music).

A year later he was attracted by the subject of Ulysses' return, a subject treated by Monteverdi in the 17th century. He even approached the young poet, Theodor Körner, asking him to adapt the subject for the stage.

It is known that Beethoven also considered Treitschke's *Romulus,* for the *Allgemeine Musikalische Zeitung* reported in the fall of 1815: "Our Genius Beethoven is supposed to write a new opera, based on a libretto by Treitschke."

According to Nottebohm, Beethoven had some sort of harmonic exoticism in mind for this opera.

Rudolf von Berge's *Bacchus* and Millner's drama of fate, *Die Schuld,* also attracted Beethoven. Bauernfeld's *Brutus* waited for his magic pen, as well as Sporschill's *Apotheosis in the Temple of Jupiter Ammon.* More important than these fleeting ideas was Beethoven's intention to compose Grillparzer's *Melusin.* Grillparzer also proposed to write a drama, *Drahomira,* for him. Collin was ordered to write a libretto for *Bradamante,* but that plan also was abandoned and Johann Friedrich Reichardt eventually received the libretto. And still the list is not complete, for *Undine* must be added as well as Goethe's *Claudina von Villabella.*

More interesting today is Beethoven's intended opera on an American subject! If we consult the third volume of *Beethovens Konversationshefte* by Prof. Schünemann, we find in a Conversation-book of Jan. 1820, that Beethoven discussed a new opera libretto by Johann Baptist Rupprecht with a couple of his acquaintances, the Janitscheks. Janitschek reported "He plans to submit the text to you for a musical composition. It is a pity it is not done." (Cf. Entries: Goethe, United States, and Grillparzer.)

Oratorio

Christus am Ölberge (*Mount of Olives*) Op. 85, for three solo voices, chorus and orchestra. First performed 1803 in Vienna at the Theater an der Wien. Published in 1811, without dedication.

The work consists of the following numbers: 1. Introduction, Recitative and Aria (Jesus) 2. Recitative and Aria (Seraph, Chorus of Angels) 3. Recitative and Duet (Jesus, Seraph) 4. Recitative (Jesus), Chorus of Soldiers and Young Men 5. Recitative (Peter, Jesus), Trio (Jesus, Peter, Seraph) with Chorus 6. Chorus of Angels.

During the summer of 1801 Beethoven was at Hetzendorf working on the *Mount of Olives* as well as the two Violin Sonatas Op. 23 and 24, the Pianoforte Sonatas Op. 26, 27, and 28, and the String Quintet in C Op. 29. He was eager to bring out another work of dramatic quality after the success of *Prometheus,* and it is possible that he may have made sketches for it as early as 1800. According to Unger and Kinsky the work was completed in March 1803 and written within a short time.

The *Mount of Olives* was composed to a text by Franz Xaver Huber, who was the author of *Die edle Rache,* music by Süssmayr, and the popular *Das unterbrochene Opferfest,* to Winter's music. In a letter of January 23, 1824, Beethoven relates that the words were written by himself, with the poet's assistance, "in a period of 14 days," and that since the poet was musical and had written much for music, he was able to discuss the work with Huber constantly.

The first performance of the oratorio occurred at the Theater an der Wien, April 5, 1803, the program on this occasion consisting of the First Symphony and three new works—the *Mount of Olives,* the Second Symphony, in D, and the Pianoforte Concerto in C minor, played by Beethoven himself. The *Mount of Olives* had an immediate popular success, attested by the fact that it received three other performances during that same year, in spite of severe critical strictures. The critics objected to the mixture of two styles, a series of operatic scenes with some items in a profoundly elevated style, but found some portions especially fine, and the music on the whole good. The general feeling was that Beethoven had shown that a composer of genius could make something even out of poor material. Beethoven himself was not entirely satisfied with the oratorio, as may be seen from the letter of August 26, 1804, to Breitkopf and Härtel, in which he says that the oratorio had not yet appeared because he had wished to change the score in several places and to add a chorus.

The *Mount of Olives* was not published for some years after its completion. Beethoven first offered the score to Breitkopf and Härtel in 1804 along with the *Eroica,* the Triple Concerto and three Pianoforte Sonatas, all for a fee of 2000 florins. The publishers found the price too high and at first refused the work. After Beethoven had offered it to several other publishers, and after much delay and correspondence about it, Breitkopf and Härtel finally bought it in October 1811. At this time Beethoven wrote the publishing firm saying "if there is anything remarkable about this oratorio, it is the fact that it is my first and earliest work of the kind, that it was written in a fortnight in the midst of continual tumult, anxiety and trouble (my brother was mortally ill at the time) . . . If I were to write an oratorio nowadays it would certainly be done very differently."

There is no record of further performance for the next eleven years. In 1814 Sir George Smart conducted ten performances of the work between February 25 and May 28 for the Lenten oratorios at Drury Lane. It was rendered into English by Arnold, then manager of the King's Theatre. Two other versions were made by Oliphant and Bartholomew respectively. In 1842 Dr. Hudson, of Dublin, made a modified version in which the story was changed to that of David, since there were some objections to the Saviour appearing as a personage in the theatre, and the title was changed to *Engedi.*

On November 16, 1815, the municipal council of Vienna conferred on Beethoven *Ehrenbürgerthum,* the freedom of the city. Perhaps as an expression of gratitude for this honor Beethoven gave a concert at the Redouten-Saal December 25, 1815, for the benefit of the Bürger Hospital. At this concert the *Mount of Olives* was performed, as well as his new Overture Op. 115 (*Namensfeier)* and *Meeresstille und glückliche Fahrt,* words by Goethe, for four solo voices and orchestra.

The renewed success of his oratorio perhaps brought about a desire to compose another, and Beethoven entered into correspondence with the Tonkünstler Societät and the Gesellschaft der Musikfreunde of Vienna regarding the proposed new work. The Gesellschaft der Musikfreunde showed great interest and agreed to accept any oratorio he might compose, leaving the subject and author of the text to his choice, and further voted him a payment of 300 gold ducats for the exclusive use of the oratorio for a period of one year. These negotiations continued until 1824—nine years—and then at last came to nothing.

Beethoven was never able to find a text that he felt was suitable. The typical oratorio text of his day was unable to inspire him, for he demanded greater profundity and spirituality. He considered many poems—among them H. J. v. Collin's *Zerstörung Jerusalems,* Kuffner's *Saul* and *Elemente,* and Bernard's *Sieg des Kreuzes.* This latter is generally thought to be the text he had in mind for his projected oratorio for the Handel and Haydn Society in Boston (see Entry: United States of America).

C. MacC.

Orchestra

Beethoven's orchestra was that which he had inherited from his predecessors. With the orchestra, as with all other phases of music, Beethoven's growth was not based on radical changes, but on the logical growth of concepts from the classic tradition. In the First Symphony Beethoven has employed a five-part string ensemble, doubled woodwinds (flute, oboe, clarinet and bassoon), two horns, two trumpets and two tympani. This is the orchestra which Haydn and Mozart employed in some of their last symphonies. As Carse has shown, the use of both oboes and clarinets was not common in the 18th century orchestra, and frequently the same player doubled on the two instruments. However, the electoral court at Bonn must have had players for each of the instruments, for the Cantata on the Death of Joseph II from 1790 uses the same orchestration which we have called the basic orchestra. Even when Beethoven made changes, it was simply an enlarging or reducing of the basic plan.

The most common change which Beethoven employs is an enlarging of the orchestra as in the Third and Ninth Symphonies, where the horns are increased to three. The woodwind section is given the additional support of the contrabassoon in the Fifth and Ninth Symphonies, and the piccolo in Symphony No. 6. Undoubtedly the most noteworthy addition is the introduction of three trombones into the symphony orchestra, as in the Fifth, Sixth and Ninth Symphonies. The trombones, which, until Beethoven's time, had been restricted to liturgical and dramatic use, naturally find a place in the *Leonore* and *Fidelio* overtures. In most of the overtures the brass section is further augmented by utilizing four horns. From this increased use of brass in the overtures (horns and trombones) it becomes obvious that for Beethoven the brass section represents dramatic force, and it is dramatic contrast which is such an outstanding characteristic of all phases of Beethoven's music. As we may expect, it is the brass section which is reduced when Beethoven desires less than the basic orchestra: the trumpets are omitted in slow and tranquil movements of the Second, Sixth, and Eighth Symphonies, while the only other reduction is the omission of one flute in the First and Fourth Symphonies.

The enlarging of the orchestra was not welcomed by all listeners of the period. A Critic of the *Allgemeine Musikalische Zeitung* in 1800 complained that the First Symphony sounded as though it were written more for a military band than for a symphony orchestra, and Spohr could not endure the "unmeaning noise" of the finale of the Fifth Symphony.

Not all the increase in sound was due to an increase in instruments, but rather to the way in which the instruments were treated as well as to a greater use of the woodwind section. It is this increase in importance of the woodwinds which is Beethoven's major advance over his predecessors. A study of the symphonies reveals a constant increase in the autonomy of the woodwind section. No longer do the woodwinds function only as a foil to the string section, or as a means of reinforcing the tone; they now participate independently in the thematic material and frequently show a complete equality with the strings. Nevertheless, the music is still conceived primarily as pure music and Beethoven uses the woodwinds more for a contrast of timbres than for a particular instrumental color. This is revealed more clearly when we observe that Beethoven generally treats the woodwinds as a homogeneous group rather than a collection of solo instruments. When the Romantic composer begins to conceive of the coloristic possibilities of the woodwinds, the section then becomes a group of solo instruments; however, in Beethoven's orchestra the individual woodwind instruments, like the individual strings parts, contribute to the whole.

Such a concept of instrumentation is carried over into the entire orchestra—it is an ensemble of instruments, each contributing its share to the over-all group. Here, perhaps, is the last vestige of the early Baroque orchestra which used those instruments which were at hand, specifying only soprano, alto, etc. Nevertheless, it is also the beginning of the Romantic orchestra, for when Beethoven employed the horns in the typical trio sections of the *scherzos*, and when he gave prominence to the tympani, he was indicating the possibilities of the individual instruments. F. T. W.

Organ and Organ playing

Beethoven had his first important contact with the organ in 1778 at the age of eight when he began keyboard lessons with the aged Bonn Court Organist, Van den Eeden. A fellow court musician and somewhat older contemporary of Ludwig van Beethoven, the composer's grandfather, Van den Eeden must have been pleased to train the grandson as his successor.

During 1780-81 after the death of Van den Eeden, Beethoven began studying the organ with Willibald Koch, a Franciscan known both as a performer and an expert organ builder. Soon he began assisting Friar Willibald, and playing 6 o'clock Mass for the Bonn Minorite Cloister, as well. The console of the latter instrument is now in the Beethoven Museum at Bonn. It was a moderate-sized instrument of three manuals, thirty-two stops and couplers, and a pedal range of twenty-six notes (*CC-d*). Beethoven made a note of the measurements of these pedals on the inside cover of one of his memoranda books. Tradition holds that Ludwig received instruction also from Hanzmann and Zensen. Of the latter, organist at the Münsterkirche in Bonn, the story is told that Ludwig composed some pieces which he could not play: when Zenser pointed this out to him, he replied, "I will when I am bigger."

Any immediate hopes that Johann van Beethoven may have had to see his son appointed successor to Van den Eeden were quenched when Christian

Gottlob Neefe got the appointment in October of 1779. Ludwig immediately established an association with this accomplished musician, and since Neefe's many enterprises made him often absent from the organ, Ludwig was made his assistant, at first unofficially, and later with a small salary of 150 *gulden* per year.

Franz Gerhard Wegeler tells the following anecdote of Beethoven's early years as assistant court organist. The young composer asked the singer, who sat with unusual firmness in the tonal saddle, if he would permit him to throw him out, and utilized the somewhat too readily granted permission to introduce so wide an excursion in the accompaniment while persistently striking the reciting note with his little finger, that the singer got so bewildered that he could not find the closing cadence. Father Ries, the first violinist, then Music Director of the Electoral Chapel, still living, tells with details how Kapellmeister Lucchesi, who was present, was astonished by Beethoven's playing. In his first access of rage Heller entered a complaint against Beethoven with the Elector, who commanded a simpler accompaniment, although the spirited and occasionally waggish young prince was amused at the occurrence. Schindler adds that Beethoven in his last years remembered the circumstance, and said that the Elector had "reprimanded him very graciously and forbidden such clever tricks in the future."

Beethoven wrote three works for organ, all dating from his youth. The first of these, a Two-voiced Fugue in D Major without opus number, may have been composed in 1783 as a demonstration of his skill when he applied for some salary in his work as assistant organist to the Bonn Court. This fugue is rather unexceptional in its regular succession of sets of two entries and an episode. As a constructional device Beethoven presents his subject twice at every degree of the scale of D major (except the seventh). (W o O. 31.)

The other organ works are Two Preludes through All the Major keys (*Zwei Praeludien durch alle Durtonarten*) composed in 1789 which did not appear until 1803 as Op. 39, Nos. 1 and 2. In both of these works are found the influence of Beethoven's study of the *Well Tempered Clavier:* in fact the title recalls the formal organization of that work. Both preludes are constructed on an ascending cycle of fifths (No. 2 actually completes the cycle twice). Beethoven's indications of dynamics, though sparse, are used to emphasize the structure of the preludes. There is no doubt that they could have been easily performed on the three-manual Minorite organ mentioned above. The arpeggios in these pieces, which some writers have described as "unorganistic," are not infrequently indicated in organ music of this period and earlier (as a notable example, cf. J. S. Bach's *Toccata and Fugue in D Minor*). (Cf. also Th.-R. I; Schiedermair: *Der junge Beethoven.*)

W. I.

Orthography

Beethoven was rather careless in his orthography when writing letters and diaries; granted, there did not exist a standardized orthography in his time. His inconsistency in writing goes even as far as his own name. Only after 1816 did he spell his name correctly. A glance through his Conversation-books shows that the famous saying of the philosopher Kant "Das moralische Gesez in unnss u. der gestirnte Himmel über unss," contains three mistakes. Much might be attributed to the fact that Beethoven, in spite of his deafness, had an aural and not a visual memory. Another factor reflected in his orthography is that Beethoven mixed his native Rhenish dialect with the Viennese colloquial language.

Overtures

Beethoven's approach to the overture is the approach of the dramatic symphonist. The essence of drama which permeates his symphonies is nowhere more apparent than in the overtures. For Beethoven the drama is the overture; here the spiritual forces which permeate the drama can be distilled out of the characters and presented in their metaphysical state. The elemental powers of human passion which ebb and flow, clash, and are resolved, need no characters for their portrayal—the characters are replaced by the master's imagination and the power of his will.

Beethoven was not the first to make the overture something more than a mere introduction, but he was the first to conceive the necessity for making the dramatic logic dictate the inner form of the work. This idea did not come suddenly or easily; he arrived at his plan only after much experimentation, for each work required its own peculiar form.

The first of his overtures, that for the ballet *Prometheus,* is little more than the traditional type of overture which treats material from the drama in a more or less formalistic manner. Only the more obvious contrasts between Prometheus and the creatures appears in the overture, but without the dramatic strife of underlying spiritual forces which they stimulate.

The three *Leonore* overtures, which are discussed more thoroughly in the article on *Fidelio,* portray most graphically Beethoven's struggles with his concept for the overture. *Leonore* No. 1, which he later called a *characteristische Ouvertüre,* is planned on lines similar to those of *Prometheus,* with the two contrasting moods of the drama appearing as the basis of a prelude and allegro. The spiritual values and dramatic possibilities of the great calamity which befalls the two principal characters appear only in the *Leonore No. 2.* Here the concept of the overture, as the condensation of the dramatic problems of the opera, finds realization, but a realization almost too concise—too abstract —to be completely grasped by the listener. Complete consummation does not come until Beethoven combines the dramatic pregnancy with the symphonic logic of sonata-allegro form in *Leonore* No. 3.

This type of overture finds its most happy fulfillment in the *Coriolanus* and *Egmont* overtures. Here Beethoven was not concerned with the play to follow—he was completely free to present the drama in its most concise state, to portray the spiritual and human values in their most abstract form.

Although there may have been outside influences which prompted the overture to *Coriolanus,* there can be little doubt that it was the elemental power of human passions which attracted Beethoven. The MS of the overture bears the date 1807 in Beethoven's own hand, while Heinrich J. von Collin's play was first performed in 1802. In the year 1807 the play had only a single performance, and, as Thayer has shown, the overture was not performed on this occasion. Thayer suggests further that Beethoven, who knew Collin, was prompted by a need for a new concert overture, and, because the play was well-known, and possibly because Collin was highly placed in official circles, decided to strengthen the friendship by composing an overture on Collin's play. Beethoven has faithfully mirrored the characters of Collin's drama in the two contrasting themes, but it is the struggle of man against society which forms the core of the idea which inspires the overture. The work was first performed at two concerts in March of 1807, and published a year later by the Kunst und Industrie Comptoir as Op. 62.

The overture which forms a companion piece to *Coriolanus* is that written for a performance of Goethe's *Egmont* in 1810. It was commissioned by the theater director Hartl (Beethoven said he wrote it out of love for Goethe's play) and Beethoven proved a fortunate choice, for the figure of Egmont, like the figure of Coriolanus, concerned itself with abstract traits of character. The integrity and heroism of Egmont inspired Beethoven to some of his greatest music, particularly in the sudden changes of mood in the final pages. The overture is one of ten numbers which Beethoven composed as incidental music for the play, and it is the only one of the group which has found a place in the concert repertoire of today. The overture was published in 1810 as Op. 84.

The performance of the *Egmont* music in connection with the drama at the Hofburg Theatre in 1811 seems to have stimulated a further commission. The incidental music to two plays by August von Kotzebue, *Die Ruinen von Athen,* and *König Stephan, oder Ungarns Erster Wohltäter,* was written for the opening of the theater in Pest on February 9, 1812. Both works were composed in 1811 and in both cases it is the overture which has proven the most lasting. Neither of the overtures can be classed among his best music, and when these, along with the *Overture in C,* were sent to the Royal Philharmonic Society in 1816 as being "new compositions written expressly for the society," the works were played through and then laid aside. Such a fate is understandable, for they are no more than arrangements of motives from the other numbers of the plays. Beethoven himself called the overture to the *Ruins of Athens* a "little recreation piece." The overture to the *Ruins of Athens,* Op. 113, was published in 1823; the *King Stephen Overture* in 1826 as Op. 117.

In 1814 Beethoven produced another overture, Op. 115 in C, the autograph of which bears the inscription, "in the first vintage month 1814, in the evening on the name day of our Kaiser." This inscription has resulted in the name *Namensfeier Ouvertüre,* although there is no indication that the work was intended for this purpose. Beethoven has himself indicated the purpose of the overture on the first sketch, "Overture for any occasion—or for use at a concert." Certainly the festive character of the piece makes it applicable as a concert overture, although the dramatic intensity which we have come to expect from Beethoven is lacking. The work was first performed at a benefit concert on Christmas Day of 1815, the other works on the program being the little cantata *Meeresstille und Glückliche Fahrt,* and the oratorio *Christus am Ölberg.* Publication was delayed until 1825 when it appeared with a dedication to Prince Anton Heinrich Radziwill.

Beethoven's last overture was written in 1822 as part of the incidental music for *Die Weihe des Hauses* (*The Consecration of the House*). According to Schindler the work on the overture was begun at Baden in July of 1822; however, in that year Beethoven did not go to Baden until September and it must have been after this month that work was actually begun. Just as with the Kreutzer Sonata, the music was not completed until the day of the performance; in fact, some of the early arrivals were already in their seats while the orchestra was still having its first reading of the overture.

The music itself shows a very skilful handling of the material, especially the fugal *allegro* with its motivic theme. Perhaps what is missing is the dramatic power of the *Egmont* overture or the Ninth Symphony. This *Consecration* overture is the work which, with the *Missa Solemnis,* interrupted the composition of the Ninth Symphony. This overture and a large part of the mass appeared on the same program which introduced the Ninth Symphony to the public.

The overture was first offered to Steiner for publication and then to Diabelli. It was finally published by Schott in 1825 as Op. 124, dedicated to Prince Galitzin.

The most productive period of Beethoven's overture output seems to have occurred during the middle of his life. The first two overtures, *Prometheus* and *Leonore* No. 1, while fulfilling their purpose as introductions to a musical drama, are not equal in quality to the works which appeared between the years 1805 and 1810. These five years saw the production of the 2nd and 3rd *Leonore* overtures, *Coriolanus* and *Egmont.* The overtures composed after 1810, with the exception of the *Consecration of the House,* are inferior both in skill and inspiration. It is interesting to observe that, of the four overtures written between 1805 and 1810, three of them are in the key of C, and the only worthwhile overture of the later years is again in the key of C. (For further information see Entry: Incidental Music.)

F.T.W.

P

Pachler, Marie Leopoldine

née Koschak, b. Graz 1794, d. there 1855. Pianist. An enthusiastic admirer of Beethoven. She was considered for some time to be the Immortal Beloved, a rumor disproved by Marie Pachler's son, Faustus Pachler, in his study: *Beethoven und Marie Pachler Koschak,* Berlin 1865. Dr. Anton Pachler, Marie's brother-in-law, came to Vienna in 1816, where he presented to Beethoven a piano fantasy written by Marie. Beethoven did not quite agree with the composition. In 1817 Marie went to Vienna, where she met Beethoven in person. In one of Beethoven's Conversation-books we read: "I never met anybody who performed my piano compositions as well as you did. . . ." When Marie's husband, Karl Pachler, came to Vienna (1817) he invited Beethoven to come to Graz. The Master even considered accepting the invitation. He met Marie again in 1823, after she had been to the spas at Baden. In Vöslau near Baden, he presented her with a "Musical Farewell," as a souvenir, containing the theme of the canon *Das Schöne zum Guten.* This fact is reported by Marie Pachler to her friend Prof. Schneller in Graz, who himself was a great Beethoven admirer. She mentioned in this letter that she found the Master in failing health. Some of Beethoven's friends in Graz belonged to the Ludlamshöhle (cf. Entry: Castelli), as stated in a letter of J. B. Jenger to Marie Pachler. From this we learn that Beethoven was in a desperate condition of health (December 29, 1826). The Pachlers were also well acquainted with Schubert. (Cf. Th.-R. III, IV, V; Wurzbach.)

Paer, Ferdinando

b. Parma 1771, d. Paris 1839. Composer, pupil of Fortunati and Ghiretti. His career as a composer is characterized by 43 operas, his style influenced by Mozart's masterpieces. *Camilla* (1799) is considered his best opera. He succeeded Naumann in Dresden as Court Kapellmeister. In 1807 he went to Paris, became Maître de Chapelle to Napoleon and conductor of the Opéra-comique. In 1812 he succeeded Spontini at the Italian Opera in Paris, with Rossini as his colleague; he resigned from his post in 1827. Paër only lived very briefly in Vienna, where his wife, Signora Ricardi, was an operatic singer (1802-1803). In Dresden he composed his opera *Leonor,* wich was performed there October 3, 1804, and somewhat later in Vienna.

In Rossini's circle there was a rumor that Beethoven had received the impetus for his *Fidelio* from Paër's opera. This rumor was denied in an article by Leopold Sonnleithner: "Beethoven and Paër." (Rezension und Mitteilungen über "Theater und Musik" Bd. VI 1860.) From this article we hear a malicious anecdote, told by Ferdinand Hiller to Berlioz, printed in the *Journal des Débats:* Beethoven, seeing Paër's *Leonora* in the Theater an der Josephstadt exclaimed: "*Que c'est beau, que c'est intéressant. Il faut que je compose cela.*" Paër was very proud that he might have stimulated the idea of *Fidelio,* but it has been fully proven that Beethoven's *Fidelio* was composed entirely independently. The funeral march of Beethoven's Sonata Opus 26 was also somehow connected with Paër. According to Ries, Beethoven added this movement after having heard Paër's *Achille.* This is another rumor, as the opera was performed July 6, 1801, a long time after Beethoven had sketched his movement. Paër's C minor theme of the funeral march has very little to do with Beethoven's music. (Cf. Th.-R. II; Frimmel: *Beethoven Handbuch;* Eric Blom: *New Ways and Means,* 1932.)

Palffy de Erdöd, Graf Ferdinand

b. Vienna 1774, d. there 1840. Promoter of art and science. When Baron Braun resigned in 1806 as head of the court theaters, a number of aristocrats such as the Princes Lobkowitz, Schwarzenberg, Esterhazy, and the Counts Esterhazy, Lodron, Zichy and Ferdinand Palffy became directors of the Burgtheater, while Lobkowitz headed the opera. In 1811 they were also put in charge of the Kärntnerthor and the Theater an der Wien. After Lobkowitz's bankruptcy, Palffy bought the Theater an der Wien (1813), which flourished considerably under his direction until 1825. During this period various operas were performed, among them Schubert's *Zauberharfe* and *Rosamunde.* He appointed the composers Seyfried, Roser, and Riotte, the tenors Jäger, Haitzinger, Wild, the buffo Spitzeder and introduced the famous Children's Ballet with Fanny and Therese Elssler, Angioletta Mayer and Therese Heberle. Palffy never favored Beethoven and a certain animosity prevented their closer cooperation. It was a Count "P....." (Palffy), who, according to Ries, was "honored" by Beethoven's classical remark "*Für solche Schweine spiele ich nicht,*" when Palffy disturbed him by a long conversation. On the other hand, Palffy overpaid two tickets for the Bridgetower concert (May 1803) when the violinist played Beethoven's Kreutzer Sonata. When Beethoven was to give a concert in November 1814 in the Redoutensaal, an unpleasant correspondence between the composer and Palffy took place, because of Palffy's financial pressure on Beethoven. The concert had to be postponed and Palffy was blamed by the courts. (Cf. Th.-R. III; Wurzbach; Rommel: *Die Altwiener Volkskomödie;* and Frimmel: *Beethoven Studien* II, p. 41.)

Paraquin, Johann Baptist

See Entry: Copyists.

Pasqualati, Johann Baptiste, Baron Osterberg

b. 1777, d. 1830. His younger brother

was Joseph Pasqualati. Both were music lovers and on friendly terms with Beethoven; the Master lived frequently in their house on Mölkerbastei (1804-1815). Johann was imperial Hofagent and belonged to the Krainischer Landstand (Yugoslavia). Both brothers were pianists; Joseph was also a composer. Beethoven consulted Pasqualati often in financial matters; when difficulties arose about his pension from Lobkowitz and Kinsky, the Master had authorized Pasqualati to cash the pension for him. Breuning in his book *Aus dem Schwarzspanierhaus* told the story, confirmed by the Pasqualati family tradition, that Beethoven once ordered a mason to break through the wall of the palace, in order to build an extra window for him. In the summer of 1814 Beethoven composed his *Elegischer Gesang* Op. 118 and dedicated it to the Baron in memory of Johann's wife Eleonora, née von Fritsch, who had died August 23, 1811. The revised copy of the composition carried Beethoven's inscription: *"An die verklärte Gemahlin meines verehrten Freundes Pasqualati von Seinem Freunde Ludwig van Beethoven;"* the poet of this composition (*Sanft wie du lebtest, hast du vollendet*) is unknown. The chorus is reminiscent in the saraband-like rhythm of the slow movement of the Trio Op. 97 and deserves a revival. Beethoven also wrote for Pasqualati the canon *Glück zum neuen Jahre.* A copy of it, written by Diabelli, bears the inscription: *"Canon, am ersten Tage des Jahres 1815 bey Bar. V. Pasqualati geschrieben und ihm gewidmet von Lud. van Beethoven."* After 1815 Beethoven left the Pasqualati palace for good, but continued his friendly relations. At the time of the Master's final sickness the Baron looked after him and sent him fruit, wine, and champagne (cf. Wurzbach; Th.-R. III-V).

Pechatschek, Franz

b. Vienna 1793, d. Karlsruhe 1840. Violinist; son of Franz Pechatschek (1763-1816), who was also a violinist and composer, writing especially dance music. The younger Pechatschek was a child prodigy, who concertized at the age of ten before the Austrian Court. After studying with E. A. Förster he worked as a second conductor at the Theater an der Wien. In 1818 he became concertmaster with the orchestra in Hanover, and toured subsequently in Germany and France. Pechatschek was an excellent violinist with pure intonation and sweet tone who excelled in graceful playing. He was well acquainted with Beethoven, as seen in a letter from the Master to his nephew Karl. Beethoven mentioned in this letter that he had met some musicians, including Pechatschek, at the station at Wiener Neudorf. In the Conversation-book of 1819 (December 12-25) Oliva remarked that Pechatschek had received 2000 gulden for a concert which had not been satisfactory at all. The violinist had played variations on a vulgar theme in the style of Hummel. He had some talent, but played without taste. (Cf. Wurzbach; Hanslick: *Geschichte des Concertwesens in Wien;* Th.-R. V. Rob., Haas in Mozart Jb. 1954.)

Penzing

Suburb of Vienna, located on the river Wien. Beethoven lived there for a short time in 1824 in the house of the tailor Johann Hörr. Breuning mentions another house in which Beethoven lived at that time: 62 Parkgasse, called the "Hadikschlössl" (cf. Th.-R. V, p. 100).

Peters

Publishing company in Leipzig, named after the Leipzig bookseller Carl Friedrich Peters who died 1827. Predecessor of the firm was the Bureau de Musique, founded by Franz Anton Hoffmeister and Ambrosius Kühnel. Beethoven had already had connections with Hoffmeister, when the latter had lived in Vienna as a book seller. The Eight Variations in F major on a theme *"Tändeln und Scherzen"* from Süssmayer's opera *Soliman II,* dedicated to the Countess Browne, were published there in December 1799. Hoffmeister and Kühnel published Beethoven's Op. 19-22, the Second Piano Concerto in B flat major, the Septet, the First Symphony and the B flat major Piano Sonata. After Hoffmeister's death (1813), Carl Friedrich Peters bought the firm, running it under the name Bureau de Musique von C. F. Peters. Peters had been in correspondence with Beethoven since May 18, 1822, but no agreement was reached, and a down payment by the firm to the Master was returned to Peters in December, 1825.

Peters, Karl

Educator in the house of Prince Lobkowitz. Together with Karl Bernard and Herr and Frau von Janitschek, he belonged to the intimate circle of Beethoven after 1816. Hofrat Peters has been immortalized by Beethoven in the canons dedicated to him: *Sankt Petrus ist ein Fels* and *Bernardus ist ein Sankt.* Many times Peters conversed with the Master on behalf of the nephew Karl and in 1820 he was made co-guardian of the boy (cf. Entry: Nephew.) In one of the Conversation-books we read: "Peters is one of the finest people" and Kanne jotted down: "Peters is limited, but good." Schindler remarked in the same Conversation-book: "Hofrat Peters is talkative, but he means well." It may be assumed that Beethoven spent many pleasant hours with him. Jokingly Peters wrote down: "The girl in the tavern Die Birne was not bad at all; I am going to procure her for you." At another time Bernard improvised a drinking song in reference to the abovementioned canon; Bernard's words were: *"Sankt Petrus ist kein Fels, auf ihn kann man nicht bauen, Bernardus war ein Sankt, der hatte sich gewaschen, er hat der Hölle nicht gewankt und nicht 10,000 Flaschen."* And Peters added: "It is a pity about your canon, maybe it's blurred already. It might have immortalized me." (Cf. Th.-R. IV, V; Schünemann: *Ludwig van Beethovens Konversationshefte,* vol. I, p. 134, 136, 183, etc.)

Pfeifer (Pfeiffer), Tobias Friedrich

Musician and actor, who taught young Ludwig keyboard playing for a short time in Bonn while he lived with the Beethoven family (1779-1780). He was a flute player, and Ludwig liked to accompany him. Of unstable character, Pfeiffer was fired from Grossmann's theatrical troupe in Frankfurt (1783) because of disorderly and sloppy behavior. The Fischer Manuscript overrates his importance considerably. (Cf. Schiedermair; Th.-R. I.)

Philharmonic Society, Boston

This Society ordered an oratorio from Beethoven in 1822. (See also Entry: United States.)

Philharmonic Society, Laibach

See Entry: Laibach.

Philharmonic Society, London

This Society was founded in London 1813 for the encouragement of orchestral and instrumental music. Through Ries, Salomon, and Georges Smart, Beethoven came in connection with that institution; the following musicians, friends, and acquaintances of the Master were members: M. Clementi, C. Neate, Bridgetower and R. Potter. In 1813 three symphonies and the septet were performed, in 1814 the *Eroica,* in 1816 the Fifth Symphony, the next year the *Fidelio* overture and Seventh Symphony, in 1823 *Die Weihe des Hauses,* in 1824 the Piano Concerto in C minor, and in 1825 the Choral Symphony. However, the *Ruinen von Athen* and the overture *König Stephan* were not permitted for performance in 1816. In 1822 and 1824 the Society had asked Beethoven to compose a symphony and come for a visit to London. The invitation was extended to the Master in a letter by Neate, dated December 1824. Beethoven considered this trip seriously, but it was never realized. The London Society was extremely generous when they learned that Beethoven was very ill. Moscheles and Stumpf acted as intermediaries. 100 pounds sterling were sent to Vienna, and the money was paid by the Eskeles firm by their Hofmeister (family educator), Heribert Rau. In his delirious fantasies Beethoven sketched some parts of a tenth symphony for the society. (Cf. Grove; Th.-R. V.)

Piano Sonatas

In order to follow Beethoven through all phases of his development, no form gives more or better information than his piano sonatas. From his early attempts up to the compositions of his later life, with the exception of the very last years which were devoted to the late quartets, the piano sonatas outnumber all other forms. This fact can be easily understood when one considers that Beethoven wrote them for his own use as one of the most outstanding performers of his time. Trained from early childhood, he received even as a young boy the greatest praise for his perfection as a piano player. It is understandable that the first printed works offered to the public were three piano sonatas. These sonatas, E flat major, F minor, and D major, were published in 1783, and dedicated to the "Most worthy Archbishop and Prince Elector of Cologne, Maximilian Friedrich." Whether Beethoven was aware of his mistake in giving his age incorrectly as eleven, or whether he was purposely misled by his father, is of no importance. The sonatas show clearly the training Beethoven had received from his excellent teacher Neefe, who introduced him to the works of Sebastian Bach as well as to the sonatas of Bach's sons, Carl Philipp Emanuel and Johann Christian. These influences can be traced even in Beethoven's later sonatas. (W o O. 47.)

Some doubts exist about the authenticity of the two sonatinas in G major and F major, published after Beethoven's death; there is also an uncertainty about another early sonata in C, that is whether Beethoven composed it while still in Bonn, or later in Vienna in 1796, as is generally accepted. Still another sonata movement which Beethoven wrote for his friend Franz Wegeler in 1785 was published recently in G. Henle's edition of the piano pieces. The sonatas in G and F were published in Hamburg by Böhme; the one in C by Dunst in Frankfurt, 1830.

The acquaintance with the works of Mozart and Haydn in the last six years of his residence in Bonn, and during his first short visit to Mozart in Vienna in 1787, brought new ideas to Beethoven's writing. A big step forward is shown in the three Piano Quartets, E flat, D, and C, which were completed in Bonn. The quartets, composed probably around 1785-86, show clearly the influence of Mozart; the one in E flat even takes Mozart's Violin Sonata in G (KV, 379) as a strict model, as Ludwig Schiedermair in *Der junge Beethoven* has convincingly proved. Mozart's sonata was published in 1781. Likewise Mozart's Quintet for piano and wind instruments, published 1784, which Mozart himself regarded as one of his best compositions, inspired the young Beethoven to his work for the E flat Quartet scored for the same instruments.

The piano quartets act as a bridge to the next set of piano sonatas, which were written after he moved to Vienna. How highly Beethoven thought of those quartets is shown by the fact that he has used parts of them in the second movement of the F minor Sonata, and in the G minor transition part of the third sonata in C major. The quartets, in spite of their great dramatic effects, so typical of Beethoven's writing, are still influenced by their models; the Piano Sonatas Op. 2 present Beethoven in all his originality and greatness—a mighty beginning foreshadowing all phases of his later development. Composed in 1795 and published in 1796 by Artaria, these Op. 2 sonatas are dedicated to Beethoven's teacher in Vienna, Joseph Haydn. This dedication is more than a formality or expression of thanks and friendship; in this case it can be understood almost as a motto, even as an explanation for many features in the working out of the sonata form. It appears as though Beethoven wanted to prove to Haydn his own achievement and mastery. This mastery is revealed in the varied character of the sonatas, in the dramatic element in the first F minor, the more lyric character in the A major, and the concert-type of virtuosity revealed in the third sonata in C major. How assiduously Beethoven worked toward the goal of artistic independence can be proven by a sketch of the F minor Sonata preserved in the library of the Society of Friends of Music in Vienna. The sketch shows that, under the influence of the F minor Sonata by Emanuel Bach, Beethoven treated the first theme in a traditional manner, with no trace of the unique and courageous idea of introducing the "consequent" in C minor. The second and third sonatas replace the *minuet* with a *scherzo.* The *rondo* of No. 2 was one of Beethoven's favorite pieces. The C major Sonata gives a clear picture of Beethoven's ability as a virtuoso and reflects his manner of improvising. In spite of all the great achievements in the Op. 2 sonata there is some unevenness in the value of the individual movements, especially the last movement of the F minor, which seems to be especially weaker than the first movement. The same is true of the *largo* of No. 2, and even the *scherzo* in No. 3.

The Sonata Op. 7 in E flat, dedicated to the Countess Babette von Keglevics, was written in 1796-97 and published in 1797 by Artaria. Czerny states that Beethoven wrote the sonata *"in passionierter Stimmung,"* and this fact is reflected throughout the four movements. Because of the balance and the perfection of every movement, Op. 7 is the first great and complete masterpiece. Here are found the mysterious surprises of the great Beethoven, for instance: the C major part in the first movement, the striking and deceiving attempt of a recapitulation in B flat in the C major *largo,* and a similar effect in the coda of the *rondo.* Even more important seems to be Beethoven's attempt to bring more coherence and connection to the *scherzo,* here called simply *allegro,* and to the *rondo* form. The *rondo* of Op. 7 may be taken as a paradigm for this form, and its perfection has never been surpassed, not even by the beautiful *rondo* of the Op. 22, which added still more original features to the form.

Op. 10 also contains three sonatas, C minor, F major and D major, and again one can recognize the contrasting character of each sonata as observed in Op. 2. Dedicated to the Countess Anna Margarete von Browne, the sonatas were published in 1798 by Joseph Eder, Vienna. The sketches (cf. Nottebohm, *Beethoveniana* II, 29ff.) indicate Beethoven's slow-working procedures, his way of starting in one fashion and entirely transforming the idea during its progress; the original beginning of the first movement of No. 3 is a fine example (Nottebohm, page 35). How highly Beethoven regarded his Op. 10, may be seen in a remark to Schindler as late as 1823. If Schindler can be trusted in his reports, Beethoven said of the *largo e mesto* of the D major Sonata that the movement expressed the "state of a melancholy man, with all the various nuances of light and shade that make up the picture of melancholy."

The *Sonate pathétique* Op. 13, C minor, even today retains its magnetic effect and demoniac power. The sonata was published in 1799 (Joseph Eder, Vienna) and its influence on Beethoven's contemporaries might be understood from some contemporary reports. For instance, it has been told that Ignaz Moscheles, when he was 10 years old (1804), copied the sonata for himself and was aroused to an adoration which he retained through his entire life. The report about Beethoven's way of playing this sonata deserves to be mentioned: "What the *Sonate pathétique* became under Beethoven's hands, one had to hear over and over again, in order to recognize that it was the same piece one had known before." Entirely new in this sonata was the dramatic introduction, and it is connected with the following *allegro* in such a dynamic way that it had to be partly repeated before the development section, and again before the very end. The treatment of the second theme, in E flat minor, contributed to the dark and stormy character. It might be mentioned that the *adagio* is written in *rondo* form, an unusual procedure which proves how interested Beethoven was in showing the new possibilities of this form. Op. 13 was dedicated to one of Beethoven's important supporters, Prince Carl von Lichnowsky. We enter quite a different world when we turn to the twin sonatas Op. 14 in E major and G major; both were published by Mollo & Co. in the same year as the Op. 13, and were dedicated to the Baronin Josefa von Braun. The highly idyllic character of both sonatas is quite obvious. The first one has only three movements with the slow movement being replaced by a scherzo-like *allegretto* in E minor. The first sketch to the first movement shows some indication that Beethoven conceived the idea of this movement as a string quartet (*Beethoveniana* II p. 45). It is not a mere coincidence that Beethoven later transcribed this sonata for string quartet, changing the key to F major—the only transcription of this kind Beethoven ever made. Schindler, in his biography of Beethoven (Münster, 1840) gives a description of Beethoven's playing of the sonatas Op. 14, pointing out the various nuances according to the musical content (cf. Heinrich Schenker's instructive comment in *Der Dreiklang* ed. Oswald Jonas, Vienna 1938). Referring to the sonata in B flat major Op. 22, Beethoven wrote to Hoffmeister in April 1802: "My sonata is beautifully printed, but it has taken a jolly long time." The sonata was composed around 1800 and published in 1802 by Hoffmeister & Kühnel, dedicated to Count Johann von Browne. The sonata shows a decisive step forward in the master's technique of writing. Beethoven himself took great pride in it: "*die Sonate hat sich gewaschen.*" Its fluency and especially the way the passagework is animated and interwoven into the texture foreshadow Beethoven's later technique in Op. 78, 81a, etc. This is true not only for the first movement but also for the *rondo,* a form difficult to treat in such a way.

Whether or not Beethoven was inspired by Mozart's Sonata in A major when he started his next sonata with a set of variations, cannot be decided. The Sonata Op. 26 in A flat major was composed in 1800-01 and published by Jean Cappi (1802) with a dedication to the Prince von Lichnowsky. The "Marcia funebre sulla morte d'un Eroe" was written after hearing a funeral march composed by F. Paër (?), and the last movement supposedly after being impressed by Cramer's playing in Vienna and by Cramer's three sonatas published at that time. It is well known that Beethoven esteemed Cramer as a pianist as well as a composer of etudes; he even wanted to edit a collection of Cramer's etudes with some commentary; the attempt in its embryonic stage was published later by Shedlock. It should be mentioned that the funeral march was orchestrated (transposed to B minor) by Beethoven himself for the play *Eleonore Prohaska* (1815/16).

As in his Op. 26, so in the two sonatas Op. 27 Beethoven avoided beginning with a movement in sonata form. Apparently he felt that he had to justify this treatment by adding "*Quasi una fantasia*" to the sonata title. Both sonatas—E flat and C sharp minor—were published in 1802 by Cappi, the first one dedicated to the Prince von Liechtenstein, the second one to the Countess Giulietta Guicciardi. The myth about the C sharp minor sonata might well be ignored; the beautiful improvisation of the three-part form in the first movement has unfortunately been neglected because of too much talk about the moonlight involved. Also apparent is the fact that in both sonatas the last movements are much more extended than the finales of the preceding sonatas, especially the finale of No. 2, which is presented in a highly dramatic sonata form.

The idyllic character of the Sonata in D major, Op. 28, has been recognized by the adoption of the title *Pastorale Sonata.* Composed in 1801 and published in 1802 at the Bureau d'arts et d'industrie, the sonata is dedicated to Joseph von Sonnenfels. The first movement shows still more progress in Beethoven's desire to bring the formal sections into closer relationship; the ingenious way in which Beethoven introduced the second theme is of extraordinary beauty. The *andante* D minor 2/4 was for a long while Beethoven's favorite piece. According to Czerny, he played it often for himself. "About the year 1803 Beethoven said to his friend Krumpholz: 'I am not satisfied with my works up to this time. From now I will try a different path.' Soon after this the three Sonatas Op. 31 were published" (from Czerny's recollections).

The three Sonatas Op. 31, G major, D minor, E flat major, were not published at the same time—the first and second were first published without opus number by Nägeli in the collection *Repertoire des Clavecinists,* next by Simrock in Bonn, and later by Cappi with the opus number 29; No. 3 was published without dedication. Some new features in these sonatas may be easily discovered. In No. 1, the second theme appears in B major instead of the usual dominant D, a device Beethoven employed later in the C major Sonata Op. 53, and which became common in Schubert's treatment of sonata form. Further evidence of this is found in No. 2, with the startling beginning in the midst of the cadence with all its consequences for the recapitulation. Finally the grand improvisation of No. 2: the unique structure of the antecedent (bars 1-18) within the dominant and consequent on the tonic, moving into the second theme on the minor dominant but starting too on the auxiliary dominant, the ghostly recitative in the recapitulation, features previously unheard in the sonata writing. The sketch to this movement shows the whole outline of the form.

The two "easy" sonatas or sonatinas Op. 49 in G minor and G major, published in 1805, were written many years before, probably in 1795/96. The *tempo di menuetto* of the second was already known from the Septet Op. 20.

In the C major Sonata Op. 53, published in 1805 and dedicated to Count Ferdinand von Waldstein, Beethoven again employed the virtuoso element (similar to the C major Op. 2 No. 3). It is certainly significant that among the sketches are found exercises in the form of various scales. In the first movement as well as in the *rondo* Beethoven tried an extension of such length that the second movement of the same length had to be replaced by a much shorter one, a mere introduction to the *rondo.* To enrich the sonata form by extending the length was a specific trend in Beethoven's compositions at that time; see for instance the "Kreutzer" Sonata Op.

47 and the "Eroica" Op. 55. In the "Waldstein," Beethoven introduced the second theme on the major chord of the mediant (as in the Op. 31/1), thereby prolonging the modulation to the dominant.

The virtuoso element was also employed in Op. 54, F major: for instance, the rather difficult octave passages in the first movement (*tempo di menuetto*) similar to the ones in the *"Andante favori"*, a work which was supposed to be the second movement of Op. 53. The Sonata Op. 54, published in 1806, contains only two movements, similar to the later sonatas, Op. 78, Op. 90, and Op. 111. The second movement, *allegretto,* is reminiscent of Scarlatti.

The next sonata, in F minor Op. 57, represents a climax in Beethoven's sonata writing. Composed about 1804 (the first sketches appear in the sketchbook to *Fidelio),* it was not published until 1807; the sonata is dedicated to Count Franz von Brunswick. In addition to the tendency towards extension and brilliant writing, the sonata reveals another attempt to unify the sonata as a whole, for the three movements are strongly linked to each other. Also unique is Beethoven's masterful treatment of the variation form in the second movement, *andante con moto.* Here the master combines the growth of figuration with a general ascent through the various registers. Until he composed the Sonata Op. 106, Beethoven regarded the Op. 57 as his greatest achievement in sonata writing.

It was a quite natural reaction for the experimenter Beethoven to turn to the opposite extreme in exploring the possibilities of sonata writing. The Sonata in F sharp major Op. 78, as well as the Op. 81a in E flat show the utmost contraction in their structure. Op. 78, dedicated to the Countess Therese von Brunswick, was published in 1810 by Breitkopf. Beethoven offered to Breitkopf both this sonata and the *Sonate facile ou Sonatine* in G major, thinking that both sonatas could be published together. For the first time since the *Sonate Pathétique* Beethoven begins with an introduction in both sonatas. In the Op. 78 he prepared the first theme, while in the second one the introduction takes part in depicting the moment of departure. Beethoven wrote the Op. 81a to commemorate the departure of his friend and devoted pupil, the Archduke Rudolph. This is the only sonata showing programmatic tendencies: *"Abschied (Lebewohl) - Abwesenheit - Wiedersehen."* Because of this program Beethoven himself called it a "characteristic sonata." Here Beethoven provides unity to the whole sonata by expressing the program through the musical structure. The "Farewell" in E flat, the "Absence" in the more remote minor keys of C and F minor, and the "Return" over the dominant seventh to E flat shows that the whole sonata is built on a large cadence: I - VI - II- V - I.

The Sonata Op. 90 in E minor was published in 1815 by S. A. Steiner, and is dedicated to the Count Moritz von Lichnowsky. Like the Op. 111, this sonata contains only two movements, and for this reason the two movements are in sharp contrast to each other: the first one is in minor, the second in major. According to Schindler the sonata gives a description of a love-affair of Count Moritz Lichnowsky with his second wife. The technique of interlocking the parts of a sonata form by using smaller motifs, as in Op. 81a, is again employed in the Op. 90. At the same time, Beethoven introduced more lyricism (Op. 101, 109, and 110). This ability to introduce a lyric element without endangering the dramatic drive of the music demonstrates one of the greatest achievements of the late Beethoven, and shows him at the summit of his art. His ability to transform simple repetitions into lyrical phrases, as in the bars 9-16 in Op. 90, or in the bars 5-11 in Op. 110, is unique. This new technique has been the cause of so much misunderstanding concerning Beethoven's treatment of form in his late sonatas.

The sonata Op. 101, dedicated to one of Beethoven's favorite pupils, the Freiin Dorothea von Ertmann, was published in 1817 by Steiner. The first movement is probably the shortest one Beethoven ever wrote; still it shows all the different sections of the form, but here interlocked and interwoven, held together by a beautiful lyric mood. The *scherzo* is replaced by a *vivace alla marcia* in 4/4 which, in its characteristic rhythm, anticipates Schumann. This movement brings a new device, the use of the old contrapuntal form, into the realm of the sonatas. Here in the trio he introduced a canon, while in the development section of the last movement he used the fugue. It is clear that this procedure also brought some change in the pianistic approach, because the increased range of Beethoven's keyboard instruments allowed a different contrapuntal treatment in spacing and doubling. Even today some movements such as the fugue of Op. 106 or the fugue of the cello sonata Op. 102 in D major, bring difficult problems to the performer. In 1816 Beethoven wrote to Tobias Haslinger in regard to Op. 101: "Some people are worrying me about the sonata being so difficult to play; who can help writing such difficulties. . . ."

In this limited space it is impossible to discuss fully the great Sonata Op. 106 in B flat major. Beethoven began to compose the sonata in 1817 but it was not published until September 1819, by Artaria, dedicated to Archduke Rudolph. In order to bring unity and still enlarge the sonata form Beethoven used a device which he had already adopted for the Pianoforte Trio Op. 97, and the Ninth Symphony: that is, to move in a broad arch to the sub-dominant by using the lower third (G) for the second theme, thus saving the effect of the dominant until the end of the development section. "The sonata was written under painful circumstances," Beethoven wrote to Ferdinand Ries (April 1819), and certainly the *adagio sostenuto* tells a most sorrowful musical story. It might be mentioned that the first measure of this movement was added after the whole sonata was finished and it seems almost like taking a deep breath before starting the song. After the magnificent dimensions of Op. 106, Beethoven returned to less extended forms. The last three sonatas are the most sublime and intimate pieces that Beethoven wrote for the instrument. They differ from each other in both the form of individual movements and the plan of the sonata as a whole. Op. 109 in E major, dedicated to Maximiliane Brentano, Op. 110 in A flat major, and Op. 111 in C minor, dedicated to Archduke Rudolph, were written at the same time as the *Missa Solemnis,* and all three were published by Schlesinger in Berlin in the years 1821 and 1822. They again offer new devices: the Op. 109 with its *adagio* second theme and the beautiful variations in the last movement (note the relationship of the *alla breve* variation to the *Credo* of the *Missa Solemnis);* the use of the fugue form in connection with a slow movement in the Op. 110; and finally, to mention only one of the outstanding features of the opening movement of Op. 111, the fantastic transformation of the C minor first theme into the second theme in A flat major. The first theme itself originated in a motif which was supposed to become the second movement of the Op. 30 Violin Sonata in A major composed in 1802. The second and last movements are Beethoven's highest achievement in writing variations in the form of figuration; a whole world, a whole life, lies between these variations and the variations found in such works as the Op. 26 Sonata in A flat.

O.J.

Pieringer, Ferdinand

b. Unterretzbach 1780, d. Vienna 1829. Music amateur, vice-conductor for the *Concerts Spirituels.* Belonged to the circle of Beethoven's friends. One of his letters to Beethoven, dealing mostly with financial matters, he signed as "Illustrissimi, Generalissimi, humillimus servus." He was a violinist and had a good bass voice; occasionally he functioned as Beethoven's proofreader. An autograph book of Pieringer is preserved to which Beethoven contributed a short piano piece; it is published by Frimmel in Robitschek's *Deutsche Kunst-und Musikzeitung* 1893.

Pinterics, Karl

d. Vienna 1831. Private secretary of Prince Palffy (Ferdinand or Franz). Schindler tells about a circle of "Josephins" (liberals), who had their meetings in the tavern Blumenstöckl; Pinterics and a captain of the Imperial bodyguard belonged to this group. Kreissle von Hellborn, in his Schubert biography, relates details about Pinterics, who was an excellent pianist and amateur handicraft artist. Beethoven was a regular visitor with this group, which exchanged highly liberal ideas. According to Schindler the canon, *Ta-ta* (Eighth Symphony, 2nd movement), was sung in the tavern, Pinterics singing the bass (Conversation-book 1820). Numerous letters from Beethoven to Pinterics are preserved. Otto Erich Deutsch in *Franz Schubert, die Dokumente seines Lebens,* reproduced a picture of a Schubert-Abend by Moritz von Schwind, showing all of Schubert's friends, including Karl and Marie Pinterics.

Pistyan

Resort place in Hungary, today Slovakia, formerly owned by Count Erdödy. Beethoven had considered this place for a possible cure during the last weeks of his life.

Piuk, Franz Xaver

Official of the Vienna Magistrate to whom Beethoven wrote July 19, 1819, concerning his nephew Karl. Piuk, Bernard, and Oliva were permitted to visit Karl at Blöchinger's institution (cf. Th.-R. IV).

Pleyel, Ignaz Josef

b. Rupperstal 1757, d. Paris 1831. Musician. When he came to Vienna at the age of 15, he took keyboard lessons from Wanhal and Haydn, enjoying the special protection of Count Erdödy, who appointed him a conductor. At the expense of the Count, he went to Italy, but returned to Vienna for a short visit in 1781. In 1783 he went to Strassburg and became assistant to Franz Xaver Richter at the cathedral. He was invited to come to London, where he spent a very successful time. After his return to Strassburg, he got into trouble with the French revolutionaries. In 1795 he moved to Paris, where he founded a publishing firm. His son, Camille Pleyel (b. Strassburg 1788, d. Paris 1855), was likewise a musician and in addition, a pianomaker.

Both Pleyels were acquainted with Beethoven. In 1805 the elder Pleyel had come to Vienna, where one of his quartets was performed in the Lobkowitz Palace. At the same gathering Beethoven was asked to extemporize; he grasped the two violin parts from the Pleyel quartet and from these he chose a short motif on which he improvised so admirably that the old Pleyel kissed Beethoven's hands. In a later concert Beethoven was less successful with his improvisation, so he took his hat and left. When the two Pleyels saw him the next day, Beethoven made up for it wonderfully. In 1807 Beethoven had planned to publish some of his works with Pleyel in Paris. He was not too enthusiastic about Pleyel's piano method (first edition 1797), preferring Clementi's method. Little Gerhard von Breuning used this method for his piano lessons in spite of Beethoven's protest. (Cf. Ries; Th.-R. Breuning: *Aus dem Schwarzspanierhaus;* Wurzbach.)

Polledro, Giovanni Battista

b. Piova (near Torino) 1781, d. there 1853. Next to Viotti, Polledro was the best pupil of Pugnani. He toured Europe and also went to Russia, where he served as a violinist with Prince Tatischeff. In 1814 he became concertmaster of the royal chapel in Dresden. Some of his works, such as the Variations Op. 3 on a theme of Païsiello's opera *La Molinara* and his Etudes, are still played today. On August 6, 1812, he visited the Bohemian resort places and with Beethoven gave a recital in Carlsbad for the benefit of the victims of a blaze in Baden near Vienna. (Cf. Max Unger: *Beethovens Badereisen;* Andreas Moser: *Geschichte des Violinspiels,* Berlin 1923.)

Potter, Philip Cipriani Hambly

b. London 1792, d. there 1871. Composer and pianist. Started his musical education at the age of seven under his father and afterward studied counterpoint under Attwood, and theory under Callcott and Crotch. Upon Wölfl's arrival in England, he received instruction from him for five years. In 1817 he came to Vienna and studied composition under Emanuel Aloys Förster, receiving also friendly advice from Beethoven. Writing to Ries in London on March 5, 1818, Beethoven said: "Potter has visited me several times; he seems to be a good man and has talent for composition." Through Potter is learned something about Beethoven's love for nature and about a project of the Master's to write an opera *Romulus* (1818). The conversation of the two was carried on in Italian or partly in French. Potter also met Beethoven's copyist Schlemmer.

"As a performer [Potter] ranked high,

and he had the honour to introduce Beethoven's concertos in C, C minor, and G to the English public at the Philharmonic. He played the C minor concerto on March 8, 1824, and the G major in 1825" (Grove). In 1825 he also introduced the Ninth Symphony in London. (Cf. Potter: *Recollections of Beethoven to the musical world,* 1836; Th.-R. IV.)

Prague

Capital of Czechoslovakia. In Beethoven's time part of the Austrian Empire. Beethoven visited the city several times. Whether or not he had been there by 1795, as stated by Dlabacz (*Künstlerlexikon aus Böhmen)* and by Stephan von Breuning in a letter, is questionable. In a letter of the Master's to his brother Johann Nikolaus, dated February 19 (no year, probably 1796), one reads that Beethoven planned to stay in the Bohemian capital for some time. He lived in the Hotel Goldenes Einhorn, visited before by Mozart in the company of Prince Carl Lichnowsky (cf. Nettl: *Mozart in Böhmen).* Beethoven also had traveled with Prince Lichnowsky. Beethoven was completing his concert aria "Ah perfido" for the Prague singer Josephine Duschek, formerly a friend of Mozart's. Nevertheless it was later dedicated to Countess Clari.

In Prague he also met the Kanka family and the aristocratic Clari and Clam-Gallas families. According to Tomaschek, Beethoven visited Prague again in 1798, but it is not possible to verify the year given by the Czech composer. He called Beethoven the giant among the pianists, who played in the Convikt Saal his C major Piano Concerto Op. 15, the *adagio* and *rondo* from Sonata Op. 2 No. 2, and improvised on a theme of Mozart's *Titus,* which had been suggested to him by Countess Sch.... (Schlick?). In his second concert, Beethoven played, according to Tomaschek, his B major Piano Concerto. Tomaschek also heard the Master play in the house of Count C.... (Clam, Clari, Canal?), where he played the *rondo* of the A major Sonata and extemporized on the theme "Ah—vous dirai-je Maman." Later, when traveling to the different Bohemian resorts, Beethoven passed through Prague in 1811 and 1812. On July 2, 1812 he met Varnhagen and Prince Kinsky, and tried in vain to reach Archduke Rudolph, who had just left. Two days later Beethoven himself left for Teplitz.

The Master had numerous friends in Prague, besides Kanka and Varnhagen, the lawyer Dr. Reger, and a number of aristocrats. He even considered for a while sending his nephew Karl to Prague for his education. Beethoven's works were performed in Prague comparatively early. *Fidelio* was given by Carl Maria von Weber, Nov. 21, 1814. The score had been sent to Prague by Treitschke and Beethoven, dated September 5; on the cover were some suggestions regarding the performance. (Cf. Frimmel: *Beethoven-Studien* II p. 359.)

Pratsch, Johann-Gottlieb

d. 1798. German musician and educator, born in Silesia, who spent most of his life in Russia. In 1789 he became a teacher of the clavichord and "note reading and writing" in the Petersburg School of the Theater. He composed the music for Empress Catherine the Second's comic operas *Gore-Bogatyr Kosometovich* and *Fevey.* Together with N. Lvov, he collected Russian folk songs, and while Lvov recorded the Russian text, Pratsch wrote the musical score. The melodies are reproduced with accuracy, although Pratsch did not sufficiently understand the harmony of Russian folk music. This collection, known as *Sobranie Russkykh Narodnykh Pesen,* was published in Petersburg in 1790, 1806, 1815, and 1897. Another work by Pratsch, *Complete School for Forte-Piano,* was published in Petersburg in 1816. Russian melodies from Pratsch's collection were used by Beethoven in his Quartets, Op. 59 (Razumovsky).

S. Z.

Preindl, Joseph

b. Marbach 1756, d. Vienna 1823. Composer and organist, student of Albrechtsberger, and representative of the conservative, polyphonic style. Besides a number of piano compositions, he wrote a theoretical work, *Wiener Tonschule* (1827), published after his death by Seyfried. He was on bad terms with Beethoven, as he despised his "modernism," especially the unprepared dissonance at the beginning of the *Prometheus* overture. Schindler spoke about a trinity of Beethoven-haters, consisting of Preindl, Dyonis Weber, later director of the Prague Conservatory, and Abbé Stadler, a former friend of Mozart's. (Cf. Schindler I, p. 79.)

Pressburg, Pozsony (Hungarian), Bratislava (Slovak)

Capital of Slovakia at the present time. Was the Hungarian capital until 1784. Beethoven visited the city a number of times. Frimmel in his article "Besuche Beethovens in Pressburg" (*Beethoven-Studien* II, p. 33) thoroughly discussed this matter. Nottebohm suggested in his article on Beethoven's Keglevich Sonata (Op. 7) that according to a note by the Master, *"Geschrieben und gewidmet das Con. B. C. (?) als Andenken seines Aufenthalts in P."*, P. means Pressburg. (Cf. Nottebohm: *Beethoveniana* II, p. 511.)

Probst, H. A.

Publisher in Leipzig. Beethoven corresponded with him in 1824, because of the possible publication of his *Missa Solemnis* and the Ninth Symphony (cf. Th.-R. V).

Prometheus

The *Creations of Prometheus,* a ballet in two acts, was first begun in the summer of 1800. The work had been commissioned by the ballet designer and dancer, Salvatore Vigano, who wished to honor Maria Theresia. Why Vigano entrusted the work to the relatively little known Beethoven has never been clearly established; however, Beethoven, who was eager to try his hand at dramatic music, certainly must have accepted with alacrity. On March 28, 1801, *Prometheus* received its first performance at the Imperial Court Theater as a benefit for Fräulein Cassentini, the prima ballerina. The premiere was followed by 15 additional performances in the same year, and 13 performances in 1802 before being withdrawn from the repertoire. The overture, however, retained its popularity and received many later performances as a concert overture. One of the performances of the ballet was witnessed by Haydn with great pleasure, although his praise was not unreserved.

The original MS of the score has been lost, as has the plot of the ballet itself. Of the latter, only a playbill remains from which we must try to reconstruct some of the choreography. Fortunately, a revised MS copy of the score has been preserved in the Imperial Court Library in Vienna. A piano score of the work, which Czerny says was made by Beethoven, was published by Artaria in 1801 as Op. 24, dedicated to the Princess Lichnowsky. Three years later Hoffmeister published the parts and a piano score as Op. 43, the opus number which the work has retained. A full score did not appear until the publication of the complete works.

The story of the ballet concerns itself with the Greek god Prometheus. In the first act, a sort of prologue, we see Prometheus striving to give life and grace to the two creatures, but he can only bring them life. Thereupon he decides to take them to Mount Olympus where they can be instructed in the arts by Apollo and the Muses. Act II shows the instruction on Mount Olympus.

The work is composed of 16 separate numbers not including the overture; three of these make up the first act and the remaining are part of Act II. The overture was originally entitled *Tempesta,* apparently being an attempt to portray the chaos of the world before the creation. The opening dominant 7th chord is similar to the opening of the First Symphony.

Each of the separate numbers is written in a closed form and there appears to be little attempt at continuity in the work as a whole. The second act is in reality a divertimento with individual dances, each of which represents one of the gods instructing the creatures in a particular art.

There are certain characteristics which warrant special mention, such as the use of 6/8 meter to represent the faint stirrings of emotion within the creatures. One of the few instances of Beethoven's use of the harp appears in Number 5, where it is used for the accompaniment to the woodwind solos; this number also contains a lovely cello cadenza and solo. The orchestral recitative is used when the creatures are being taught the art of the drama. Numbers 14 and 15 are solo dances for the creatures, where they exhibit their newly acquired skills; as we may expect, the form of these two movements is a series of variations. Number 14 contains a long solo for basset horn, a seldom used instrument. The final number is a general dance and possibly holds more interest for us because of the later appearance of the theme as the finale of the *Eroica* symphony.

This ballet and the *Eroica* symphony are not the only appearances of the theme in Beethoven's works; it also appears in a small contredanse, and as a basis for the Op. 35 Piano Variations. In fact, when the Op. 35 first appeared Beethoven wrote to the publishers (Breitkopf and Härtel) asking that the front cover contain a reference to the use of the theme in the ballet. Nevertheless, the use of the theme in a ballet about Prometheus and again in the very heroic and noble *Eroica* symphony leads us to speculate as to whether or not Beethoven attached any extra-musical significance to the theme. On the other hand, there can be little doubt that Beethoven was intrigued by the developmental possibilities offered by the theme and its accompanying bass line. Apparently only in the finale of the *Eroica* was he completely satisfied with the treatment, and it is significant that the theme never again appears in his works.

The instrumentation employed in the ballet is the classic orchestra, with paired woodwinds, plus some additional instruments as mentioned above. Perhaps the outstanding characteristic of the scoring is the frequent use of solo instruments, much more than customarily employed. This unusual use of solo instruments and rare instruments can undoubtedly be attributed to exigencies of the drama and the character of the music itself.

In spite of the excellence of the music, the ballet has been denied to the modern public. It has been revived only once since 1802—a performance at Paris in 1929 with the choreography by Serge Lifar. The work received only a few performances and contemporary critics complained that the quality of the music far overshadowed the drama. (Cf. Th.-R.; Nottebohm: *Beethoveniana* II, p. 236-7 with sketches of the composition; Riemann: "Beethovens Prometheusmusik, ein Variationenwerk" in *Die Musik* IX; Entries: Dance music; Vigano.) F. T. W.

Punto, Johann Wenzel

b. Zechužice (near Caslav) 1748, d. Prague 1803. World-famous horn player. His German name was Stich, his original Czech name Štěch, hence the Italian translation Punto. His father was a servant of Count Joseph Thun's, who sent the boy to Munich in order to study horn with a Czech horn player Sfindelař (Šindelař?) and later to Dresden, where Anton Hampel and Carl Haudek became his teachers. After his return to Prague, Johann secretly escaped from Thun's estate and toured with greatest success, soon becoming the most famous horn player in Europe. He served in the orchestras of the Prince Bishop of Würzburg and Count Artois, later Charles X of France. When the French Revolution broke out, he left Paris and toured again through Europe.

In 1800 he met Beethoven, probably in the house of Count Deym (Hofstatuarius Müller), who gave splendid musical soirées in honor of the Countesses Brunswick. In a letter of Josephine Brunswick's to one of her sisters, we read in questionable French: "Nous avions une charmante musique. Punto, Beethoven, Schuppanzigh, Zmeskall. Tu penses que cela donne quelkue choses du bien. Punto joue vraiment merveilleusement. Ils déjeunèrent tous chez nous et ensuite on fit de la musique toute l'après-midi." (Cf. Hevesy: *Les petites amies de Beethoven.)*

Beethoven wrote for Punto his Horn Sonata Op. 17, which he dedicated to Baroness Braun, and which was published by Mollo (1801). Ries related that Beethoven promised Punto to perform the sonata with him. The concert had already been advertised, but Beethoven had not even started his composition. However, on the day of the performance, April 18, 1800, he was ready with his work. It is amazing that no sketches exist, a fact which seems to verify the almost unbelievable report of Ries. However, Nottebohm mentioned a sketch of six bars, belonging to the *adagio* of the sonata. Czerny reported that Punto instructed Beethoven how to compose for his instrument. The theme of the first movement is a typical horn theme. The short second movement, stressing the melancholic character of the instrument, leads to a refreshing *rondo,* similar to the typical instrumental "chasses" of that time. Punto gave two concerts in the Theater an der Wien (1801), returned to Bohemia thereafter, went back to Paris, and returned once more to Prague. There he fell sick and died.

It should be mentioned that Mozart was well acquainted with Punto. His famous *Sinfonia Concertante* (K. Anh. 9) for Oboe, Clarinet, Horn and Bassoon was written in Paris for the virtuoso. Punto himself wrote many works for his instrument. One of them, a *Concert Rondo,* was recently recorded by *Anthologia Musicae Bohemicae.* Hanslick in his *Geschichte des Konzertwesens* commented about Punto: "No nation produced an equal rival for Punto," and one may add that the Czechs were the first to bring the French horn to Germany and Bohemia. (Cf. Wurzbach; Th.-R. II; Nettl: "Franz Anton Graf von Sporcks Beziehungen zur Musik" in *Die Musikforschung* 1953/Heft 4.)

Puton, Johann Baptist, Freiherr von

Head of the firm G. I. Schüller and Co., director of the Austrian National Bank. His and his wife's names appear several times in the Conversation-books. In 1822 Beethoven improvised at Puton's. Peters noted at the beginning of 1820: "Baron Puton would love to see you." (Cf. Schünemann: *Konversationshefte,* vol. I.)

Q

Quintets

There can be no doubt that Beethoven's favorite chamber music group was the string quartet, while essays in other chamber combinations represent a sort of peripheral activity. The various quintets are no exception and among themselves reveal a lack of consistency in treatment. There are only four works of importance for such a combination, and of these, only two, Op. 16 and Op. 29, were considered originally as quintets. Even here there is a diversity: Op. 29 being written for a quintet of strings, 2 violins, 2 violas and cello, and Op. 16 for piano, oboe, clarinet, bassoon and horn. The two remaining quintets, Op. 4 and Op. 104, were arrangements of existing works in different mediums.

There remain two other works of lesser importance for a combination of five instruments: the first is an arrangement of the First Symphony made by the publisher Mollo without Beethoven's knowledge; the second a Fugue in D Major for Five String Instruments, which was prepared for a projected manuscript collection of Beethoven's works by Haslinger. The latter was published soon after Beethoven's death in 1827 as Op. 137.

The Quintet Op. 16 in E flat was probably composed between the years 1796 and 1797; sketches can be found in connection with the Piano Sonata Op. 10 and there is evidence that the work was played at a concert for Schuppanzigh in 1797. The quintet was published by Mollo and Co. in 1801 with a dedication *"a son Altesse Monseigneur le Prince Regnant de Schwarzenberg."* This is the work in which Beethoven, during a performance with the famous Munich oboist Ramm, took advantage of a *fermata* to improvise a cadenza. Each time he approached the final 6/4 chord the players would prepare to play, only to find that Beethoven had gone off on a new idea; it is reported that Ramm became very indignant. The work is in three movements and shows some similarity in form and instrumentation to Mozart's quintet in the same key.

The Quintet Op. 29 in C major was first published in 1802 by Breitkopf and Härtel, after having been composed in the previous year. A pirated edition was also issued in 1802 by Artaria, the copies of which Beethoven managed to acquire. These copies were given to Ries for correction, with instructions to make the corrections both numerous and heavy. However, Beethoven apparently forgave Artaria, for these plates were later used with the composer's permission and his corrections. This quintet, frequently called the "Storm" Quintet because of the sixteenth notes in the finale represent a point midway between the Op. 18 and Op. 59 String Quartets, revealing the classic transparency of Op. 18 and some of the boldness of invention found in Op. 59. The additional viola gives an increased warmth and depth of sonority not found in the quartets.

The Quintet Op. 4 in E flat was published in 1796, described as a completely new work. Although it is frequently called an arrangement of the Wind Octet, Op. 103, it actually goes further than an arrangement, for Beethoven omits one part completely, changes registers in order to accommodate the new instruments, and even changes the themes themselves. In accounting for the existence of this quintet, Wegeler reports that in 1795 Beethoven was commissioned by Count Apponyi to write a string quartet; however, the result was this quintet and the String Trio, Op. 3. In the case of the trio, Thayer has shown this to be untrue, but there is no evidence that it is not true of the quintet. If so, we may date the quintet 1796, otherwise we can give only the approximate dates of 1792-97. The work is scored for 2 violins, 2 violas and cello.

The Quintet Op. 104 in C minor is another arrangement. According to one source, an unnamed musician presented to Beethoven a string quintet arrangement of the Trio Op. 1 No. 3 during the summer of 1817. The work apparently interested Beethoven enough to cause him to produce his own arrangement. The manuscript, in the Royal Library in Berlin, is in a copyist's hand, but the cover bears an inscription in Beethoven's autograph. Apparently Beethoven attached some significance to the work, for he mentions it in several letters and allowed it to be performed at a meeting of the Gesellschaft der Musikfreunde in 1818. The work, scored for the usual 2 violins, 2 violas and cello, was published by Artaria in 1819.

There remains a sketch for a quintet, dating from the year 1826, which appears to have been almost completed. Jahn reports that the first movement of a quintet in C minor, for Diabelli, had been completed in Beethoven's mind but not fully written out. This is probably the partially completed quintet in C which Diabelli bought at the sale of Beethoven's posthumous effects and which was published by the firm in a two- and four-hand piano arrangement. However, the original autograph is lost and it is impossible to know how much of the work had been completed by Beethoven and how much by the arranger.

F. T. W.

R

Radziwill, Prince Anton Heinrich

b. Wilna 1775, d. Berlin 1833. Music amateur. He was married to the daughter of Prince Ferdinand of Prussia, and consequently a brother-in-law of Prince Louis-Ferdinand. Prince Radziwill attended the Vienna Congress (1815). Varnhagen in his *Denkwürdigkeiten* related that the Prince had expressed a desire to meet Beethoven, but because of the Master's increasing deafness and bad humor, he was admitted only reluctantly. It was only because of his relationship to Prince Louis Ferdinand that Beethoven received him. When Beethoven intended to sell copies of the *Missa Solemnis* (1823), he negotiated with Deetz, representative of Radziwill. Deetz notated in a Conversation-book: "Prince Radziwill speaks continuously about you with greatest admiration." According to a letter of Prince Galitzin from St. Petersburg (1824), Radziwill spoke enthusiastically about the performance of the *Missa Solemnis* in St. Petersburg. Finally Beethoven dedicated to Radziwill his overture *Zur Namensfeier*, written in honor of the feast day of Emperor Franz. The Prince played an important role in the correspondence between Zelter and Goethe, who admired the music Radziwill had written to his *Faust*. Many years later Robert Schumann enjoyed it less. (Cf. Th.-R. III and V; Kalischer: *Beethoven und Berlin.*)

Rampel

Musician. He worked as Beethoven's copyist between 1823 and 1826. (Cf. Frimmel: *Beethoven Handbuch.)*

Rau, Heribert

Teacher in the family of Baron Eskeles. It was he who handed Beethoven the gift of money which the Philharmonic Society in London sent him on the order of the banking firm Eskeles. Rau was the author of a historical novel, entitled *Beethoven* (1859), which contains many stories that must be considered fictitious. Rau was in correspondence with Moscheles.

Razumovsky, Andrey Kirillovich

1752-1836. Russian count and prince of the German Roman Empire. Russian ambassador in Vienna, well-known Maecenas, and friend of Beethoven. Andrey Razumovsky was the son of Cyril Razumovsky (1728-1803), the last hetman (chief of state and Cossack army commander) of Little Russia (Ukraine), and the nephew of Alexis Razumovsky, morganatic husband of the Russian Empress Elizabeth. Alexis Razumovsky, a Ukrainian Cossack, became a singer in the court capella choir in Petersburg in 1731 and shortly after became a favorite of Elizabeth, at that time still princess. He later became a courtier and *Hofintendant* of Elizabeth's court. After Elizabeth's accession to the throne in 1742 Alexis Razumovsky became *Kammerherr* and a lieutenant general, and married the empress. In 1744 he became a count of the Holy Roman Empire (Reichsgraf). Alexis' brother, Cyril, became president of the Academy of Sciences and in 1750 *hetman* of Little Russia (now Ukraine).

Andrey Razumovsky had a brilliant career at the Russian court. He received an excellent education, served with the navy, and in 1772 became *Kammerjunker* at the Russian court. Handsome, well educated, and witty, he was one of the most brilliant representatives of the Russian aristocracy and enjoyed great success at the court and among women. In 1779 he was appointed ambassador to the court of Naples, where he soon became a close friend of the all-powerful Queen Carolina Maria (who later was closely associated with Admiral Nelson and Lady Hamilton). In 1784 Razumovsky was transferred to Copenhagen, and in 1786 to Stockholm. In 1790 he was appointed Russian ambassador at the court of the German Roman Empire in Vienna. In all these positions he displayed his ability as a capable diplomat, and his reports furnished an excellent analysis of European political entanglements. He participated actively in the diplomatic preparations of the second and third partitions of Poland. Emperor Paul, dissatisfied with Razumovsky's close friendship with the Viennese court, recalled him to Russia, but Alexander I sent him back to Vienna in 1801, where he remained ambassador until he retired in 1807. Razumovsky continued to live in Vienna until his death in 1836.

During the Congress of Vienna he was appointed Russia's main representative at the Congress and played an important role in the negotiations. For his participation in the Congress, Razumovsky was granted the title of prince.

The tremendous wealth which Razumovsky inherited from his father and uncle made him one of the richest men in Europe. His generosity and lavish way of life, however, undermined his fortune, and he spent the last years of his life in difficult financial conditions. The Russian state on many occasions furnished Razumovsky financial support.

Razumovsky was the most generous Maecenas of his time, supporting artists, musicians, and painters. His picture gallery and musical parties were famous throughout all Europe. A well-educated, liberal, and generous aristocrat, and brilliant *causeur,* he was one of the most popular and renowned European aristocrats of the late 18th and early 19th centuries. His influence and wealth won for him among the Viennese the nickname "Archduke Andrew." Toward the end of his life, Razumovsky, under the influence of his second wife, Countess Türkheim, was converted to Catholicism. (Cf. Prince A. Vasichikoff: *Semeistvo Razumovskih,* Vols. 3, 4, Petersburg, 1882/87.) S. Z.

Razumovsky, who had already worked as a clerk for the Russian Embassy in Vienna (1777-79), met Haydn and Mozart in musical and aristocratic circles. In 1808 he established a permanent string quartet with Schuppanzigh (first violin), Louis Sina (second violin), Franz Weiss (viola), and Joseph Linke (cello). Often he played the second violin part himself. His acquaintance with Beethoven was already established in 1796. Razumovsky's name appears on the subscription list of Beethoven's Trios Op. 1, and he regularly purchased tickets for the Master's concerts. On the occasion of the first performance of the "Kreutzer" Sonata (May 24, 1803) Razumovsky bought five tickets. In 1806 he intended to study music theory with Beethoven, with emphasis on quartet composition. The Master refused the offer and recommended instead his friend E. A. Förster. It is well known that Beethoven's Quartets Op. 59, composed in 1805-06, were dedicated to Razumovsky. To please the Russian aristocrat, he used Russian themes in the first and second quartets of the group; these he took from Pratsch's collection (cf. Entry: Pratsch). Furthermore Beethoven introduced in the second movement of the third quartet (C major) a definite exotic theme, designated by Schering as Spanish. The three quartets Op. 59 are all written in the same style. They reflect a magic world of distant countries as visualized by Beethoven.

Razumovsky was considered one of the wealthiest men of Vienna, but after his palace burned down on New Year's Eve, 1815, the Prince restricted all his musical activities and dissolved his quartet. On the day of the blaze, Czar Alexander and Emperor Franz appeared on the scene and Razumovsky not only received the title of Prince from the Czar, but was given a considerable loan for rebuilding his palace. For a long time Princess Marie Esterhazy was Razumovsky's mistress. Beethoven dedicated to her his three four-hand Piano Sonatas Op. 45. Countess Thürheim, Razumovsky's sister-in-law, vividly described Marie Esterhazy's jealousy. She later became the mistress of Meyer Rothschild, the financier of the Vienna Congress and founder of the Vienna line of the Rothschilds. Lulu von Thürheim's memoirs, in four volumes, ed. by René van Rhyn, Munich 1913, give ample information on the family life of Razumovsky; they fail, however, to inform us of the Prince's musical activities. The name of Beethoven is hardly mentioned. Beethoven's Symphonies Nos. 5 and 6 are dedicated simultaneously to Razumovsky and Prince Lobkowitz. (Cf. Th.-R.; Wurzbach; Reichardt: *Vertraute Briefe*; Max Unger: *Neue Musikzeitung,* 1917; Hanslick: *Geschichte des Concertwesens.*)

Reading

Beethoven was an attentive reader of all categories in literature. He did not own a real library, a fact connected with his irregular life. According to Schindler he did not even own a bookcase. However, reading was of the greatest importance to him. He liked to make personal notes on the margins of the books and his diaries and Conversation-books are full of allusions to his readings. In his Beethoven biography, Schindler gave some information about the books in Beethoven's possession. After Beethoven's death Schindler took some of the Master's books from the estate to his home and with Schindler's estate they finally ended up in the Royal Prussian Library of Berlin. These are the books: Homer: *Odyssey,* transl. by Voss; two volumes of the Mannheim Edition of Shakespeare, transl. by Eschenburg; Goethe: *West-Östlicher Divan;* Christian Sturm: *Betrachtungen der Werke Gottes im Reiche der Natur,* two volumes; Shakespeare: *Tempest,* transl. by Schlegel, Vienna 1825; Schiller: *Sämtliche Werke,* six volumes, Vienna 1810, containing the *Jungfrau von Orleans* and *Wilhelm Tell;* Scheller-Lünemann: *Latein-deutsches u. deutsch-latein. Handlexicon, vornehmlich für Schulen,* three volumes, Leipzig 1807 (fourth volume missing); de la Veaux: *Dictionnaire français-allemand et allemand-français, à l'usage des deux nations,* three volumes, Strasbourg et Paris 1793 (fourth volume missing); Jagemann *Italien.-deutsches und deutsch-italien. Wörterbuch,* two volumes, Leipzig 1785; and *Nouvelle Grammaire à l'usage des dames,* two volumes, Berlin 1782 (third volume missing). The first four of the abovementioned books show characteristic signs of use; dog's-ears, notations, pencil marks, crosses, exclamation and question marks, many of them indicating the emotions of the reader. Schindler remarked: "No Hogarth would have been able to draw grimmer looking question marks." Beethoven's remaining library was auctioned on Nov. 5, 1827. It consisted of about 44 books, some of which had to be confiscated, as they were forbidden in Austria. The confiscated works included some volumes of Seume, Kotzebue's *Vom Adel;* W. C. Müller's *Paris im Scheitelpunkte* and Fessler's *Ansichten von Religion und Kirchentum.* It is interesting to know that Fessler was a well-known Freemason. The remainder (40 books) include such works as Kant: *Naturgeschichte und Theorie des Himmels;* Hufeland: *Praktische Übersicht der vorzüglichsten Heilquellen Deutschlands;* Sailer: *Kleine Bibel für Kranke und Sterbende;* Goethe: *Sämtliche Schriften,* 24 volumes, Vienna 1811; Schiller: *Sämtliche Werke,* Graz 1824. Among the musical books the following are worth mentioning: Forkel: *Allgemeine Literatur der Musik;* Burney: *General History of Music* (four volumes); Mattheson: *Der vollkommene Kapellmeister*; Marpurg: *Abhandlung von der Fuge;* and the *Missale Romanum,* Venice 1777. It is natural that Beethoven knew many other books besides those in his library. He might also have lost some in his frequent moves. Schindler related that his music library was pretty limited. From the ancient Italian composers he knew only a collection of short pieces by Palestrina, Nanini, Victoria, and others, published in 1824 by Artaria. There was nothing by Haydn or Cherubini. Mozart was represented by a part of his *Don Giovanni* score and many sonatas. Beethoven also owned all the sonatas by Clementi and the etudes by John Cramer. Johann Sebastian Bach was hardly represented at all, except for some motets, sung in van Swieten's house. Beethoven only owned the *Well Tempered Clavier,* three books of the Exercises, the Inventions and Symphonies and a Toccata in D minor. His copies of Bach's music were bound all in one volume. Arnold Schering in his book, *Beethoven und die Dichtung,* has attributed great significance to Beethoven's knowledge of poetry, as he assumes that a great many of the Master's works were written under the influence of his reading. (Cf. Entry: Schering; Leitzmann: *Ludwig van Beethoven,* vol. II, p. 379; Schindler.)

Recke, Elisabeth von der

b. Courland 1756, d. Dresden 1833. Writer and poetess. Daughter of Count Friedrich von Medem. In 1771 she married Baron Magnus von der Recke, from whom she separated five years later. After 1779 she lived at the court of her stepsister, the Dutchess von Courland in Mitau, where she supposedly revealed Cagliostro's charlatanism. For some time she accompanied the poet Tiedge on his travels to Italy, and she remained his steady companion. Many times she visited the Bohemian resorts, especially Teplitz, where she met Beethoven in 1811 in the circle of Varnhagen von Ense, Rahel Levin, Amalie Sebald, Bettina von Arnim and Oliva. One might assume that it was Elisabeth who led Beethoven to Seume's tomb in Teplitz. It is obvious that Beethoven had in mind to compose one of Elisabeth's poems, as revealed in a letter the Master wrote her October 11 (?), 1811, with an apology for being unable to attend a musical church service. A deep friendship had developed between Beethoven and Tiedge, dating from his visit in Teplitz, which is shown in a letter the Master wrote on the reverse side of his letter to Elizabeth. There he addressed Tiedge with the brother-word *du*. When Beethoven returned to Teplitz the following year, he missed Elisabeth and Tiedge, who had left shortly before.

Elisabeth was an occasional visitor of Count Waldstein's in Dux, where she happened to meet Casanova. (Cf. Moriz Geyer: *Der Musenhof in Löbichau,* 1882; Brunier: *Elisabeth von der Recke*; Th.-R. III.)

Reger, Josef

One of Beethoven's lawyers in Prague about 1813, who represented him in his law suit against Kinsky's estate. In the Beethoven literature Reger's name is occasionally read erroneously as Beyer.

Reicha, Anton

b. Prague 1770, d. 1836. Composer, nephew of Joseph Reicha (b. Klattau (Bohemia) 1764, d. 1795). Joseph had been a cellist with the Oettingen-Wallerstein Orchestra, and later director of the Bonn Orchestra. He lived in Bonn from 1785. Anton Reicha came with his uncle to Bonn, and he was matriculated together with Beethoven and one of the Kügelgen brothers at the University there. After the French invasion of Bonn, Reicha moved to Hamburg, and in 1799 to Paris. He met Beethoven again in Vienna in 1801. According to Thayer, Reicha excelled Beethoven in musical scholarship and general education, but was inferior to Beethoven as a composer and pianist.

Reicha definitely had some influence over Beethoven. He was frequently mentioned in Beethoven's correspondence, as in a letter to Zmeskall, November 1802. In a letter to Breitkopf and Härtel, dated January 22, 1803, Beethoven offered several works by Reicha to the Leipzig firm, stating: "These compositions are well done." Reicha wrote in his unpublished autobiography: "We spent fourteen years together, in close friendship like Orestes and Pylades. After a separation of eight years we met again."

Reicha was commissioned by Empress Maria Theresia to write an opera *Argene, Regina di Granata.* In 1808 Reicha returned to Paris, where he became professor of composition (1818), as the successor of Méhul. He was the teacher of many prominent composers, including Liszt, Gounod, Dancla, Berlioz, and César Franck. (Cf. Bücken: *Reichas Leben und Kompositionen*; Bücken: "Beethoven and Reicha," *Die Musik* XII/12; Prod'homme: "The Unpublished Autobiography of Anton Reicha" *Musical Quarterly*, New York, 1936; Th.-R. I and II.)

Reichardt, Johann Friedrich

b. Königsberg 1753, d. Giebichenstein (near Halle) 1814. Composer, critic, and writer on music. Son of a lutenist, he studied philosophy and music theory at Königsberg. Reichardt came to Leipzig, where he composed singspiele under the influence of J.A.P. Hiller. In 1775 he succeeded Agricola as Kapellmeister for Frederick the Great. Two years later he married a daughter of Franz Benda. In 1782 Reichardt traveled in Italy, France, and England, and returned, after the death of Frederick II, to Berlin, where he tried to Germanize Italian opera. Because of his sympathy for the French Revolution, he was forced to give up his position in 1794. Reichardt, until then on good terms with Schiller and Goethe, lost their friendship on account of his attitude. The two poets attacked him bitterly in their *Xenien.* Reichardt retired to his home in Giebichenstein, where he became inspector of the salt mines. In 1806 the French invasion drove him to Königsberg, and because of Jerôme Bonaparte's threat to confiscate his property, Reichardt joined him at Cassel, and became his court conductor. He was soon granted a leave of absence and visited Vienna to produce his operas and singspiele. The trip was unsuccessful, and he remained in Giebichenstein until his death.

Reichardt was one of the most prolific music critics of his time. Rooted in a North-German tradition, represented by Kirnberger, Marpurg, Zelter, Benda, and others, he certainly had a cool approach towards Beethoven. Among his many travelogues, his *Vertraute Briefe, geschrieben auf einer Reise nach Wien* (1808), were especially important to Beethoven. As his journey progressed, his attitude toward the Master became warmer, and finally even enthusiastic. Reichardt heard Beethoven play in the house of Countess Erdödy; he reported that he enjoyed the art of the pianists Ertmann and Bigot, and made many comments on Beethoven's quartets, played by Schuppanzigh. However, there is a certain arrogance and impertinence in Reichardt's way of writing, which Beethoven certainly did not like. In November 1808 Reichardt reported: "At last I succeeded in finding the good Beethoven. People care so little about him that nobody could give me his address. Finally I found him in his desolate and disorderly apartment. In the beginning he looked as gloomy as his place did . . . finally he became more cheerful . . . and spoke in an honest and friendly way." Letters of this superficial type were written by Reichardt, and one is not surprised at Beethoven's critical attitude towards a man who was out of favor with Beethoven's hero, Goethe. In a letter from Beethoven to Breitkopf and Härtel (1809-1810) he remarked: "How do you like Reichardt's scribbling?" (Cf. Reichardt's "Autobiography" in *Berliner Musikalische Zeitung;* Bode: *Die Tonkunst in Goethes Leben;* Zentner: *Johann Friedrich Reichardt,* 1941; Schletterer: *Johann Friedrich Reichardt,* 1865; Th.-R. III; Max Faller: *Johann Friedrich Reichardt und die Anfänge der musikalischen Journalistik,* 1929.)

Religion

Beethoven's education was based on Roman Catholic principles. However, the strong rationalistic atmosphere at the Electoral Court should not be overlooked. True, Beethoven was Court Organist, and in this capacity he was more than familiar with the Catholic liturgy, which in itself must have had a tremendous effect on him. It is significant that Beethoven in his Bonn period never composed sacred music. Elector Maximilian Franz, brother of Joseph II, certainly was not the man to promote church music. Beethoven's religious feelings were fluctuating; however, his deep belief in God runs through his entire life like a red thread. If the report of Major Blöchinger's memoirs is trustworthy (he was the son of Joseph Blöchinger, owner of Karl van Beethoven's boarding school), Beethoven made the following statement in 1819: "Christ was nothing but a crucified Jew."

Beethoven certainly felt attracted by the philosophy of deism, which teaches that the fundament of the world is a god, different from the world itself (contrast to pantheism), a god who neither is of personal nature, nor interferes in the course of the world. In that respect his philosophy came close to that of Freemasonry or to that of Voltaire and the German Rationalists (Lessing, Mendelssohn, etc.). This is confirmed by Schindler. The Master himself was very reluctant to talk about religion, which he took for granted and compared to knowing the figured bass. But he speculated about the relations of God and the world and was often searching in foreign literature to find the secrets of this world. In a notebook of 1816 he wrote: "God is immaterial. He is therefore beyond conception. As He is invisible, He can not have a form; but from the manifestation of His works we must conclude that He is eternal, omnipotent and omnipresent. Whatever is free from desire and greed, is the Mighty One. He alone. There is none greater than He. Brahma: His Spirit is bound up in itself. He, the Almighty, is present in every part of space. His omniscience is of His own comprehension and His comprehension includes every other. Of all all-comprehending qualities, onmiscience is the greatest: there is no threefold being for it—it is independent of all. O, God, Thou are the true, the everblessing unchangeable light of all time and space. Thy wisdom recognized thousands of laws, and yet, Thou ever acteth freely and to Thine glory. Thou standeth for everything that we revere: all glory and worship to Thee. Thou alone art the All Blessed One (Bhagavan)—Thou, the essence of all laws, the image of all wisdom, present to all the world, Thou, who bearest within thyself all things."

Frequently he called on God, as in the *Heiligenstädter Testament.* There is no doubt that Kant's ideas had a strong influence on him, as seen in a note of 1820 which reads: "The ethical law within us and the starred heaven above us—Kant." Beethoven's feelings were quite profound when composing such works as the *Missa Solemnis,* the C major Mass and the Gellert songs. Particularly in the *Missa Solemnis* is he obviously overwhelmed by the depth of the liturgical text, as for instance in *Et vitam venturi* or the *Crucifixus.* It would seem as if his rationalism gradually subsided. By 1802, when Hoffmeister and Kühnel in Leipzig asked him for a revolutionary sonata, he declined and offered instead a *Missa pro Sancta Maria:* "I would like to take a brush into my hand and write down in weighted notes 'Credo in unum Deum.' "

Rellstab, Heinrich Friedrich Ludwig

b. Berlin 1799, d. there 1860. Composer and writer on music. His father, Johann Karl Friedrich was a musician, printer, and his teacher. Later Ludwig became an artillery officer, teacher of mathematics and history at the Brigade-Schule in Berlin, which he left in 1821. He lived afterward in Frankfurt a.O., Heidelberg, Bonn, and at last settled for good in Berlin, where he became editor and music critic of the *Vossische Zeitung*. It was he who gave impetus to the sensational dismissal of Spontini as Royal Prussian Kapellmeister. In his memoirs *Aus meinem Leben* 2 vol., 1861, he spoke extensively about his visit to Beethoven in 1825. Zelter had provided him with a letter of recommendation to the Master. At that time Beethoven lived at Krügerstr. 767 on the fourth floor.

"When I had ascended the quite considerable number of steps I found at my left a bell pull with a name half erased, yet which I thought I could decipher as that of Beethoven. I rang; steps drew near; the door opened; and my pulse raced. Actually I am no longer able to say whether a maid or a young man, Beethoven's nephew, who then was living with him, and whom later I met once or twice, opened the door for me. My high inner tension had robbed me of all consciousness of external happenings. I only recollect that I could not manage to get out the question: 'Does Mr. Beethoven live here?' How the gigantic weight of a great name demolishes the pigmy rules and barriers of convention, behind which the immeasurable pettiness of the everyday safeguards its vain rights.

"These forms, however, in this case also refused to relinquish their petty claims. I was announced, handing over my letter from Zelter as a card of admission, and stood waiting in the anteroom. I could still paint it from memory in its half-void, half-disordered confusion. On the floor stood a number of emptied bottles, on a plain table a few plates and two glasses, one of them half-filled. 'Could Beethoven have left this half-emptied glass?' I wondered. And the desire seized me to drink what was left, as a secret theft of brotherhood by which German custom binds two hearts.

"The door of the adjoining room opened; I was asked to enter. As I stepped timidly over the sacred threshold, I could hear my heart beat. I had already stood in the presence of various great men whom I, the youthful poet, saw tower above me at the same immeasurable height; I will mention only Goethe and Jean Paul.

"Yet this sensation which now filled me I had not experienced when confronted with the two I have mentioned. I will not arrogantly say that it was an *anch' io sono pittore** which had made access to them free from constraint and which made it easier to set up the bridge of intellectual communication; yet for all that, I belonged to the same artistic realm over which they ruled, we spoke the same language. I had a more valid right to be answered; I could more securely ground that right and, finally, in the field of poetic thought a greater number of connecting threads spun themselves out between us, from one to the other. And this to say nothing of the well-nigh impassable barrier which Beethoven's deaf ear opposed to every more intimate sympathetic approach. And yet, that which in the first moments seemed to separate us, the difference in our creative fields, later helped us approach one another. A mediocre musician, perhaps, would have struck Beethoven as the most negligible, the most tiresome person in the world; a passably talented poet, at least, still gave him something which he himself did not possess, yet valued and loved.

"As I entered, my very first glance was for him. He was carelessly seated on a disordered bed against the rear wall of the room, one on which he appeared to have been resting only the moment before. In his one hand he held Zelter's letter, the other he stretched amiably out to me with a look of such kindness and at the same time of such suffering that suddenly every separating wall of unease fell, and I advanced toward him whom I so profoundly reverenced glowing with the fullest warmth of affection. He rose, gave me his hand, pressed my own heartily in true German fashion, and said: 'You have brought me a fine letter from Zelter. He is a real protector of true art.' Accustomed to defray the larger part of the burden of conversation, since he could only with difficulty gather what was said in reply, he continued: 'I am not quite well, I have been ill. You will not find me very entertaining, for I am very deaf.' What I replied, whether I replied—really, I am unable to say. My looks, my repeated pressures of the hand, will best have expressed that for which, perhaps, words would have failed me, even if, in this instance, I could have spoken as I did to others. Beethoven invited me to take a seat; and he himself sat down on a chair in front of the bed, moving it over to a table which, two paces away, was completely covered with treasures, with notes in Beethoven's own hand, and with the work with which he was busy at the moment. I took a chair next to his. Then I surveyed the room with a rapid glance. It was as large as the anteroom and had two windows. Beneath the windows stood the grand piano. Otherwise nothing which in any way betrayed comfort or convenience, to say nothing of luxury, was visible. A writing cabinet, some chairs and tables, white walls with old, dusty hangings—such was Beethoven's room. What cared he for bronzes, mirrored walls, divans, gold and silver. He, to whom all the glory of this world was but vanity, dust and ashes compared with that divine spark which, outshining everything else, flames up from his soul."

In this interview Rellstab discussed

operatic projects, such as Attila, Antigone, Belisar, Orestes, etc., with Beethoven. He obtained permission to attend the rehearsal of the String Quartet Op. 127, which he certainly did not fully understand. Before Rellstab left Vienna, he tried to approach the Master again, but did not find him at home. On the reverse side of Beethoven's apologetic letter to Rellstab, he wrote a canon *Das Schöne zu dem Guten.* Rellstab had written a number of poems which Beethoven planned to compose, some of them later set to music by Schubert. It is well known that the name "Moonlight" sonata goes back to Rellstab, who compared the first movement of the Piano Sonata Op. 27 No. 2 with the moonlight scenery of Lake Lucerne. It is worthwhile mentioning that this sonata has nothing to do with Rellstab's vision. It rather suggests contrasting feelings: an excellent example of the aesthetic misunderstanding of the general public. Needless to say that the title *Mondscheinsonate* was unknown to Beethoven. (Cf. Blengert: *Ludwig Rellstab,* Dissertation, Leipzig 1918; L. E. Kossak: *Aphorismen über Rellstabs Kunstkritik*; Nohl: *Beethoven nach den Schilderungen seiner Zeitgenossen;* Leitzmann: *Berichte der Zeitgenossen,* Leipzig 1921. A section of Rellstab's Autobiography is published by Schirmer: *Beethoven, Impressions of Contemporaries,* Schirmer, N. Y. 1926.)

Requiem (Project)

For many years Beethoven had in mind composing a requiem. In a sketchbook of 1809 the Master jotted down the following words: "The funeral march could be used in the requiem." After Prince Kinsky's sudden death in 1812, the Master again thought of writing a funeral mass. In the different Conversation-books this project is mentioned over and over again. Holz writes the following about this matter: "In the Requiem the Devil should be lured out of Hell." According to the conversation between Holz and Nikolaus Lenau, Beethoven believed Mozart's *Requiem* to be too wild and awesome; he wanted to compose one in a more subdued mood. According to the same source, the Master estimated Cherubini's *Requiem* to be greater than Mozart's. (Cf. Entry: Wolfmayer; and Frimmel: *Beethoven Handbuch.*)

Ries

A family of musicians from Bonn. Franz Anton Ries (born Bonn 1755, died there 1846) was the son of the court trumpeter and violinist, Johann Ries. Franz Anton was concertmaster and later musical director of the Electoral Orchestra of Maximilian Franz in Bonn. He became Beethoven's violin teacher. Franz Anton's son was Ferdinand Ries, born Bonn 1784, died Frankfurt a.M. 1838. Ferdinand came to Vienna in 1801, where he received piano instruction from Beethoven. Beethoven recommended him to Albrechtsberger for theory instruction, which was of only short duration. In 1805 Ferdinand Ries returned to Bonn in order to join the army, but was not accepted. He toured France, England, Scandinavia, and Russia as a pianist and finally settled in London 1813; he remained there till 1824, corresponding continuously with Beethoven. In London Ferdinand met his father's friend and countryman, Salomon, who received him cordially and introduced him to the Philharmonic concerts.

Many of Ries' works appeared on the programs of the Philharmonic. In the meantime his marriage to an English lady tied him even closer to Great Britain. Ferdinand accumulated a fortune, adequate for a life of comfort, and in 1824 he decided to move to Godesberg, located in the neighborhood of Bonn, and there purchased some property. In 1830 he moved to Frankfurt, where he came in close contact with the Lower Rhine Festivals, which he often directed. Ries was the composer of a great number of chamber music works, six symphonies, piano works, operas, and oratorios which, according to Grove's Dictionary, are "dead" today. Beethoven said of Ries' compositions: "He imitates me too much," and, as Grove puts it, he caught the style and the phrases but not the immortality, of his Master. Ries will be forever connected with Beethoven's life through his *Biographische Notizen über Ludwig van Beethoven,* which was published together with Dr. F. G. Wegeler in Koblenz by Baedeker (1838). The two writers kept their contributions separate, Ries taking pages 76-163. The work was translated into French by Le Gentil and parts of it into English by Moscheles, as an appendix to Schindler's *Life of Beethoven.* The *Biographische Notizen* was republished in a facsimile edition by Kalischer (Schuster and Löffler, Berlin 1906). In 1808 and 1809 Ries spent many months in Vienna and experienced the siege of Vienna by the French. It was at that time, that he came in close connection with Beethoven. Ries' biographical contributions belong to the most important sources for Beethoven's life, a fact which Schindler tries to belittle somewhat. Schindler, in his Beethoven biography, criticized Ries for having stressed Beethoven's titanic attitude and he always tried to rectify Ries' opinions. Nevertheless Ries' work was published quite independent of any suggestions by Schindler, who had met the Master much later than Ries. In the first edition of Schindler's biography, published 1840, Ries was still criticized, whereas in the third and fourth editions Ries' biographical notes were used extensively. As in the case of Holz, Moscheles and others, Schindler considered Ries a competitor and tried to question his authenticity; he even belittles his studies with Beethoven. The Master certainly had a good opinion of Ries, to whose family he was closely attached. He introduced Ries to Count Browne and Prince Lichnowsky, on whose estate in Silesia Ries spent several weeks. (Cf. Entries: Browne; Lichnowsky; Nägeli.) A short quotation concerning Ries' piano studies with Beethoven follows:

"When Beethoven gave me a lesson he was, I might almost say, unnaturally patient. This as well as his friendly treatment of me, which seldom varied, I must ascribe principally to his attachment and love for my father. Thus he often would have me repeat a single number ten or more times. In the Variations in F major, Op. 34, dedicated to Princess Odescalchi, I was obliged to repeat almost the entire final *adagio* variation seventeen times; and even then he was not satisfied with the expression in the small cadenza, though I played it as well as he did. That day I had well-nigh a two-hour lesson. When I left out something in a passage, a note or a skip, which in many cases he wished to have specially emphasized, or struck a wrong key, he seldom said anything; yet when I was at fault with regard to the expression, the crescendi or matters of that kind, or in the character of the piece, he would grow angry. Mistakes of the other kind, he said, were due to chance; but these last resulted from want of knowledge, feeling or attention. He himself often made mistakes of the first kind, even when playing in public. Once we were taking a walk and lost our way so completely that we did not get back to Döbling, where Beethoven lived, until eight o'clock. Throughout our walk he hummed and, in part, howled, up and down the scale as we went along, without singing any individual notes. When I asked him what it was he replied: "The theme for the final *allegro* of the sonata (in F minor, Op. 57) has occurred to me." When we entered the room he ran to the piano without taking off his hat. I sat down in a corner and soon he had forgotten me. Then he raged on the keys for at least an hour, developing the new finale of this sonata (which appeared in 1807) in the beautiful form we know. At last he rose, was surprised to see me still there and said: 'I cannot give you a lesson today; I still have work to do.'"

Cf. Th.-R.; Grove: *Dictionary of Music and Musicians;* Entry: Ries; Schiedermair: *Der junge Beethoven.*)

Rio (Del Rio), Cajetan Giannatasio Owner of an educational institution in Vienna. Of Italo-Spanish origin. According to Frimmel, he owned the school as early as 1798. In 1875 Ludwig Nohl published a book titled *Eine stille Liebe zu Beethoven, nach dem Tagebuch einer jungen Dame.* The young lady who admired Beethoven was Fanny del Rio, the daughter of the educator. She was born in 1790; her younger sister, called Nanni, in 1792. As Fanny had been disappointed in love, she found some satisfaction in her emotional admiration for Beethoven. Her feelings are expressed in a diary which she had started in 1812. The connections of the del Rio family with Beethoven stemmed from the fact that Johann Friedrich Duncker, chief secretary of the King of Prussia, lived in the del Rio house (cf. Entry: Duncker). In Fanny's diary Beethoven's music to *Leonore Prohaska,* by Duncker, is mentioned. Fanny saw Beethoven for the first time on January 24, 1816, when the Master brought his nephew to the del Rio school. Karl entered the institution February 2, 1816.

From this time on, friendly relations between the del Rios and Beethoven continued. Fanny's diaries mention Beethoven's changing moods. He mourned the death of his brother and complained about the loss of his hearing. The diary also speaks of Beethoven's happy moments, when he went bowling with the school boys, had fun with them, accompanied his lieder sung by Fanny and her sister, and talked to them about his own childhood. Beethoven used to discuss with Fanny his different love affairs, and she questioned the Master about the Distant Beloved, referring to the song cycle *An die ferne Geliebte,* text by Jeitteles, which Beethoven had just composed. One friend of the del Rios' was Josef Karl Bernard (see Entry: Bernard), who was responsible for Beethoven's friendship with them. Beethoven seems to have preferred Nanni del Rio, whose refreshing temperament he enjoyed more than Fanny's silent reserve. For a while Beethoven even planned to move to the del Rios. It is impossible to discuss Fanny's diaries in detail. They reflect Beethoven's emotional attitude toward his nephew Karl. When Nanni del Rio married Leopold Schmerling on February 6, 1819, Beethoven composed a wedding song. (Cf. Hitzig: "Das Hochzeitslied für Giannatasio del Rio von Beethoven" in *Zeitschrift für Musikwissenschaft* VII, p. 164.)

The last time Fanny mentioned Beethoven was April 9, 1820: "Tonight we saw Beethoven after an absence of almost a year. He was evidently glad to see us again. He felt well, in general, at least he has some respite from being troubled by Karl's mother. I deeply regret that our connection with that wonderful man was severed. His hearing has deteriorated, and I have to write down every conversation. He gave me another beautiful song: Abendlied unter dem gestirnten Himmel, which I like very much." This song had been composed by Beethoven on March 4, 1820; Beethoven later dedicated it to Dr. Braunhofer (cf. Entry: Braunhofer). Among the many celebrities who met in the del Rio house, the poet Bauernfeld should be mentioned. The del Rios were also related to the poet Emanuel Geibel. (Cf. Leitzmann: *Ludwig van Beethoven, Berichte der Zeitgenossen etc.;* Th.-R.; Kaznelson: *Beethovens Ferne und Unsterbliche Geliebte.*)

Ritterballet (Equestrian Ballet)

See Entries: Dance; Dance music.

Rochlitz, Johann Friedrich

b. Leipzig 1769, d. there 1842. Writer on music. Studied under Doles at the Thomas School in Leipzig; later became a private teacher and dedicated himself to his own literary studies. From 1798 to 1818 he was the most influential editor of the *Allgemeine Musikalische Zeitung*, Breitkopf and Härtel, to which he contributed until 1835. From 1805 on he was a member of the Gewandhaus in Leipzig. He was one of the best writers of his time. His description of the battle of Leipzig, written in a letter to Goethe, was characterized by the great poet as one of the "most miraculous productions." It was also Goethe who was responsible for Rochlitz's title of Hofrat. Rochlitz was one of those who fully recognized Beethoven's greatness. In the spring of 1822 Breitkopf and Härtel asked Beethoven, through Rochlitz, to compose an opera *Faust*. The report of Rochlitz about his visit to Vienna can be found in his book *Für ruhige Stunden* (1828) and later in 1832 in the fourth volume of *Für Freunde der Tonkunst* in the form of two letters (one to Gottl. Christian Härtel, dated June 28, 1828, and the other one "To my house," dated Baden, June 9, 1828). An extract of the two letters follows, the translation taken from *Beethoven, Impressions of Contemporaries* (Schirmer).

"I never had seen Beethoven and hence wished all the more that our meeting might take place as soon as possible. No later than the third day after my arrival I spoke about it to N. N., his intimate friend. 'He lives out in the country,' said the latter. 'Then let us drive out there.' 'That we can do, but his unfortunate deafness has little by little made him quite unsociable. He knows that you want to visit him; he wishes to make your personal acquaintance; but at the same time we cannot be sure that when he sees us arrive, he will not run away because, just as he is sometimes full of the most spontaneous merriment, so he often is seized by the profoundest melancholy. It strikes him out of the blue, without any cause, and he is unable to make headway against it. But he comes to town at least once a week, at which times he always sees us, because we attend to his letters and the like. Then he usually is in good spirits and we have him where he cannot escape. So if you are willing to humor the poor, tortured soul to the extent of letting us inform you at once and then—it is only a matter of a few steps—come in as though by chance. . . .'

"Of course, I was more than glad to accede to his proposal. The next Saturday morning the messenger came to me. I went and found Beethoven conducting a lively conversation with N.N. He is used to the latter and understands him fairly well, reading his words from the movements of his face and lips. Beethoven seemed to be pleased, yet he was disturbed. And had I not been prepared in advance, his appearance would have disturbed me as well. Not his neglected, almost uncivilized outward semblance, not the thick black hair which bristled about his head and the like, but his appearance as a whole. Picture to yourself a man of approximately fifty years of age, small rather than of medium size, but with a very powerful, stumpy figure, compact and with a notably strong bone structure, about like that of Fichte, but fleshier, and, especially, with a rounder fuller face; a red, healthy complexion; restless, glowing, and when his gaze is fixed, even piercing eyes; not given to movement and when moving, moving hastily; with regard to his facial expression, especially that of the eyes, intelligent and full of life, offering a mingling or an occasional momentary alternation of the heartiest amiability and shyness; in his whole attitude that tension, that uneasy, worried striving to hear, peculiar to the deaf who are keenly sensitive; now a merrily and freely spoken word; again, immediately after, a relapse into gloomy silence; and in addition, all that which the thinker and meditator himself contributes and which is continually sounding together with all the rest—such is the man who has given happiness to millions, a purely spiritual happiness.

"In broken sentences he made some friendly and amiable remarks to me. I raised my voice as much as I could, spoke slowly, with sharp accentuation, and thus out of the fullness of my heart conveyed to him my gratitude for his works and all they meant to me and would mean to me while life endured. I singled out some of my favorites, and dwelt upon them; told him how his symphonies were performed in model fashion in Leipzig, how all of them were played each recurring winter season, and the loud delight with which the public received them. He stood close beside me, now gazing on my face with strained attention, now dropping his head. Then he would smile to himself, nod amiably on occasion, all without saying a word. Had he understood me? Had he failed to understand? At last I had to make an end, and he gave my hand a powerful grip and said curtly to N. N.: 'I still have a few necessary errands to do.' Then, as he left, he said: 'Shall we not see each other again?' N. N. now returned. 'Did he understand what I said?' I queried. I was deeply moved and affected. N.N. shrugged his shoulders. 'Not a word.' For a long time we were silent and I cannot say how affected I was. Finally I asked, 'Why did you not at least repeat this or that to him, since he understands you fairly well?' 'I did not wish to interrupt you and, besides, he very easily gets sensitive. And I really hoped he would understand much of what you said, but the noise in the street, your speech, to which he is unaccustomed and, perhaps, his own eagerness to understand everything, since it was perfectly clear to him that you were telling him pleasant things. . . . He was so unhappy.' I cannot describe the sensation which filled me as I left. The man who solaced the whole world with the voice of his music, heard no other human voice, not even that of one who wished to thank him. Aye, it even became an instrument of torture for him. I had my mind made up not to see him again, and to send Mr. Härtel's proposal to him in writing.

"Some two weeks later I was about to go to dinner when I met the young composer, Franz Schubert, an enthusiastic admirer of Beethoven. The latter had spoken to Schubert concerning me. 'If you wish to see him in a more natural and jovial mood,' said Schubert, 'then go and eat your dinner this very minute at the inn where he has just gone for the same purpose.' He took me with him. Most of the places were taken. Beethoven sat among several acquaintances who were strangers to me. He really seemed to be in good spirits and acknowledged my greeting, but I purposely did not cross over to him. Yet I found a seat from which I could see him and, since he spoke loud enough, also could hear nearly all that he said. It could not actually be called a conversation, for he spoke in monologue, usually at some length, and more as though by hapchance and at random.

"Those about him contributed little, merely laughing or nodding their approval. He philosophized, or one might say politicized, after his own fashion. He spoke of England and the English, and of how both were associated in his thoughts with a splendor incomparable —which, in part, sounded tolerably fantastic. Then he told all sorts of stories of the French, from the days of the second occupation of Vienna. For them he had no kind words. His remarks all were made with the greatest unconcern and without the least reserve, and whatever he said was spiced with highly original, naive judgments or humorous fancies. He impressed me as being a man with a rich, aggressive intellect, and unlimited, never resting imagination. I saw him as one who, had he been cast away on a desert isle when no more than a growing, capable boy, would have taken all he had lived and learned, all that had stuck to him in the way of knowledge, and there have meditated and brooded over his material until his fragments had become a whole, his imaginings turned to convictions which he would have shouted out into the world in all security and confidence.

"When he had finished his meal he rose and came over to me. 'And is all well with you in this old Vienna of ours?' he asked amiably. I answered in the affirmative by signs, drank to his health and asked him to pledge me. He accepted, but beckoned me to a little side room. This suited me to a T. I took the bottle and followed him. Here we were by ourselves, save for an occasional peeper who soon made himself scarce. He offered me a little tablet upon which I was to write down whatever my signs did not make clear. He began by praising Leipzig and its music; that is to say, the music chosen for performance in the churches, at concerts and in the theatre. Otherwise he knew nothing of Leipzig and had only passed through the city when a youth on his way to Vienna. 'And even though nothing is printed about the performances but the dry records, still I read them with pleasure,' he said. 'One cannot help but notice that they are intelligent and well inclined toward all. Here, on the contrary. . . .' then he started in, rudely enough, nor would he let himself be stopped. He came to speak of himself: 'You will hear nothing of me here,' he cried. 'What should you hear? *Fidelio?* They cannot give it, nor do they want to listen to it. The symphonies? They have no time for them. My concertos? Everyone grinds out only the stuff he himself has made. The solo pieces? They went out of fashion here long ago, and here fashion is everything. At the most Schuppanzigh occasionally digs up a quartet, etc.' And despite all exaggeration in what he said, a modicum of reason and truth remains. At last he had relieved himself and harked back to Leipzig. 'But,' said he, 'you really live in Weimar, do you not?' He probably thought so because of my address. I shook my head. 'Then it is not likely that you know the great Goethe?' I nodded my head vigorously. 'I know him, too,' said Beethoven, throwing out his chest, while an expression of the most radiant pleasure overspread his face."

Beethoven thought a lot of Rochlitz, whom he designated as his future biographer. Schindler reported this in his own biography. It was Schindler who transmitted Beethoven's wish to Rochlitz, September 12, 1827. Rochlitz answered in the negative six days later, being too overworked. Shortly after having written to Rochlitz, Schindler wrote to Moscheles, September 14, 1827: "A certain Herr Schlosser in Prague has published a miserable biography on Beethoven, and another one has been advertised by Herr Gräffer in Vienna, though Beethoven designated Hofrat Rochlitz in Leipzig as his biographer. The Master has given to me important documents for Rochlitz and Breuning." Finally, Schindler was the actual executor of Beethoven's wish. (Cf. Th.-R. V; Biedermann: *Goethes Briefwechsel mit Friedrich Rochlitz;* H. Ehinger: *Friedrich Rochlitz als Musikschriftsteller,* Leipzig 1928.)

Röckel, Josef August

b. Neuenburg (Upper Palatinate) 1783, d. Köthen 1870. Singer, private secretary to the Bavarian chargé d'affaires in Salzburg. When Baron Braun, theatrical director in Vienna, sent an agent to Salzburg to select some good voices, he discovered Röckel, at that time an amateur with a tremendous voice. He was chosen as first tenor for the Vienna opera. When *Fidelio* was to be revived, the role of Florestan was assigned to him. Röckel wrote a long letter to Thayer about Beethoven February 26, 1861, and gave him additional information when he met him in England. Röckel told Thayer about his invitation by Prince Lichnowsky to the discussions of the changes in the score of *Fidelio*. Princess Lichnowsky played the whole score on the piano, whereupon Clement, sitting in a corner of the room, played the whole opera from memory on his violin. As Beethoven did not want to sacrifice a single note, he became infuriated whenever cuts were suggested. Frequently the Princess had to act as an intermediary, and in one instance on her knees she had to implore the Master to yield to the requests. Röckel sang the whole opera from the score. The discussions lasted until 1 o'clock in the morning. After the whole affair was settled, an excellent supper was served, and nobody was happier than Beethoven himself. This famous musical session at Lichnowsky's was utilized in the form of a short story by Rud. Bunge in the *Gartenlaube* (1868), and some of Röckel's stories are found in Ries: *Notizen*, and Schindler: *Beethoven-Biography*. (Cf. Th.-R. II; Frimmel: *Beethoven Handbuch*.)

Rode, Pierre

b. Bordeaux 1774, d. Damazon (Lot-et Garonne) 1830. Famous violinist, student of Viotti in Paris, where he made his debut in 1790. From 1795 to 1803 he was Professor of violin at the Conservatory of Paris, and Concertmaster of the Grand-Opéra until 1799. Between 1803 and 1808 he was a solo violinist in St. Petersburg, and after 1811, in Paris. He went to Vienna in 1812, where he became acquainted with Beethoven. At the suggestion of Archduke Rudolph, Beethoven composed for Rode his Violin Sonata Op. 96, later dedicated to the Archduke. According to a letter from Beethoven to the Archduke, dated December 1812, the Master was not too much impressed by Rode's playing. The sonata was performed at an evening concert in the Lobkowitz Palace. Glöggl's Music Magazine reported on this performance on January 4, 1813, remarking that the Archduke played better than Rode. During his stay in Vienna, Rode became acquainted with musicians from Graz, as seen in a letter of Beethoven's to Josef von Varena (see Entry: Varena). (Cf. Th.-R. III, p. 350; A. Pougin: *Notices sur Rode*, 1874; Andreas Moser: *Geschichte des Violinspiels*, 1923; H. Ahlgrimm: *Pierre Rode*, 1929.)

Rolland, Romain

See Entry: France.

Romances for Violin and Orchestra

Beethoven wrote two romances for violin and orchestra. Both have identical instrumentation of one flute, two oboes, two bassoons, two horns, and the usual strings, and both have but a single movement of a free sectional form.

The first of these works, the Romanze in G, Op. 40, was published without dedication by Hoffmeister and Kühnel in 1803, the same year as the Violin Sonatas Op. 30, and the Piano Sonatas Op. 31. The second work, the Romanze in F, Op. 50, was published in 1805 by the Kunst-und Industrie-Comptoir, although it was possibly written in 1802. This work also contains no dedication.

Both of the romances are examples of Beethoven's expressive cantabile and brilliant scale passages. While they are not performed as frequently as the Violin Concerto Op. 61, they are an integral part of every violinist's repertoire.

Romberg

Family of musicians from Muenster, Westphalia. Andreas Romberg (b. Wechta, Oldenburg 1767, d. Gotha 1821), was a violinist who came to Paris in 1784, where he played for the Concerts Spirituels. Between 1790 and 1793 Andreas, together with his cousin Bernhard Romberg, a cellist, played in the Bonn Orchestra as colleagues of Beethoven. Both Rombergs were visitors of the Zehrgarten and participated in the musical excursion to Mergentheim. When the cellist Bernhard gave a concert in Vienna in 1821, Beethoven, in a letter dated February 12, apologized for his absence. Andreas Romberg was the composer of a choral work *Die Glocke,* after Schiller's poem. (Cf. Rochlitz: *Für Freunde der Tonkunst* I; H. Schäfer: *Bernhard Romberg,* Münster, 1931.)

Römischer Kaiser (Roman Emperor)

Famous inn in Vienna with a spacious hall for musical performances. The building is still standing at Freyung and Renngasse. Emanuel Eppinger, an acquaintance of Beethoven's, was manager of the inn. Beethoven lived there temporarily in 1815 or 1816. He frequently took lunch there. The performances of the Schuppanzigh Quartet took place in the music hall of the inn.

Rondo a Capriccio

"The Rage Over a Lost Penny," Op. 129. This little piano work has for many years been played by young pianists as a *tour de force.* The work has recently been the subject of an exhaustive study by Erich Hertzmann. For a number of years the autograph of the work was lost and only the first edition, published by Diabelli in 1828, was known. Otto Albrecht discovered the original autograph in 1945 in the possession of Mrs. Eugene Allen Noble, and a comparison of this autograph with the first edition reveals many discrepancies. Furthermore, the discovery of the autograph makes possible an almost exact dating of the work, a feat heretofore impossible. Until a few years ago the work had been variously ascribed to all three periods of the master's life.

The autograph exists in four single leaves written on both sides; the Rondo occupies pages 2 to 7 with page 1 containing sketches for the Rondo itself and page 8 containing extraneous sketches.

On the basis of the handwriting, Hertzmann places the work in the first period, although not as early as the Bonn years. Further, the sketches on the last page reveal a great similarity to the First Symphony and the C major Piano Concerto. Sketches containing similar material have been published by Nottebohm, who first attributed them to the First Symphony but later to an unfinished symphony in C major, preceeding the First Symphony. The sketches for the C major Concerto help us to date the manuscript still more closely, for Beethoven himself played the concerto in Prague in 1798 and therefore the sketches must antedate that year. Moreover, the sketches of the unfinished C major symphony published by Nottebohm were found along with counterpoint exercises written under the guidance of Albrechtsberger, with whom Beethoven last studied in 1795. Therefore, these sketches must have originated at about this time. On the basis of this evidence it is possible to place the date of composition of the Rondo between the years 1795 and 1798.

A comparison of the autograph with the first edition reveals that the work must have been edited by someone when published by Diabelli. In the first place, the work was left unfinished and had to be completed. Many measures have been omitted from the first edition and many places in the manuscript which were only sketched have been filled in and harmonic parts added. In numerous cases accidentals in the autograph have been misread and are incorrect in the first edition.

In view of the incomplete state of many parts of the manuscript, and the existence of sketches for the Rondo on page 1 (many appearing as variants of similar places in the work), Hertzmann conjectures that this may have been a work which Beethoven kept for himself and which formed the basis of many of his improvisations. It is well known that Beethoven was considered the foremost pianist during his early years in Vienna, particularly in improvising. Hertzmann's deductions seem highly logical although not conclusive. (Cf. Hertzmann: "The Newly Discovered Autograph of Beethoven's Rondo â Capriccio, Op. 129," *Musical Quarterly,* Vol. XXXII, p. 171).

F. T. W.

Rossini, Gioacchino Antonio

b. Pesaro (Romagna) 1792, d. Ruelle (near Paris) 1868. Celebrated operatic composer. When the operatic troupe of Barbaja, whose mistress Isabella Colbran later became Rossini's wife, came to Vienna in 1821, Rossini, as conductor and composer, had a tremendous success. All Vienna was in a frenzy about Rossini. Consequently Beethoven and Schubert were somewhat neglected. Rossini tried several times to approach Beethoven through Artaria, but with no success. Finally he succeeded in locating the Master, who lived in the Leimgrube. Schindler's information about this visit is rather vague, and a Conversation-book of that period is not preserved. Hanslick, visiting Rossini in Paris in 1867, heard the following about this visit: "I remember well being introduced to Beethoven by Carpani, who had introduced me previously to Salieri. The visit did not take long, and the conversation with Beethoven was almost painful. His hearing was very bad that day and his Italian questionable." In 1856 Rossini told Hiller similar reminiscences about Beethoven. (Cf. Th.-R. IV, p. 292; Edgar Itsel: "Rossiniana," *Die Musik* 1912.)

Rovantini, Franz Georg

b. Bonn 1757, d. there 1781. Violinist in Bonn. He was the son of an army physician, Anselm Rovantini, whose wife was closely related to Beethoven's mother. According to the Fischer Manuscript, Rovantini lived in the same house with the Beethovens. A daughter of the violinist, Anna Maria Magdalena, was governess in the house of a rich Dutch lady in Rotterdam. It is presumed that Johann van Beethoven went to see his relative in Holland and took young Ludwig with him on this trip. (Cf. Schiedermair: *Der junge Beethoven;* Th.-R. I.)

Rudolph

Archduke of Austria; b. Florence 1788, d. Baden (near Vienna) 1832. Son of the Grand Duke of Tuscany (later Emperor Leopold II) and Maria Ludovica. He was the grandson of Empress Maria Theresia and the nephew of Joseph II. Arriving in Vienna in 1790, after his father had assumed the Imperial throne, he received his own staff, headed by his Oberhofmeister Graf Ferdinand von Laurencin d' Armont. Rudolph's educator and librarian was Jos. von Baumeister.

According to reports by contemporaries, Rudolph was of a happy disposition. Later he suffered from the typical Hapsburg disease, epilepsy. Rudolph was musically very gifted, a talent inherited from his forefathers. One of his first teachers was Anton Teyber, chamber composer and teacher of the Imperial Princes. Rudolph soon realized the mediocrity of his teacher and shifted to Beethoven, whom he had met at the house of Prince Lobkowitz. According to Schindler, Beethoven had composed his Triple Concerto Op. 56 for the Archduke; it is well known that he finally dedicated it to Prince Lobkowitz. Rudolph took piano and theory lessons from Beethoven, which were given frequently in his palace in Baden. According to reports given to Thayer by Theresa von Bauer, née Dürfeld, "unions" (gatherings) took place in Baden, Hotel Stadt Wien, and Beethoven appeared there many times in the company of Archduke Rudolph. Paul Tausig in his book *Berühmte Besucher in Baden* mentioned the years 1812, 1813, 1816, and 1819 for the Archduke's visits at this resort place. When Beethoven was called to Cassel as Kapellmeister for Jerôme of Westphalia, Archduke Rudolph, Prince Lobkowitz, and Kinsky offered him a yearly pension for staying in Vienna. It was the Archduke alone who kept his promise after the deaths of Kinsky and Lobkowitz, for their heirs were not willing to continue the contribution. Originally Rudolph had been destined for an ecclesiastical profession. He was named Archbishop of Olmütz in 1819, a fact which caused Beethoven to compose his *Missa Solemnis* for Rudolph's enthronization. Beethoven recognized the Archduke as his full-fledged student. He shared this honor only with Ferdinand Ries. The Archduke was certainly an excellent pianist, and a remarkable composer. In 1819 Beethoven gave the Archduke a theme to be used for variations, and this set of forty variations, dedicated to Beethoven, was advertised by Steiner and Co. in the *Wiener Zeitung* of January 19, 1819. Certainly the Master did not stoop to Rudolph. Another contribution of the Archduke was a variation on a theme by Diabelli in the *Vaterländischer Künstlerverein*, a fugal variation in the style of Beethoven. A third printed composition by the Archduke was a sonata for clarinet and piano, dedicated to Count Ferdinand Troyer, Rudolph's chamberlain, a clarinet amateur. None of the other compositions have been printed. Variations by the Archduke are mentioned in three letters of Beethoven (no. 60, 61, 62 in Köchel's collection of Beethoven's letters to the Archduke). Some of the compositions are preserved in the archives of the Archbishopric of Olmütz, the Castle Kremsier (cf. Paul Nettl: "Erinnerungen an Erzherzog Rudolph," *Zeitschrift für Musikwissenschaft,* vol. IV). Furthermore, Archduke Rudolph composed eight variations on a Czech folk song, "To jsou kone," and another variation on a theme of his own. The Czech variations show pencil marks by Beethoven.

The Archduke owned a large music library in Vienna, containing all of Beethoven's works. Today it is part of the library of the Gesellschaft der Musikfreunde. Some of the books used by the Archduke are found in Kremsier also, among them Burney, Chladni, and others. One of Rudolph's most interesting compositions is the sketch of a chorus with the following text: "Dear Beethoven, I thank you for your New Year wishes, and accept my own wishes for you with indulgence." This might have been the answer to Beethoven's own canon of 1820, "To his Imperial Highness. To Archduke Rudolph. To the Ecclesiastic Prince. All the best." Among Beethoven's compositions dedicated to the Archduke, the following should be mentioned: The Piano Concerto in G Op. 58; the Piano Concerto in E flat major Op. 73; the Piano Sonata "Les Adieux" Op. 81a; the piano score to *Fidelio* Op. 72b; the Violin Sonata in G major Op. 96; the Piano Trio in B flat major Op. 97; the Hammerklavier Sonata Op. 106; the *Missa Solemnis* Op. 123; the Great Fugue Op. 133 and its arrangement for four-hand piano, Op. 134; the canon *Alles Gute* and the Lied "Gedenke mein." The dedication of Sonata Op. 111 was done by the publisher Schlesinger, not by Beethoven himself. (Cf. Th.-R. III-V; Entry: *Missa Solemnis;* Köchel: *83 neu aufgefundene Originalbriefe Ludwig van Beethovens an Erzherzog Rudolph,* Wien 1865.)

Ruins of Athens (Ruinen von Athen)
Music composed by Beethoven for the German theater in Pest (Budapest) in 1811, first performed on February 9, 1812, on the occasion of the opening of the above-mentioned theater. After Collin had refused in 1810 to write a play dealing with a Hungarian subject, Kotzebue took over the job. The poet wrote three plays: *Hungary's First Benefactor, Bela's Escape,* and the *Ruins of Athens.* The second was omitted because of Emperor Franz's recent flight from Vienna; it was replaced by *Elevation of Pest to a Royal Capital.* Shortly before Beethoven left Vienna for Teplitz in the summer of 1811, he received the text of the *Ruins of Athens.* In Teplitz he composed the complete music to *King Stephan* containing the Overture, male Chorus: *"Ruhend von seinen Thaten"* and *"Auf dunklem Irrweg,"* Victory March, female Chorus *"Wo die Unschuld,"* Melodrama, Chorus: *"Eine neustrahlende Sonne,"* Melodrama, Ghostly March, Melodrama with Chorus: *"Heil unserm Könige,"* and Final Chorus *"Heil, heil."* It is well known that *King Stephan* does not belong to Beethoven's masterpieces, due to Kotzebue's boisterous and bombastic text. The text was later rewritten by Karl Meisel for the Theater in der Josephstadt (1821) and again by Robert Heller. Meisel's text is found in Nottebohm's *Beethoveniana* II, p. 385, under the title *Zur Weihe des Hauses.* In 1822 the text was completely rewritten by Johann Sporschill under the title *Die Apotheose im Tempel des Iupiter Am-*

mon, ernste Oper in Zwei Akten. The hero of this play is Alexander the Great. The *Ruins of Athens* was given originally in the following order: Overture, Chorus: *"Tochter des mächtigen Zeus,"* Duet of the two Greeks *"Ohne Verschulden Knechtschaft dulden,"* Chorus of the Dervishes, *Marcia alla Turca,* Chorus: *"Schmückt die Altäre,"* Recitative and Aria *"Mit reger Freude,"* Chorus: *"Wir tragen . . .",* Aria *"Will unser Genius,"* and Final Chorus: *"Heil unserem König." Marcia alla Turca* in B flat major (No. 4), typical Janizary music, was later used by Beethoven in his variations in D major Op. 76, dedicated to Oliva. (Cf. Volkmann: *Neues über Beethoven;* Th.-R.)

Rupprecht, Johann Baptist

b. Wölfelsdorf (Silesia) 1776, d. Vienna 1846. Writer, hortologist and book censor. His father was a schoolmaster and an excellent organist. He studied in Breslau at the Josephine Convent and at the University. After coming to Vienna, he concentrated on hortology, introducing new methods in this line. As an expert on the English language, he published metrical translations of English poems in 1812. Furthermore he was interested in American culture and history, and wrote a biography of James Monroe in 1832. His association with Beethoven stems from Rupprecht's poem *Merkenstein,* for which the Master wrote two different melodies. In addition Rupprecht wrote a libretto which was to be composed by Beethoven under the title *Die Begründung von Pennsylvanien* (cf. Entry: United States of America).

In a Conversation-book of 1820 Janitschek wrote: "Rupprecht has written an excellent sketch for an opera, entitled *Die Begründung von Pennsylvanien oder die Ankunft des Pen (?) in Amerika.* He planned to hand you the text for a composition. Too bad that it has not been realized." (Cf. Schünemann: *Konversationshefte,* Vol. I, p. 209.) In Schünemann, Vol. I, p. 160, Bernard remarked that Rupprecht might be willing to travel with Beethoven (England?). Rupprecht was always on bad terms with Grillparzer, as the latter censored his poems. (Cf. Wurzbach; Th.-R.)

Russel, John

b. London 1792, d. 1863. In 1825 he published in Edinburgh a travel book entitled *A Tour in Germany.* Russel met Beethoven at a party in 1820 or 1822, where he described the Master's habits in a colorful way. At another time, he met Beethoven in a tavern. When some stranger took a seat at Beethoven's table, Russel noticed that the Master spat until the stranger left the table in disgust; thereupon Beethoven remarked about the man's apish face. On another occasion the Master made favorable remarks about English pianos. (Cf. Frimmel: *Beethoven Handbuch.*)

Russia

Beethoven's music became known in Russia in the first years of the nineteenth century. However, only after the Congress of Vienna in 1815, during which the Russian court resided in Vienna, did Beethoven's music gain its great popularity with Russian musicians and Russian society. Many Russians often had an opportunity to meet Beethoven and hear his personal execution of his works at the famous musical parties of Prince Andrey Razumovsky, Russian ambassador in Vienna, famous Maecenas and personal friend of Beethoven. The leading Russian musicians—contemporaries of Beethoven—M. I. Glinka and Prince B. F. Odoevsky, greatly appreciated and admired Beethoven's music. Beethoven's *Missa Solemnis,* composed in 1823, was first performed in Petersburg in 1824, and since that time Beethoven's music has remained an integral feature of the Russian musician's repertoire.

A. N. Serov, well-known Russian composer and a leading music critic in the mid-nineteenth century, devoted a large number of articles to Beethoven and contributed greatly to his popularity in Russia. A. N. Stasov, the ideologist of the Russian "Great Five" in music (Moussorgsky, Balakireff, Borodin, Rimsky-Korsakoff and Cui), considered Beethoven the greatest representative of European musical culture and admired his programmatic development. Stasov qualified Beethoven's work as "victory through struggle." Beethoven's music found a particular echo in P. I. Tschaikovsky, who was especially influenced by Beethoven's symphonic ideas. Important Russian writers and critics such as V. G. Belinsky, A. I. Herzen, and N. G. Chernishevsky qualified Beethoven as one of the great geniuses of the world and considered him the founder of realism in music. Since the revolution of 1917 Beethoven has become particularly popular in Russia. It is interesting to know that Beethoven found one of his greatest admirers in V. Lenin, who once remarked to Gorky, "There is no better musical work in the world than the *Apassionata.* I enjoy listening to it every day. Formidable, super-human music. I always think with pride that man has been able to create such a miracle." The well-known Soviet minister of education, A. V. Lunacharsky, wrote a number of studies on Beethoven. It is indicative of the degree of official recognition of Beethoven in Russia that on the day of the proclamation of Stalin's constitution the final part of Beethoven's Ninth Symphony, mentioned as the anthem of human freedom, concluded the official concert performed before the Supreme Soviet. (Cf. Alexeev, M. P. and Ya. Z. Berman: *Beethoven: Materials for the Bibliographical Guide of Russian Literature about Beethoven* (in Russian), Vols. 1, 2, Odessa, 1927-28; Shaverdan, A.: *Symphonies of Beethoven* (in Russian), Moscow, 1936; Lunacharsky, A. B., see *In the World of Music* (in Russian), Moscow, 1926; Stasov, V. V., see *Complete Works,* Vol. 4, Petersburg, 1909; Serov, A. N., see *Critical Articles and Notes,* Petersburg, 1892; Tschaikovsky, P. I.: *Music Feuilletons and Notes,* Moscow, 1898; *Russkaya Kniga o Beethovene,* Moscow, 1927.)

S. Z.

S

Sali

Beethoven's last housekeeper and cook. In contrast to many other servants this "gem" was faithful and devoted to the Master, assisting him during the last hours of his life. Sali had come to Beethoven's house at the recommendation of the von Breunings. (Cf. Entry: Servants; Breuning: *Aus dem Schwarzspanierhaus.*)

Salieri, Antonio

b. Legnago (near Verona) 1750, d. Vienna 1825. Famous operatic composer. He studied with his brother Francesco, a pupil of Tartini, with the organist Simoni, the Maëstro di Capello Pescetti and the tenor Pacini in Venice. In 1766 he met F. L. Gassmann, who took him to Vienna, where he attended to his further education. In 1777 Antonio made his debut with the comic opera *Le donne letterate,* which impressed Gluck. After the performance of a second opera, *La fiera di Venezia,* his reputation was established. When Gassmann died in 1774, he succeeded him as chamber composer and conductor of the Italian opera in Vienna. After Gluck's fame had overshadowed his own, he began to compose opera in the reformed style and tried to follow Gluck's patterns. Gluck sponsored him and gave him a chance to appear in front of the Paris audience. Salieri's opera *Les Danaïdes,* with Calzabigi's libretto, was introduced in Paris under the names of Salieri and Gluck, and Gluck's name did not disappear from the playbill until after the twelfth performance, when its success was certain. In addition Salieri composed for the Paris opera *Les Horaces* and *Tarare,* libretto by da Ponte, later renamed *Axur re d' Ormus* (piano score by Neefe). This was the first to be given a Polish performance at the National Court Theater in Warsaw. In 1788 Salieri became Giuseppe Bonno's successor, but was dismissed after the death of Joseph II in 1790. He thenceforth worked as a conductor of the Imperial Chapel and as an operatic composer. He retired in 1824.

When Beethoven came to Vienna, he chose Salieri as his instructor in dramatic composition. Whether or not Beethoven took regular lessons from him is uncertain. Beethoven dedicated to Salieri his three Violin Sonatas Op. 12, evidently as a token of his gratitude. When Salieri's opera *Falstaff* had its first performance in Vienna (1799), Beethoven was impressed by the aria *"La stessa la stessima*" and later used the theme for his B flat major Variations, dedicated to Countess Barbara Keglevitsch. Moscheles reported that when he came to see Salieri for a lesson in 1806, he found on a table a sheet of paper on which the following words were written in big letters: "The pupil Beethoven was here."

It may be assumed that Salieri, as the last exponent of Italian art, was not too friendly with Beethoven. His jealousy of Mozart was already proverbial, and there were even rumors that Salieri had poisoned Mozart. Pushkin used this story as the plot for his play *Mozart and Salieri.* It is certain that Beethoven took advantage of Salieri's abilities. The Master's comparatively good knowledge of Italian might be due to Salieri. On the other hand Salieri's poor understanding of Beethoven should be excused. According to Bauernfeld's recollections, Schubert, also a pupil of Salieri, had to hide his enthusiasm for Beethoven from Salieri. Rochlitz in *Für ruhige Stunden* (1822) gave a picturesque description of Salieri, describing him as a little vivacious man who still spoke broken German with fragments of Italian and French. (Cf. E. von Mosel: *Antonio Salieri,* 1827; A. von Hermann: *Antonio Salieri,* 1897; Th.-R. II-V; Wurzbach.)

Salomon, Johann Peter

b. Bonn 1745, d. London 1815. Violinist, member of the Electoral Orchestra in Bonn. His father, Philip, was also a member of that orchestra, while two sisters, Anna Maria (later married Geyers) and Anna Jacobina, were Electoral court singers. In 1765 Salomon became concertmaster for Prince Heinrich of Prussia (brother of Frederick the Great) in Rheinsberg. When the orchestra was discontinued, he went to Paris and, in 1781, to London. Here he made himself a considerable reputation as a quartet violinist. After he became an independent concert impresario he invited Haydn to London. From London he paid occasional visits to Bonn, as in 1790 when he met Beethoven for the first time. During Beethoven's stay in Bonn, the Salomon family lived in the neighborhood of the house of the baker, Fischer, whose connections with Beethoven are well known. For the remainder of his life Salomon was always in contact with Beethoven, negotiating on his behalf with publishers, and with Smart and Ries promoting the Master's works in London. (Cf. Th.-R. II and III; C. F. Pohl: *Haydn in London,* Wien, 1867; Grove.)

Sanft wie du lebtest

Funeral cantata for Johann Pasqualati (see Entry: Pasqualati).

Schaden, Dr. von

Lawyer in Augsburg who received Beethoven in his home in 1787, when the latter returned from Vienna to Bonn. Nanette Schaden née Frank, from Salzburg, the lawyer's wife, was an excellent pianist and singer. Reichardt called her the greatest clavirist and unexcelled by any virtuoso. Schiedermair printed an intimate letter from Beethoven to Schaden, dated September 15, 1787, in which the Master described the death of his mother, complaining about his own personal difficulties. (Cf. Schiedermair: *Der junge Beethoven;* Th.-R. I, p. 216.)

Schechner, Nanette

b. Munich 1806, d. there 1860. Excellent singer who studied the role of Fidelio in 1826. Holz, in a Conversation-book of May 22, 1826, said "Today Schechner will sing in *Schweizer Familie* [by Joseph Weigl]. She sings almost as well as Milder, but with more flexibility in her throat." Later Holz noted: ". . . almost like Milder, but with better acting. Pure intonation and clear diction." Schindler remarked in June: "I am approaching you, my great Master, asking your permission to introduce to you Mlle. Schechner, who is longing to meet you. A true *portentum naturae*. Vienna never heard anything equal . . ." During Beethoven's last days, Nanette, her mother, and her fiancé, the operatic singer Ludwig Cramolini, came to visit Beethoven frequently. (Cf. Th.-R. V.)

Schenk, Johann

b. Wiener Neustadt 1753, d. Vienna 1836. Composer and theoretician, student of Wagenseil and a free-lancing music teacher. He gained fame as the composer of the singspiele *Der Dorfbarbier* (1796), *Der Bettelstudent* (1796), and *Die Jagd* (1797). His acquaintance with Beethoven started in the summer of 1792 (Schenk) or 1793 (Thayer). Schenk left an autobiography in the form of a letter addressed to Aloys Fuchs (1799-1853), in whose possession it remained for a long while. It was Schenk who, at Abbé Gellinek's house, heard the young Beethoven playing and became highly enthusiastic about his talent. When he visited Beethoven, he found on his desk some compositions in counterpoint which proved that the young composer didn't know too much about that art. He advised Beethoven to study the Fux *Gradus ad Parnassum*. When Schenk heard that Beethoven was studying with Haydn, and when he learned that Haydn hadn't been too eager to correct Beethoven's contrapuntal mistakes, he accepted him as a pupil, with the condition that the whole affair was to be done secretly, so that Haydn wouldn't learn about Schenk's teaching of Beethoven. Beethoven was supposed to recopy all the exercises which Schenk corrected in order to avoid Haydn's suspicions; but the secret was betrayed by Gellinek and Beethoven's brothers. Schenk's short autobiography was preserved in his own manuscript. Beethoven's study with Schenk lasted only until May 1793/94. At that time Beethoven was called to Esterhazy in Eisenstadt. Schenk notated in his autobiography: "The day of Beethoven's departure was not yet set. One day in the beginning of June I came to give him his lesson as usual—but my good Louis was no longer there. He had left me the following note which I copy word for word:

'Dear Schenk,

I wish I had not been compelled to leave for Eisenstadt today. I would have liked to talk to you before I left. But meanwhile be assured of my gratitude for all the kindness you have shown to me. I shall try to be worthy of it as best I can. I hope I'll see you soon again and have the pleasure of your company. Farewell and do not entirely forget your

Beethoven.'

"It was my intention to touch upon my relationship with Beethoven only briefly; but the circumstances which brought me together with him and made me become his guide in musical composition, demanded a more detailed explanation. For my endeavor (if endeavor is the right word for it) I received the costliest gift from my good Louis, namely the strong tie of friendship which remained intact to the day of his death."

According to Schindler, Schenk met Beethoven once more, in the spring of 1824. The Master was overwhelmed with joy to see his old friend, took his hand and dragged him into the tavern Zum Jägerhorn. They discussed all sorts of happenings and when the events of 1793/94 were mentioned, Beethoven burst into roaring laughter over having deceived good old "Papa Haydn." Beethoven complimented his old teacher and their farewell was touching. (Cf. Nettl: *Forgotten Musicians* [Translation of the authentic text of Schenk's Autobiography]; Schindler I, p. 33; Th.-R. I.)

Schenker, Heinrich

(1868-1935) Eminent Viennese theorist, whose monograph *Beethovens Neunte Symphonie* (U. E. Vienna, 1912) is one of the most important works on the subject. The commentary edition of the last five sonatas of Beethoven (U. E. Vienna, 1913-1921; Sonata Op. 106 has not been published) contains a most lucid analysis, and based on the original manuscripts in the edition of the Sonata Op. 101, we find the recommendation of the Photogrammarchiv at the Vienna National Library (Anthony van Hoboken; cf. Entry: Manuscripts). Schenker also published the "Urtext" Edition of all the Beethoven sonatas (U. E. Vienna). Further publications concerned with Beethoven are: "Analysis of the Sonatas Op. 2 No. 1 and Op. 57" (*Tonwille* Gutmann Verlag Vienna, issue 2 and 7), "Fifth Symphony," (*Tonwille,* issue 1, 5 and 6), "Beethovens metronomische Bezeichnungen" (*Tw.* issue 5), "On Beethoven's Op. 127" (*Tw.* issue 7). In *Das Meisterwerk in der Musik* (Dreimasken Verlag, Munich): "Noch einmal zu Op. 110" (vol. 1, 1925); "Vom Organischen der Sonatenform" (vol. 2, 1926); "Rameau oder Beethoven" (vol. 3, 1930) and "Beethoven's *Eroica*" (vol. 3).

One of Schenker's most outstanding pupils is Dr. Oswald Jonas, now living in Chicago, Illinois. Dr. Jonas, a member of the faculty of Roosevelt College, has published the following articles on Beethoven: "The Manuscript of Beethoven's Violinconcerto" (*Z.f.MW* May 1931); "Beethoven's Sketches and his Finished Works" (*Z.f.MW* Oct. 1934); "Beethoveniana" (*Der Dreiklang* Vienna, 1937); "The Autograph of Beethoven's VIII Symphony" (*Music & Letters,* 1939); and in *Musical Quarterly:* "An Unknown Sketch by Beethoven" (1940) and "A Lesson with Beethoven" (1952).

Schering, Arnold

b. Breslau 1877, d. Berlin 1941. Famous musicologist and professor at the Universities of Halle, Leipzig, and Berlin. He was a representative of the symbolic interpretation of music, a method which he applied also to Beethoven's instrumental works. According to his opinion, Beethoven wrote the major part of his instrumental works under the impression of famous poetical works. Accordingly many, if not all, of Beethoven's compositions belong to the category of "esoteric programmatic" music. He quotes many of Beethoven's contemporaries, including Carpani, Kanne, and

Schindler as witnesses for his theory. Schindler, in particular, spoke often about the poetic ideas on which Beethoven's works were based. In fact, however, there are only few instances of a possible link between a poetic work and the corresponding instrumental composition. Once Schindler asked Beethoven about the poetic idea of his Piano Sonata Op. 31 No. 2. The master answered shortly: "Read Shakespeare's *Tempest.*" Schindler said in his Beethoven biography: "Only Beethoven's closest friends knew how well versed he was with the literature of former days and the present time, and how deeply he dived into the spirit of the works of Shakespeare, Schiller, and Goethe. If he had only mentioned at one single occasion what he had in mind, thus giving us the key to one or the other of his great instrumental compositions, it would not be so difficult to understand them and many an enigma would be solved . . . I very often urged him to do so . . . Beethoven seemed to be ready to follow my suggestion, but he did not do so. Unfortunately—because of all the unrecognizable figures, the disguised operas, mummeries—I do not know what kind of dreams of the poetic world that appear in his music, would have been explained in the most natural way." In 1816 Hoffmeister in Leipzig, who intended to publish a complete edition of Beethoven's works, told Beethoven that one of the conditions for publication would be that he agreed to give with each one of his compositions an explanation about his poetic idea. Beethoven declared that he was ready to do so, but Hoffmeister's plan was not realized.

Schering's conclusions are often more than odd. The String Quartet Op. 74 in E flat major is based, according to Schering, on *Romeo and Juliet;* the String Quartet Op. 95, on *Othello;* Quartet Op. 127 on *Falstaff;* Op. 130 on *Midsummer Night's Dream* and Op. 131 on *Hamlet.* The "Moonlight" Sonata appears as the *King Lear* Sonata, and the "Appassionata" as a *Macbeth* Sonata. Beethoven's Ninth Symphony is a Friedrich Schiller Symphony, the first movement of which is based on the poem *Gruppe aus dem Tartarus,* the second movement on the poem *Der Tanz,* the third on *Das Glück.* Beethoven's Seventh Symphony is based on the scenes of Goethe's novel *Wilhelm Meister.* The String Quartets Op. 59 are based on *Wilhelm Meister,* on Jean Paul's *Flegeljahre,* and on Cervante's *Don Quixote.* The String Quartets Op. 132, 133, and 135 are based on scenes of Goethe's *Faust,* etc. It must be admitted that Schering's interpretations are highly suggestive.

Symbolism and representation play a great part in Schering's concept of Beethoven's music and give impetus to psychological associations. Apparently Beethoven himself believed in the poetic function of his music, for he called himself a "Tone poet," but it is doubtful that Beethoven had precise poetic ideas when conceiving a work. He may have begun with symbolic ideas, as in his Third and Fifth Symphonies, but these ideas developed into gigantic metaphysical creations surpassing the visible and materialistic world. In some instances Beethoven gave a belated interpretation, as in the "Tempest" Sonata, or the String Quartet Op. 18, No. 1, the *adagio* of which, he explained to his friend

Amenda, was the farewell of two lovers (Romeo and Juliet). Schering's ideas could be extremely useful, if presented as a personal impression and not in such an authoritative way. (Cf. Schering: *Beethoven und die Dichtung,* Berlin, 1936; Schering: *Beethoven in neuer Deutung,* Leipzig, 1934; Schering: "Zu Beethoven's Klaviersonaten," *Zeitschrift f. Musikwissenschaft,* 1936; Schering: *Das Symbol in der Musik.)*

Schickh, Johann

b. Vienna 1770, d. Gastein 1835. Writer and editor of the *Wiener Zeitschrift für Kunst, Literatur, Theater und Mode* which he directed from 1816 to 1836. His name appeared frequently in the Conversation-books; in 1824, for instance, when he acidly criticized Bernard's oratorio text *Der Weg des Kreuzes,* which Beethoven was supposed to set to music (Th.-R. V, p. 13). Evidently Schickh and Bernard were on bad terms. In December 1819, Bernard improvised a whole poem making a pun of Schickh's name. About the same time Schickh jotted down: "I beg you [Beethoven] to compose a poem of Count Loeben." At some other occasion Schickh asked the Master to delay the composition of his Requiem in order to compose Grillparzer's opera *Melusina.* (Cf. Th.-R. IV and V; Schünemann: *Ludwig von Beethoven, Konversationshefte.)*

Schiller, Johann Christoph Friedrich von

b. Marbach (Württemberg) 1759, d. Weimar 1805. Famous German poet. B. L. Fischenich, professor of law in Bonn, wrote to Charlotte von Schiller, the poet's wife, on January 26, 1793, that Beethoven was going to compose Schiller's *Lied an die Freude.* He enclosed in this letter Beethoven's song "Feuerfarb" and mentioned that something perfect and sublime might be expected from the composer. Beethoven became familiar with Schiller's plays in Bonn when *Die Räuber* and *Fiesko* were performed by the Grossmann Troupe.

Beethoven frequently used quotations from Schiller's plays. A quotation from *Don Carlos* is found in a Nürnberg autograph album of 1793, belonging to Vocke, a Nürnberg merchant. One of the Master's favorite quotations was *"Nicht ohne meine Fahne darf ich kommen,"* pointing to his sketchbooks. His canon *Kurz ist der Schmerz,* written for Ludwig Spohr, was taken from the same drama *Don Carlos,* whereas *"Rasch tritt der Tod den Menschen an,"* composed for three male voices (see Entry: Krumpholz) was taken from *Wilhelm Tell* (1817). He was also well acquainted with the *Braut von Messina.* In a letter to the Wiener Gesellschaft der Musikfreunde (1824), Beethoven mentioned that he planned to compose Homer, Klopstock, and Schiller, rather than Bernard's oratorio *Der Weg des Kreuzes* (cf. Entry: Reading). It is well known how important Schiller's *Lied an die Freude* became during Beethoven's life. For a while the Master had in mind to write a "Schiller" Symphony as proved by the sketches of his Ninth Symphony, containing the following words by Beethoven: *"Lasst uns das Lied des unsterblichen Schiller singen."* It is well known that he made some additions of his own to Schiller's text, which he changed around many times himself, as seen by the sketches. (Cf. Entry: Schering; Nottebohm: *Beethoveniana* II, p. 190.)

Schimon, Ferdinand

b. Pest (Budapest) 1797, d. Munich 1852. Bavarian court singer and painter. He was appointed as a tenor to the Royal Theater in Munich (1821), after Franz Schubert had advised him to give up painting. Schimon, who belonged to Schubert's circle of friends, was introduced to Beethoven through Schindler. Because Beethoven was involved with his *Missa Solemnis* at that time, Schimon was not able to paint Beethoven's portrait immediately. After some secret sketches, Beethoven finally yielded, because he was taken by the open character of the young artist. The Master became more and more interested in him, invited him for the famous "60 beans of coffee" and it was then that the painter was able to finish the details of the portrait. Schimon's portrait, which is in Bonn at the present time, gave impetus to many modern portraits of the Master, such as the etching by Reyherr, a lithograph by Rohrbach, and others. (Cf. Schindler II, p. 288; Frimmel: *Beethovens äussere Erscheinung,* Munich, 1905.)

Schindler, Anton Felix

b. Medl (Moravia) 1795, d. Bockenheim (near Frankfurt) 1864. Musician and devoted friend of Beethoven during the last twelve years of the Master's life. Studied law in Vienna, where he became a clerk in Dr. Bach's law office. At the same time he was a musician. In 1820 he abandoned his law career and became first violinist and orchestral director of the Theater in der Josephstadt; in 1825 he obtained the same position at the Kärntnerthor Theater. During the winter of 1823-24 he performed all of Beethoven's symphonies, under the supervision of the Master. His acquaintance with Beethoven began in 1814, when Schindler played in an orchestra at the house of Pettenkofer, a music lover. A student of Schuppanzigh, his desk-neighbor, had asked Schindler to hand a ticket to Beethoven, which he did. Shortly afterward Schindler became involved in trouble with the police, having participated in some student riots. He had to escape to Brünn, where he was seized and jailed, but soon released. Beethoven, who had heard about these mishaps, invited him to report about it in the tavern Blumenstöckl. In 1816 Schindler became a member of a student organization with German nationalist tendencies. He got into close contact with Beethoven in Dr. Bach's law office. As late as 1822 Schindler became Beethoven's secret private secretary without salary. At that time Schindler turned out to be a full-fledged musician. There is no doubt that Schindler's devotion to Beethoven was honest and ethical. The Master's frequent suspiciousness of Schindler—such as on the occasion of the Akademie in 1824—was unjustified. It was well known that Beethoven often treated Schindler very badly, taking advantage of his submissive nature. Schindler had to do all the degrading errands for Beethoven, deal with the police, handle his correspondence, rent apartments, hire servants, and undergo the ordeal with the Master's nephew. A letter from Beethoven to Schindler (May 1824) is self-explanatory: ". . . I would like to make you a small gift now and then, instead of remunerating your services only with free meals; your low standards would always misinterpret my generosity . . ." In a letter to Ries (1822), Beethoven had the following to say about Schindler: ". . . I have never, on God's earth, met a bigger wretch . . ." Even Beethoven's joking with Schindler was often offensive, for instance, when he called him "Papageno," indicating that Schindler should act discreetly. Sometimes Schindler himself signed "Fidelissimus Papageno." In 1823 Schindler lived with Beethoven, but the Master soon considered him a burden, and, in a letter to Grillparzer, called him his "appendix." Between March 1825 and August 1826 the connections between Schindler and Beethoven were severed, but after the nephew's suicide attempt, the Master called back his former friends, Schindler and Breuning. In the meantime Holz had partly taken over Schindler's job, but faithful Schindler fulfilled his duties up to the Master's last breath. Shortly after Beethoven's death, Schindler started collecting material for his biography, after Rochlitz had refused to write it. Schindler completed the biography in 1839 in Aachen, where he had been living since 1835 as municipal music director and conductor of the Cathedral. Previously he had worked in the same capacity in Budapest (1827), where his sister was a singer. Schindler performed all the quartets of Beethoven in the house of Brunswick. In the spring of 1829, he returned to Vienna where he remained till 1831. Before going to Aachen, he spent a short time in Münster. The biography of Beethoven was published in 1840 by Aschendorff in Münster. A second edition of 1845 brought some additions, but kept in general the text of the first edition. The third and fourth editions (1860, 1871) showed many changes (cf. Entry: Jews). Schindler owned a great part of Beethoven's estate, which he offered to the British Museum and the Belgian Government; it was finally purchased by the Royal Prussian Library, Berlin (1845). When Schindler visited Paris in 1841-42, he was celebrated by French musicians, which caused Heinrich Heine to spread the false story about Schindler's calling card: "Anton Schindler, ami de Beethoven." In his article on Schindler, Wurzbach discussed the story and was inclined to trust Heine, in spite of Schindler's denial. It is necessary to distinguish between Schindler, the honest friend of Beethoven from 1814 to 1827, and the somewhat ridiculous Professor Schindler of a later time. In his later years, Schindler was jealous of everybody who had had the honor of knowing the Master (cf. Entry: Moscheles). The authenticity of Schindler's biography has frequently been questioned; many facts and dates up to 1814 might be wrongly represented, but as a whole the work is authentic, and has been used by such biographers as Thayer, Frimmel, etc., as a sound source of information. (Cf. E. Hüffer: "Anton Schindler," dissertation, Leipzig, 1909; Th.-R.; Reinhardt Zimmermann in *Allgem. Musikzeitung,* 1925; Wurzbach.)

Schlegel, Hermann

b. Altenburg 1804, d. Leyden 1884. Scientist. In his autobiography he told about his musical experiences in Vienna (1825). (Cf. Hermann Schlegel: *Lebens-*

bild eines Naturforschers, Altenburg 1886; Frimmel: *Beethoven Handbuch.)*

Schlemmer

Citizen of Vienna, with whom Beethoven's nephew, Karl, lived 1825-26. His residence was Alleegasse 72, near the Karlskirche, as indicated in several of Beethoven's letters (cf. Th.-R. V, p. 525.)

Schlemmer

Copyist. See Entry: Copyists.

Schlesinger

Music publishers in Berlin and Paris. The business in Berlin was founded in 1795 by Adolf Martin Schlesinger, continued by his son Heinrich in 1851 and purchased by Robert Lienau in 1864. The firm was enlarged by adding other firms, Haslinger of Vienna in 1875, Wernthal of Berlin in 1925, and Köster of Berlin in 1928. The Lienau firm was still in existence until recently. Moritz Adolf Schlesinger, the oldest son of Adolf Martin, founded the French firm in 1822. He met Beethoven in 1819 in the office of Steiner and Haslinger. Beethoven invited him to Mödling. In a letter to A. B. Marx, published in his Beethoven biography, Moritz Adolf Schlesinger wrote the following:

"Stepping from my carriage I entered the tavern, and there found Beethoven stalking out of the door, which he slammed to after him, in a rage. After I had removed some of my travel stains, I went to the house pointed out as his dwelling. His housekeeper told me that I probably would be unable to speak to him, since he had returned home in a rage. I gave her my visiting card, which she took to him, and, to my great surprise, returned a few minutes later and told me to enter. There I found the great man sitting at his writing desk. I at once wrote down how happy I was to make his acquaintance. This (what I had written) made a favorable impression. He at once gave free rein to his feelings and told me he was the most wretched man in the world; he had but just returned from the tavern, where he had asked for some veal which he felt like eating—and none had been available. All this he said in a very serious, gloomy way. I consoled him, we talked (I myself writing) about other things, and thus he kept me for nearly two hours; and though, afraid of boring or molesting him, I several times rose to go, on each occasion he prevented me from taking my departure. Leaving him, I hurried back to Vienna in my carriage; and at once asked my innkeeper's son whether he had some roast veal ready. When he said he had, I made him put it in a dish, carefully cover it and, without a word or explanation, sent it back to Baden by the man, in the carriage I had kept, to be presented to Beethoven with my compliments. I was still lying in bed the following morning when Beethoven came to me, kissed me and embraced me, and told me I was the most kind-hearted person he had ever met; never had anything given him such pleasure as the roast veal, coming at the very moment when he so greatly longed for it."

Castelli told in his memoirs that after a dinner given by Schlesinger in 1819, Beethoven started improvising. Castelli, who had no ideas at all about piano playing, was asked by Beethoven for a theme. He just pressed four keys upwards and downwards with his index finger, and this was satisfactory for the Master, who improvised a full hour on this "theme." In 1820 Beethoven offered Schlesinger several works, of which only 25 Scotch songs were printed, but the plates were discarded (Marx). These songs finally appeared in 1821 (?) as Op. 108, and were dedicated to Prince Radziwill. Other works published by Schlesinger were the Sonatas Op. 109, 110, 111, and after Beethoven's death the Quartets Op. 132 and Op. 135. Schlesinger's name appeared frequently in the Conversation-books. There is a letter from Schlesinger Sr. to Beethoven, dated June 9, 1817, which proved a most cordial relationship between the two.

An odd story about Adolf Martin was told by Holz. It referred to the shortness of the Quartet Op. 135 for which the old Schlesinger paid Beethoven 80 ducats in paper, instead of gold. According to Holz, Beethoven used one of his famous puns in an offensive anti-Semitic way (*"Beschnittene Dukaten, beschnittenes Quartett"*). A closer investigation proved Holz' hypothesis wrong, as Schlesinger knew in advance that this quartet would be short.
(Cf. Max Unger: *Beethoven, Freundschaftsverkehr und Briefwechsel mit Steiner, Haslinger, Schlesinger*, 1920, p. 24; Th.-R. III, IV, V; Nottebohm: *Beethoveniana* I and II; Frimmel: *Beethovenstudien* II; Kalischer: *Beethoven und Berlin;* Kaznelson: *Beethovens ferne und unsterbliche Geliebte.* Cf. Kinsky p. 309.)

Schlösser, Louis

b. Darmstadt 1800, d. there 1886. Musician. Studied first in Darmstadt with von Rinck, later in Vienna with Seyfried, Mayseder, Worzischek, and Salieri, and finally in Paris with Le Sueur and Kreutzer. Became concertmaster and Hofkapellmeister in Darmstadt. His best known works were the operas *Das Leben ein Traum, Die Braut des Herzogs* and a melodrama *Die Jahreszeiten.* He also composed the music to Goethe's *Faust* and numerous other works, of which about 70 were republished. Schlösser made the acquaintance of Beethoven in 1822, but did not record his impressions in print until 1885 in "Persönliche Erinnerungen an Beethoven", published in the magazine *Hallelujah* VI, 20-21. They are reprinted in part in Th.-R. IV, p. 417. Schlösser attended (November 1822) the performance of *Fidelio,* which he described as follows:

"Wilhelmine Schröder in the title role, Haitzinger as Florestan, Forti as Pizarro, and so on, all the other parts taken by artists of the first rank. What a plentitude of enjoyment did that evening promise me, who never yet had heard this unique dramatic creation by Beethoven. A whole hour before the opera began I pushed my way up to the box office, in order to secure a decent seat; for *Fidelio* had not been given for years. I listened to a performance which was a model in every respect and the impression it made upon me was overpowering.

"Napoleon's headquarters had been established at Schönbrunn (1805), and then French soldiers had filled the body of the opera house. Is it conceivable that the ethic purity and chaste beauty of a work whose very language they did not understand could have aroused a familiar echo in these passing guests used to a more frivolous fare? Feverishly excited by the wonderful closing hymn, that apotheosis of faithful conjugal devotion,

I hardly noticed that the house was gradually growing empty; until my faithful friend Franz Schubert seized my arm to accompany me to the exit. Together with us, three gentlemen, to whom I paid no further attention because their backs were turned to me, stepped out of a lower corridor; yet I was not a little surprised to see all those who were streaming by toward the lobby crowding to one side, in order to give the three plenty of room. Then Schubert very softly plucked at my sleeve, pointing with his finger to the gentleman in the middle, who turned his head at that moment, so that the bright light of the lamps fell on it and—I saw, familiar to me from engravings and paintings, the features of the creator of the opera I had just heard, Beethoven himself. My heart beat twice as loudly at that moment; all the things I may have said to Schubert I now no longer recall; but I well remember that I followed the Desired One and his companions (Schindler and Breuning, as I later discovered) like a shadow through crooked alleys and past high, gable-roofed houses, followed him until the darkness hid him from sight."

He reported the following about his visit to Beethoven:

"Opposite, in a workshop open to the street, a herculean bell-founder, like Vulcan the Smith, swung a most hefty hammer, so that the strident blows made the air tremble within a wide radius, and drove me as quickly as possible into the interior of the house at No. 60, where without paying any attention to a man, presumably the proprietor, who stepped forward to meet me on the threshold, I at once hurried up the uncomfortable, nearly dark stairs to the first story, the door at the left. At times one is overtaken by moods which do not admit of verbal expression and which instinctively, at the thought of soon confronting some extraordinary celebrity, occasion a shyness beyond control. This was my case when, since neither servant nor maid appeared, I carefully opened the outer door and, quite unsuspecting, found myself standing in a kitchen, through which one had to pass to gain the living rooms. At any rate, I never knew of any other way, for on every subsequent occasion when I came to Beethoven and remained a long time, he himself, at parting, invariably led me through this kitchen anteroom to the stairs. After repeatedly knocking in vain at the real living room door, I entered and found myself in a rather commodious but entirely undecorated apartment; a large, foursquare oak table with various chairs, which presented somewhat chaotic aspect, stood in the middle of the room. On it lay writing books and lead pencils, music paper and pens, a chronometer, a metronome, an ear trumpet made of yellow metal and various other things. On the wall at the left of the door was the bed, completely covered with music, scores and manuscripts. I can recall only a framed oil painting (it was a portrait of Beethoven's grandfather for whom, as is known, he had a childlike reverence) which was the sole ornament I noticed. Two deep window niches, covered with smooth paneling I mention only because in the first a violin and a bow hung from a nail, and in the other Beethoven himself, his back to me, stood busily writing down figures and the like on the wood, already covered with scribblings. The deaf Master had not heard me enter, and it was only by stamping vigorously with my feet that I managed to attract his notice and he at once turned around, surprised to see a young stranger standing before him. Yet before I could address a single word to him, he commenced to excuse himself in the politest manner imaginable because he had not sent out his housekeeper, and no one had been in attendance to announce me, the while quickly drawing on his coat; and then first asking me what I wished. Standing so near this artist, crowned with glory, I could realize the impression which his distinguished personality, his characteristic head, with its surrounding mane of heavy hair and the furrowed brow of a thinker, could not help but make on every one. I could look into those profoundly serious eyes, note the amiably smiling expression of his mouth when he spoke, his words always being received with great interest.

"My visit probably occurred shortly after he had eaten breakfast, for he repeatedly passed the napkin lying beside him across his snow-white teeth, a habit, incidentally, in which I noticed he often indulged. Steeped in my contemplation of him I entirely forgot the unfortunate man's total deafness, and was just about to explain my reason for being there to him when, fortunately, I recalled the uselessness of speaking at the last moment, and instead reverentially handed him the letter with its great seal. After he had carefully opened it and read its contents, his features visibly brightened; he pressed my hands gratefully, and after I had given him my visiting card, expressed his pleasure at my visit and added (I shall use his very language): 'These are heartening words which I have read. Your Grand Duke expresses himself not only like a princely Maecenas, but like a thorough musical connoisseur with comprehensive knowledge. It is not only his acceptance of my work which pleases me, but the value he attaches to art in general, and the recognition he concedes my activities.' He had seized his ear trumpet, so I explained the unbounded veneration accorded his genial works, with what enthusiasm they were heard, and what an influence the perfection of his intellectual creations had exercised on the cultural level of the day. Though Beethoven was so impervious to flattery of any kind, my words, which came stammering from the depths of my soul, nevertheless seemed to touch him, and this induced me to tell about *Fidelio*. 'But what prevented you from coming to see me in person?' he asked. 'I am sure you have been told any amount of contradictory nonsense; that I have been described as being an uncomfortable, capricious and arrogant person, whose music one might indeed enjoy, but who personally was to be avoided. I know these evil, lying tongues, but if the world considers me heartless, because I seldom meet people who understand my thoughts and feelings, and therefore content myself with a few friends, it wrongs me.'

"He had put down his ear trumpet, for speaking into it agitated his nerves too greatly; his complaint, so he insisted, did not lie in the weakness of the auditory canals, but was seated in the intestines; his physicians in treating him had made a false diagnosis their point of departure, etc. In fact, our conversation continued as follows: I wrote down briefly the short questions and bits of information, which I addressed to him on the sheets of paper lying at hand, and he then answered in the greatest detail, so that not only did no hiatus ever occur but his calmness and patience when I asked him to explain certain passages in his scores actually astonished me. Under these circumstances, in which the sovereignty of his genius breaks through every constricting barrier, whereas a critical pedantry would consider such ventures insurmountable, he expressed himself with a conviction which carried one away with it. At times, in these conversations, he let fall many sarcastic remarks about the actual art currents of the day in Vienna, which slumbered profoundly under the spell of Italian superficiality, and with no less sharpness did he express himself anent the speechlessness of various princely gentlemen, a matter which was not made clear to me until later, and then in a far more drastic manner."

Schlösser's recollections belong to the most valuable sources about Beethoven, as they provide us with a deep insight into the workshop of the Master.

"One day I brought him a new, somewhat complicated composition I had written, and after he had read it he remarked: 'You give too much, less would have been better; but that lies in the nature of heaven-scaling youth, which never thinks it possible to do enough. It is a fault maturer years will correct, however, and I still prefer a superfluity to paucity of ideas.' 'What shall I do to find the right way and—how did you yourself attain that lofty goal?' I added, timidly. 'I carry my thoughts about with me for a long time, sometimes a very long time, before I set them down,' he replied. 'At the same time my memory is so faithful to me that I am sure not to forget a theme which I have once conceived, even after years have passed. I make many changes, reject and reattempt until I am satisfied. Then the working-out in breadth, length, height and depth begins in my head, and since I am conscious of what I want, the basic idea never leaves me. It rises, grows upward, and I hear and see the picture as a whole take shape and stand forth before me as though cast in a single piece, so that all that is left is the work of writing it down. This goes quickly, according as I have the time, for sometimes I have several compositions in labor at once, though I am sure never to confuse one with the other. You will ask me whence I take my ideas? That I cannot say with any degree of certainty; they come to me uninvited, directly or indirectly. I could almost grasp them in my hands, out in Nature's open, in the woods, during my promenades, in the silence of the night, at earliest dawn. They are roused by moods which in the poet's case are transmuted into words, and in mine into tones, that sound, roar and storm until at last they take shape for me as notes.'"

Schmidt, Johann Adam

b. Aub (near Würzburg) 1759, d. Vienna 1809. Famous physician. Originally an army doctor, he became Professor of Anatomy at the Academy of Military Medicine in Vienna in 1789. Wurzbach listed his many publications. Around 1800 Beethoven was among his patients. Dr. Schmidt and his family were very fond of music; the Doctor played the violin. Beethoven dedicated to him the Piano Trio in E flat major, identical with the Septet published by the Bureau d'Arts et d'Industrie. The dedication on the third page is somewhat unusual, being rather elaborate and showing the Master's devotion. He stressed in his dedication that this work was easy to perform and might therefore be especially enjoyable for the Doctor and his talented young daughter. Evidently Beethoven shifted the difficult part in the arrangement to the piano, and left the easy part to the clarinet, which could be substituted for by the violin. In a letter to Wegeler, dated November 16, 1801, Beethoven mentioned the Doctors Gerhard von Vering and Schmidt and a new method of "Galvanism," which might possibly be used to improve his hearing. In the *Heiligenstädter Testament* he stated: "If after my death Prof. Schmidt should be still alive, please beg him in my name to give a description of my illness. . . ." (Cf. K. Op. 38.)

Schnaps, Frau

One of Beethoven's housekeepers when he lived (1823) in the house of the baker Obermayer, brother-in-law of his brother Johann. In a humorous letter to Schindler, dated June or July 2, he called her "my quick-sailing frigate." Every second day she rushed from Hetzendorf to Vienna to clean Schindler's apartment. (Cf. Th.-R. IV, p. 447; Entry: Servants.)

Schneider, Eulogius

b. Wipfeld (Lower Franconia) 1756, d. Paris 1794. French revolutionary, a former Franciscan monk, 1786-89 court preacher of Duke Carl Eugen of Wurttemberg, 1789-1791 professor of Greek literature in Bonn. From there he moved to Strasbourg. In 1793 he was the public prosecutor of the tribunal in Alsace, where he ordered numerous executions, whereupon he was seized himself and guillotined at the order of St. Just. In 1790 his revolutionary poems were published and impressed Beethoven highly. It might be assumed that Schneider had a considerable influence on Beethoven's development. Beethoven's liberal and revolutionary philosophy, expressed in many of his works and in his daily life, seemed to be foreshadowed by the enthusiastic poems of Schneider. It was Schneider who was responsible for Beethoven's composition of the funeral cantata on the death of Joseph II. Schneider's name appeared as late as 1819 in a political conversation between Beethoven and Oliva. (Cf. Schiedermair: *Der junge Beethoven;* Entry: Cantatas.)

Schneller, Julius Franz Borgias

b. Strasbourg 1777, d. Freiburg im Breisgau, 1832. Writer and poet. His pseudonym was Velox. In 1796 he came to Austria, lived in Vienna and Linz and later became professor of history in Graz. In Vienna he had joined the circle around Caroline Pichler to which belonged Toni Adamberger, Kotzebue, Collin, Castelli, and Hammer-Purgstall. Gleichenstein was one of his closest friends. Through him he became acquainted with Beethoven. In a letter of March 19, 1807, Schneller asked Gleichenstein if Beethoven would consider composing a comic opera. In 1811 Schneller worked as an enthusiastic promoter of Beethoven's music in Graz, where Louis Bonaparte, Napoleon's third brother, was one of his close friends. Schneller was an ardent admirer of Great Britain and the United States, which he thought to be model countries. These progressive ideas made him many enemies in Graz and resulted in his moving to Freiburg in 1823. (Cf. Wurzbach; Th.-R. II-IV; Ernst Münch: *Julius Schnellers Lebensumriss,* Leipzig 1834.)

Schnyder von Wartensee, Xaver

b. Lucerne 1786, d. Frankfurt a.M. 1868. Swiss composer. He came to Vienna in 1811 in order to study with Beethoven, at that time the most celebrated composer. As Beethoven did not accept any pupils, he became a pupil of J. Ch. Kienlen. On December 17, 1811, Schnyder wrote to Nägeli in Zürich: "I was very well received by Beethoven, and I saw him frequently. He is a very peculiar man. His sublime ideas can only be expressed through music. He has no command of words. His education has been neglected and except for his art, he is crude, however, honest and without falsehood. From his youth to this day he has had to face many difficulties. This makes him moody and gloomy. He says everything that is bad about Vienna, which he would like to leave as soon as possible. All Viennese are no good, from the Emperor down to the shoeshine man. I asked him whether or not he would accept any pupils. He refused. There was only one pupil, whom he would like to get rid of. . . . Archduke Rudolph." (Cf. Th.-R. III; *Lebenserinnerungen von Schnyder von Wartensee, nebst musikalischen Beilagen und einem Gesamtverzeichnis seiner Werke,* Zürich 1888; Refardt: *Hist. Biogr. Musikerlexikon der Schweiz,* Zürich 1928.)

Scholl, Karl

b. Zolkiew (Poland) 1778, d. Vienna 1854. Flutist. His father was Kapellmeister of Radziwill. Karl's flute teacher was Karl Kreith (cf. Wurzbach). In 1797 he was appointed to the Burgtheater; in 1813 to the Opera in Vienna. Schindler reported that Scholl had been Beethoven's only adviser in the field of flute technique. (Cf. Wurzbach; Th.-R. II, p. 127.)

Schott

Famous music publishing company, founded by Bernhard Schott in Mainz 1770. Bernhard died in 1809, and bequeathed his firm to his sons, Andreas (1781-1840) and Johann Josef (1782-1855). From that time the name of the firm was B. Schott, Söhne. In the beginning of the 19th century, a Belgian branch was added under the name of Schott Frères, Antwerp and Brussels. The firm of Schott published more than 50,000 works, including Richard Wagner's operas. The following works by Beethoven were published by Schott: *Opferlied* Op. 121b; *Bundeslied; Missa Solemnis* Op. 123; overture *Weihe des Hauses* Op. 124; Ninth Symphony Op. 125; 6 Bagatelles, Op. 126; E flat major String Quartet Op. 127; ariette "Der Kuss" Op. 128 and the C sharp minor String Quartet Op. 131. Schott was also the publisher of the magazine *Cäcilia,* which contained the ironic and jocose biography of Haslinger by Beethoven on April 7, 1825. (Cf. Haslinger; Th.-R. V, p. 171.)

Schreivogel (Schreyvogel), Joseph

b. Vienna 1768, d. there 1832. Writer. Also known under the pseudonyms

Thomas West, Karl August West, and Gebrüder West. In 1793-94 he contributed to Alxinger's *Monatsschrift.* In 1794 he went to Jena, where he wrote for Schiller's *Neue Thalia* and contributed to Wieland's *Mercur.* Returning to Vienna in 1797, he became secretary to the Court Theaters (1802), after Kotzebue had left the city. In 1804 he resigned from this position, and founded, together with Köhler, the Kunst und Industriecomptoir, which was given up in 1811. In 1814 Schreivogel returned to his old theater job. In 1832 he resigned on account of differences with the theater administration. Shortly afterward he died a victim of cholera. His epitaph was written by Grillparzer, who compared him with Lessing. There are numerous connections between Schreivogel and Beethoven, and the writer's name appears many times in letters and Conversation-books. (Cf. Wurzbach; Karl Glossy: *Josef Schreivogel, eine biographische Skizze als Anleitung zu dessen Tagebüchern,* Wien, 1903; Franz Gräffer: *Kleine Wiener Memoiren und Wiener Dosenstücke,* München, 1922.)

Schröder-Devrient, Wilhelmine

b. Hamburg 1804, d. Koburg 1860. Famous singer, daughter of the baritone Friedrich Schröder and the renowned actress Sophie Schröder. She was educated by Joseph Mozatti in Vienna, made her debut as Pamina 1821 in Vienna, and sang as a guest the same role in Prague and Dresden. When Beethoven's *Fidelio* was revived in 1822, she was entrusted with the part of Fidelio. Schindler, Schlösser, and Kanne have written much about that famous performance (cf. Entry: Schlösser). There is no doubt that the tremendous success of *Fidelio* was due mostly to the genial interpretation of the artist. Bäuerle's *Theaterzeitung* reported, November 9, 1822: "The role of Fidelio was given by Dem. Schröder with such diligence, concentration and ardor, that she was a great surprise, in spite of the fact that we are used to vivid and splendid performances. She surpassed all expectations." In 1823 the young artist married the actor Karl Devrient. The marriage broke up in 1828, and she remarried twice thereafter. Her second husband was Herr von Dőring, divorced 1848, the third Baron Bock. In 1849 the singer participated in the revolution in Dresden, and was expelled from the city. She was scheduled to come to the U.S.A., but sickness prevented the realization of her plans. About her relation to Richard Wagner, see Wagner's letters from the Burrell Collection, published by Macmillan Co., New York 1950. (Cf. Th.-R. IV; Richard Wagner: *Uber Schauspieler und Sänger,* publ. 1872, and dedicated to her memory; Claire von Glűmer: *Erinnerungen an Wilhelmine Schröder-Devrient,* 1862.)

Schubert, Franz Peter

b. Lichtenthal (near Vienna) 1797, d. Vienna 1828. Celebrated composer and contemporary of Beethoven. There is no doubt that Schubert and Beethoven knew each other, in spite of the fact that the stories circulating about them lack authenticity. Schindler in his Beethoven biography II, p. 176 noted the following: "Schubert had an unhappy experience when, in 1822, he presented to the Master a copy of his Variations for four hands, which he had dedicated to him.

The shy and speechless young composer contributed to his own embarrassment, in spite of the fact that he was introduced by Diabelli, who interpreted for him his feelings towards the great man. The courage which had sustained him as far as the house forsook him completely in the presence of the prince of composers. And when Beethoven expressed the wish that Schubert himself should write down the answers to his questions, his hand was as if paralyzed. Beethoven ran through the Variations and discovered a harmonic inaccuracy. He gently drew the young man's attention to this, but at once added that it was not a mortal sin; whereupon Schubert completely lost control of himself, perhaps as a direct result of this kindly observation. He rushed out of the house and bitterly reproached himself. He could never again summon up the courage to present himself before the great man."

The four-hand Variations in question are those on the song *Reposez bon chevalier* (1822) which just had been published by Cappi and Diabelli, dedicated to Beethoven, April, 1822. Schubert's friend Spaun reported that Schubert did not find the Master at home when he called on him. Later Beethoven played these variations with his nephew. Whether or not these variations impressed Beethoven is unknown. Anyway the finale of the Variations revealed an affinity to the Master. One has to agree with Alfred Einstein, who said: "How much wiser it would have been to dedicate three or even half a dozen songs to him." In fact, Beethoven was later deeply impressed by Schubert's songs. Beethoven's statement: "A divine spark dwells within Schubert; he will even surpass me" should be considered authentic. It is well known that Schubert had the greatest admiration for Beethoven and that he developed a kind of inferiority complex towards the Master. According to Schubert's biographer, Kreissle von Hellborn, Schubert said many times: "Who can add anything to Beethoven?"

Shortly before Schubert entered the "convikt," the orchestra of the institution had been called to Schönbrunn for a performance, attended by Teyber and Beethoven. Young Schubert liked to hear the story again and again. Schindler reported in the *Niederrheinische Zeitung* that during the time of Beethoven's last sickness, he showed Beethoven about sixty songs by Schubert, partly in manuscript. Schindler's purpose was to divert Beethoven, who had stopped composing at that time. The Master was astonished at Schubert's output and his great art. For many days he could not get away from the songs and he loved to read over and over *Iphigenie, Grenzen der Menschheit, Allmacht, Junge Nonne, Müller-Lieder,* etc. It was at that time that Beethoven made the above-mentioned remark adding: "If I had known this poem I would have liked to compose it myself. . . ."

Beethoven's esteem for Schubert grew continuously and he wanted to hear his piano works and operas. But the Master's sickness developed so rapidly that he could not realize his desire. He prophesied that Schubert's compositions would some day be sensations. The Master deeply regretted not having met Schubert earlier in his life. It is well known that Anselm Hüttenbrenner, learning of Beethoven's sickness, hastened from Graz to Vienna to assist him in his last hours (cf. Entry: Hüttenbrenner). A few days before Beethoven's passing, Josef Hüttenbrenner, the painter Teltscher, and Schubert went to see Beethoven. This was probably Schubert's only personal visit to the Master. Schubert's brother Ferdinand, when asked about Franz's relations with Beethoven, had only the following to say: "They saw each other very seldom."

Schubert participated in Beethoven's funeral in the company of Franz Lachner and Josef Randhartinger. The latter told Kreissle that the three, returning from the cemetery, visited the Auf der Mehlgrube tavern. They emptied the first glass of wine in memory of the deceased Master, the second to the one who would follow Beethoven in death. Nobody suspected that Schubert would be the next. Schubert had expressed the desire to be buried at Beethoven's side. His wish was fulfilled.

There are many relations between the works of Schubert and those of Beethoven. Many reminiscences could be enumerated, e.g., Schubert's song *Der Neugierige,* which recalls melodically Beethoven's *Lied aus der Ferne.* Schubert's *Wanderer* and *Doppelgänger* might have been influenced by Beethoven's Gellert-Lied *Vom Tode,* and Schubert's *Wanderer* appears almost identical to Beethoven's sketch *Erlkönig.* More important was Beethoven's influence on Schubert's piano works. One has to realize the basic differences between the two personalities and their styles. Whereas Beethoven shapes his ideas like a craftsman, Schubert, like Mozart, presents a variety of ideas in emotional oblivion. His natural melodic wealth prevents him from presenting classical developments and recapitulations. That is why many repetitions are found in his music, often transposed to the subdominant. If Schubert tried to follow Beethoven in fugal treatments as in the *Wanderer-Phantasie,* he exposes this weakness, from which not only he, but all the Romanticists suffered. Characteristic of Schubert is his neglect of the variation form. Compared to Beethoven, there is a lack of balance in form. Beethoven's great achievements in the field of sonority were surpassed by Schubert's piano and chamber music works. He was even able to overshadow Beethoven in the field of the Lied, inasmuch as he not only exhausted the contents of a poem, but also presented a new creation. Whereas Beethoven as a personality was the type of autonomous man, governing his own fate, Schubert, like a number of his romantic successors (Schumann, Weber, Mendelssohn, Chopin) seemed to be governed by fate. In contrast to Beethoven's balanced forms, in Schubert's work, huge (C major Symphony) or small, lyric forms (Impromptu, Lied) predominate. Schubert himself felt this discrepancy, which caused his inferiority complex towards Beethoven.

Schulz, Edward

(n.d.) English musician. He published an article entitled "A Day with Beethoven," an extract of a letter from Vienna to a friend in London, in the musical magazine *The Harmonicon.* He signed the article (Jan. 1824) with the Greek letter *sigma.* This report was used by Schindler (1824) in his book *Beethoven in Paris.* A German translation of Schulz's article was given by Chrysander in his essay "Beethoven's Verbindung mit Birchall und Stumpff in London," *Jahrbücher der musikalischen Wissenschaft,* Leipzig 1863. The following quotation from this essay runs:

"The 28th of September, 1823, will be ever recollected by me as a *dies faustus;* in truth, I do not know that I ever spent a happier day. Early in the morning, I went in company with two Vienna gentlemen—one of whom, Mr. H. (Holz), is known as the very intimate friend of Beethoven—to the beautifully situated village of Baden, about twelve miles from Vienna, where the latter usually resides during the summer months. Being with Mr. H., I had not to encounter any difficulty in being admitted into his presence. He looked very sternly at me at first, but he immediately after shook me heartily by the hand, as if an old acquaintance; for he then clearly recollected my first visit to him in 1816, though it had been but of very short duration. A proof of his excellent memory. I found, to my sincere regret, a considerable alteration in his appearance, and it immediately struck me that he looked very unhappy. The complaints he afterwards made to Mr. H. confirmed my apprehensions. I feared that he would not be able to understand one word of what I said; in this, however, I rejoice to say, I was much deceived, for he made out very well all that I addressed to him slowly and in a loud tone. From his answers it was clear that not a particle of what Mr. H. uttered had been lost, though neither the latter, nor myself, used a machine. From this you will justly conclude that the accounts respecting his deafness lately spread in London are much exaggerated. I should mention though, that when he plays on the pianoforte, it is generally at the expense of some twenty or thirty strings, he strikes the keys with so much force. Nothing can possibly be more lively, more animated and—to use an epithet that so well characterizes his own symphonies—more energetic than his conversation, when you have once succeeded in getting him into good humour; but one unlucky question, one ill-judged piece of advice—for instance, concerning the cure of his deafness—is quite sufficient to estrange him from you forever. He was desirous of ascertaining, for a particular composition he was then about, the highest possible note of the trombone, and questioned Mr. H. accordingly, but did not seem satisfied with his answers. He then told me that he had in general taken care to inform himself, through the different artists themselves, concerning the construction, character, and compass of all the principal instruments. He introduced his nephew to me, a fine young man of about eighteen, who is the only relation with whom he lives on terms of friendship, saying: 'You may propose to him an enigma in Greek, if you like'; meaning, I was informed, to acquaint me with the young man's knowledge of that language. The history of this relative reflects the highest credit on Beethoven's goodness of heart; the most affectionate father could not have made greater sacrifices on his behalf than he has made. After we had been more than an hour with him, we agreed to meet at dinner, at one o'clock, in that most romantic and beautiful valley called das Helenenthal, about two miles from Baden. After having seen the baths, and other curiosities of the village, we called again at his house about twelve o'clock, and, as we found him already waiting for us, we immediately set out on our walk to the valley. B. is a famous pedestrian, and delights in walks of many hours, particularly through wild and romantic scenery. Nay, I was told that he sometimes passes whole nights on such excursions, and is frequently missed at home for several days. On our way to the valley, he often stopped short, and pointed out to me its most beautiful spots, or noticed the defects of the new buildings. At other times he seemed quite lost in himself, and only hummed in an unintelligible manner. I understood, however, that this was the way he composed, and I also learnt that he never writes one note down till he has formed a clear design for the whole piece. The day being remarkably fine, we dined in the open air, and what seemed to please Beethoven extremely was that we were the only visitors in the hotel, and quite by ourselves during the whole day. The Viennese repasts are famous all over Europe, and that ordered for us was so luxurious that B. could not help making remarks on the profusion which it displayed. 'Why such variety of dishes?' he exclaimed, 'Man is but little above other animals, if his chief pleasure is confined to a dinner table.' This and similar reflections he made during our meal. The only thing he likes in the way of food is fish, of which trout is his favorite. He is a great enemy to all *gêne,* and I believe that there is not another individual in Vienna who speaks with so little restraint on all kinds of subjects, even political ones, as Beethoven. He hears badly, but he speaks remarkably well, and his observations are as characteristic and as original as his compositions. In the whole course of our table talk, there was nothing so interesting as what he said about Handel. I sat close by him, and heard him assert very distinctly, in German, 'Handel is the greatest composer that ever lived.' I cannot describe to you with what sublimity of language he spoke of the *Messiah* of this immortal genius. Every one of us was moved when he said, 'I would uncover my head, and kneel down on his tomb.' H. and I tried repeatedly to turn the conversation to Mozart, but without effect; I only heard him say, 'in a monarchy we know who is the first'—which might, or might not, apply to the subject. Mr. C. Czerny—who by the by, knows every note of Beethoven by heart, though he does not play one single composition of his own without the music before him—told me, however, that B. was sometimes inexhaustible in his praise of Mozart. It is worthy of remark that this great musician cannot bear to hear his own earlier works praised; and I was apprized that a sure way to make him very angry is to say something complimentary of his Septetto, Trios, etc. His latest productions, which are so little relished in London, but much admired by the young artists of Vienna, are his favorites. His second Mass he looks upon as his best work, I understood. He is at present engaged in writing a new opera, called *Melusina,* the words by the famous, but unfortunate poet, Grillparzer. He concerns himself very little about the newest productions of living composers, insomuch that when asked about the *Freischütz,* he replied, 'I believe one Weber has written it.' You will be pleased to hear that he is a great admirer of the ancients. Homer, particularly his Odyssey, and Plutarch he prefers to all the rest; and, of the native poets, he studies Schiller and Goethe in preference to any other; this latter is his personal friend. He appears, uniformly, to entertain the most favourable opinion of the British nation; 'I like,' said he, 'the noble simplicity of English manners,' and added other praises. It seemed to me as if he had yet some hopes of visiting this country together with his nephew. I should not forget to mention that I heard one trio of his, for the pianoforte, violin, and violoncello, which I thought very beautiful and it is, I understood, to appear shortly in London. The portrait you see of him in the music shops is not now like him, but may have been so eight or ten years back. I could tell you many things more of this extraordinary man, who from what I have seen and learnt of him, has inspired me with the deepest veneration; but I fear I have taken up your time already too much. The friendly and hearty manner in which he treated me, and bade me farewell, has left an impression on my mind which will remain for life. Adieu."

In a letter from Schulz (December 24, 1824) to Haslinger and his wife, he asked the publisher for several of Beethoven's compositions, among others *Die Weihe des Hauses* and wanted the biography of Mayseder and Carl Czerny. The relationship between Schulz and Beethoven has not been clearly revealed.

Schuppanzigh, Ignaz

b. Vienna 1776, d. there 1830. Famous violinist and chamber musician. His father was a professor at the Vienna Realakademie. The Augarten Concerts, prominent in Mozart's times, declined after the death of Joseph II, but they got a new start with Schuppanzigh as concertmaster. He inaugurated the morning concerts which continued up to 1816. Wegeler in his *Notizen* reported that Prince Lichnowsky engaged a string quartet every Friday morning: Schuppanzigh, Weiss, Krafft and a cellist (Linke). According to Schindler the quartet consisted of Schuppanzigh, Franz Weiss and the two Kraffts. The *Jahrbuch der Tonkunst für Wien und Prag* (1796) mentioned Schuppanzigh as originally a viola player. "He is known to all musical societies, popular and in high demand. He is obliging and pleasant, a disposition responsible for his many friends." In Hanslick's *Geschichte des Konzertwesens,* one of the best sources for the history of music in performance in Vienna, there is printed a playbill of a concert by *"Herr Ignaz Schuppanzigh in der Himmelpfortgasse in dem Saale des Herrn Hofträteurs Jahn"* (cf. Jahn). The following compositions were played: 1. A Symphony of the late Mr. Mozart; 2. Aria by Herrn von Beethoven, sung by Mme. Willman; 3. A violin-concert played by Mr. Schuppanzigh; 4. An aria by Sarti, sung by Mr. Codecasa; 5. A quintet for the pianoforte, accompanied by four woodwinds, played and composed by L. v. Beethoven; 6. Variations for the violin, played by Herr Schuppanzigh; 7. A final symphony.

According to Hanslick, Schuppanzigh was the first to perform string quartets in public, starting in 1804. They first took place in a private house, Heiligenkreuzerhof, later in the Römischer Kaiser (Freiung) of which Eppinger was the manager. Schuppanzigh played the first violin; Mayseder, the second violin; Schreiber, a chamber musician of Prince Lobkowitz, the viola; and Anton Krafft, the cello. In 1808 Schuppanzigh organized the private quartet of Count Razumovsky, which was disbanded in 1816, after the palace of the Count had burned down.

Schuppanzigh had always been a devoted friend and admirer of Beethoven. When the "Battle" Symphony was performed in 1813, Beethoven wrote a note of thanks to all performers, in which he mentioned especially Schuppanzigh as leader of the first violins, emphasizing his lively and expressive way of performing. Beethoven in turn had the highest esteem for Schuppanzigh, who later came into competition only with Josef Böhm. While Böhm was a more fragile type, and a more refined musician, Schuppanzigh was more of the "Musikant" type, rather stout with plump fingers. Beethoven liked to call him "Falstaff" or "Lump" (scoundrel), "Eselskopf" (jackass), etc. In a letter to Ferdinand Ries, Beethoven remarked that his offenses toward Schuppanzigh should serve the latter as a reducing cure. The canon *Falstafferl lass' dich sehen* (Little Falstaff) was meant for Schuppanzigh, whom the Master would address in the following way: "To Schuppanzigh, offspring of the ancient English dynasty of my lord Falstaff." Another funny way of addressing Schuppanzigh read: *"Al Signore Milord stimatissimo Nominato Scuppanzig grand uomo della città di Vienna."*

After the Razumovsky quartet had been disbanded, Schuppanzigh went to Russia, and returned in 1823, performing Beethoven's last quartets many times. He was one of the torchbearers at the funeral of the Master, whom he would follow three years later. He died at one of the famous Saturday suppers, given by Dr. Rudolf von Vivenot when he was about to drink a cup of coffee. As a soloist Schuppanzigh was hampered by his stoutness, but his name will live on in the history of chamber music. (Cf. Th.-R. II-V; Wurzbach; Kinsky: *Beethoven und das Schuppanzigh-Quartett.)*

Schwan, Gasthaus "Zum Weissen Schwan"

See Entry: Taverns.

Schwarzenberg, Prince Josef Johann

b. Vienna 1796, d. Frauenberg 1833. Beethoven dedicated to him the Quintet Op. 16 for Piano and Woodwinds, performed for the first time in a concert of Schuppanzigh's on April 6, 1797. Josef Johann was the husband of Princess Pauline, Caroline Iris von Arenberg-Archot, who died while rescuing her thirteen-year old daughter from a fire that broke out at a dance given by her brother-in-law Karl Philipp, the victor of Leipzig. The latter had hardly any connections with Beethoven, except for the fact that the Septet Op. 20 had its first performance in his palace, according to Dolezalek. (Cf. Wurzbach; Th.-R. II.)

Schwarzspanierhaus

Beethoven's last apartment in Vienna, today Schwarzspanierstrasse 15 in the Alserstadt (Alserstädter Glacis 200). The house was originally a convent of the Spanish Benedictines, called the "Schwarzspanier." The building does not exist today, having been wrecked in

1903. For a while a section of the Vienna Medical School was located on these premises. In Beethoven's times the entrance to the house was through a broad gate. A beautiful broad stairway led to Beethoven's apartment on the third floor (European second floor). The apartment was spacious and consisted of a hall, a kitchen, a servant's room, a large living room and two smaller rooms. A sideboard was against the right wall of the hall where a portrait of Beethoven's grandfather hung. The living room was almost unfurnished. Beethoven's own portrait by Mähler hung from the wall. The floor of the room was scattered with piles of music. In the adjacent smaller rooms there were two pianos, one Broadwood, one Graf. There were also bookshelves and drawers, Beethoven's bed, a wardrobe rack. The next small room was Beethoven's study. (Cf. Breuning: *Aus dem Schwarzspanierhaus,* 1874; Karl Kobald: *Wiener Musikstätten,* Wien, 1929.)

Schwind, Moritz von

b. Vienna 1804, d. Munich 1871. Famous painter of the Romantic School. Belonged to the circle of Franz Schubert and might have known Beethoven in person. His drawings for the *Marriage of Figaro* were enjoyed by Beethoven during the last days of his life. The painter made the following annotations in his drawing book: "This book was kept by Beethoven during his last days, and returned to me after his death." Schwind sketched Beethoven's head occasionally. (Cf. Frimmel: *Beethovens äussere Erscheinung,* München, 1905.)

Seal

Beethoven was in possession of three seals engraved: L.v.B. Two of them are preserved in the Beethoven House in Bonn. Beethoven called the larger one his state seal.

Sebald, Amalie

b. Berlin 1787, d. there 1846. Singer, possibly already known to Beethoven in 1796, when the Master stayed in Berlin. The Sebalds were a highly musical family, belonging to the Zelter circle around the Singakademie. In 1811 Amalie had come to Teplitz, together with Elisabeth von Recke and Christoph August Tiedge. Amalie was a charming woman, and there is no doubt that Beethoven, spending his vacations in Teplitz (1811, 1812), was enchanted by her. On August 8, 1811, he wanted to pay her a visit, did not find her at home and left his card with the following words: *"Ludwig van Beethoven, den Sie, wenn Sie auch wollten, doch nicht vergessen sollten"* (Ludwig van Beethoven, whom you should not forget, even if you would like to do so). On September 6 the Tiedge-von Recke party had already left Teplitz, whereas Beethoven continued to stay in the Bohemian resort. On that day the Master wrote a letter to Tiedge, asking him to transmit a tender and devoted handshake to Countess Recke and to Amalie an "ardent kiss, if nobody should be around." Next summer, 1812, both Amalie and Beethoven were in Teplitz again, but not at the same time. Beethoven asked Breitkopf and Härtel (July 17) to send some of his compositions to "a charming lady in Berlin. Her address is: Amalie Sebald, Bauhof No. 1, Berlin. She is a pupil of Zelter and we are very fond of her." There are extant some other letters of Beethoven to Amalie, written from Teplitz. Obviously she had once called him a tyrant and Beethoven thereupon answered: "I should be your tyrant? Only some misunderstanding could have caused this name. I only have to report that the tyrant is enslaved to his bed." In other letters from Beethoven to Amalie a warm feeling towards the singer can always be observed. Amalie later married an employee of the Berlin police, Krause. Thomas San Galli in his book *Die unsterbliche Geliebte Beethovens Amalie Sebald,* Halle claims that Amalia Sebald was the Immortal Beloved, but there is no doubt that the available sources do not justify this claim. Beethoven's letters to Amalie were written in a more friendly tone, and are in sharp contrast to the passionate feelings expressed in the famous love letter to the Immortal Beloved. (Cf. Entry: Immortal Beloved; Kaznelson: *Beethovens ferne und unsterbliche Geliebte.)*

Sechter, Simon

b. Friedberg (Bohemia) 1788, d. Vienna 1867. Musician, student of Koželuch, from 1811 music teacher at the Institute of the Blind in Vienna; from 1824 on court organist and after 1851 professor of composition at the Vienna Conservatory. His famous book *Die Grundsätze der musikalischen Komposition,* 1853-54 is one of the best manuals of harmony and counterpoint. Anton Bruckner was his most famous pupil. His reputation in Beethoven's time was already so well established that Franz Schubert, shortly before his death, had planned to take lessons in counterpoint from Sechter. Among his many compositions his Four Fugues for Pianoforte Op. 5 were dedicated to Beethoven. A list of his compositions is given by Wurzbach, who used Sechter's *Autobiography* as his main source (Archiv Gesellschaft der Musikfreunde). Among the numerous works is a song "Bei dem Leichenbegängnisse des L. von Beethoven," poem by Castelli, published by Kettner. His oddest composition is his 104 Variations on an original subject of 104 bars. Nottebohm was one of his pupils. (Cf. Wurzbach; C. F. Pohl: *Simon Sechter,* 1868.)

Sedlaczek, Johann

b. Oberglogau (Silesia) 1789, d. Vienna 1866. Famous flutist; the son of a tailor, he had learned tailoring from his father. At the age of 21 he wandered as a journeyman tailor through Austria. After he settled in Vienna, he became a professional musician and a member of the Court Orchestra. In 1820 he began extensive concert tours. In 1825 Beethoven recommended him to Cherubini and Kreutzer. Beethoven's letters of recommendation are printed in Th.-R. V, p. 245. In about 1826 he went to London, married an Englishwoman, and settled in the English capital. In 1845 he returned to Vienna. In a Conversation-book of 1825 Karl wrote the following: "Everybody was enthusiastic about your (Beethoven) improvisation, above all Sedlaczek." Beethoven had improvised in the Prater tavern Zum Wilden Mann. (Cf. Hanslick: *Geschichte des Konzertwesens in Wien;* Wurzbach; Th.-R. V.)

Seibert, Johann

Surgeon and Master in Surgery in the General Hospital in Vienna (cf. Entry: Diseases).

Seitzerhof

Viennese tavern, visited by Beethoven (cf. Entry: Taverns).

Selig, Heinrich

Owner of a delicatessen and wine store, frequently mentioned in the Conversation-books. These conversations were often held in Selig's store, between January and March 1824. Qualities of wine were often discussed among Selig, Peters, and Beethoven. From a quotation of Schünemann: "This wine is too cold, you will get another one." Peters: "Your Ofen wine No. 3 is the best wine." Selig: "The claret must be warm." Selig was also a collector of paintings, as seen in a note of Peters: "Selig owned a Leonardo da Vinci of extreme beauty. This painting was worth 20,000 Fl." The Conversation-books mentioned that Selig's merchandise was twice as expensive as anyone else's.

Sellner, Josef

b. Landau (Alsace) 1787, d. Vienna 1843. Important oboist. His father, originally in French service, switched with the Corps Condé to the Austrians (1792). As a soldier he learned trumpet, horn and clarinet. In 1808 he went to Prague for further training, and soon became an accomplished oboist. In that capacity he was appointed first oboist of the Prague Orchestra by Carl Maria von Weber. He was also an established guitarist and had such command of this instrument that he concertized in public with the most famous guitarist, Mauro Giuliano. J. W. Tomaschek was Sellner's theory teacher. In Vienna Sellner was a member of the Beethoven circle and had the Quintet Op. 29 performed in one of his concerts. In 1825 he participated in the party given by Kuhlau in Baden in honor of the Master. Sellner's improvements of the oboe were of interest to Beethoven. (Cf. Wurzbach; Hanslick: *Geschichte des Konzertwesens in Wien;* Th.-R. V, p. 234.)

Septet

One of the most popular chamber music works of Beethoven, published as Op. 20 in 1802 by Hoffmeister and Kühnel in Leipzig. It was composed between 1799 and 1800, possibly for Prince Karl Philipp Schwarzenberg, the victor of Leipzig, at whose house it was performed for the first time. According to a report by Doležalek to Otto Jahn, the work was received enthusiastically. Beethoven was supposed to have said: "That is my own creation." The fact that Beethoven held this work of his in such high esteem is reflected in the dedication to Empress Maria Theresia, second wife of Franz I. The Septet, arranged for violin, viola, French horn, clarinet, bassoon, cello and bass, consists of seven movements and belongs therefore to the category of serenades of divertimenti, an outgrowth of the suite. The first public performance took place on April 2, 1800, and one thousand performances followed. Wagner in his short story "A Pilgrimage to Beethoven" made Czech musicians play the Septet when the hero of his story entered Bohemia. The legendary beauty of that work is based on the marvelous *cantabile* in A flat major, and mainly the variation theme, which is identical with a Rhenish folk song *Ach Schiffer, lieber, Schiffer,* also sung to the text: *"Nun bricht aus allen*

Zweigen . . ." Nottebohm doubted that Beethoven took his theme from the folk song, but the possibility exists that Beethoven's song in turn became a folksong, like many works of Haydn and Mozart. Beethoven transcribed his Septet for Trio (Op. 38). (Cf. Entries: Schmidt; Serenades.)

Serenades

Beethoven used the serenade in the sense of a cyclic form, related to the Baroque suite rather than to the classical sonata (symphony) form at large. Similar forms are the Divertimento, the Cassation, the Notturno (Nachtmusik) and Finalmusik, as written by the two Haydns, Mozart, and many Austrian composers of that time. Often these forms are used as open-air music and are distinguished from the symphonies and regular chamber forms by additional movements, mostly by the introduction of two minuets and two slow movements. The Septet Op. 20 belongs to that group, as do also the Serenade Op. 8 in D major for Violin, Viola and Cello (string trio) with the famous *Alla Polacca*, and Serenade in D major for Flute, Violin and Viola Op. 25. The latter starts with an *entrata*, exactly as 17th century suites began, followed by a *tempo di minuetto* and *allegro, andante con variazioni, allegro scherzando, adagio* and *allegro vivace*. It was published in 1802 by Cappi, whereas Op. 8 appeared with Artaria in 1797. A text was added later to the *andante* Op. 8 *Sanft wie die Frühlingssonne.*

Servants

It would be unfair to judge Beethoven's attitudes towards servants by applying American standards of the 20th century. In spite of his democratic philosophy, Beethoven frequently showed an autocratic manner towards his numerous servants. As a bachelor he had to depend greatly on them as he was completely absorbed by his musical creations. He was frequently helpless in dealing with servants. In 1802 he consulted Zmeskall to learn whether or not he had to give a certificate to a pretentious and dissatisfied servant.

Well known is the attack against a cook who served rotten eggs. Mistrusting the cook, he started fixing his own eggs and buying his own food supplies at the market. Beethoven's cooking was more than questionable. In about 1814, according to Schindler, Beethoven hired as a servant a tailor, who carried out his profession in the anteroom. Though the tailor's wife did not sleep in, the couple took good care of the Master until 1816. In that same year the Master had an actual fight with a new servant in Baden. Somewhat later a new servant, Wenzel Braun, was hired, who locked Beethoven out of his own apartment. Beethoven's diaries reflect his untold miseries with his different servants. According to his diaries, he changed servants at least five times between January 31 and July 20, 1819, and he adds the characteristic words: "*Miser et pauper sum.*" In 1820 he changed servants at least eight times. In 1817, according to Fischhof's manuscript, he notated: "The best would be to order the food from a tavern." The numerous "Baberls," "Nanis" and "Pepis" were a real headache for the Master. In 1823 Frau Schnaps served Beethoven. He called her "*Meine schnellsegelnde Fregatte, die wohl edel geborene Frau Schnaps*" in a letter to

Schindler (II, p. 51). In addition to her, another servant, Therese Kaufmann, appeared in 1823. Another servant laughed at Beethoven's measure-beating and composing; the Master simply kicked her out. Michael and Sally Kren were much better, the latter recommended by the Breunings. They took care of Beethoven in his last days. (Cf. La Mara: *Klassisches und Romantisches.)*

Seyfried, Ignaz Xaver, Ritter von

b. Vienna 1776, d. there 1841. Composer and theoretician. A student of Mozart and Koželuch in piano and of Albrechtsberger and Peter von Winter in composition, he studied at the universities of Prague and Vienna. Originally a clerk in a commercial firm, he decided to devote himself to music. Between 1797 and 1828 he was Kapellmeister in Schikaneder's theater, and composed more than a hundred dramatic works, masses and other sacred music, symphonies, sonatas, etc. Today only his singspiel *Das Ochsenmenuet* with motives by Haydn, is performed and that only now and then. He was one of the first to recognize Beethoven's genius. Shortly after the Master's death he published (1831) Beethoven's *Studien im Generalbass.* But erroneously he took Beethoven's preparatory studies for Archduke Rudolph as Beethoven's own studies. Nottebohm was the first to recognize this error in his book: *Beethoven Studien, Beethovens Unterricht bei J. Haydn, Albrechtsberger und Salieri,* (Leipzig, 1873). As an appendix Seyfried's book contains *Biographische Notizen* and *Charakterzüge und Anekdoten* to be used cautiously. Beethoven had already been acquainted with Seyfried as early as 1803, when he worked on *Fidelio* and lived in the Theater an der Wien. Beethoven's *Heiligenstädter Testament* was first printed in Seyfried's book. Ignaz's brother was Josef von Seyfried, editor of the *Wiener Allgemeine musikalische Zeitung* 1819-1820. He too was acquainted with Beethoven, and belonged to the circle of Castelli. He was born in 1780 and died in 1849. (Cf. Wurzbach.)

Simrock, Nikolaus

b. Mainz 1752, d. Bonn 1833. Musician, later publisher. From 1774 on, he was a horn player in the Electoral Orchestra in Bonn, and had at the same time a business dealing with music, wallpaper, prayer books, stationery and musical instruments. His acquaintance with Beethoven in Bonn was continued in Vienna, as seen by a letter of the Master's from the year 1794. A letter of August 2 of the same year characterized the Austrians as people who would never rebel as long as they had beer and frankfurters. The following works have been published by Simrock: the three Sonatas for Piano, Op. 31; "Kreutzer" Sonata for Violin and Piano Op. 47; the Sextet in E flat major for two violins, viola, cello and two horns Op. 81b; two Sonatas for Cello and Piano Op. 102; Variations on 10 Folk Melodies for Piano Op. 107. (Cf. Leopold Schmidt: *Beethoven Briefe an Nikolaus Simrock;* Entries: Wegeler; Eleonore von Breuning; Ferdinand Ries.)

Simrock, Peter Joseph

1792-1868. Son of Nikolaus. He was Nikolaus' successor in the publishing firm of Simrock and Co. According to Thayer, Simrock saw Beethoven often in the Sailerstätte apartment or in the tavern Zur goldenen Birne, located on Landstrasse Hauptstrasse 42. Simrock was successful in talking into Beethoven's left ear, but confidential matters had to be written down, as the servants liked to listen to the conversations. One day, the Master said to Simrock: "Let's talk loud again. I gave 5 fl. to my servant, gave him a kick in the pants, and sent him to the devil." Simrock introduced to Beethoven the young violinist K. M. Berg (1785-1852), who wanted to dedicate several of his own trios to the Master. Beethoven, who did not think too much of these compositions, said to Berg: "Well, all right, if you don't have anything better." These trios were published by Steiner in 1817 as Op. 11. According to Simrock Beethoven was angry with the Emperor Franz because of the devaluation of the Austrian currency, and Thayer believed it best that he omit Beethoven's strong outbursts. Simrock related to Thayer that Beethoven spent much money in the taverns, ordering meals at random and sending them back the same way. (Cf. Th.-R. III, p. 566.)

Sina

Violinist in Beethoven's time, mentioned by Schindler as a member of the Razumovsky quartet. Sina later promoted Beethoven's music in Paris. Frimmel in his *Handbuch* mentioned a slip written by Beethoven: "Dear Sina, for Heaven's sake, come tonight." Probably an SOS call for a quartet session.

Sisters-in-Law

Johanna, née Reiss, married Beethoven's brother Karl and was the mother of Beethoven's nephew Karl. Therese, née Obermayer, married Beethoven's brother Johann.

(Cf. Entries: Brothers; Karl v. Beethoven; Gneixendorf; Obermayer.)

Sketchbooks

No composer has left as many sketches as Beethoven, and from these sketches it is possible to learn about his working procedure from the first little germ to the finished score. The number of these sketches, books and single sheets, is amazingly large and it is almost inconceivable that there are still about 4000 pages of Beethoven's handwriting not yet published (cf. *Sketchbooks to the "Missa Solemnis,"* Bonn, Beethovenhaus, 1952).

That the musical world has not taken more advantage of the quite unique opportunity of looking behind the scene of the creative process is not entirely due to the indolence of the public. Everyone who has ever dealt with Beethoven's sketches in manuscript knows the enormous difficulties in reading and deciphering them and how the greatest insight and intuition are often inadequate to understand certain passages. It is the great merit of Gustav Nottebohm to have devoted himself to an eager study of Beethoven's sketches and to have published some of the results of his investigation; it might be of interest that no less a person than Brahms recommended Nottebohm's *Beethoveniana,* a collection of articles, to the publisher Rieter in 1870. Another volume *Zweite Beethoveniana* was published after Nottebohm's death in 1887. In order to show the great variety of the material, Nottebohm gave only a cross section of the sketchbooks. In his two earlier publications: *Ein*

Skizzenbuch von Beethoven (1865) and *Ein Skizzenbuch von Beethoven aus dem Jahre 1803* (1880), both volumes republished by Paul Mies, Nottebohm gave a detailed though incomplete description of the second of those sketchbooks which deals with the *Eroica.*

Nottebohm approached the study of the sketches from the standpoint of the historian and his conclusions were mostly concerned with fixing the correct dates of Beethoven's works. It was Heinrich Schenker who first used the sketches to arrive at a deeper understanding of Beethoven's method of composing (cf. his *Beethovens Neunte Symphonie* and the commentary edition of the last sonatas). Further, a book by Paul Mies, *Die Bedeutung der Skizzen Beethovens zu Erkenntnis seines Stiles* (Leipzig, 1925), should be mentioned as an attempt to systematize features frequent in Beethoven's creative process.

Only a very few complete editions of sketchbooks have thus far been published: the sketchbook of the Ninth Symphony (in facsimile reproduction, Verlag W. Engelmann, 1913) and, transformed into regular print, *Ein Notierungsbuch von Beethoven,* edited by Karl Mikulicz, Breitkopf and Härtel, 1927. Recently the director of the Beethovenhaus in Bonn has started the great project of publishing all the sketchbooks that are available; the first of the *Missa Solemnis* sketchbooks is only the beginning of a long series.

Investigating Beethoven's sketches, we must keep in mind that his writings present a kind of shorthand for his memory, and very probably do not present a complete picture of his inner hearing. This is obvious from the fact that, for the most part, he indicates only one line and one staff.

The sketches show also that Beethoven worked on different works at the same time. How such common threads can later be observed in finished scores is revealed by a comparison of the sketches and scores of the Fifth Symphony and the G major Concerto. That both use the same rhythm in their themes is quite obvious. The sketches to the concerto show another noteworthy characteristic, namely, that of using a motif which was later discarded and used in a quite different work. Who would suspect that the melody of the chorus of the prisoners in *Fidelio* was originally intended as the main theme of the last movement of the concerto? The ingenious stroke of starting the orchestra in B major after the G major entrance of the piano did not appear in the first sketch; here the B major chord appears within the theme as an incidental passing chord. Furthermore, who would suspect that the main theme of the Sonata Op. 111 in C minor occurred first in F sharp minor in slow tempo in the sketchbook of the year 1801, where it was intended as the slow movement of the A major violin Sonata Op. 30? Sometimes Beethoven jots down the idea of an entire work as in the sketch for the D minor Sonata Op. 31, first movement; on the other hand he seems to have the greatest difficulty in shaping a rather short theme, even to such a degree that the final form cannot be recognized in the first attempts, as in the second movement of the G major Violin Sonata Op. 30 or in the introduction to the Second Symphony, where the simple beginnings in the sketch do not betray any of the individual features of the final version. It might also be of interest to learn that the well-known second theme in the "Appassionata" Sonata in A flat major does not appear at all in the first sketch, where a theme in minor serves in its stead. One of the most striking facts came to light in a recent publication, the sketchbook to the *Missa Solemnis* mentioned above; here Beethoven tries out some counterpoint in eighth notes against the Credo melody; this counterpoint does not show up in the final score but appears in the *Alla breve* variation of the Sonata Op. 109 on which, according to the sketchbook, Beethoven worked at the same time.

Beethoven struggled especially hard when setting words to music. Nottebohm shows in the *Beethoveniana* (II, 332) how Beethoven rewrote the beginning of the song *Sehnsucht* sixteen times. The same hard work is apparent from the sketches to the song *Adelaïde* and the cycle *An die ferne Geliebte.*

The study of Beethoven's sketches could well be a school for composers, and it can be hoped that the publication of the Sketchbooks, which has just begun, will arouse more concern with the art of composing practiced by the masters.

O. J.

Smart, Sir George Thomas

b. London 1776, d. there 1867. Famous English musician. Son of George Smart, a music publisher and double-bass player. In his early youth George Thomas was organist of Saint James' Chapel, Hampstead Road, and at the same time a violinist with Salomon's Concerts. The story is well known in England of how he once received a free drum lesson from Haydn in a symphony rehearsal of Salomon's orchestra. In 1811, having successfully conducted some concerts in Dublin, he was knighted by the Lord-Lieutenant. In 1813 he was chosen one of the original members of the Philharmonic Society, and between that date and 1844 conducted 49 of its concerts. From 1813 to 1825 he conducted the Lenten oratorios at one of the Patent Theaters, where (1814) he introduced Beethoven's *Mount of Olives* to the English public (Grove). Smart conducted Beethoven's Battle Symphony in the Drury Lane Theater, whereupon he received a note of appreciation by Johann Hering, a Viennese merchant and musician who was well known in London musical circles. Hering's letter, dated April 9, 1815, addressed to Smart, enclosed a letter of Beethoven's. In 1825 Smart made a continental tour and visited Beethoven in Vienna. In his account of his travels he told of interesting experiences in Austria, Bohemia, and Germany. He described his visit to the Master in the following way:

"On Friday, September 16th at half-past eight in the morning, young Ries came and we went in a hired carriage from Mödling to Baden. The distance is about six miles south of Mödling and sixteen miles southwest of Vienna. The journey cost five florins in paper money and took us about an hour. After walking in the little park and looking at the baths we went to Beethoven's lodgings according to his invitation. These are curiously situated, a wooden circus for horsemanship has been erected in a large court before his house. He has four large-sized rooms opening into each other, furnished à la genius; in one is the grand pianoforte, much out of tune, given him by Broadwood, in which is written, besides the Latin line, the names of J. Cramer, Ferrari and C. Knyvett. Beethoven gave me the time, by playing the subjects on the pianoforte, of many movements of his symphonies, including the Choral symphony, which according to his account took three-quarters of an hour only in performance. The party present —namely: Holz, the amateur violinist, Karl Beethoven, the nephew, besides young Ries—agreed that the performance at Vienna only took that time; this I deem to be totally impossible. It seems at Vienna the Recit was played only with four 'celli and two contra bassi which certainly is better than having the tutti bassi. Beethoven and we deservedly abused Reicha's printed specimen of fugueing. He told me of a mass, not yet published, which he had composed. We had a long conversation on musical subjects conducted on my part in writing. He is very desirous to come to England. After ordering his dinner with his funny old cook and telling his nephew to see to the wine, we all five took a walk. Beethoven was generally in advance, humming some passage. He usually sketches his subjects in the open air; it was on one of these occasions, Schuppanzigh told me, that he caught his deafness. He was writing in a garden and was so absorbed that he was not sensible of a pouring rain, till his music paper was so wet that he could no longer write. From that day his deafness commenced, which neither art nor time has cured. The water at Baden, whither he goes every summer, has been of service to his chest and gout, and his health is better than formerly. He would show me Prince Charles' beautiful chateau in the mountains and also some of the baths. On our return we had dinner at two o'clock. It was a most curious one and so plentiful that dishes came in as we came out, for, unfortunately, we were rather in a hurry to get to the stage coach by four, it being the only one going to Vienna that evening. I overheard Beethoven say, 'We will try how much the Englishman can drink.' He had the worst of the trial. I gave him my diamond pin as a remembrance of the high gratification I received by the honour of his invitation and kind reception and he wrote me the following droll canon as fast as his pen would write in about two minutes of time as I stood at the door ready to depart: "Ars longa, vita brevis." The castle of Prince Charles is of course the Weilburg of Archduke Karl.

Beethoven's name is often mentioned in Smart's memoirs. Schindler notified Smart of Beethoven's death. The English musician had always shown deep sympathy and understanding for the master's sickness. (Cf. H. Bertram Cox and C. L. Cox: *Leaves from the Journals of Sir George Smart*, London, 1907, with a Facsimile of Beethoven's canon *Ars longa, vita brevis;* T. H. Rand Charles Maclean: "Sir George Smart, Musician-Diarist" *Sammelbände der Internationalen Musikgesellschaft,* No. X, 1909.)

Smetana (Smettana)

Surgeon in Vienna, who performed a hernia operation on Beethoven's nephew Karl in 1816. Beethoven himself consulted him frequently about his deafness, and Smetana's name appeared in many letters. On the occasion of the nephew's ill-famed suicide attempt, Smetana was consulted again. Schindler (II, p. 12) described the way in which Beethoven dealt with Smetana's prescriptions. The physician would prescribe a teaspoon of a medicine; Beethoven would quickly change the teaspoonful to a tablespoonful, and correct the prescription in his own handwriting as though it were a musical score. In 1823 Smetana was Beethoven's guest. (Cf. Th.-R. V; Entry: Diseases.)

Smoking

Beethoven was a moderate smoker. In one of the Conversation-books of 1823 the Master wanted to be reminded to buy some tobacco in town. When the Master expected the great singers Sontag and Unger as guests, Schindler notated humorously: "Invite the girls for a pipe." During the last years of his life, Beethoven acquired a liking for cigars. According to Holz, he smoked only in taverns. He did not own any pipes and used snuff only seldom. (Cf. Volkmann: *Neues über Beethoven.*)

Songcycle

See Entry: Jeitteles, Aloys.

Sonnleithner

Family of musicians and scholars. Christoph Sonnleithner was a musician and jurist, born Szegedin (Hungary) 1734, died Vienna 1786. Christoph's compositions, especially symphonies, sacred music, and quartets were well known in his time, and were performed by the "Esterhazy Kapelle" and the concerts of Baron Keess. One of Christoph's sons was Joseph Sonnleithner, born Vienna 1766, died there 1835. He followed his father's career, being a musician and a jurist. As a youth he founded a printing firm (1782) which was liquidated. Emperor Franz commissioned him to travel in Germany and Scandinavia to collect portraits and biographies for the Imperial private library. Sonnleithner, together with Holer, West (Schreyvogel) and Rizy, formed in 1801 the Kunst-und Industrie-Comptoir, which was dissolved in 1805. In 1804 Sonnleithner had become Kotzebue's successor as K. K. Hoftheater-Sekretär and director of two theaters. He was responsible for the flourishing of the opera until 1814. It is well known that Sonnleithner was the librettist of the original version of *Leonore,* which was later remodeled as *Fidelio* by Treitschke. In addition, Sonnleithner was the first editor of the Taschenbuch *Aglaia,* as well as the founder of the Gesellschaft der Musikfreunde, responsible for its by-laws.

Beethoven was often in contact with Sonnleithner and consulted him in matters of law, as in his famous struggle with Artaria about the reprint of his Quintet Op. 29. Beethoven was often a guest in Sonnleithner's house; his wife, Johanna Wilhelmine, née Mariboe, was of Danish extraction. It was there that the Master met Grillparzer. Sonnleithner collected a large amount of material for a history of music which was never published. This material, in forty-one handwritten volumes, was donated by him to the Gesellschaft der Musikfreunde, and is one of the most valuable sources for the music historian. Ignaz Sonnleithner (1770-1831), another son of Christoph, was also acquainted with Beethoven. He was a lawyer and a great music lover, in whose house were held a number of memorable performances of works by Schubert,

Beethoven, Worzischek, and Hellmesberger between the years 1815 and 1854. Ignaz Sonnleithner was a professor of commercial law at the Polytechnicum in Vienna, where Beethoven's nephew was a student in 1825. In one of the Conversation-books a note of nephew Karl's is found, indicating that Dr. Sonnleithner paid him much attention as "he knows you very well." Ignaz's son Leopold (1797-1873) was likewise a jurist and music lover. He was known to Beethoven, who mentioned him in a letter of 1824. Leopold knew a great deal about Beethoven and his works, and contributed many articles to different magazines on this subject. According to Leopold, Beethoven was dissatisfied with the last movement of his Ninth Symphony, which he thought to be a failure. This statement is found in the *Allgemeine musikalische Zeitung* (1864) in an article entitled: "Ad vocem: Contrabass-Recitative der 9. Symphonie von Beethoven." In addition, there is a remark by Leopold that in the times of Beethoven the double-bass recitatives were played rapidly. Sonnleithner's article "Beethoven und Paër" was printed in Czartoryski's *Recensionen und Mittheilungen über Theater und Musik* (1860).

The family tree of those Sonnleithners who were prominent in the music field is found in Wurzbach. (Cf. Wurzbach; Paul Friedrich Walther: Obituary for Joseph Sonnleithner in *Oesterreichische Zeitschrift für Geschichts- und Staatskunde* (1836); Th.-R.; Entry: Gesellschaft der Musikfreunde.)

Sontag, Henriette Gertrude Walpurgis

b. Koblenz 1806, d. Mexico (of cholera) 1854. Famous singer. Her father, a basso buffo, was of Spanish-Portuguese extraction. The child grew up in a theatrical environment, making her debut at the age of eight in Kauer's *Donauweibchen.* In 1815 Henriette arrived at Prague with her mother Franziska, also a famous actress. In Prague she began as a student in the Conservatory, studying with Triebensee, Pixis and Mme. Czeska. Having successfully performed at the opera in Prague, Henriette went to Vienna in 1822, where the Italian opera flourished under Barbaja. Her first important role was Donna Anna in *Don Giovanni.*

Henriette's acquaintance with Beethoven dates from September 1822, as indicated in a letter from Beethoven to his brother on September 8, of that year: "Today I had the visit of two singers who felt like kissing my hands. As they were pretty girls, I offered them my mouth. They were Caroline Unger and Henriette Sontag." As late as 1873 Caroline Unger wrote: "Jette (Henriette) and I entered [Beethoven's] room as though it were a church, but our attempt to sing for the Master was unfortunately in vain." Friendly connections developed between Beethoven and the "lovely witches," who tried several times to persuade him to attend social gatherings. The names of both singers appeared many times in the Conversation-books.

Toward the end of 1823 Beethoven decided to entrust the two singers with the solos of the Ninth Symphony and the *Missa Solemnis.* In March 1824 the Master invited them both for lunch, and Caroline Unger jotted down in the Conversation-book: "Schindler informed us, and everybody seems happy, that you finally decided to give a concert. We

SPEECH-HABITS

shall appreciate it if you find us worthy to participate." The housekeeper served capon, and several helpings of meat, catered from a restaurant, and a Gugelhupf as a dessert. A few days later Schindler reported the sad news that the heavy lunch had not agreed with the ladies. "The two beauties want to be recommended to you," Schindler wrote in a Conversation-book, "they hope for a better time on the next occasion." The two singers were not the only ones with whom Beethoven's meals did not agree.

Shortly after this incident the rehearsals for the Ninth Symphony began. Henriette confessed to Schindler that never in her life had she sung such a difficult part. Schindler coached her and even gave her some voice lessons according to the methods of Durante, Leo, and Porpora. The two singers knew little about Beethoven's requirements and the sonority of their voices was by no means satisfactory to the deaf Master. They both asked for changes in the score; Sontag was not able to keep up the high pitch in the passage of the Ninth Symphony: *Küsse gab sie uns und Reben.* When the Master stubbornly repeated "No," Sontag would answer: "All right, keep on torturing us!" The famous concert took place May 7, 1824, an enthusiasm knew no bound er, the
deaf Master, with his audience, could not hea endous
applause until Sont brilliant
idea of turning him e could
see his public. This imulant
to the general enth

The colorful car tte Son-
tag was described ncke in
"Henriette Sontag bstverlag
der Gesellschaft f ichte. In 1828 Henriette had married the Sardinian diplomat, Count Rossi, after having been previously engaged to Count William Clam-Gallas in Prague, and to another "Clam," Lord Clamwilliam in Berlin. When Ludwig Rellstab wrote his novel *Henriette, or The Beautiful Singer* under the pseudonym Freimund Zuschauer, he satirized the amorous and social adventures of the singer so acidly that he was jailed for six months.

Sontag's entire career was a great and unique triumph; whenever she appeared in concerts, on the stage or in private, in Europe or the Western Hemisphere, she was acclaimed. Among her great admirers we find Zelter, Börne, and, above all, Goethe, who glorified her in two of his poems. Her voice was described as not exceedingly voluminous, and there were other singers with a more attractive coloratura. Her forte was unsurpassable acting, with indescribable gracefulness and a beautiful *mezzavoce.* She competed successfully with Malibran and Catalani, the latter having judged her in the following way: "*Elle est unique dans son genre, mais son genre est petit.*" The actor Karl Sontag, her brother (1828-1900), wrote many reminiscences of Henriette in his autobiography: *Vom Nachtwächter zum türkischen Kaiser,* 3rd edition 1878. In addition, she has been the subject of many novels, for instance, Gundling: *Henriette Sontag* (1861).

(Cf. Rellstab: *Aus meinem Leben*; Hans Kühner: *Genien des Gesanges,* Basel, 1951.)

Speech-habits

It may be assumed the Beethoven's original speech was the Rhenish dialect spoken in Bonn. In 1792 he had to face a new dialect, one already known to him through Elector Maximilian Franz, Count Waldstein and Haydn. This Austrian dialect was also familiar to Beethoven from his trip to Vienna in 1787. Frau Kissow-Bernhard, the governess for the Secretary of Russian Ambassador von Klupfeld, was struck by the strangeness of Beethoven's dialect (cf. Nohl: *Beethoven nach den Schilderungen seiner Zeitgenossen*, 1867). Gradually the Master assumed elements of the Viennese dialect. We might visualize his way of speaking as a strange mixture of Rhenish and Viennese. Karl Holz told Otto Jahn that everybody could recognize Beethoven's Rhenish accent in his speech. Beethoven spoke softly, but later, when he became deaf, he often shifted from soft to very loud, even shouting, especially if emotionally disturbed. His singing voice was a sonorous bass. Schlösser in his biography mentioned that Beethoven's voice, after he became deaf, lost its sonority. His laugh was kind of yelling, and his voice was proverbially called the voice of a lion.

Spiker, Samuel Heinrich

Berlin 1786, d. there 1858. Royal Prussian Librarian. From 1807 he was a member of the Berlin Singakademie, and from 1810 on, a member of the Zelter Liedertafel. When Beethoven dedicated his Ninth Symphony to Friedrich Wilhelm III, the Prussian king, Dr. Spiker came to Vienna to bring the Ninth Symphony back to Berlin and hand it to the Prussian king. It was a revised copy by Beethoven with an autographed title page bearing the dedication in Beethoven's own hand. Spiker described his visit with the Master in an obituary printed in No. 96 of the *Berliner Nachrichten von Staats- und Gelehrten Sachen*, dated April 5, 1827. The report is reprinted in Th.-R. V, p. 370. In Castelli's memoirs we find a reference to Spiker, whom Castelli called editor of the *Spenersche Zeitung*. Spiker is described as a "bon vivant, witty, highly educated, and a remarkable gourmet." (Cf. Kalischer: *Beethoven und Berlin*; Castelli: *Memoiren meines Lebens*, München 1913.)

Spohr, Ludwig

Braunschweig 1784, d. Cassel 1859. Famous composer and violinist. He received his first violin lessons in Braunschweig from the organist Hartung and concert-master Maucourt, later (1802) from Franz Eck. He became a sensational success in 1804, when he toured Germany as a violinist and composer, and in 1805 he became concertmaster in Gotha, as successor to Franz Anton Ernst. After his marriage to the famous harpist, Dorette Scheidler, he toured and came to Vienna in 1812, competing with Rode. Count Palffy appointed him Kapellmeister of the Theater an der Wien, but he left the Austrian capital in 1816 to start another concert tour. He had met Beethoven in Vienna and he wrote about him extensively in his autobiography, published in 1860-61. This autobiography was translated into English in 1865; an excerpt from it, referring to Beethoven, shows the vividness of his impressions.

"Upon my arrival in Vienna I immediately paid a visit to Beethoven; I did not find him at home, and therefore left my card. I now hoped to meet him at some of the musical parties to which he was frequently invited, but was soon informed that Beethoven, since his deafness had so much increased that he could no longer hear music connectedly, had withdrawn himself from all musical parties, and had become very shy of all society. I made trial therefore of another visit; but again without success. At length I met him quite unexpectedly at the eating house where I was in the habit of going with my wife every day at the dinner hour. I had already given concerts, and twice performed my oratorio. The Vienna papers had noticed them favourably. Beethoven had therefore heard of me when I introduced myself to him, and he received me with an unusual friendliness of manner. We sat down at the same table, and Beethoven became very chatty, which much surprised the company, as he was generally taciturn and sat gazing listlessly before him. But it was an unpleasant task to make him hear me, and I was obliged to speak so loud as to be heard in the third room off. Beethoven now came frequently to these dining rooms, and visited me also at my house. We thus soon became well acquainted. Beethoven was a little blunt, not to say uncouth; but a truthful eye beamed from under his bushy eyebrows. After my return from Gotha I met him now and then at the Theater an der Wien, close behind the orchestra, where Count Palffy had given him a free seat. After the opera he generally accompanied me to my house, and passed the rest of the evening with me. He could then be very friendly with Dorette and the children. He spoke of music but very seldom. When he did, his opinions were very sternly expressed, and so decided as to admit of no contradiction whatever. In the works of others, he took not the least interest; I therefore had not the courage to show him mine. His favorite topic of conversation at that time was a sharp criticism of the management of both theatres by Prince Lobkowitz and Count Palffy. He frequently abused the latter in so loud a tone of voice, while we were yet even within the walls of his theatre, that not only the public leaving it, but the Count himself could hear it in his office. This used to embarrass me greatly, and I then always endeavored to turn the conversation upon some other subject.

"Beethoven's rough and even repulsive manners at that time arose partly from his deafness, which he had not learned to bear with resignation, and partly from the dilapidated condition of his pecuniary circumstances. He was a bad housekeeper, and had besides the misfortune to be plundered by those about him. He was thus frequently in want of common necessaries. In the early part of our acquaintance, I once asked, after he had absented himself for several days from the dining rooms: 'You were not ill, I hope?' 'My boot was, and as I have only one pair, I had house-arrest,' was his reply.

"But some time afterwards he was extricated from this depressing position by the exertions of his friends. The proceeding was as follows:

"Beethoven's *Fidelio,* which in 1804 (or 1805) under very unfavorable circumstances (during the occupation of Vienna by the French), had met with very little success, was now brought forward again by the director of the Kärntnerthor Theater and performed for his benefit.

Beethoven had allowed himself to be persuaded to write a new overture for it (in E), a song for the jailer, and the grand air for Fidelio (with horn obligati) as also to make some alterations. In this new form the opera had now great success, and kept its place during a long succession of crowded performances. On the first night, the composer was called forward several times, and now became again the object of general attention. His friends availed themselves of this favorable opportunity to make arrangements for a concert in his behalf in the great Redouten Saal at which the most recent compositions of Beethoven were to be performed. All who could fiddle, blow, or sing were invited to assist, and not one of the most celebrated artists of Vienna failed to appear. I and my orchestra had of course also joined, and for the first time I saw Beethoven direct. Although I had heard much of his leading, yet it surprised me in a high degree. Beethoven had accustomed himself to give the signs of expression to his orchestra by all manner of extraordinary motions of his body. As often as a *sforzando* occurred, he tore his arms, which he had previously crossed upon his breast, with great vehemence asunder. At a piano, he bent himself down, bent the lower the softer he wished to have it. Then when a *crescendo* came, he raised himself again by degrees, and upon the commencement of the *forte*, sprang bolt upright. To increase the *forte* yet more, he would sometimes also join in with a shout to the orchestra, without being aware of it.

"Upon my expressing my astonishment to Seyfried at this extraordinary method of directing, he related to me a tragicomical circumstance that had occurred at Beethoven's last concert at the Theater an der Wien.

"Beethoven was playing a new pianoforte concerto of his, but forgot at the first *tutti* that he was a solo player, and springing up, began to direct in his usual way. At the first *sforzando* he threw out his arms so wide asunder that he knocked both the lights off the piano upon the ground. The audience laughed, and Beethoven was so incensed at this disturbance that he made the orchestra cease playing, and begin anew. Seyfried, fearing that a repetition of the accident would occur at the same passage, bade two boys of the chorus place themselves on either side of Beethoven, and hold the lights in their hands. One of the boys innocently approached nearer, and was reading also in the notes of the piano part. When therefore the fatal *sforzando* came, he received from Beethoven's outflung right hand so smart a blow on the mouth that the poor boy let fall the light from terror. The other boy, more cautious, had followed with anxious eyes every motion of Beethoven, and by stooping suddenly at the eventful moment he avoided the slap on the mouth. If the public were unable to restrain their laughter before, they could now much less, and broke out into a regular bacchanalian roar. Beethoven got into such a rage that at the first chords of the solo, half a dozen strings broke. Every endeavor of the real lovers of music to restore calm and attention were for the moment fruitless. The first *allegro* of the concerto was therefore lost to the public. From that fatal evening on Beethoven would not give another concert.

"But the one got up by his friends was attended with the most brilliant success. The new compositions of Beethoven pleased extremely, particularly the Symphony in A major (the Seventh); the wonderful second movement was encored and also made upon me a deep and lasting impression. The execution was a complete masterpiece, in spite of the uncertain and frequently laughable direction by Beethoven.

"It was easy to see that the poor deaf maestro of the piano could no longer hear his own music. This was particularly remarkable in a passage in the second part of the first *allegro* of the symphony. At that part there are two pauses in quick succession, the second of which is *pianissimo.* This Beethoven had probably overlooked, for he again began to give the time before the orchestra had executed this second pause. Without knowing it, therefore he was already from ten to twelve bars in advance of the orchestra when it began the *pianissimo.* Beethoven, to signify this in his own way, had crept completely under the desk. Upon the now ensuing *crescendo,* he again made his appearance, raised himself continually more and more, and then sprang up high from the ground, when according to his calculation the moment for the *forte* should begin. As this did not take place, he looked around him in affright, stared with astonishment at the orchestra that it should still be playing *pianissimo,* and only recovered himself when at length the long expected *forte* began, and was audible to himself. Fortunately this scene did not take place at the public performance, otherwise the audience would certainly have laughed again.

"As the salon was crowded to overflowing and the applause enthusiastic, the friends of Beethoven made arrangements for a repetition of the concert which brought in an almost equally large amount. For some time, therefore, Beethoven was extricated from his pecuniary difficulties; but, arising from the same causes, these recurred to him more than once before his death.

"Up to this period, there was no visible falling off in Beethoven's creative powers. But as from this time, owing to his constantly increasing deafness, he could no longer hear any music, this of necessity must have had a prejudicial influence upon his fancy. His constant endeavor to be original and to open new paths could no longer, as formerly, be preserved from error by the guidance of the ear. Was it then to be wondered at that his works became more and more eccentric, unconnected, and incomprehensible? It is true there are people who imagine they can understand them, and, in their pleasure at that, rank them far above his earlier masterpieces. But I am not of the number, and freely confess that I have never been able to relish those last works of Beethoven. Yes! I must even reckon the much admired Ninth Symphony among them, the first three movements of which, in spite of some solitary flashes of genius, are to me worse than all of the eight previous symphonies; the fourth movement of which is in my opinion so monstrous and tasteless, and in its grasp of Schiller's *Ode* so trivial, that I cannot even now understand how a genius like Beethoven could have written it. I find in it another proof of what I already remarked in Vienna, that Beethoven was wanting in aesthetical feeling and in a sense of the beautiful.

"And at the time I made Beethoven's acquaintance, he had already discontinued playing both in public and at private parties; I had therefore but one opportunity to hear him, when I casually came to the rehearsal of a new trio (D Major ¾ time) at Beethoven's house. It was by no means an enjoyment; for in the first place the pianoforte was woefully out of tune which, however, troubled Beethoven little, since he could hear nothing of it, and, secondly, of the former so admired excellence of the virtuoso scarcely anything was left, in consequence of his total deafness. In the *forte*, the poor deaf man hammered in such a way upon the keys that entire groups of notes were inaudible, so that one lost all intelligence of the subject unless the eye followed the score at the same time. I felt moved with the deepest sorrow at so hard a destiny. It is a sad misfortune for any one to be deaf; how then should a musician endure it without despair? Beethoven's almost continual melancholy was no longer a riddle to me now."

Sporschill, Johann Chrysostomus

b. Brünn 1800, d. Vienna 1863. Writer. Studied in Brünn, later in Vienna, where he finished his studies in law and political science in 1823. In that year he met Beethoven. In 1827 he went to Leipzig, where he wrote a number of books, among them an English dictionary. In 1858 he left Leipzig for political and religious reasons, and settled in Vienna, where he became a successful journalist. Among his translations from English into German the following authors should be mentioned: Ainsworth, Bulwer, Brougham, Cooper, Gibbon, Goldsmith, Hazlitt, Montesquieu, Say, Miss Trollope, etc.

In 1823 Sporschill approached Beethoven through the latter's brother Johann. Beethoven agreed to compose music for a libretto by Sporschill under the title: *Die Apotheose im Tempel des Jupiter Ammon.* The manuscript of the libretto came through Schindler's estate into the hands of the Library of Berlin, and was described by Hans Volkmann in his book: *Neues über Beethoven,* 2nd Edition 1905. The persons of the play are: Alexander the Great, his friend Clitus, Roxanne, Alexander's wife, and his friend Hephaestion. It is worth mentioning that Beethoven had attempted a similar project about 1803, when he started composing an opera with the following characters: Porus, Volivia, Sartagones, etc. In Sporschill's libretto King Porus was also introduced. Beethoven's early Porus libretto was written by Schikaneder. Sporschill's libretto might be called a failure. On November 5, 1823, he wrote an article on Beethoven in the *Stuttgarter Morgenblatt für gebildete Stände,* and after Beethoven's death an obituary in the Dresden *Abendzeitung,* July 11-12, 1827, an excellent characterization of the Master. Sporschill's name appeared many times in the Conversation-books; for instance, the nephew Karl jotted down: "Sporschill spends all day in the coffee houses, playing." (Cf. Wurzbach; Th.-R. IV; Entry: *Vestas Feuer;* Nottebohm: *Beethoveniana* I, p. 92.)

Stadler, Maximilian

b. Melk (Austria) 1748, d. Vienna 1833.

Abbé and composer, Stadler was the son of a baker and received his education in a Jesuit college in Vienna; he became abbot in Lilienfeld 1786, and in Kremsmünster in 1798. For several years Abbé Stadler lived in Vienna, where he became friendly with Haydn, Mozart, Gassmann, Reuter, Bonno, Vanhall, and other musicians. In 1806 he became rector (Pfarrer) in Altlerchenfeld near Vienna, later also in Böhmisch-Krut. He finally settled in Vienna in 1815. In the discussion about Mozart's Requiem, he defended the authenticity of the work, when consulted by Nikolaus von Nissen and Mozart's widow Konstanze (at this time the wife of Nissen). The results of Stadler's findings can be seen in some of his writings of 1826-27. In 1813 Stadler's oratorio *Die Befreiung von Jerusalem* was performed by amateurs at the Vienna University under the direction of Mosel. This text, by Collin, is the same one that Beethoven was considering.

According to Castelli, Stadler called Beethoven's works "sheer nonsense," and would walk out of concerts where Beethoven's works were performed. However, Beethoven liked the kind-hearted old gentleman and enjoyed joking with him. As late as 1803 the Master intended dedicating to the Abbé a set of variations in E flat (probably Op. 35 Eroica Variations). In 1826 Stadler had sent Beethoven his *Verteidigung des Mozartschen Requiems*, whereupon the Master answered him in a touching letter of appreciation, begging the Abbé for his blessing. Whether or not Beethoven took him seriously as a priest, is not certain. Castelli in his memoirs tells the following story: One afternoon Stadler met Beethoven at Steiner's. Beethoven knelt before Stadler, asking him: "Honorable Reverend, give me your blessing." Stadler was not embarrassed, made the sign of the cross over him, as if mumbling a prayer, and said: "If it does no good, it will do no harm." This incident goes well with Beethoven's Canon No. 13 of the complete works: "*Signore Abbate io sono ammalato. Santo Padre vieni e date mi la benedizione. Hol' Sie der Teufel, wenn Sie nicht kommen.*" (Cf. Th.-R. II-V; Hanslick: *Geschichte des Conzertwesens in Wien*; Castelli: *Memoirs*; Wurzbach with an extensive catalogue of Stadler's works.)

Stainer, von Felsburg

A talented amateur pianist who performed Beethoven's Sonata Op. 90 (February 1816) in a concert given by Schuppanzigh. He was one of those who signed the address of devotion to Beethoven in February 1824 with his professional title of Bank Liquidator. (Cf. Schindler II, p. 63; Th.-R. V, p. 69.)

Starke (Starcke), Friedrich

b. Elsterwerda 1774, d. Döbling (near Vienna) 1835. Musician, military bandmaster. In his youth he was an itinerant musician and Kapellmeister of the famous Kolter circus. Later in Salzburg, a clavier teacher in the house of Countess Pilati in Wels (Upper Austria). In addition he was Kapellmeister of an Austrian regiment which fought in the Napoleonic wars. After the end of the war, he settled down in Vienna and studied composition with Albrechtsberger. Recommended by Beethoven, he became first horn player of the Vienna Opera. Starke was a prolific composer whose tone poem *The Battle of Leipzig,* a monstrous composition, might compete with Beethoven's Battle Symphony (cf. Hanslick: *Patriotische Konzerte in Wien,* Neue Freie Presse 1866 No. 641). Starke's reputation stems from his book, *Wiener Pianoforte Schule.*

Beethoven permitted the reprinting of the *andante* and *rondo* of his Piano Sonata Op. 28 (Sonnenfels). These two movements have educational value because of Beethoven's fingerings and remarks. The third part of the *Pianoforte Schule* contains "Kleinigkeiten" with Beethoven's Bagatelles No. 7-11, from Opus 119, and a "Concert Finale von Ludwig van Beethoven," which is a kind of arrangement of the last movement of the Piano Concerto in C minor Op. 37. In addition, this part contains Exercise No. 3 with some passages of Piano Sonata 31 No. 2 in D minor ("Tempest"). Exercise No. 34 consists of Beethoven's theme *"O, Hoffnung,"* and some variations written by Archduke Rudolph on that theme. Starke was often invited by Beethoven for lunch. Beethoven's *Egmont* was arranged by Starke for "Turkish Music," and published by Haslinger. He was in addition the arranger of the Alexander March, falsely attributed to Beethoven. (Cf. Th.-R. IV; Wurzbach.)

Staudenheim, Jakob, Ritter von

b. Mainz 1764, d. Vienna 1830. Famous physician, personal physician of Emperor Franz, in 1826 the personal physician of the Duke of Reichstadt. In 1812 he accompanied the Imperial family to the Bohemian resorts, where he met Beethoven, whom he advised to go from Teplitz to Carlsbad and Franzensbad. Staudenheim kept in touch with Beethoven as late as the spring of 1824. By the summer of 1824, the Master seemed to prefer Dr. Braunhofer. Because of Beethoven's unreliability, both doctors withdrew, and could not be persuaded to see the Master during the last days of his sickness. (Cf. Wurzbach; Th.-R. IV, V.)

Steibelt, Daniel

b. Berlin 1765, d. St. Petersburg 1823. Celebrated piano virtuoso and composer of piano music. According to Tomaschek's autobiography (Libussa printed in Prague 1848, p. 377), Steibelt came to Prague in 1799. Tomaschek described vividly a concert by Steibelt, who was a kind of fake pianist. He appeared, together with an English lady, who accompanied his playing on the tamburin, a combination for which he had written several rondos. This arrangement electrified the Prague aristocracy to such an extent that the aristocratic ladies expressed the desire to play the tamburin. Such a course was given by the English lady on request at a fee of 12 gold ducats for 12 lessons. Steibelt received the same price for the sale of a tamburin, and made a fortune with this financial transaction.

Steibelt went from Prague to Vienna, where he met Beethoven in the palace of Count Fries (1800). There Beethoven's Trio Op. 11 was performed. Steibelt praised Beethoven in an affable way, but could not persuade him to play. Ries in his *Notizen* told that a week later another concert took place at the Count's palace. Steibelt performed a quintet of his own, and improvised on the theme *"Pria ch'io l'impegno"* from

Weigl's opera *L'Amor marinaro,* the same theme on which Beethoven's Variations of the last movement of Op. 11 are based. Beethoven's friends were aggravated, and persuaded the Master to improvise. In his informal and undisciplined way he went to the piano, taking along the cello part of Steibelt's Quintet, put it on the stand upside down, picked a few notes, and began to improvise in such a way that Steibelt left the room before Beethoven had finished.

Steiner, Sigmund Anton

b. Weitersfeld (Lower Austria) 1773, d. Vienna 1838. Publisher. He was educated in Langenlois, and came to Vienna, working there as a clerk in a law-office. In 1803 he acquired Senefelder's Chemische Druckerei, which he operated with Rochus Krasnitzky until 1812. In 1810 Tobias Haslinger came from Linz to Vienna and was appointed by Steiner as a bookkeeper. In 1814 Haslinger became associated with the firm. By that time the emphasis was on publishing music. In 1826 Steiner retired but remained active with the Gesellschaft der Musikfreunde. Beethoven's works were published by Steiner between 1814 and 1820. His letters to the firm were usually addressed to Haslinger. The firm was located on Paternostergasse. Many of these letters and notes Beethoven signed "Generalissimus." He addressed Steiner "Lieutenant General," Haslinger "Adjutant," and Diabelli "Diabolus" (cf. Entries: Haslinger; Diabelli).

The Master did not like the invoices the firm sent him, particularly because Steiner charged him interest for borrowed money. The complicated calculations between Beethoven and Steiner may be checked in Reinitz' book: *Beethoven im Kampfe mit dem Schicksal* and Th.-R. Other disagreements between Beethoven and Steiner occurred because of the title pages, which did not satisfy the Master. Among Beethoven's works published with Steiner during the composer's lifetime were: Piano Sonata Op. 90 (advertised June 9, 1815) and the Battle Symphony Op. 91. On July 24, 1815 the song "Es ist vollbracht," from Treitschke's singspiel *Die Ehrenpforten* was performed, and announced for publication with Steiner August 11; in 1815 the songs "Merkenstein," "Der Mann von Wort" and "An die Hoffnung" Op. 94; in 1816 the song cycle *An die ferne Geliebte,* and shortly thereafter the Seventh and Eighth Symphonies. Other Steiner publications were the String Quartet Op. 95 in F minor, the Violin Sonata Op. 96, the B flat major Trio Op. 97, the Theme with Variations by Archduke Rudolph and finally the *Elegische Gesang* Op. 118 for Pasqualati. (Cf. Th.-R. III; Max Unger: *Beethoven über eine Gesamtausgabe seiner Werke,* Bonn, 1920.)

Sterkel, Johann Franz Xaver

b. Würzburg 1750, d. there 1817. Composer. Studied Catholic theology, became court chaplain and organist in Mainz (1778). Concertized in Italy as a pianist. Became Canon in Aschaffenburg (1781) and Court Kapellmeister 1794-1797. Returned to Würzburg and Aschaffenburg and became Episcopal Court Music Director. When the Bonn musicians traveled to Mergentheim in 1791, Beethoven visited Sterkel en route. Sterkel played one of his own piano sonatas with violin accompaniment. Later he asked Beethoven to play his

Righini Variations on the theme *Vieni Amore*, as they were too difficult for Sterkel to play. Evidently Sterkel thought that Beethoven himself would not be able to play them. Beethoven performed them brilliantly.

Schiedermair suggested that the Master was influenced by Sterkel. Some of the slow movements of the latter seemed to anticipate Beethoven's *adagios*, as seen in the "Romance" of the First Sonata by Sterkel Op. 17. Likewise a *moderato* from Sterkel's Sonata No. 3 is almost identical with the second theme in Beethoven's first movement of his Piano Concerto No. 3 in C minor. Sterkel also contributed to the collection *In questa tomba oscura*. His composition has a striking similarity to that of Beethoven. (Cf. D. Augustin Scharnagl: *Johann Franz Xaver Sterkel*, Würzburg, 1943.)

Stich (Stech), Johann Wenzel

See Entry: Punto.

Stiebitz (Tavern)

See Entries: Kameel; Taverns.

Streicher, Johann Andreas

b. Stuttgart 1761, d. Vienna 1833. Composer and piano manufacturer. Famous in German literature because of his friendship with Schiller. They escaped together from the Karlsschule to Mannheim and Frankfurt (cf. Streicher's book *Schillers Flucht*, 1836, and Gutzkow's famous play *Die Karlsschüler*). Streicher, after his escape, went to Munich, where he became an established musician, and partner in a music shop. Since he went frequently to Augsburg, he met there and married Nanette Stein (1769-1833), the daughter of the famous organ and piano manufacturer. The couple moved to Vienna in 1794, where Streicher established a branch of the Augsburg firm in partnership with Nanette's brother, Mathäus Andreas Stein, under the name of Geschwister Stein. In Vienna, Streicher at first dedicated himself to piano playing and composing, but gradually he came to devote all his time to piano manufacturing. Under his supervision a private concert hall was opened, at Ungargasse 334, later No. 375, and in recent days No. 46. In 1812 statues of musicians sculptured by Franz Klein were placed in this concert hall. Here many magnificent concerts took place; for instance, in 1812 Handel's oratorio *Timothy* was performed with 579 artists and amateurs participating. These concerts finally paved the way for the foundation of the Gesellschaft der Musikfreunde. More details about the concerts were given by Reichardt in his *Vertraute Briefe* (1808) and Hanslick: *Geschichte des Konzertwesens in Wien*.

Another important source of information about Streicher's concerts is Carl Bertuch's diaries (cf. Egloffstein: *Karl Bertuchs Tagebuch vom Wiener Kongress*, 1916), and the unprinted memoirs of a candidate of theology, Traugott Alberti, who was a tutor in the Streicher family. Starke also gives details about the concerts at Streicher's. He related that Beethoven was a regular guest at the performances between 1816 and 1818. Often Beethoven took along his nephew Karl, who was then nine or ten years old, and who fell asleep many times on his uncle's lap during the music. When a composition of Beethoven's was played, Karl woke up at the first chord. Asked about the reason for his sudden awakening, the boy would answer abruptly: "This is the music of my uncle." Beethoven, who had met Nanette Streicher in Augsburg (1787), must have known Streicher as well. A letter from Streicher to Beethoven, written September 5, 1824, reads: "My opinion, uttered in this letter, comes from a friend whom you have known for over 36 years." The relation between the two always showed sincerity and dignity.

Nanette Streicher proved to be a helpful friend to Beethoven in all his domestic troubles. According to a note by Otto Jahn, Beethoven's C minor Variations were played (1807) by a daughter of the Streichers'. When the Master entered the room he asked: "Whose is this?" "Yours." Whereupon said Beethoven: "This trash, oh, Beethoven, what a jackass have you been!" Streicher visited the sick Beethoven on his deathbed. He came with Hummel and Ferdinand Hiller and provided the patient with wine. Streicher was among the torch bearers at Beethoven's funeral. (Cf. Wurzbach; *Allgemeine musikalische Zeitung,* Leipzig, 1834, No. 7. About Nanette Streicher, see *Allgemeine musikalische Zeitung,* 1833, No. 23; Kalischer: *Beethovens Frauenkreis.*)

String Quartets

Although not so numerous as the piano sonatas, the sixteen string quartets render a perfect reflection of Beethoven's musical and artistic development. Generally speaking, there are three main types of musical expression found in Beethoven's works, and they occur in three utterly different media: the monumental creation of the symphonic works; the piano solo music, as a means of experimental improvisation; and the chamber music, representing a balance between the independence of the single line and the limitations of the ensemble.

The Op. 18 Quartets were composed between 1798 and 1801 and published in two parts in the latter year by Mollo and Co. in Vienna; the quartets were dedicated to Prince Lobkowitz. Beethoven came to string quartets after having written for other string combinations such as the trio, the quintet and piano quartet; thus he was not completely inexperienced in string writing. These Op. 18 quartets show a decided advance over the quartets of Haydn and Mozart in perfectly balancing the four voices and in extending the range of all instruments. Nevertheless, the clarity of form brings a classic purity to these compositions.

Quartet No. 1 in F major was originally No. 2, being preceded by the one in D, but on Schuppanzigh's advice Beethoven reversed the order for publication. The opening movement is one of the most obvious examples of Beethoven's ability to create an entire movement from the germ of a single motive. Sketches from the Sketchbooks show varying experimental versions of this motive before it achieved its present concise form. The high point of the quartet, however, is the *adagio* movement which the Master related to the burial scene in Romeo and Juliet. The *scherzo* and *finale* return to the gay mood, allowing each instrument to revel in its brilliant virtuosity.

The second quartet of the group, in G major, offers an almost feminine charm and grace. The character of tender and obliging conversation is retained through the opening *allegro,* the witty *scherzo* and the whispering *finale*. Only the *adagio cantabile* resounds with more serious matters.

Quartet No. 3 in D major was the first to appear among the sketches for this group of quartets. The first three movements retain a lyric mood, offset by the brilliant tarantella of the final *presto*.

The C minor quartet, the fourth of the Op. 18, stands outside the general character of the other five quartets. It is the only one of the six in the minor key and it shares its depth and seriousness with other works in C minor. The energetic opening theme of the *allegro* is admirably transformed to serve also as a second theme. The *andante scherzoso* of the second movement undoubtedly required a *minuetto* third movement in place of the usual boisterous *scherzo*, while the *minuetto* retains the classic third movement form. The finale resumes the energy and seriousness of the opening movement. The fifth quartet of the group, in A major, reflects the splendour of the concerto style. The 6/8 runs of the *allegro* seems to require the *minuet* and *trio* as the second movement. The *andante* is a set of variations on a rather simple melody.

Op. 18, No. 6 in B flat major foreshadows the orchestral concept of the Op. 59 quartets. The affective *allegro* is relieved by a melancholic *adagio*, in turn balanced by a *scherzo* of shifting accent and unexpected stresses. The finale is preceded by a "Malinconia" section as in the late quartets, while the finale proper is a delicately skipping *allegretto* with a victorious *prestissimo* which rushes to the end of the work.

The three quartets of Op. 59, F major, E minor and C major, were composed in 1805 and 1806 and published by the Kunst-und Industrie-Comptoir in 1808. The three quartets were first mentioned in a letter to Count Brunswick in 1806 and in the same year the Master began sketching the works. The impetus for this set of quartets came from Count Razumovsky, who in 1805, had asked Beethoven to write a number of quartets with Russian themes. Razumovsky received the dedication.

The Op. 59 quartets reflect a much different concept of chamber music than the previous group. Being so surrounded by great works in the field of the symphony, it is understandable how they could assume some of the characteristics of the larger medium. It is this basic structural increase which moved the quartets beyond the comprehension of most of Beethoven's contemporaries.

The first of the group, in F major, reflects in its first movement this new style of writing, particularly in its large development section, harmonic perseverance and greater scope. The repeated notes in the cello, which open the *allegretto* movement, were considered a joke at the first performance. The *scherzo* contains a depth and profundity seldom found in similar movements. The finale employs a Russian theme according to the wishes of Razumovsky.

The E minor quartet, second in the series, is one of the few compositions by the Master in the key of E minor. The work opens with a 6/8 *allegro* followed by a second movement marked *molto adagio*. The *scherzo* departs slightly from the form usually employed by Beethoven: the *scherzo* and trio sections are repeated a second time after the normal repetition. In this quartet the

Russian theme appears in the trio; the theme is the well-known Russian folk song, frequently used by Russian composers (such as in Moussorgsky's *Boris Godunov*). The finale is full of exuberance and driving motion.

Op. 59 No. 3 is the least problematic of the group; there is a relatively simple structure in all movements. An actual slow movement has no part in this work, being replaced by an *andante con moto*. The almost Mozartian *menuetto* acts as a foil to the contrapuntal finale.

The Op. 59 quartets were the last to appear as a group; henceforth each quartet will possess its own opus number. The first of these, Op. 74 in E flat major, was composed in 1809 and published by Breitkopf and Härtel in 1810. It was dedicated to one of the Master's patrons, Prince Lobkowitz.

The years 1808 and 1809 show a curious affinity with the key of E flat major, including among others the Emperor Concerto and this quartet, frequently known as the Harp Quartet because of accompaniment figure in the coda of the first movement. The work itself, in its extended form, shows a tendency toward an orchestral style, particularly in the first movement. The *adagio* second movement and the *scherzo-presto* are more traditional in scope as is the final set of variations.

A year after the composition of the Op. 74 Quartet, another work for the same medium appeared from the pen of the Master. Publication was delayed until 1816, when it appeared as Op. 95 under the imprint of Steiner and Co., dedicated to the Baron von Zmeskall. This "quartetto serioso" as Beethoven called it, is frequently included in the third period of the Master's stylistic development. Although the work may not approach the depth of emotion and profundity of expression found in the last five quartets, there are, nevertheless, certain technical aspects which are typical of the third period: for instance, the chromatic harmonies and restless modulations, or the wealth of contrapuntal writing. The fantasia sections of the third period compositions are missing from this quartet. Here Beethoven follows a strict formal plan. The opening movement is constructed on a short motif, similar to the Op. 18, No. 1 Quartet and the Fifth Symphony. The second movement, an *allegretto ma non troppo* is remarkable for a chromaticism which reappears in the third relationship of the modulation found in the *scherzo*. The finale is almost completely contrapuntal.

A period of fourteen years separates the Op. 95 Quartet from the last five, a period marked by the great suffering caused by his nephew and the failure to achieve complete public recognition. These last five quartets are regarded by many persons as the epitome of Beethoven's art and of the string quartet medium in general.

Op. 127 in E flat major: This work was composed in 1824 and published in 1826 by Schott in Mayence. The work was dedicated to Prince Galitzin as one of three which had been requested by the prince two years previously. The work does not show as many revolutionary tendencies as the last four. The first movement opens with a slow introduction followed by a rather severe *allegro* in which the opening introductory theme functions as thematic material.

The reiterative rhythm, found also in the *scherzo* and finale, is one of the outstanding features of the movement. The *adagio* second movement is a set of variations, while the *scherzo* follows the common form as used previously by Beethoven. Most noteworthy is the use again of a motivic theme for the *scherzo,* although the treatment of the motive is somewhat different than previously. The rhythmic figure of the scherzo, taken from the opening introduction to the work, and the theme of the *adagio* are discontinued in the final *allegro.*

The second of the quartets requested by Galitzin was the Op. 130 in B flat major, written in 1825. The work was published posthumously by Artaria in 1827, dedicated to Galitzin. This quartet and the A minor and C sharp minor are linked together not only by the close relationship in date of composition, but also by musical relationships. Sketches in the note books reveal that themes of the A minor and of the B flat were worked on simultaneously. The opening theme in the introduction of the A minor was used again in the original finale of the B flat. The finale of the C sharp minor is likewise derived from themes which are to be found in the above-mentioned movements. The opening *allegro* is again based on a motive which serves both as thematic material and as a constructive element. The next four movements represent two pairs of contrasting movements: the whirling *scherzo* is followed by an ethereal *andante*; the *danza alla tedesca,* is succeeded by a masterpiece of touching personal expression. The original finale of this work was the Grosse Fuge, later published separately as Op. 133. At the first performance of the quartet in 1826, the fugue was felt to be much too long and profound; thus it was replaced by the present *allegro.* This *allegro* adds another colour to the variety of the previous movements. Since this was the last piece of music Beethoven completed, it is surprising in its rather simple outline.

The Quartet Op. 131 in C sharp minor was composed in 1826 and published in 1827 by Schott. It was first dedicated to Wolfmayer and later to Baron von Stutterheim. The seven movements of this quartet can actually be reduced to four, with the other three movements serving as transitions between the main movements. The quartet opens with a fugal *adagio,* serving as an introduction to the following *allegro molto vivace.* The instrumental recitative of the short *allegretto* harks back to K. P. E. Bach; it serves as a transition to the *andante* variation movement. The term variation is here to be understood in a much broader sense than before; Beethoven uses only the approximate form and hardly more than fragmentary references to the melodic and harmonic basis. The *presto* (*scherzo*) and the final *allegro* are separated by an *adagio* section.

The third quartet requested by Prince Galitzin and dedicated to him is the Op. 132 in A minor. The work was written in 1825, possibly before Op. 131 and 132, but it was not published until 1827. The first sketches date from 1824, mainly for the first movement, and are intermingled with sketches for the Grosse Fuge. The introduction is built on the theme which is so familiar from the Grosse Fuge, and fragments of the theme are inserted into the following *allegro,* a movement which is full of overflowing exuberance. Beethoven had finished the work as far as the second movement, the *allegro ma non tanto,* when further work was delayed by a serious illness. His gratefulness for his recovery is reflected in the inscription which he gave the slow movement: "Hymn of Thanksgiving to God of an Invalid on his Convalescence, in the Lydian mode."

Beethoven's last quartet, Op. 135 in F major, was composed in 1826, while Beethoven was staying with his brother at Gneixendorf near Vienna. It was published the following year by Schlesinger, dedicated to Johann Wolfmayer. The quartet is full of a mature serenity that comes only after a long struggle with life. This detachment of mind produces a work, concise and brief, collected and yet relaxed, which enjoys playing with the emotions rather than getting involved in them. Four relatively short movements make up this last quartet. The first *allegretto* reflects a deep contemplation, and the *scherzo* second movement contains the last outburst of wild humour. The *lento,* occurring as the third movement, returns to the contemplation of the *allegretto,* while the finale is introduced by the famous "*Muss es sein?—Es muss sein.*"

The sixteen quartets by Beethoven reflect an entire lifetime. From the classic formal balance of Op. 18 to the monumental, philosophical tomes of the last five quartets, there is revealed the Master's development both technically and psychologically. Beethoven was the last of the great string quartet composers; other composers after him wrote for the medium but none practiced it so assiduously nor attained the perfection which Beethoven achieved.

A. R.

Stumpff, Joseph Andreas

b. Ruhla 1769, d. London 1846. Musician and manufacturer of harps. For many years Stumpff lived in London. He came to Vienna in 1824, when he approached Beethoven through Haslinger and Andreas Streicher. Streicher had given him a letter of recommendation to the Master which ran as follows: "Herr Stumpff is a fine German who has lived in London for 34 years. . . . He is going to Baden, my dearest Beethoven, in order to see the man of whom Germany is proud. Receive him kindly and friendly as a saint receives a pilgrim from abroad." Stumpff left his reminiscences to his business successor T. Martin. Thayer made some excerpts which are published in Th.-R. V, p. 122. Stumpff was received by Beethoven with extraordinary cordiality. The composer accepted an invitation to dinner, entertained his host at dinner in return, played for him on his Broadwood pianoforte (after Streicher, at Stumpff's request, had restored its ruins), and at parting gave him a print of one of his portraits and promised to stop at his house if ever he came to London. Much of his conversation, which Stumpff records, is devoted to a condemnation of the frivolity and bad musical taste of the Viennese, and excessive praise for everything English. "Beethoven," Stumpff remarks, "had an exaggerated opinion of London and its highly cultured inhabitants," and he quotes Beethoven as saying: "England stands high in culture. In London everybody knows something and knows it well; but the man of Vienna can only talk of eating and drinking, and sings and pounds away at music of little significance or of his own making." He spoke a great deal about sending his nephew to London to make a man of him, asked questions about the cost of living there and, in short, gave proof that an English visit was filling a large part of his thoughts. The incidents of the conclusion of the dinner which he gave to Stumpff may be told in the latter's words:

"Beethoven now produced the small bottle. It contained the precious wine of Tokay with which he filled the two glasses to the brim. 'Now, my good German-Englishman, to your good health.' We drained the glasses, then extending his hand, 'A good journey to you and to a meeting again in London.' I beckoned him to fill the glasses again and hurriedly wrote in his notebook: 'Now for a pledge to the welfare of the greatest living composer, Beethoven.' I arose from my chair, he followed my example, emptied his glass and seizing my hand, said: 'Today I am just what I am and what I ought to be—all unbuttoned.' And now he unbosomed himself on the subject of music, which had been degraded and made a plaything of vulgar and impudent passions. 'True music,' he said, 'finds little recognition in this age of Rossini and his consorts.' Thereupon I took up the pencil and wrote in very distinct letters: 'Whom do you consider the greatest composer that ever lived?' 'Handel,' was his instantaneous reply, 'to him I bend the knee,' and he bent one knee to the floor. 'Mozart,' I wrote. 'Mozart,' he continued, 'is good and admirable.' 'Yes,' I wrote, 'who was able to glorify even Handel with his additional accompaniments to the *Messiah*.' 'It would have lived without them,' was his answer. I continued writing, 'Seb. Bach.' 'Why is he dead?' I answered immediately, 'He will return to life again.' 'Yes, if he is studied, and for that there is now no time.' I took the liberty of writing: 'As you, a peerless artist in the art of music, exalt the merits of Handel so highly above all, you must certainly own the scores of his principal works.' 'I? How should I, a poor devil, have gotten them? Yes, the scores of the *Messiah* and *Alexander's Feast* went through my hands.'

"If it is possible for a blind man to help a cripple, and the two attain an end which would be impossible to either unaided, why might not in the present case a similar result be effected by a similar cooperation? At that moment I made a secret vow: Beethoven, you shall have the works for which your heart is longing if they are anywhere to be found."

Stutterheim, Joseph, Freiherr von

b. Mährisch-Neustadt 1764, d. of cholera Lemberg 1831. Austrian general. For bravery in the battle of Aspern, he received the Order of Maria Theresia, highest military award. Beethoven dedicated to him his C sharp minor quartet Op. 131 as a token of his gratitude. The general had acted as an intermediary in placing Beethoven's nephew Karl in the Regiment Archduke Ludwig in Iglau (Moravia). The quartet was supposed to have been dedicated to J. N. Wolfmayer. Beethoven changed his mind, and wrote about it to Schott in Mainz on March

10, 1827. Evidently Beethoven had met Stutterheim in the house of Stefan von Breuning, who had introduced the nephew to the General. (Cf. Th.-R. V; Wurzbach.)

Swieten, Gottfried van, Baron

b. Leyden 1733, d. Vienna 1803. Diplomat and music lover. Son of the celebrated Gerhard van Swieten, personal physician to Empress Maria Theresia. Wurzbach in his *Biographisches Lexikon des Kaiserthums Oesterreich* offers a family tree of the Austrian branch of the Swieten family. Gottfried became K.K. Wirklicher Geheimer Rat, commander of the Royal St. Steven's Order and director of the Imperial Library in 1777, after he had been ambassador in Brussels, Paris, Warsaw and Berlin. Swieten was responsible for an extensive enlargement of the library. His influence on cultural matters at the time of Maria Theresia was stupendous, especially in his capacity as head of the Austrian education department. While in Berlin, he joined the circle around Philipp Emanuel Bach, Marpurg, and Kirnberger, and became acquainted not only with the works of Philipp Emanuel, but also with those of Sebastian Bach and Handel. On his return to Vienna he brought with him numerous compositions by Bach and Handel. Through Swieten, Mozart became interested in the polyphonic style of the late Baroque, which led to Mozart's transcriptions of works of Bach and Handel. Swieten played an important part in Mozart's life, and was responsible for the pauper funeral Mozart was given.

When Beethoven came to Vienna the musical soirées at van Swieten's were flourishing. Schindler related that the old gentleman was musically insatiable. He usually dismissed Beethoven very late, because the Master had regularly to fulfill his requests for playing a number of fugues by Johann Sebastian Bach as a sort of evening prayer. One of the letters from Swieten to Beethoven reads as follows: "To Herrn Beethoven, 45 Alsergasse in the house of Prince Lichnowsky. If you are free next Wednesday, I am requesting your presence at 8:30 p.m. with the nightcap in your pocket. Please reply immediately. Swieten." In one of Beethoven's diaries of 1792, the Master notated: "Dined in Swieten's house. Gave 17 cents to the superintendent as a tip for opening the door. . . ." Beethoven dedicated his First Symphony to van Swieten. It was performed for the first time April 2, 1800. (Cf. Jahn: *Mozart;* Mosel: *Geschichte der Hofbibliothek;* Wurzbach; Hanslick: *Geschichte des Konzertwesens in Wien;* Pohl: *Joseph Haydn.*)

Symphonies

As a symphonist, Beethoven continued in the tradition of Haydn and Mozart, and through a logical extension and expansion of the forms and styles, arrived at the place where any further expansion necessitated a completely new departure from the former aspect of symphonic logic. Nevertheless certain revolutionary characteristics appeared, but these were not in the external concept of the forms, rather, in the filling of these forms.

Perhaps his success as a symphonist can be traced to the essentially symphonic aspect of his material. These were not merely musical ideas which lent themselves to symphonic elaboration, but rather ones that demanded exploitation by all the resources of the orchestra. We know from the sketchbooks that the final form of his material was arrived at only after long periods of trial and error. These were periods of gestation, years in which the sketches were pounded and shaped on the anvil of his imagination until they were pared down to the unadorned and unembellished nucleus of symphonic thought.

It is this ability to give every thought a symphonic aspect which distinguishes Beethoven from other symphonists before and after him and which even today makes his symphonies a constant source of pleasure and a storehouse for student and composer alike.

In 1911 Professor Fritz Stein discovered among the archives of the University of Jena the MS score and parts of a symphony which had Beethoven's name inscribed on it. The work is in C major and stylistically would have to belong to the Bonn period. There is little doubt that the work is spurious, possibly having been written by one of the Mannheim group or perhaps by Franz Anton Rösler (Francesco Antonio Rosetti), a composer of 34 symphonies often in a style similar to Beethoven's. Rösler's Piano Concerto in B major was at one time attributed to Beethoven.

The Symphony in C major Op. 21, was given its initial performance at Beethoven's first public concert in Vienna on April 2, 1800. It can be traced back to 1794-5, where sketches for the finale can be found intermingled with counterpoint exercises which he prepared for Albrechtsberger.

This work, while showing its affinity to the classic tradition, nevertheless has indications of the future Beethoven in its breadth, and a seriousness heretofore unknown in the medium. There are certain innovations which set the work apart from its predecessors; perhaps the most obvious being the opening dominant seventh chord in F which caused so much concern among Beethoven's contemporaries. The introduction of only 12 measures does not surpass many of Haydn's symphonic introductions but it is a harbinger of such mature thoughts as the introductions of the Second and Seventh symphonies.

The "Mannheim Rocket" in the third measure of the Mozartean first theme is very typical of Beethoven's first period and it is possible that the fugal treatment of the theme at the opening of the second movement reflects the counterpoint lessons with Albrechtsberger. Perhaps the most indicative movement is the *minuet* and trio which so clearly contains the seed of future *scherzos*.

The entire work reflects the growing independence of the instruments and a tendency to treat the woodwind section as equal with the strings. This symphony already shows the basic woodwind family which Beethoven would retain throughout his works: flutes, oboes, clarinets and bassoons in pairs. The use of two horns is also standard, although he will use three in the *Eroica* and four in the Ninth.

The symphony was dedicated to Baron Gottfried van Swieten, the translator and arranger of Haydn's Creation libretto and friend of Mozart. It was not particularly well received by contemporary critics, and yet, after the production of the Third Symphony, it was to the style of this and the Second Symphony that Beethoven was advised to return.

Symphony D-Major Op. 36 dedicated to Prince Lichnowsky, was composed in 1802 and first performed in April of the following year at the Theater an der Wien in a program which included the oratorio *The Mount of Olives*, the C major Symphony, and the C minor Piano Concerto.

With this work Beethoven established the peculiar sequence which finds the even-numbered symphonies brighter, more serene and relaxed. The peaceful mood of the Second Symphony is unruffled throughout, this in spite of the fact that it was conceived during one of the most trying periods of the master's life. The famed *Heiligenstadt Testament* was written during the same summer of the year 1802, but at no place in the symphony does this cry of anguish disturb the confidence and contentment of the music.

Sketches for this symphony appear in the notebooks of 1802, mostly of the finale which is in more or less complete form. This sketch book was published by Nottebohm in 1865.

The symphony, in the customary four movements, shows a great advance over the first, particularly in its formal compactness and ease of expression. It is undoubtedly the beautiful *larghetto* which comes to mind when we recall the Second Symphony. It is curious that in a Paris performance of 1821, the *larghetto* was replaced by the *allegretto* movement from the Seventh Symphony. For sheer beauty and contentment, this *larghetto* is highly worthy of the master, even though there is little of the emotional intensity which we will later come to expect in slow movements.

It was the final *allegro molto* movement with its large skips, bursts of chords and audacious modulations which was most highly castigated by the contemporary critics, particularly the Leipzig *Zeitung für die elegante Welt,* after the first performance there.

As a whole, the symphony shows a great advance in instrumental color and idiomatic writing. The instrumentation does not go beyond that employed in the First Symphony, and again we see the characteristic way in which Beethoven pits the wind instruments against the strings, although here he seems to achieve a more perfect assimilation of the groups into a homogeneous unit. The work was later arranged as a Trio for Piano and Strings by Beethoven himself.

It is doubtful if any single work of art in the history of mankind marks such a bold and decisive step as does the Third Symphony in E flat major. This work is more vast in scope than the first two, both in length and magnitude of concept. (Op. 55.)

The work itself was conceived between the years 1802 and 1804, most of the actual composition being done in 1803. The earliest known sketch book to contain references to the work appears in 1802 and gives evidence that he began his movements conventionally enough (the third movement first appears as a *minuet*) but no sooner was the thought committed to paper than his imagination seized upon it and began expanding and transforming it.

SYMPHONIES

The first private performance in 1804 was at the house of Prince Lobkowitz, to whom it was eventually dedicated; the first public performance in the following year was at the Theater an der Wien. We are indebted to Ferdinand Ries for the story of Beethoven's destroying the title page containing the dedication to Napoleon. We can well understand Beethoven's disillusionment upon hearing that the man believed to be the savior of the people and friend of the downtrodden had been proclaimed Emperor. Hereafter the symphony would be known as the *Eroica*.

The work itself does not depend upon a new plan; the broad outlines of the form are no different than those used by Haydn or Mozart or even some of the pre-classic composers, but the inner contents of every movement reveal a completely new concept of the medium. In the first movement such traits as the use of thematic groups instead of single themes, and the inclusion of new thematic material in the development section mark a new and mature Beethoven. The *marcia funebre* retains the rough outlines of the march form but the noble sorrow of the opening theme is unlike any symphonic movement heretofore written.

The *scherzo* enters like a whisper of resurging life, constantly striving upwards only to fall back again. An early sketch for the trio showed a great similarity to the opening theme of the symphony; this theme was soon abandoned however, and an embryonic form of the present theme appears. This theme we can trace through several versions before it takes its present shape. The finale returns to the *Prometheus* ballet of 1800 for thematic material and perhaps a comparison of the two works reveals the essence of Beethoven's growth. What frequently appears redundant and unsure in the ballet music is stripped away in this finale; Beethoven seems to know precisely what the material demands and will allow, and his unerring sense of proportion penetrates immediately to the heart of the material. It is interesting that at three different times previous to this symphony, in a contradance, the Op. 35 Piano Variations and the *Prometheus* ballet, Beethoven had used this theme. The finale marks the realization of a tendency to make the final movement the equal of the first; further, it is the first appearance of the magnificent variation form which we have come to recognize as so distinctly Beethoven.

After experiencing the full magnitude of this enormous work, we perhaps find it somewhat of a surprise to realize that it has all been accomplished with the same orchestra used for the first two symphonies, with only the addition of a single horn. Perhaps the secret of the feeling of increased power is the skill of the idiomatic writing and the realization of the complete equality of the winds and strings.

The symphony was not gratefully received, and even critics sympathetic to Beethoven found it too long and difficult and sometimes redundant. His enemies proclaimed it harsh, odd, wild and often lost in confusion, and Schindler tells us that at the Conservatorium in Prague, of which Dionys Weber was the head, it was considered a dangerously immoral composition. Even as late as 1824 a London critic found that the symphony had "parts of such exquisite beauty and effect as to make ample compensation for the many strange and unconnected thoughts in which he has but too frequently indulged."

The Symphony in B flat major Op. 60, was the fourth symphony to come from the master's pen and represents a pleasant interlude between two milestones, or, as Robert Schumann has phrased it, "like a slender Greek maiden between two Norse giants." After the magnitude of the Third Symphony it is only natural that Beethoven's genius should seek relief in a more genial work, which under his hand has become a superb expression of tenderness and nostalgia.

Very little is known of the composition of the work except that it was composed in 1806, possibly at Martonvasar. Few of the sketches have been preserved, although some are found among the sketches for *Fidelio.* The original MS was once the property of Mendelssohn and was preserved among other musical treasures at the Mendelssohn house in Berlin. The symphony, which received its first performance at the house of Lobkowitz in Vienna during March of 1807, was dedicated to the Silesian nobleman Count Franz von Oppersdorf, who had commissioned a symphony from Beethoven.

It appears that work on the Fifth Symphony was laid aside for the composition of the B flat Symphony, although we do not know the circumstances for such action. We only know that the first two movements of the C minor were virtually completed in 1805.

It is almost impossible to single out any one movement as being superior or more interesting; perhaps in the very balance lies its value. It is noteworthy that Beethoven returns to the term *minuet* for the third movement although it is far removed from the 18th century prototype.

The instrumentation is the same basic one which Beethoven always employs except that here he limits himself to only one flute. Many of the string passages require a virtuosity which was unusual for the time and undoubtedly instigated Carl Maria von Weber's unjust attack on the work. Weber was not the only detractor, but the symphony by no means received the mockery and ridicule accorded the previous opus number, the Razumovsky Quartets.

The Fifth Symphony in C minor (Op. 67) will always remain the ultimate in symphonic logic. Composition of the work seems to have covered the years 1804 to 1808, being interrupted by the composition of the Fourth Symphony. The first performance took place in Vienna at the Theater an der Wien in December of 1808, a program which included the *Pastorale* Symphony, which was listed as No. 5 and the C minor as No. 6, a numbering which they retained in Vienna as late as 1820. The MS of the Pastorale is numbered 6 in Beethoven's own hand. It is obvious that the two symphonies are related in external circumstances; in fact, each of the symphonies is dedicated to the same two men, Prince Lobkowitz and Count Razumovsky.

Numerous sketches for this symphony are in existence, the first of which appears along with sketches for the G major Piano Concerto and reveals the characteristic four note rhythm of the first theme, but in a rather meandering fashion and without the concentrated drive which the theme later assumed. A curiosity in the sketches occurs in relation to the *scherzo,* whose theme is so similar to the finale of Mozart's G minor Symphony. The similarity is recognized by Beethoven for he wrote, on the adjoining page, the first 29 bars of the Mozart finale.

The first movement theme has occasioned many discussions about its germinal qualities. If, however, we understand a germinal theme to be the smallest, most succinct expression of the dominating thought in a work, then this is certainly a germinal theme *par excellence.* The rather mysterious *scherzo* is full of shifting accents which, however, do not destroy the "swing." This movement is not indicated as a *scherzo* in the autograph, merely *allegro.* The final *allegro* calls for the addition of trombones, piccolo and double bassoon to strengthen the tumultuous joy. The recall of the *scherzo* at the end of the development was a sheer stroke of genius.

The addition of trombones and double bassoon marks their first appearance in the symphony. Adam Carse conjectures, however, that the choice fell on the double bassoon merely because it was available in Vienna; had Beethoven been in Paris he would probably have scored for the ophicleide.

Even from its first performance, the elemental power of this symphony was recognized, and its popularity has certainly increased with time. Nevertheless, it has not always been received without reservations. Berlioz, usually the champion of Beethoven, felt a certain repetitiousness in the finale and Ludwig Spohr, while recognizing the opening theme's aptness for contrapuntal manipulation, nevertheless felt that it lacked the dignity which was indispensable for the opening theme of a symphony. Neither could he endure the "unmeaning noise" of the finale. In spite of this, the sureness of its musical logic and succinctness of its expression will undoubtedly continue to captivate audiences for many generations to come.

The Sixth or *Pastorale* Symphony in F major forms a companion piece to the C minor, but only in external connections, as we have seen. In character the two works lie at emotional extremes; where the Op. 67 is peculiar for its tension and terseness, this Op. 68 is completely relaxed. It reflects the contentment of a summer's afternoon when one can loll lazily among the wonders of nature. The work has received innumerable programmatic connotations in spite of the fact that Beethoven has warned that it is "more an expression of feeling than painting."

The work received its first performance along with the Fifth Symphony at the Theater an der Wien in 1808, in a program which included, among other works, the G major Piano Concerto and the Choral Fantasia. Like the C minor Symphony, this work is dedicated to both Lobkowitz and Razumovsky.

Each of the movements, in spite of its title, is clearly a structure of symphonic logic. The opening movement "Impressions on arriving in the Country" is as clearly *allegro* sonata form as any of the other first movements. As early as 1803 Beethoven had recorded in his sketch book the sound of a brook as he heard it, using a triplet figure as he does in the "Scene at the Brook" in the symphony. The *scherzo,* "Jolly Gathering of peasants," is followed by a section which represents a thunderstorm but is so completely a logical musical movement that even the flashing lightning manages to lend itself to symphonic development. The opening *Ranz de Vaches* of the finale is shown by the sketch book to be an afterthought, the movement originally beginning with the first theme in the violins.

The symphony was received with rather mixed reactions, the length of the *andante* being particularly castigated. It is perhaps in this movement that Beethoven is most sinned against, for it is frequently performed with long and numerous cuts.

The instrumentation consists of the usual paired woodwinds, two horns and strings, with the addition of two trumpets and two trombones for the storm and the finale, and a piccolo for the storm movement.

The Symphony No. 7 in A major Op. 92 was completed during the summer of 1812 and was first performed at the University of Vienna in December of 1813. This work and the Eighth Symphony are bound together in much the same manner as the Fifth and Sixth; both were completed in the year 1812 and both received their first performance at about the same time. The work is dedicated to the Count Moritz von Fries.

The sketch book for this symphony, published by Nottebohm in the *Zweite Beethoveniana*, dates from 1809 and shows page after page of sketches which were later to appear in the *allegretto* and finale of this work, as well as the first and final movements of the Eighth Symphony and projected overture on Schiller's *Ode to Joy*. The MS is another of those belonging to the Mendelssohn family and contains the date in Beethoven's own hand; unfortunately, the binder has inadvertently cut off the month so that we cannot tell with certainty whether the work was finished in May, June, or July, although he mentions in a letter of July 19, from Teplitz, that the work was ready.

The symphony, which Wagner has called the apotheosis of the dance, is marked by its rhythmic drive; each movement has its own rhythmic figure which permeates the entire movement. The 72 bar introduction has the distinction of being the longest of any of the symphonies, but it is undoubtedly the *allegretto* which is the most popular. It was encored at the first performance, and in France was frequently substituted for the second movements of the Second and Eighth Symphonies. The final movement is the most boisterous and most frankly rhythmic of the four.

The Seventh Symphony made its first appearance at a benefit concert for injured soldiers, and this frankly exciting music was almost as well received by the masses as was the more ostentatious *Battle of Victoria*. The orchestra contained most of the important musicians then in Vienna and was conducted by Beethoven himself. The concert was repeated on the same program with the Eighth. There is little doubt that it was a great success in Vienna, although not so well received in Leipzig. The work likewise met with approval in both France and England, the *allegretto* being particularly singled out for acclaim.

The customary scoring for paired woodwinds, horn and trumpets, along with strings, is carried out in this work.

The Eighth Symphony in F major Op. 93 was completed in the short space of four months, or at least between the time of completion of the Seventh Symphony and October of the same year. The MS in the Royal Library at Berlin bears the inscription, "*Sinfonia-Linz im Monath October 1812.*" The months during the composition of the work were partially spent traveling from Teplitz to Carlsbad, back to Teplitz and to Linz. The work received its first performance at the Redoutensaal in Vienna in February of 1814 on a concert with the Seventh and the "Battle" Symphonies.

Sketches for this work go back to 1809, along with sketches for the A major. The largest number of sketches, however, belong to the summer of 1812. Thayer points to an 11 bar introduction in A major which leads to a theme similar to the present first theme but in D major. Nottebohm also points to a passage which occupies 26 pages of the sketch book before finally evolving into the present theme. In spite of the brevity of the second movement there exist numerous sketches for it.

This work is often characterized as the "humorous" symphony, and indeed seems to have more boisterous horseplay than any of the others. It is also frequently referred to as the "metronome" symphony because of the apparent reference to Mälzel's chronometer in the ticking opening of the *allegretto.* The symphony is the shortest of the nine, excepting the first, and in a way is a return to the more classic concept of the form, although filled of course with Beethoven's more mature thoughts and much freer key relationships. The work is in the customary four movements although the traditional slow movement is replaced by an *allegretto scherzando.* The opening theme of the *allegretto* was taken from a canon extemporized at a dinner party in 1812 and addressed to Mälzel. This theme takes a different form in one of the sketches, although it is impossible to discover which is earlier.

Beethoven restricts himself to a very simple orchestra for this work, using, basically, the same orchestra as in the Seventh Symphony, although the trumpets and drums are omitted in the *allegretto.* In the finale the drums are tuned in octaves.

With the possible exception of the Second, this symphony is the least performed of the Beethoven symphonies. Its fate seems to be that, while it is not disliked, there are others which are preferred. In its first performance it was overshadowed by the Seventh, and even Berlioz seems to treat it somewhat patronizingly.

Beethoven's last and greatest symphony was not ready for actual performance until the end of 1823 or the beginning of 1824, eleven years after the composition of the Eighth Symphony. The original MS of the first three movements is in the Royal Library in Berlin along with the first MS by the copyist, which contains the dedication to King Frederick William III. The first of these contains an interesting discrepancy in that the trio of the *scherzo* is in 2/4 time but put into 4/4 by canceling every other bar line. There is another MS copy which is inscribed to the London Philharmonic Society, for which Beethoven received 50 pounds in return for exclusive rights to the symphony for

18 months. In spite of this agreement Beethoven allowed the symphony to have its first performance on May 7, 1824, in the Kärntnerthor Theater in Vienna.

Although the sketches for the work are very profuse, we know little about the actual scoring and final completion of the work. A letter to Ries in London on September 5, 1823, says that the score had just been finished by the copyist, and Schindler tells us that Beethoven returned to Vienna from Baden at the end of October and plunged immediately into the first movement. The score was not offered for sale until March of 1824 and it is doubtful if the work was complete before that date.

Schiller's *Ode to Joy* had held a fascination for Beethoven for many years and there is an indication he intended setting it as early as the Bonn period. The first appearance of the words in the sketch books occurs as early as 1798 and again among the sketches for the Seventh and Eighth Symphonies in 1811. Numerous sketches follow, mostly in 3/4 meter, until in 1822 appears a new theme which eventually becomes the one we know today. The sketch books are also full of various fragments of the poem, revealing Beethoven's efforts to decide upon the portions and order of verses which he would use. The Choral Fantasia of 1808 acted as an early study for this type of work also.

The first sketches for an instrumental movement appear in a sketch book of 1815 among sketches for the Op. 102 No. 2 Cello Sonata and a definite memoranda for a B flat symphony. This sketch is a fugue subject which would appear later as the *scherzo*. In 1817 appear sketches for the first and *scherzo* movements, the *scherzo* appearing as the third movement. On a separate sheet from around 1822 appears a thematic catalogue of all the movements except the slow one, with the *scherzo* being second. The slow movement was the last to appear, with the second section making its appearance first. Even as late as June or July of 1823 he appears to consider an instrumental finale as evidenced by sketches which eventually appear in the A minor String Quartet.

The symphony falls into the customary four movements, with the *scherzo* appearing second. However, within the movements there are great departures from the expected schemes. Particularly noteworthy in the first movement are the abundance of secondary themes and the way they appear to be generated out of the first theme.

The final movement is the one which employs Schiller's *Ode*. It opens with a long introductory passage which recalls each movement in order and represents a connection between the three instrumental movements and the vocal section. The cello recitative has its precedent in the instrumental recitatives of C. P. E. Bach, as well as other 18th century composers, but this is its first appearance in the classic symphony. The theme of the choral section appears also. The baritone recitative, between the instrumental introduction and the choral part, was written by Beethoven to act as a transition into the final section.

Beethoven has employed his usual instrumentation for this symphony to which he has added: two horns, bringing the total to four for the first time, three trombones in the second and fourth movements, and the double bassoon, piccolo, triangle, cymbals and bass drum only in the fourth movement.

The first performance of the work encountered difficulties from the beginning. In spite of his contract with the London Philharmonic Society, Beethoven made attempts to have the work first performed in Berlin, whereupon a group of his admirers in Vienna prevailed upon him to have the first performance in Vienna. Even so, the exact date could not be decided upon and when the date was finally set the work was performed with only two rehearsals. In spite of this, Beethoven received an ovation, the *scherzo* being interrupted by applause. Well known is the story of how Madame Unger induced him to turn toward the audience so that he could see the applause which he could not hear.

The reception of the symphony outside Vienna was not nearly so enthusiastic. In neither Frankfurt nor Aix-la-Chapelle the following year was the work well received. It was quite a different story in Leipzig, however, when the work was performed on March 6, 1826; the work had to be repeated at a later concert, even though the local critic was not convinced of its worth. The first performance in England occurred in 1825 and the critic of the *Harmonicon* objected to its length, repetitiousness and verbosity. Paris produced the work in 1831, after almost two years of rehearsal, and the New York Philharmonic in 1846. Ludwig Spohr felt the first three movements to be inferior to any of the previous eight symphonies, and the finale absolutely tasteless and monstrous.

Undoubtedly length and obscurity prevented the work from being popular in its day, but probably one of the greatest drawbacks to its acceptance was the novelty of the vocal movement and the extreme difficulty in both the instrumental and vocal parts. In spite of all, however, Beethoven acknowledged its superiority in a letter to the Russian Ambassador in Vienna in which he says, "I am just publishing the greatest symphony I have yet written."

Nottebohm tells us that if Beethoven had completed all the symphonies which he had contemplated there would be well over 50. As early as 1785-86 there is a long sketch for a movement in C minor and the sketches continue to fill the sketch books throughout his life. In 1818 a memorandum for a symphony in the old modes appears in the sketch books. Schindler at one time possessed a sketch book containing 30 measures of a C minor *scherzo,* 9 measures of a 6/8 finale and 5 measures of an A flat *andante* which he claimed were material for a tenth symphony. Schindler's erstwhile successor, Karl Holz, tells of Beethoven's playing to him on the piano an introduction in E flat major and a powerful *allegro* in C minor which were intended for a tenth symphony.

There can be little doubt that the symphony under Beethoven grew amazingly. Possibly most obvious is the overall growth in the size of each movement and the gradual shift in emphasis from the first movement to the last. Within the movements we find certain technical innovations such as the frequent introduction of new thematic material in the development sections as well as the more consistent use of thematic groups instead of single themes. The increase in size and importance of the introductions and codas is another advance, as is the use of the *scherzo* in place of the *minuet*. A noteworthy point is the complete autonomy of conception in the individual movements; no two corresponding movements are alike, each single movement has its particular structure as a necessary outgrowth of its material.

In spite of his innovations and freedoms Beethoven never quite stepped beyond the bounds of the classic concept, but, in these alterations and particularly in the power of expression and poetic feeling, he showed the way to the Romantic period. F.T.W.

T

Taverns (Restaurants, Coffeehouses)

As a housekeeper, Beethoven was certainly a failure. The Master as a result was a frequent visitor of the Viennese coffee houses, where the 18th century patrons had already established the custom of leisurely reading their local newspapers. For many years the tavern Zum weissen Schwan in midtown Vienna was one of Beethoven's favorite spots. There a well-known event took place, as reported by Ries: the waiter brought him a dish he had not ordered; a short argument followed resulting in Beethoven's throwing the whole dish at the poor waiter, who in turn could not help but lick with his tongue the Viennese gravy that was running down his face. A great feature of an Austrian tavern is its almost infinite uses. Beethoven, like many intellectuals, was most absorbed by his work; once he attempted to pay for a meal which he had never eaten (Doležalek and Breuning).

Beethoven's Quintet Op. 16 was first performed in the Hotel Ignaz Jahn. Other hotels and restaurants visited by Beethoven were Greif (later Erzherzog Karl) about 1800, where the Brunswicks lived; the Fischtrüherl (Little Fishtrough), Seitzer Hof, Blumenstöckl, the tavern Schwarzes Kameel, whose co-owner was Arlet, a friend of the Master. After 1814 Beethoven was frequently seen at the Römischer Kaiser, in Renngasse near Freiung. Other favorite places were Jägerhorn (Dorotheergasse), Brauner Hirsch (Rote Turmstrasse), Birne and Roter Hahn (Landstrasse), and the first coffee house in the Prater. Many a conversation recorded in the Conversation-books took place in taverns, and sometimes Beethoven even asked his partner to find out what the guests at the neighboring tables were discussing. (Cf. Volkmann: *Neues über Beethoven*; Frimmel: "Beethoven als Gasthaus Besucher in Wien," *Neues Beethoven Jahrbuch* I.)

Tayber (Teyber), Anton

b. Vienna 1754, d. there 1822. Musician. He was secretary to Salieri, a cembalist in the Imperial orchestra and for many years the music teacher of the Habsburg princes. As a student of Padre Martini he had a considerable knowledge of composition. He was the first teacher of Archduke Rudolph and very jealous of Beethoven. (Cf. Schindler II, p. 27; Wurzbach; and Hanslick: *Geschichte des Konzertwesens in Wien.*)

Teltscher, Josef

b. Prague 1802, drowned in the port of Phaleron about 1837. Excellent painter from the circle around Schubert. He portrayed Beethoven on his deathbed.

Teplitz

World-famous resort in Bohemia, a most fashionable spa visited by many celebrities. Malfatti and Bettina Brentano advised Beethoven to use the springs. The master arrived in Teplitz August 2, 1811, and his name was announced in the list of visitors two days later. He took a room in the "Harfe." During that season a great many aristocrats and artists were assembled in Teplitz, such as Elisabeth von der Recke, August Tiedge, Amalie Sebald, the Esterhazys, Count Bentheim, with his aid Varnhagen von Ense, who had come to see his beloved Rahel Levin (Robert); also Theresia Lobkowitz, Dr. Kanka from Prague, Beethoven's friend Oliva, and Varena from Graz. The violinist Polledro was Beethoven's roommate at the "Harfe" and the two became acquainted with each other. Beethoven saw Varnhagen frequently and also played for Rahel. Another acquaintance from Vienna was Pasqualati. Beethoven's stay in Teplitz lasted till the beginning of October; by October 29 he was back in Vienna. More important was Beethoven's second visit to Teplitz in 1812. He traveled via Prague where he made a stopover on July 2. On July 7 his name appears in the "Kurliste" as guest number 806. At that time he took a room in the "Eiche." The season of 1812 was made especially splendid by the presence of the Austrian Court, Prince Karl von Lichnowsky, and many other aristocratic families, as well as Achim von Arnim and his young wife Bettina. Another highlight of the season was Goethe's presence. (Cf. Entries: Oliva; Varnhagen; Goethe; Travels.) Beethoven's cure was interrupted toward the end of July, and the Carlsbad guest list shows his name on July 31st. Somewhat later the Master visited Franzensbad but returned to Teplitz in September. Beethoven's stay in Teplitz cannot be considered successful in regard to his health. He returned to Vienna about the middle of September via Prague and Linz, where he stopped several days at his brother Johann.

Thayer, Alexander Wheelock

b. South Natick, Mass. 1817, d. Trieste 1897. Graduate of Harvard (1843), where he became an assistant librarian. He decided to undertake a detailed and trustworthy biography of Beethoven. Between 1849 and 1851 he lived in Germany, collecting material for this work. He returned to the U.S.A. in 1852, joining the staff of the New York Tribune, and then returned again to Europe in 1854 where he remained, except for two years (1856-1858) when he lived in Boston. In 1862 Thayer was appointed to the American embassy in Vienna and in 1865 he became American consul in Trieste, a position he held throughout his life. Thayer's Beethoven biography was first published in German in a translation by H. Deiters (5 vols. I, 1866, (1901); II, 1872; III, 1879; IV, 1907; V, 1908: Vols. IV and V were edited by Hugo Riemann, who also revised the other volumes). Deiters used the manuscripts of only the first 3 volumes. The remainder had to be completed from incoherent material. The

English edition was edited by H. E. Krebiehl in 3 volumes (1921), and published by the Beethoven Association in New York. Thayer also wrote *Chronologisches Verzeichnis der Werke L. van Beethovens, ein kritischer Beitrag zur Beethoven-Literatur* (1877). Thayer's biography was an extremely detailed and accurate description of Beethoven's life, but it contained no aesthetic evaluation of the Master's works. Thayer's ideas were partly spoiled by the aesthetic judgments added by Deiters and Riemann, which necessarily are subjective and dated. Riemann especially, with his overemphasis on the Mannheim School, cannot be considered a faithful executor of Thayer's will. (Cf. Krebiehl in *Musical Quarterly*, October 1917; Entry: United States.)

Thomson, George

See Entry: Folk Music.

Thun, Countess Maria Wilhelmina

b. Vienna 1744, d. there 1800. Née Uhlefeld, wife of Count Franz Joseph Thun. One of her three daughters was the first wife of Prince Razumovsky, and her daughter Christine was married to Prince Lichnowsky. Beethoven might have been introduced to the Thun family in 1796. According to a report of Fräulein Kissow, later Frau von Bernhard, Countess Thun had once on her knees begged Beethoven to play. She had formerly patronized Mozart, Haydn, and Gluck. (Cf. Entry: Lichnowsky; Dr. Adolf Deutsch: *Sammlung von Wiener-Schattenrissen aus dem Jahre 1784.*)

Tiedge, Christoph August

b. Gardelegen (Altmark) 1752, d. Dresden 1841. Poet. For many years he had lived as the companion of Elisabeth von der Recke. His fame stemmed from his educational poem *Urania,* professing in a splendid way the ideas of Kant. Among his lyrical poems, two won widest acclaim: *An Alexis send ich dich* and *Schöne Minka, ich muss scheiden,* written on an Ukrainian folk tune. In 1800 Beethoven composed *An die Hoffnung* from Tiedge's *Urania* (1805). He met Tiedge in Teplitz in 1811, and they started a correspondence. Beethoven even offered Tiedge the brotherly "du," as he felt emotionally attached to the poet. As a result he recomposed *An die Hoffnung* about 1813. The first rendering bears the opus number 32. (Cf. Th.-R. III; Entry: Recke.)

Tomaschek, Johann Wenzel

b. Skutsch (Bohemia) 1774, d. Prague 1850. Composer. Studied with the local teacher, Wolf, in Chrudim; was chorister at the Minorite Monastery in Iglau, and took a law course at Prague University (1790-1793). Later he became chamber musician of Count Bucquoy-Longueval and a highly renowned private music teacher in Prague. Among his students the following should be mentioned: Dreyschok, Kittl, Kuhé, Schulhof, Bocklet, Dessauer, Woržischek, and Würffel. Hanslick as well belonged to this host of pupils. According to his memoirs, Tomaschek was full of self-confidence and the proverbial phrase of Dingelstedt: "You can't imagine how much praise I can bear," could easily be applied to Tomaschek. Tomaschek was a prolific composer of sacred music, chamber music and songs. Goethe enjoyed especially Tomaschek's compositions of his poems and rated his composition *Kennst du das Land* higher than Beethoven's. It was he who introduced the lyrical piano pieces into the literature with his eclogues and rhapsodies, a form taken over by his pupil Woržischek and above all by Schubert in his impromptus and *moments musicaux*. Tomaschek published his autobiography in the Prague yearbook *Libussa* (1847-1849), where he told about his experience with Beethoven, whom he had heard perform in Prague in 1797. (Cf. Entry: Prague.) He heard the C major Concerto Op. 15, then the *adagio* and the graceful *rondo* in A major, Op. 2, then he improvised on the theme: *"Ah tu fossti il primo oggetto!"* from Mozart's *Titus*, given to him by Countess Sch[lick]. Tomaschek was so shaken by Beethoven's grandiose performance that he did not feel like touching the piano himself. On the second occasion he heard Beethoven play the B major Concerto, which according to Tomaschek, was composed in Prague. The third time, he heard the young Master play in the house of Count C[anal], where he played the graceful *rondo* from the A major Sonata and improvised on the theme *"Ah vous dirai-je maman."* This time he watched Beethoven more objectively. Although he admired his powerful and splendid technique, he criticized the audacious jumpings from one motif to the other which lacked organic connection. The original and sensational in his composition seemed to be of greater importance than anything else. When a lady asked Beethoven if he liked Mozart's operas, he answered: "I don't know them and I don't like to listen to other people's music, because I don't want to jeopardize my originality." Tomaschek's further criticism of Beethoven may be read on p. 374 ff. of his autobiography, which also contains a report, "A visit to Beethoven in 1814." On account of its importance, it may be reproduced here.

"On the morning of October 10th, my brother and I visited Beethoven. The poor man's hearing was particularly bad that day, and we had to scream rather than talk to be understood at all. The reception room was furnished with anything but grandeur, and the disorder reigning therein was as great as that in his hair. I found an upright pianoforte, and, on its stand, the text of a cantata: *Der Glorreiche Augenblick* by Weissenbach. On the piano, there lay a pencil with which he had sketched his work. Side by side with this I found, on a small piece of paper, all sorts of ideas, without the least connection, jotted down; the most heterogeneous details thrown together, just as they came into his mind. However, this was the material of the new cantata.

"His conversation was just as haphazard as was this medley of musical details. As is usual with the deaf, he carried on the conversation in a very loud voice, always stroking his ear with one hand as though seeking the weakened power of hearing. Some parts of this conversation, which for me were without a meaning, I shall herewith report, omitting certain names the mention of which seems to me without importance.

"I: Herr van Beethoven, you will pardon me for disturbing you. I am Tomaschek of Prague, compositeur of Count Bucquoy. I am taking the liberty of visiting you, in company of my brother.

Beethoven: I am very pleased to make your acquaintance, and you are not disturbing me in the least. I: Dr. R. [Dr. Josef Reger, lawyer] wishes to be remembered to you. Beethoven: How is he? It is a long time since I have heard from him. I: He would like to know how you have progressed with your lawsuit. Beethoven: There are so many formalities that little progress is made. I: I hear that you have composed a Requiem. Beethoven: I wanted to write a Requiem as soon as this business was over. Why should I write before this affair is settled? Now he began to tell me all about it. And here too, he spoke without coherence, more rhapsodically. Finally the conversation changed to other matters. I: Herr van Beethoven seems to be very industrious. Beethoven: Must I not? What would become of my fame? I: Does my pupil Worzischek often come to see you? Beethoven: He was here several times, but I did not hear him. Not long ago he brought me some of his compositions, which, for a young fellow like him, are well done. (Beethoven was alluding to the twelve rhapsodies for the pianoforte which, dedicated to me, later appeared in print.) I: I suppose you seldom go out? Beethoven: Hardly anywhere. I: Tonight there is a premiere of Seyfried's opera; I have no desire to listen to such music. Beethoven: Lord, there must be composers like that. What otherwise would the masses do? I: I was also told that a young foreign artist has arrived here, who is said to be an extraordinary piano player [G. Meyerbeer]. Beethoven: Yes, I too have heard of him, but I have not heard him play. Lord, just let him stay here three months, and then we will hear what the Viennese think of his playing. I know how everything new takes here! I: I don't suppose you have met him? Beethoven: I did meet him at the performance of the *Schlacht* (*Battle of Victoria*), at which occasion several of the local composers played some instrument. The big drum was assigned to that young man. Ha ha ha! And I was not at all satisfied with him. He did not strike it correctly, and always came in too late, so that I had to give him a good calling down. Ha ha ha! That angered him. There is nothing to him. He hasn't the courage to strike at the right time. This observation made both my brother and myself laugh heartily. Refusing Beethoven's invitation to stay for a meal, we left him, with the promise to visit him again before my departure.

"November 24th. I visited Beethoven again, for I had a great longing to see him before leaving Vienna. I was announced by his servant and admitted at once. If, on the occasion of my first visit his apartment had been untidy, it was all the more so this time; for in the middle of the room I met two copyists who were writing down, in great haste, his before-mentioned and now finished cantata. In the second room, parts of scores, which were probably being corrected by Umlauf (to whom he introduced me) were lying all over the place, on tables, chairs, etc. Herr Umlauf seemed to be of a happy disposition, for he was neither cold nor warm at our first meeting. The mutual impression we made on each other remained; but he went and I stayed. Beethoven received me very cordially but seemed more deaf than ever before and I had to exert all my power to make myself understood. I will reproduce the dialogue here:

"I: I have come to see you once more before my departure. Beethoven: I thought you had already left Vienna. Have you been here all this time? I: Yes, with the exception of a few excursions to Aspern and Wagram. You have been well? Beethoven: O, as ever, I had much annoyance; it is hardly possible to continue living here. I: I see you are very busy with your academy—I should not like to disturb you in your work. Beethoven: Not in the least, I am glad to see you. There are, believe me, annoyances and corrections without end connected with an academy. I: I just read a notice that you have postponed it. Is that right? Beethoven: Everything was copied wrong. I was to have a rehearsal on the day of the performance, and that is why I was obliged to postpone the academy. I: I wonder whether there is anything more troublesome or unpleasant than the preparations for an academy. Beethoven: You may be right there. Stupidity prevents all progress. And last but not least—all the money it costs. It is inexcusable how art is now handled. I have to give one third of the proceeds to the theatre management, and a fifth to the prison. The devil take it all! When the event is over, I am going to inquire whether the art of tones is a free art or not. Believe me, there is nothing doing with art these days. How long are you going to stay in Vienna? I: I intend to leave on Monday. Beethoven: Then I must give you a ticket for my academy.' I thanked him and begged him not to bother. He, however, went into the other room, but returned immediately with the words that his servant, who had charge of the tickets, was not at home. I was to give him my address, and we continued our conversation as follows:

"I: Did you see Meyerbeer's opera? Beethoven: No, I understand it is very bad. I had to think of you; you were right when you said that his composition would not become a success. I spoke to some of the opera singers, after the performance, in the Weinstube where they generally meet. I told them flatly: 'There you distinguished yourselves once again! What asses you made of yourselves! You ought to be ashamed of yourselves not to know better, not to understand, not to be able to judge, and to make such a hubbub over this opera. Is it right to live to see old and good singers so wanting in judgment? I should like to talk it over with you, but you do not understand me. . . .' I: I was there. It began with Hallelujah, and ended with a Requiem. . . . Beethoven: Ha ha ha! And it is just like that with his playing. I have often been asked whether I had heard him play. I said: 'No.' But judging from what my friends, who have some knowledge in the matter, told me, I could assume that, while he had skill, he was on the whole a very superficial person. I: I was told he played at Mr. ...'s home, before his departure for Paris, but that he was little liked. Beethoven: Ha ha ha! What did I tell you? I know all about that. Just let him stay here half a year, and you will hear what they say about his playing. All that does not mean a thing. It has always been known that the greatest piano players have also been the greatest composers, but—how did they play? Not like the piano players of today, who merely run up and down the keyboard, with drilled passages: putsch, putsch, putsch—what does that signify? Nothing. The true piano virtuosi, when they played—that was something coherent, something unified, something whole! It would—when written down immediately—have been recognized as a well thought out piece of work. That is what piano playing means. All the rest means nothing. I: I think it is ridiculous that Fuss, who himself has very limited knowledge of piano playing, has declared Meyerbeer to be the greatest of all piano players. Beethoven: He has no idea of instrumental music. He is a miserable creature. I would tell him so to his face. He at one time praised a composition from which the ears of jackasses and goats peeped out all over. I had to laugh heartily at his ignorance. He does know something about singing and he should have left it at that. Of composition he knows bloody little. I: I am taking with me a very poor opinion of Fuss! Beethoven: As I said before, outside of singing he knows nothing. I: I understand that Moscheles is creating quite a sensation here. Beethoven: O Lord! He plays well, nicely, nicely. Outside of that, he is a—he will come to nothing. Those people have their social connections, where they often go and where they are praised, and praised again, and then it is all over with their art. I tell you he will never get anywhere. I have been harsh in my opinions and thus have made enemies; now I judge no one for the simple reason that I do not wish to harm any one. And I finally think: if the work is really good, it will stand, in spite of all attacks and envy; but if it is not solid and not firm, it will fall apart—sustain it and hold it up as much as you will! I: That is also my philosophy. Beethoven had in the meantime dressed, and prepared for going out. I left him. He wished me a pleasant journey, and asked me, should I stay longer in Vienna, to come and see him again.

"But more interesting still for me was the 28th, which brought me to the great Redoutensaal, at eleven o'clock in the morning, when the rehearsal of Beethoven's academy took place. I met Spohr and the Regierungsrat Sonnleithner, and I stayed with them until the end of the rehearsal. The vivacious mentality and brilliant wit of the latter formed a delightful contrast to Spohr's calm and equanimity.

The Symphony in A major to which I could not warm up, was rehearsed, and then followed the new cantata, which undeniably showed Beethoven's genius, but the declamation and the organic tonal arrangement!!!!! The solution of this musical problem was, I repeat, entirely outside the limits of his genius. The colossal voice of Mme. Milder was heard even in the remotest corner of the hall; but, as a contrast, the violin solo sounded faint, although clearly and nicely performed by Herr Mayseder. Beethoven had miscalculated mightily when he intended a violin solo for so big a hall. The cantata did not take. Its defects are such as could not be hidden either by genius or by renown. The academy closed with the *Schlacht von Victoria,* over which the greater part of the audience was beside itself, but which affected me painfully, inasmuch as I found a Beethoven to whom providence had allotted the highest throne in the realm of music, among the crassest of materialists. It is true, I have been told that he himself designated the work as a piece of stupidity, and he cared for it only so far as he therewith wished to win over the Viennese totally. I, however, believe that he has won over the Viennese gradually, by his glorious compositions, and not by the *Schlacht.*

"When the orchestra was almost drowned by the noise of the drum's rattling and pounding, and when I put into words my disapproval of the uproarious applause, Herr von Sonnleithner made a sarcastic remark. The academy was performed under the direction of Umlauf; Beethoven stood next to him, and beat time with him; but owing to his deafness, he did it most incorrectly, which in fact, however, caused no disturbance, for the orchestra followed Umlauf alone. Quite benumbed from the cataract, I was glad to get out into the fresh air."

(Cf. Hanslick: *Aus meinem Leben;* W. Kahl: *Das lyrische Klavierstück Schuberts und seiner Vorgänger* Archiv f. Musikwissenschaft III; Paul Nettl: "Schubert's Czech Predecessors," *Music and Letters* Vol. 23; and *Forgotten Musicians.)*

Traeg, Johann

Art dealer and publisher. Beethoven's Variations on the Duet *"Nel cor più non mi sento"* (1796) from Païsiello's *La Molinara* and his Variations on *"Quant e più bello"* from the same opera (1795) were published with Traeg. The opera *La Molinara* was first performed in Vienna, June 1795. The Variations *"Quant e più bello"* were dedicated to Prince Lichnowsky. Traeg also published Beethoven's three Trios Op. 9 for violin, viola and cello, dedicated to Count Browne.

Travels

If one compares the traveling done by the different composers, one finds that Handel, Haydn, and Mozart were great travelers, whereas Bach and Beethoven preferred to stay at home. A certain split in Beethoven's personality might explain that phenomenon. Just as he was frequently in love, but never got married, so he had an unceasing desire to travel, but whenever the realization of a travel project came close, the idea was dropped. In the last analysis he was the exclusive servant of his own genius, who did not permit any deviation from his creative activities. Wegeler and Ries exaggerated somewhat by stating that Beethoven hardly traveled at all. As a child he visited Rotterdam, besides making various excursion trips from Bonn. For his travels to Vienna in 1787 and to Mergentheim, see Entries: Mozart; Mergentheim. His route to Vienna ran probably via Frankfurt, Nürnberg, Regensburg and Linz. On his return from Vienna he made a stopover in Augsburg. His second important trip coincided with his moving to Vienna in 1792. During his first years in Vienna he hardly left the city and its environs. Whether or not he was a guest of Lichnowsky in Grätz near Troppau is uncertain. In 1793 or 1794, and again in 1807, the Master paid a visit to the Esterhazys in Eisenstadt. In 1796 there was a trip to Berlin with stopovers in Dresden, Leipzig and Prague (cf. Entries: Prague; Leipzig). In the following year Beethoven visited Hungary, as guest of the Brunswicks and Esterhazys (cf. Entries: Brunswick; Esterhazy; Pressburg). About his sojourn in Grätz, see Entry: Lichnowsky. Bohemia was visited in 1811 and 1812, when the Master made use of the spas in Teplitz, Carlsbad and Franzensbad. On his way he stopped in Prague and Linz. At that time he often expressed his desire to visit London in the company of Oliva. In a Conversation-book of April 1819, Oliva jotted down: "Those Englishmen only talk about your coming to England. They maintain that you would earn enough money in one winter in England, Scotland and Ireland, that you could live on the interest for the rest of your life" (cf. Th.-R. IV, p. 162). In another Conversation-book, a trip to Italy with Bernard is discussed and later, in 1825, the invitation of the London Philharmonic Society is a matter for serious discussion. Beethoven's very last trip was to Gneixendorf for a visit to his brother.

Treitschke, Georg Friedrich

b. Leipzig 1776, d. Vienna 1842. Playwright, poet, actor. His father, a businessman in Leipzig, had planned to make a businessman out of his son and sent him to Switzerland for further study. But in the house of Salomon Gessner (1730-1788) he discovered his love and talent for art and science. After his return to Leipzig he joined his father's firm, but after the latter's death he liquidated the business, dedicating himself to literature. He wrote a number of plays; his *Der Stammbaum* and *Das Bauerngut* were widely known in the theatrical world of that time. In 1802 Treitschke came to Vienna, where he met Baron Braun, who had been director of the two Imperial Theaters since 1794. Braun appointed Treitschke as poet and stage director. In 1809 he became vice-director of the Theater an der Wien, but resumed in 1814 his duties as stage director of the Imperial Theaters. In 1822 he became the business manager of the Court Theaters, a position he kept up until his death.

Treitschke had known Beethoven since 1811. There is a letter of July 6 by Beethoven addressed to Treitschke, dealing with an operatic project, possibly a translation or arrangement of *Ruines de Babylon.* When the allies invaded Paris in 1814, Treitschke's one-act singspiel *Gute Nachricht* was successfully performed in the Kärntnerthor Theater; the music was by Gyrowetz, Hummel, Kanne, Mozart and Weigl. For this occasion Beethoven composed the final chorus: *Germania, wie stehst du jetzt im Glanze da,* for chorus and orchestra. In addition to this patriotic play, Treitschke produced *Die Ehrenpforten* given in the Kärntnerthor Theater in June and October 1815, a *Pasticcio* with compositions by Hummel, Seyfried, B. A. Weber. Beethoven again was the composer of the Schlussgesang *Es ist vollbracht* for chorus and orchestra. Beethoven had planned to compose Treitschke's *Romulus* around 1814 or 1815, but finally Johann Ev. Fuss (1777-1819) composed the text under the title *Romulus and Remus.* (Cf. Th.-R. III, p. 457 ff.) It is well known that Treitschke rewrote the libretto of *Fidelio.* In 1841 he published an article under the title "Die Zauberflöte—der Dorfbarbier—Fidelio" in August Schmidt's music magazine *Orpheus,* in which he told the facts about this matter (cf. Entry: Fidelio). Treitschke is also mentioned in Max Maria von Weber's biography of his father Carl Maria von Weber. There he is described as a passionate collector of butterflies, and owner of 2582 items. After his death, this collection was bought by the Hungarian National Museum in Budapest. Treitschke wrote a scholarly work *Die Schmetterlinge Europas* and a well-known handbook on butterflies, started by Oxenheimer. Treitschke's wife was Magdalena Caro, a famous ballet dancer (1788-1816), sister of Maria de Caro. Both sisters had been students of Noverre. (Cf. Wurzbach with an extensive list of Treitschke's works, incl. a biography of Magdalena Treitschke.)

Trémont, Louis-Philippe-Joseph Girod de Vienney

d. 1852. Trémont, who was created a baron of the French Empire in 1810, had met Beethoven in the previous year, while on a diplomatic mission in Vienna; he was a musical enthusiast and Maecenas for the remainder of his life. Trémont's diary, consisting of 5 volumes, is preserved in the National Library of Paris, and was partly edited by Michel Brenet in *Guide Musical 1892* and by Jean Chantavoine in *Die Musik* (1902). Trémont prided himself on having musical reunions at his home for 50 years (1798-1848), at which all the celebrated musicians, both French and foreign, were pleased to display their talents. Trémont has the following to say of Beethoven:

"I admired his genius and knew his works by heart when, in 1809, as Auditor to the Council of State while Napoleon was making war on Austria, I was made the bearer of the Council's dispatches to him. Although my departure was hurried, I made up my mind that in case the army should take Vienna I must not neglect the opportunity to see Beethoven. I asked Cherubini to give me a letter to him. 'I will give you one to Haydn,' he replied, 'and that excellent man will make you welcome; but I will not write to Beethoven; I should have to reproach myself that he refused to receive some one recommended by me; he is an unlicked bear!'

Thereupon I addressed myself to Reicha. 'I imagine,' said he, 'that my letter will be of no use to you. Since the establishment of the Empire in France, Beethoven has detested the Emperor and the French to such a degree that Rode, the finest violinist in Europe, while passing through Vienna on his way to Russia, remained a week in that city without succeeding in obtaining admission to him. He is morose, ironical, misanthropic; to give you an idea of how careless he is of convention it will suffice to tell you that the Empress (princess of Bavaria, the second wife of Francis II) sent him a request to visit her one morning; he responded that he would be occupied all that day, but would try to come the day after.'

This information convinced me that any efforts to approach Beethoven would be vain. I had no reputation, nor any qualification which might impress him; a repulse seemed all the more certain because I entered Vienna after its second bombardment by the French army, and besides was a member of Napoleon's Council. However, I intended to try.

I wended my way to the unapproachable composer's home, and at the door it struck me that I had chosen the day ill, for, having to make an official visit thereafter, I was wearing the everyday habiliments of the Council of State. To make matters worse, his lodging was next the city wall, and as Napoleon had ordered its destruction, blasts had just been set off under his windows.

The neighbors showed me where he lived: 'He is at home (they said), but he has no servant at present, for he is always getting a new one, and it is doubtful whether he will open.'

I rang three times, and was about to go away, when a very ugly man of ill-humored mien opened the door and asked what I wanted.

'Have I the honor of addressing M. de Beethoven?' 'Yes, sir! But I must tell you,' he said to me in German, that I am on very bad terms with French!' 'My acquaintance with German is no better, Sir, but my message is limited to bringing you a letter from M. Reicha in Paris.' He looked me over, took the letter, and let me in. His lodging, I believe, consisted of only two rooms, the first one having an alcove containing the bed, but small and dark, for which reason he made his toilet in the second room, or salon. Picture to yourself the dirtiest, most disorderly place imaginable—blotches of moisture covered the ceiling; an oldish grand piano, on which the dust disputed the place with various pieces of engraved and manuscript music; under the piano (I do not exaggerate) an unemptied pot de nuit; beside it, a small walnut table accustomed to the frequent overturning of the secretary placed upon it; a quantity of pens encrusted with ink, compared wherewith the proverbial tavern pens would shine; then more music. The chairs, mostly cane-seated, were covered with plates bearing the remains of last night's supper, and with wearing apparel, etc. Balzac or Dickens would continue this description of the dress of the illustrious composer; but, being neither Balzac nor Dickens, I shall merely say, I was in Beethoven's abode.

I spoke German only as a traveler on the highways, but understood it somewhat better. His skill in French was no greater. I expected that, after reading my letter, he would dismiss me, and that our acquaintance would end then and there. I had seen the bear in his cage; that was more than I had dared hope for. So I was greatly surprised when he again inspected me, laid the letter unopened on the table, and offered me a chair; still more surprised, when he started a conversation. He wanted to know what uniform I wore, my age, my office, the aim of my journey; if I were a musician, if I intended to stay in Vienna. I answered that Reicha's letter would explain all that much better than I could.

'No, no, tell me,' he insisted, 'only speak slowly, because I am very hard of hearing, and I shall understand you.'

I made incredible conversational efforts, which he seconded with good will; it was a most singular medley of bad German on my part and bad French on his. But we managed to understand each other; the visit lasted nearly three-quarters of an hour, and he made me promise to come again. I took my leave, feeling prouder than Napoleon when he entered Vienna. I had made the conquest of Beethoven!

Do not ask how I did it. What could I answer? The reason can be sought only in the bizarrerie of his character. I was young, conciliatory and polite, and a stranger to him; I contrasted with him; for some unaccountable reason he took a fancy to me, and, as these sudden likings are seldom passive, he arranged several meetings with me during my stay in Vienna, and would improvise an hour or two for me alone. When he happened to have a servant he told her not to open when the bell rang, or (if the would-be visitor heard the piano) to say that he was composing and could not receive company.

Some musicians with whom I became acquainted were slow to believe it. 'Will you believe me,' I told them, 'if I show you a letter he has written me in French?' 'In French? that's impossible! he hardly knows any, and he doesn't even write German legibly. He is incapable of such an effort!' I showed them my proof. 'Well, he must be madly in love with you,' they said; 'what an inexplicable man!'

This letter—so precious an object to me—I have had framed. Call to mind the reflection which heads this article; my vanity would have scarcely have moved me to do as much for Papa Haydn.

I fancy that to these improvisations of Beethoven's I owe my most vivid musical impressions. I maintain that unless one has heard him improvise well and quite at ease, one can but imperfectly appreciate the vast scope of his genius. Swayed wholly by the impulse of the moment, he sometimes said to me, after striking a few chords: 'Nothing comes into my head; let's put it off till—.' Then we would talk philosophy, religion, politics, and especially of Shakespeare, his idol, and always in a language that would have provoked the laughter of any hearers.

Beethoven was not a man of esprit, if we mean by that term one who makes keen and witty remarks. He was by nature too taciturn to be an animated conversationalist. His thoughts were thrown out by fits and starts, but they were lofty and generous, though often rather illogical. Between him and Jean Jacques Rousseau there was a bond of erroneous opinion springing from the creation, by their common misanthropic disposition, of a fanciful world bearing no positive relation to human nature and social conditions. But Beethoven was well read. The isolation of celibacy, his deafness, and his sojournings in the country, had led him to make a study of the Greek and Latin authors and, enthusiastically, of Shakespeare. Taking this in conjunction with the kind of singular, though genuine, interest which results from wrong notions set forth and maintained in all good faith, his conversation was, if not specially magnetic, at least original and curious. And, as he was well affected towards me, by a whimsey of his atrabilious character he preferred that I should sometimes contradict him rather than agree with him on every point.

When he felt inclined to improvisations on the day appointed, he was sublime. His tempestuous inspiration poured forth lovely melodies, and harmonies unsought because, mastered by musical emotion, he gave no thought to the search after effects that might have occurred to him with pen in hand; they were produced spontaneously without divagation.

As a pianist, his playing was incorrect and his mode of fingering often faulty, whence it came that the quality of tone was neglected. But who could think of the pianist? He was absorbed in his thoughts, and his hands had to express them as best they might.

I asked him if he would not like to become acquainted with France. 'I greatly desired to do so,' he replied, 'before she gave herself a master. Now, my desire has passed. For all that, I should like to hear Mozart's symphonies (he mentioned neither his own nor those of Haydn) in Paris; I am told that they are played better at the Conservatoire than anywhere else. Besides, I am too poor to take a journey out of pure curiosity and probably requiring great speed.' 'Come with me, I will take you along.' 'What an idea! I could not think of allowing you to go to such expense on my account.' 'Don't worry about that, there's no expense; all my charges for the post are defrayed, and I am alone in my carriage. If you would be satisfied with a single small room, I have one at your disposal. Only say yes. It's well worth your while to spend a fortnight in Paris; your sole expense will be for the return journey, and less than fifty florins will bring you home again.' 'You tempt me; I shall think it over.'

Several times I pressed him to make a decision. His hesitation was always a result of his morose humor. 'I shall be overrun by visitors!' 'You will not receive them.' 'Overwhelmed by invitations!' 'Which you will not accept.' 'They will insist that I play, that I compose!' 'You will answer that you have no time.' 'Your Parisians will say that I am a bear.' 'What does that matter to you? It is evident that you do not know them. Paris is the home of liberty, of freedom from social conventions. Distinguished men are accepted there exactly as they please to show themselves, and should one, especially a stranger, be a trifle eccentric, that contributes to his success.'

Finally, he gave me his hand one day and said that he would come with me. I was delighted—again from vanity, no doubt. To take Beethoven to Paris, to have him in my own lodgings, to introduce him to the musical world, what a triumph was there!—but, to punish me for my pleasurable anticipations, the realization was not to follow them.

The armistice of Znaim caused us to occupy Moravia, whither I was sent as intendant. I remained there four months; the Treaty of Vienna having given this province to Austria, I returned to Vienna, where I found Beethoven still of the same mind; I was expecting to receive the order for my return to Paris, when I received one to betake myself immediately to Croatia as intendant. After spending a year there, I received my appointment to the prefecture of l'Aveyron, together with an order to wind up an affair at Agram with which I had also been charged, and then to travel in all haste to Paris to render an account of my mission before proceeding to my new destination. So I could neither pass through Vienna nor revisit Beethoven.

His mind was much occupied with the greatness of Napoleon, and he often spoke to me about it. Through all his resentment I could see that he admired his rise from such obscure beginnings;

his democratic ideas were flattered by it. One day he remarked, 'If I go to Paris, shall I be obliged to salute your emperor?' I assured him that he would not, unless commanded for an audience. 'And do you think he would command me?' 'I do not doubt that he would, if he appreciated your importance; but you have seen in Cherubini's case that he does not know much about music.' This question made me think that, despite his opinions, he would have felt flattered by any mark of distinction from Napoleon. Thus does human pride bow down before that which flatters it . . .

When Napoleon took possession of Vienna for the second time, his brother Jerôme, then King of Westphalia, proposed to Beethoven that he should become his maître de chapelle, at a salary of 7000 francs. As I was then at Vienna, he asked my advice, in confidence. I think I did well in advising him not to accept the offer, but to observe his agreement with regard to the stipulated pension (from Archduke Rudolph and Princes Kinsky and Lobkowitz); not that I could already foresee the fall of that royalty, but Beethoven would not have stayed six months at Jerôme's court . . .

To show how little thought Beethoven gave to those who were to execute his music, we only need examine the *grande sonate* for piano and violin dedicated to his friend Kreutzer. This dedication might almost be taken for an epigram, for Kreutzer played all the passages *legato,* and always kept his bow on the string; now, this piece is all in *staccato* and *sautillé* and so Kreutzer never played it." (Schirmer, *Impressions.)*
(Cf. Th.-R. III p. 142.)

Trios

The trio combinations employed by Beethoven fall easily into three groups. The best known and most popular are the piano trios, and it is this combination which is the most frequently used. The second group would be the string trios, and the last, those trios employing wind instruments. The trios do not show the consistent high quality to be found in the string quartets; nevertheless there are works of great beauty among them.

It is interesting to note that all but four of the trios date from the early years in Vienna when Beethoven was a struggling young composer trying to make his name known, and we may be sure that the trio combination offered many advantages. First, the prodigious amount of amateur music making among the dilettantes created a large demand for this form and increased the young composer's chance of publication. Furthermore, the smaller number of players increased the opportunities for performance and assured the composer of numerous hearings. Finally, for the trios employing the piano, the piano was a popular instrument and its ability to produce full harmonies covered up many weak violin and cello parts in the amateur groups of the day.

Because of the popularity of the combination we can understand why Beethoven chose the piano trios to introduce his music to the Viennese public as his Opus Primum. It was an auspicious beginning; the clarity of the themes, the adroit handling of the forms, the careful blending of the instruments, announced to the public of Vienna that Beethoven was a name to be reckoned with as a composer, no less than as the foremost piano virtuoso of the city.

The first two trios of Op. 1, E flat major and G major, show the 18th century world from which Beethoven was emerging. There is a galante character about the works, although the slow movement of the G major reflects the patrimony of K. P. E. Bach's *Empfindsamer Stil.* The third of the group, in C minor, is more advanced in its emotionalism than either of the first two. Perhaps this is the reason Haydn advised Beethoven to delay its publication. The C minor later appeared as a quintet for 2 violins, 2 violas and cello, Op. 104. The date of composition for these three trios of Op. 1 is unknown. Certainly, Beethoven must have withheld them until he was quite sure they were ready. Mannerisms in thematic structure even suggest that they may go back to the Bonn period. According to Ries they were first performed at Prince Lichnowsky's where they were heard by the foremost musicians of Vienna. It was upon this occasion that Haydn heard and praised them, even though he felt the third should be withheld. The trios were published as Op. 1 in 1795, the year of their first performance, dedicated to Prince Lichnowsky.

Although the three trios of Op. 1 were the first to be published, they were not the first written. An early work in E flat undoubtedly originated in the Bonn period. The work is in only three movements, omitting the slow movement, and has the rocket-like thematic material so typical of the early period. It was published posthumously. (W o O. 38.)

The second set of trios to appear were the two of Op. 70, in D major and E flat major. These two trios, completed at the end of 1808, are far advanced over the Op. 1 group both in technical skill and poetic expression. The three movements of the D major may suggest a concertante style, but it has no place in this melancholy work which has been given the name "Ghost" Trio. The E flat trio is in the traditional four movements. The two works were published in 1809, dedicated to the Countess Erdödy.

The next trio, the "Archduke," is one of the great masterpieces of his output. Here we meet the heroic Beethoven of the Third and Fifth Svmphonies. The broadly conceived themes, the virtuoso character of the parts, and the inevitability of its musical logic, all mark this as one of the few great trios in the entire literature. The work is in four movements, although the third passes into the finale without a break. The trio was completed in the year 1811, but publication was delayed until 1816 when it appeared as Op. 97 dedicated to the Archduke Rudolph.

Another work in this medium was written for his "little friend, Maximiliane Brentano" in 1812. It was designed as a stimulant to her piano playing and is a cheerful little work of only a single movement. It was published posthumously in 1830. (W o O. 39.)

Sketches for a trio in F minor belong to the year 1816, but the work did not materialize and as a final appearance of this combination we have only the set of variations on the theme *"Ich bin der Schneider Kakadu"* from Wenzel Müller's opera *Die Schwestern von Prag.* These variations, published in 1824 as Op. 121a, are much more advanced than the many sets of variations composed during the early Vienna years, such as the set of 14 variations in E major for the same combination, written in 1803 and published in 1804 as Op. 44.

In two trios, the clarinet replaces the violin. However, the one in B flat major, which appeared as Op. 11 in 1798 dedicated to the Countess von Thun, has nothing worthwhile to recommend it. The second of these, in E flat major, is a transcription of the Septet, Op. 20. The trio version was published in 1805 as Op. 38.

The string trios occupy a position much inferior to the string quartets, and since all the trios were written between 1796 and 1798, we may conclude that they were a result of Beethoven's attempt to gain fame. The first of these, Op. 3 in E flat, is in reality a divertimento consisting of 6 movements, 2 of the movements being minuets. This work was possibly first sketched while Beethoven was still in Bonn, and is marked by a cheerful 18th century style. It was published in 1796.

The trio Op. 8 in D major is a serenade of sunny good humour, first published in 1797.

The three string trios of Op. 9, G major, D major and C minor, are by far the most ambitious of the works for this combination, and at the time of their appearance, the most advanced works to come from the Master's pen. In dedicating them to Count von Browne, Beethoven called them the best of his works, revealing that he realized himself that their gravity and mastery of form set them apart. The D major perhaps still sounds like charming entertainment music, but the other two reveal the high degree of expressiveness of which Beethoven was capable.

The serenade for flute, violin and viola in D major, Op. 25, belongs to the year 1796, although unpublished until 1802.

Among the trios for wind instruments, there exists a work for piano, flute and bassoon in G major. The work was composed in 1787 in Bonn, possibly for Count Westerhold.

A woodwind trio of 2 oboes and English horn, in C major, was written in 1794 but not published until 12 years later as Op. 87. It was probably inspired by the three Teimer brothers, important oboists in Vienna at the time. The work later appeared for two violins and viola, and still later as a sonata for violin and piano. For the same combination Beethoven composed a set of variations on Mozart's *"La ci darem,"* which probably dates from the same time as Op. 87.

F. T. W.

Troxler, Ignaz Paul Vitalis

b. Münster (Switzerland) 1780, d. Aarau 1866. Physician and philosopher. A devoted follower of Schelling's "Philosophy of Nature," he taught philosophy in Lucerne, Basel and Bern. His name appeared several times in the Conversation-books; in a letter of Beethoven's (1807) the Master addressed him "Lieber Doktor" and signed "Ihr Freund Beethoven." Beethoven wanted to take Troxler to Clementi for a visit. In Vienna Troxler belonged to the circle of Malfatti. Beethoven might have been familiar with Troxler's work *Über das Leben und sein Problem,* Göttingen 1807.

Typology

According to the findings of Edward

Sievers and Becking, every human being has its adequate *Schallform*, an expression of his personality by which one understands the total configuration of all those audible characteristics which cling to the spoken word or even can be heard as an echo from the written word. This *Schallform* is a combination of acoustic characteristics which are indivisible and inter-related. According to findings of Franz Saran, the constituents of the *Schallform* are rhythm, i.e. the gradation and grouping of the syllables, speech, melody, pitch, timbre, sonority, tempo, loudness and elision (legato and staccato). Among the various methods of investigating the *Schallformen* of separate individuals or groups, that of Eduard Sievers is most striking. According to Sievers, every physical speech occurrence has an intellectual counterpart. The acoustic quality and the rhythmic movement of each individual or group (nation, clan, contemporaries, types) can be represented by graphic curves. These curves correspond to the type or the character of the person in question, and were named by Sievers after their discoverer, the musicologist Gustav Becking, the Becking curve or personal curve. Every human being is born with his personal curve. In general, Sievers distinguishes three different types of personal curves; or, to state it in another way, one of these curves is the property of every human being, disregarding the specific difference of single individuals.

It is interesting that Sievers came to his three types as a result of an acquaintance with theories of the voice teacher, Josef Rutz. Rutz wished his pupils to obtain as far as possible complete rendition of the spirit of vocal compositions by greatest emphasis upon his observation of posture and upon the use of body muscles as they expressed the physical and psychological attitude of the composer in question. He found that when one sings Wagner one's body muscles from the back of the larynx are used differently than when one sings Mozart or Schubert. Therefore hand in hand with the muscle set goes the psychological attitude. Rutz is responsible for the three types on which Sievers' typology is based. Becking and Sievers took over Rutz's three types; corresponding to the Goethe, Schiller, and Heine types, in music are Mozart, type one; Beethoven, type two; Bach, type three.

Let us examine first from this point of view the difference between Beethoven and Mozart. Beethoven's music strides along firmly, securely and unfalteringly. Every beat has its effect. The accented beats are strong—we might say they are saturated with weight. A Beethoven downbeat is firm and sometimes, as in the beginning bars of the Fifth Symphony, falls thunderously. Therefore, the conductor reacts as follows: he will begin the downbeat gently; then, however, he will press down the accent firmly and, finally, almost with clenched fist and bated breath, as if groaning with exertion, will complete the beat. A completely different typological reaction can be observed in the case of Mozart. The Mozart beat is more graceful and symmetrically curved. The conductor will begin with a kind of little aerial flourish, as if he were using an imaginary grace note. Then, toward the middle he will swell the beat a little, as if for a fraction of a moment he

TYPOLOGY

were about to let the baton fall freely—but only for a split second—and then throw down his lower arm perpendicularly, and only at the very end allow the complete arm movement, together with the play of the wrist, to set in.

Again quite different is the picture of the third type, Bach. If Mozart and Beethoven have strong accents, those of Bach are weaker, divided equally along the melody. Bach has not the rhythmic elan, as do Mozart and Beethoven, and Bach's predecessors, such men as Schütz and Pachelbel, have it even to a lesser degree. Where the Mozart conductor allows the baton at first to fall freely and then takes it into his hand, the Beethoven director from the very beginning of the measure takes the baton almost belligerently into his hand, and imposes his will upon the beat. The Bach director scarcely bothers about this weightiness; the rhythm of Bach pulsates as if flowing freely on dictation of Nature itself. The Bach beats are low and pointed. They are associated with superiority, calm and divinity. The majority of the composers of Bach's time and before his time follow the same beat pattern, which Sievers also establishes in the case of personalities like Heine and Richard Wagner.

And this brings us to the philosophy of the great composers. Mozart's philosophy is pantheism. He sees, like Goethe, a world with a soul with which he feels himself one. The rhythmic figures of Mozart and Goethe swing harmonically and joyously, and so we see in the work of the poet Schiller and of the composer Beethoven that they are idealists in literature and music, who subdue substance (in the case of Beethoven the rhythmic weight) and attempt to build up another world. This is the point of view which the greater number of German composers have, while the Italians for the most part have the psychology and rhythmic attitude of Mozart. While Mozart regards himself as part of a world, Bach thinks as an outsider facing a world which is the product of a superior might. Thus resulted the natural and uninhibited but also transpersonal language of his music, which has an unbelievable pictorial power. Strange as it seems, Bach belongs to the group of naturalists, among whom are found most frequently the Anglo-Saxons and the French with their particular rhythmic form.

These three types into which the philosopher, Dilthey, also divides all human character, permeate the whole musical history which under the influence of the Sievers school can now be seen in an entirely new and highly fascinating light. From that point of view, we gain new insight into the personality and art of Beethoven.

U

Umlauf, Ignaz

b. Vienna 1746, d. Mödling 1796. Composer. His *Die Bergknappen* was the first German *Singspiel,* performed in Vienna under the sponsorship of Joseph II, February 18, 1788. It has been republished in the *Denkmäler der Tonkunst in Oesterreich,* XVIII, 1. Among the other *Singspiele* by Umlauf, *Die schöne Schusterin oder die pucefarbenen Schuhe* had some significance for Beethoven, because the Master composed for it two arias: *"O welch' ein Leben"* for tenor, and *"Soll ein Schuh nicht drücken"* for soprano. This *Singspiel* was performed in Vienna in 1779 and revived in 1795, for which occasion Beethoven had made his contributions. Nottebohm found a sketch of the aria *"Soll ein Schuh nicht drücken."* (Cf. *Beethoveniana* II, p. 30; Th.-R. II, p. 30; Haas in his edition of *Denkmäler der Tonkunst in Oesterreich.*)

Umlauf, Michael

b. Baden 1781, d. Vienna 1842. Son of the composer Ignaz. Excellent conductor, famous for his score-reading ability and his musicianship. He conducted the first performance of Beethoven's Ninth Symphony, May 7, 1824. In the literature he is often mixed up with his father, for instance in Th.-R. V (cf. Index), where Michael Umlauf is called Ignaz.

Unger-Sabathier, Caroline

b. Székesfehérvár c. 1805, d. near Florence 1877. Famous singer, student of the voice teacher Mozatti. At the age of 15 she performed a difficult Mozart aria in public. She succeeded Karoline Wranitzky, after the latter had left the Kärntnerthor Theater in 1819. Rossini took great interest in the excellent singer, who was highly acclaimed in operas by Cimarosa, Carafa, Rossini, and Kreutzer. On May 7, 1824, together with Henriette Sontag, she sang the soprano solo in Beethoven's Ninth Symphony and selected parts of the *Missa Solemnis.* Her name appeared often in the Conversation-books. It is well known that Nikolaus Lenau was in love with the great singer. For her gastronomic adventure with Beethoven, see Entry: Sontag; Wurzbach; Kalischer: *Beethovens Frauenkreis,* II.

United States, Autographs in the

Many autographs from Beethoven's hand have found their way to America, most of them in the form of sketches or portions of completed works. There are three autographs which exist in complete form: the song *In Questa Tomba Oscura,* now in the Memorial Library of Music, Stanford University; the score of the Romance for Violin and Orchestra Op. 50, owned by the Library of Congress, and the autograph of the "Rage over a Lost Penny" (see Entry: Rondo a Capriccio), which is in the hands of a private collector. The entire body of autographs found in America represents almost every medium in which the Master wrote, as well as some of his canons and the counterpoint lessons. There are also several unidentified sketches.

Of the forty-three autographs in the United States, over half are the property of libraries, the rest being in the hands of private individuals. Eleven of these are in the Library of Congress, four in the New York Public Library, three in the Memorial Library of Music, Stanford University, and one each in the libraries of Yale, Harvard, Peabody Conservatory of Music and the Sibley Music Library. (Cf. Albrecht: *A Census of Autograph Music Manuscripts of European Composers in American Libraries.)*

United States, Beethoven in the

So far as is known, the first public performance of Beethoven on any American program occurred in Lexington, Kentucky, November 12, 1817. It was the *Sinfonia con Minuetto* (fragment), played by "Full Band," under the direction of Anthony Philip Heinrich, a migrant musician who spent a few years of his Bohemian existence in Kentucky. One year later, in 1818, a *"Minuetto*—Full Orchestra" is included in a program performed in Boston, which was then the cultural center of America. Philadelphia did not lag. A fragment of the *Grand Sinfonia in C* was performed April 24, 1821 at the first concert of the newly formed Musical Fund Society. Although the artistic climate of New York was then not as salubrious as that of Boston and Philadelphia, nevertheless a performance of the *Prometheus* Overture is reported in 1823. The following year, the *Hallelujah* Chorus, from his *Mount of Olives* (performed in Boston several years earlier) was given its first New York performance by the newly-organized New York Choral Society.

This is not to imply that the early reputation and fame of Beethoven in America actually depended on these scattered and inadequate performances, even though one assumed that there were still earlier dates unrecorded. There is ample evidence that Beethoven was known by reputation from European sources, principally by way of England, with whom cultural and economic ties were very close. The literary and musical works of William Gardiner enjoyed wide circulation in America, and familiarized the people with the name of Beethoven, to whose melodies he had set sacred words. The order book of the Boston musician and dealer, Gottlieb Graupner, carries an entry dated March, 1819, for two copies of a Beethoven symphony for duet. As early as 1824, the announced ambition of the aforementioned New York Choral Society was to bring before the public the choicest selections of the "great masters: Handel, Haydn, Mozart, Beethoven, Jomelli, Pergolesi, &c." That Beethoven, even before his death, had been placed in company with the Masters is further attested by the fact that John Rowe Parker devoted six pages (material derived from Gardiner) to him in *A Musical Biography*, which was published in Boston also in 1824. The Boston Handel and Haydn Society had approached the composer in 1822 on the subject of a commission for an oratorio. It was, of course, never fulfilled. It was even reported that Beethoven had been urged to compose an opera on the subject *Die Gründung von Pennsylvanien*. Beethoven seemed aware of his contacts with the New World when in 1826 he referred to Haslinger (Vienna publisher) as his "best North American music dealer."

Early performances were more likely to be choral works or quartets than the symphonies with which he became associated in the mind of the concertgoers later in the century. Many of these were under private and semi-private auspices. Thus in 1816 the Beethoven quartets were performed in private soirées in Philadelphia, but it was not until about 1840 that his symphonies were given in their entirety either in Boston, Philadelphia, or New York. Chicago, Cincinnati, and St. Louis had to await the tours of the Germania orchestra to hear the first complete symphony of Beethoven in 1853. On the other hand, in London (1813), Paris (1828), Vienna (1812), and Munich (1811), the established concert orchestras at once cultivated the taste for Beethoven's new music.

The reasons for this American cultural lag are not far to seek. In contrast to the large European centers built around castle and court of the nobility, Boston, New York and Philadelphia were frontier cities without the accoutrements of the rich tradition, material wealth and noble pride so necessary for the sustenance of full musical life. In fact, the two most potent social forces—Puritans in Boston and Quakers in Philadelphia—officially frowned on the cultivation of the arts, both secular and religious. Before 1835, instrumentalists were scarce and audiences were immature. Hence Beethoven's reputation was rather a derivative one, imported to this country in the tastes of the British and German immigrants who had heard his music at first hand, and who were trying to emulate European concert life in so far as the pathetically meagre facilities and talents would permit.

If Beethoven's fame had outrun his American performances before 1840, his symphonies from this point on assured him a predominant place in what was to become in the United States the concert medium of the highest prestige: the symphony orchestra. The initiative in this musical venture was taken by New York, as a primary result of the completion in 1825 of the Erie Canal, which channeled trade and migration by way of the New York harbor. By 1840 that city had forged ahead of its colonial rivals, Boston and Philadelphia, in population, wealth and cultural progress. The New York Philharmonic Society, an orchestra of professional musicians, opened its first season in 1842 with Beethoven's Fifth, which had been given its first American performance only the preceding February.

After these beginnings, Beethoven entered into a period of absolute preeminence, with Haydn and Mozart being reduced to stars of definitely second magnitude. During these early decades, about a third of the playing time of the orchestra's programs was devoted to Beethoven, but by the close of the century, American orchestras were devoting only about 18 per cent of their time to his music. The reasons for this slow decline may be summarized as follows. In mid-century there was only one orchestra and it could afford only infrequent rehearsal periods; repertoires were therefore limited, and tastes were likewise restricted and conservative. However, after 1875 additional orchestras were organized, philanthropic financial patronage permitted more rehearsals, and new conductors were imported from Europe who subscribed to the newer cults of Brahms, Wagner and Tschaikowsky. Hence, Beethoven was nudged by these contemporary geniuses until he had settled down almost to their level in statistical volume. It is all the more remarkable then to find that in 1950 he still occupies first place among all composers, with 12 per cent of the total orchestral repertoire to his credit in the national average.

Toscanini, who conducted the New York Philharmonic from 1926 to 1936, never did espouse the newer romantic trends. Well known for his conservatism, he accorded Beethoven during that period over 20 per cent of the repertoire, while the national average was about half of that figure.

Although Beethoven's choral works have practically disappeared with the decline in the cultivation in the choral organizations, his only opera, *Fidelio,* has modestly maintained itself in the repertoire of the Metropolitan with a total of 62 mountings between 1884 and 1950. It had been first produced in New York (14 nights) and Philadelphia in 1839 in English. Toscanini offered the opera in concert form with his radio orchestra and chorus in December, 1944.

The Beethoven concertos have competed well with newer trends. In 1885, it was the Violin Concerto struggling for priority with Mendelssohn and Bruch; today Brahms has challenged him, while the Tschaikowsky and Mendelssohn violin concertos display somewhat lesser strength. In the piano concertos, it was Schumann's A minor which shared priority with the "Emperor" in 1885; in 1950, Brahms' No. 2 and Rachmaninoff's No. 2 are on a par with Beethoven's Fifth in frequency of rendition. The Fourth and Third Concertos of Beethoven still retain a reasonable hold on the public, successfully holding their own against the Brahms No. 1 and Tschaikowsky's B flat minor concerto.

The string quartet has never enjoyed the prominence in America that was accorded to it in Central Europe. However, there was some cultivation of chamber music throughout American musical history. The Beethoven quartets were specifically mentioned in Philadelphia before 1820. In the programs of the pioneer Mason-Thomas Chamber Concerts in New York, 1855-1868, Beethoven compiled a proportion of about 25 per cent of the items on the program. The Kneisels, the Flonzaleys and other quartets in subsequent years relied on Beethoven as the cornerstone of the repertory.

In the Beethoven literature, America took an early lead with the noted biography by Alexander Wheelock Thayer

(1817-1897). This author searched the European archives and conferred with the surviving friends of Beethoven, and published his life work in Germany in three volumes between 1860 and 1872. These volumes, together with a fourth volume completed by others, still constitute a revered and authoritative work.

Thus, after late beginnings, Beethoven maintained the same continuous preeminence he enjoyed in Europe. The First World War, which expunged Richard Strauss and Wagner from the American repertoires, did not affect the universal Beethoven, although some writers "patriotically" deprived him of his German blood and emphasized his Flemish heritage. His uniquely secure status, which was capable of no accretion, was indicated by the fact that in 1927, the centennial of his death, his repertoire remained practically stationary.

Since 1900, Brahms, Wagner and Tschaikowsky have been his great competitors. The cycles of symphonies in the orchestras of America which were first introduced by Henschel in Boston in 1882 and continued by Walter Damrosch and Mahler in New York, are still the staple ingredient of the American repertoire. As for the future, there seems to be no indication of a recession.

J. H. M.

United States, Letters in the

Oscar Sonneck lists a total of 35 Beethoven letters in the United States. These letters, covering almost the entire period of Beethoven's life in Vienna, range from the short note to Carl Friedrich Müller, a Berlin musician, to the long and interesting letter to Prince Galitzin concerning the proper note in a figure from one of the three quartets dedicated to the Prince.

Several of these letters are written to his publishers concerning items of publication. There are letters to the publishers Diabelli, Haslinger, B. Schott, Söhne and S. A. Steiner & Co.; those to the last-named publisher are perhaps the most interesting to the scholar, as they offer many problems of identification.

There are also three letters to Karl Holz, the Austrian Treasury official who succeeded Schindler as Beethoven's *factotum* from 1825 to shortly before his death. Holz's name, meaning wood, offered the Master many opportunities for his favorite pastime of punning and these letters reflect the coarse humor which was so much a part of the Master's personality. There is also a letter to Schindler, the man who devoted his life to Beethoven's comfort and welfare and whose biography of the Master has been an invaluable source of reference.

A series of four letters to Amalie Sebald, dated Teplitz, 1812, although now owned by three different individuals and the New York Public Library, actually compose a complete set. The series has caused Sonneck to join the ranks of those authors attempting to solve the problem of the Immortal Beloved (cf. Entry: Immortal Beloved; O. G. Sonneck: *The Riddle of the Immortal Beloved).*

There are several letters to members of the nobility whom Beethoven numbered among his personal friends. Besides the one to Prince Galitzin already mentioned, the best known names among these letters are Baron Gleichenstein, Lichnowsky, and Zmeskall. Oliva, a bank clerk, and Charles Neate, who served as liaison between Beethoven and the English publishers as well as the London Philharmonic Society, are represented by one letter apiece.

A total of 22 of these letters were in the hands of private collectors when Sonneck made his compilation in 1927. The remainder of the letters are in the possession of libraries and museums. Besides the letter to Treitschke, which Sonneck learned of too late to include in the compilation, there are undoubtedly additional specimens which have found their way into the United States since the publication of Sonneck's study (cf. Sonneck: *Beethoven Letters in America*).

F. T. W.

V

Varena, Joseph von

b. Marburg (Styria) 1769, d. Graz 1843. His father was administrator of the princely Schwarzenberg vineyards. Joseph received his LL.D. from the University of Budapest in 1790, whereupon he moved to Graz. There he became Kammerprokurator. As an enthusiastic musician, he was one of the founders of the Grazer Musikverein. In 1811 he met Beethoven in Teplitz. In Graz he continuously promoted Beethoven's music, such as the performances of the Sixth Symphony July 25 and September 8, 1800. (Cf. Entries: Graz, and Teplitz; Bischoff: "Beethoven und die Grazer musikalischen Kreise," in Frimmel: *Beethoven Jahrbuch I;* Bischoff: "Beethovens Briefwechsel mit Varena." *Beethoven Jahrbuch II.*)

Variations

In the first printed notice of a very young pupil of Christian Gottlob Neefe, it is mentioned that Neefe was then "training him in composition and for his encouragement has had nine variations for the pianoforte—written by him on a march by Ernst Christoph Dressler (an opera singer in Cassel)—engraved at Mannheim" (*Cramer's Magazine,* 1783). Before this young composer left Bonn for Vienna in 1792, and during the early days in Vienna, many more sets of variations, either on original themes or popular airs, found their way into print.

Probably those sets of variations, which we may confidently assume were written in the Bonn period, include the 12 for violin and piano (pub. 1793) on the aria *Se vuol ballare* from Mozart's *Figaro,* and the 24 for piano alone (pub. 1801) on the arietta *Venni Amore* by Vincenzo Righini (1756-1812). Similarly, although they were not published until 1793, the pianoforte variations on *Es war einmal an alter Mann,* from Dittersdorf's *Das rote Käppchen,* and the variations for four hands on a theme by Count Waldstein, belong to the Bonn period. In view of Beethoven's well-known association with Waldstein during this period, and the fact that a performance of *Das rote Käppchen* was given in Bonn during the winter of 1791-2 we have added support for this assumption.

Most of Beethoven's work in the variation form belongs to the early days in Vienna, when this form of composition was very popular. The variations themselves are generally based on either popular arias, or simple popular tunes (volkstümliche Lieder) from contemporary Singspiele. To the former category belongs the set of 9 variations on *Quant è più bello* (pub. 1795), and 6 (pub. 1796) on *"Nel cor più non mi sento"* from Giovanni Paisiello's (1740-1816) *La Molinara. La Molinara,* composed in 1788 for performance in Naples, was performed in Vienna in 1794, where Beethoven probably heard it for the first time. The 12 variations on the Minuet à la Vigano from the ballet *Le Nozze disturbate* by J. J. Haibel (1761-?) also belong to the same period. Vigano, of course, was later to be the choreographer of *Prometheus.*

Variations on tunes from Singspiele include the 7 (pub. 1799) for piano on *Kind, willst du ruhig schlafen* from Peter Winter's (1754-1825) *Das unterbrochene Opferfest* (1796), and the 8 (pub. 1799) on *Tändeln und Scherzen* from F. X. Süssmayer's *Soliman II* (1799). Both Winter and Süssmayer, like Beethoven, were former pupils of Antonio Salieri (1750-1825). Joseph Weigl (1760-1846), another pupil of Salieri's, wrote the ballo eroico, *Riccardo Cuor di Leon* (1795), which was the source of *"Mich brennt ein heisses Fieber."* However, this particular aria, upon which Beethoven wrote a set of 8 variations (pub. 1798), ultimately comes from an opera by Grétry. Beethoven also wrote 10 variations (pub. 1799) on *La stessa, la stessissima,* an aria from his former teacher's opera, *Falstaff, ossia le tre Burle* (1799).

Beethoven found a favorite source of material for variation in Mozart's operas. Thus, in addition to the previously mentioned variations on *Se vuol ballare,* he also wrote 7 Variations for Piano and Violoncello on *Bei Männern welche Liebe fühlen,* and 12 for the same combination of instruments on *Ein Mädchen oder Weibchen* (pub. 1798), both from Mozart's *Magic Flute;* and the variations for the unusual combination of two oboes and English horn (pub. 1914) on *Là ci darem* from *Don Giovanni.*

Other variations on borrowed themes from this same period include the 12 Variations on a Russian Dance from Paul Wranitzky's (1756-1808) ballet *Das Waldmädchen* (pub. 1797); the 12 variations for pianoforte and violoncello (pub. 1797) on *See the Conquering Hero Comes* from Handel's *Judas Maccabaeus;* and the 6 variations for four hands on *Ich denke Dein,* written in the family album of the Countesses Josephine Deym and Therese Brunswick in 1800, and later published in 1805.

The Six Easy Variations on a Swiss Air (pub. ca. 1798), for harpsichord or harp, are of some interest in that the air is quoted in a somewhat lengthy essay by J. F. Reichardt which forms the preface to a song collection for men's voices published by him in 1781. Possibly, Reichardt's ideas about the simple aesthetics of the folk song influenced Beethoven in this particular setting. Beethoven also wrote several sets of Variations on National Airs for the folk song publisher George Thomson (cf. Entry: Folk Song), as well as those for piano on *God save the King* and *Rule Britannia* (both pub. in 1804). The 8 variations (pub. 1831) on the German folk song *Ich hab' ein kleines Hüttchen nur* are somewhat doubtful in origin. This song, known in earlier sources as *Vetter*

Michel, was very popular in the late 18th and early 19th centuries, and often quoted in theoretical sources because it was an eminent example of a *Schusterfleck.* (Cf. Marpurg: *Historisch-Kritische Beyträge* (1754); Burney: *Present State of Music in Germany;* Koch: *Musikalisches Lexikon* (1802); etc. See the discussion of the Diabelli Variations, below, for the meaning of the term.)

Beethoven also composed sets of variations on original themes, or themes taken from his own works. To this category belong the 14 Variations (Op. 44, pub. 1804) for Piano, Violin, and Violoncello, and the 6, Op. 76, for piano, on a theme later used as the Turkish March in the incidental music to Kotzebue's play, *The Ruins of Athens.* The theme of these variations was traditionally considered a Russian folk song, probably due to its similarity to one of the Russian folk songs varied in Op. 107, the *Air de la Petite Russie,* but this seems unlikely in view of the fact that it was used for a Turkish march. The 6 Variations, Op. 34, and 15 Variations on a theme from *Prometheus,* Op. 35, were both written in 1802 and published in 1803. The *Variations très faciles,* also an original theme, were sketched and probably written in 1800. Somewhat more ambitious are the 32 Variations in C minor, composed in 1806-7, and published in the latter year, which Beethoven often assigned as material for study to his piano students.

Beethoven's greatest achievement in this area of his creative work is certainly the 33 Variations on a Waltz by the Viennese publisher, Anton Diabelli. Diabelli conceived the idea of having variations written by a number of the popular composers of the day on his melody, and Beethoven was approached through Schindler. (Other composers invited to write variations on the same tune included Franz Schubert and Wolfgang Amadeus Mozart, the son of the great composer.) According to Schindler, Beethoven was at first reluctant to contribute to Diabelli's enterprise, and further disparaged Diabelli's little tune by calling it a *Schusterfleck.* (The term refers generally to unimaginative repetitions of the same motive on different scale degrees, and specifically to modulation and repetition to the second above the tonic.) The variations themselves (Op. 120, pub. 1823) present great differences in tempi and mood, and are so free in character that another theme, from *Don Giovanni,* is unobtrusively woven into the twenty-second variation.

Beethoven's last work in the field of variations is found in the second movement of the Trio for Piano, Violin, and Violoncello Op. 121a (pub. 1824). The theme in question is derived from Wenzel Müller's (1767-1835) Singspiel, *"Die Schwestern von Prag"* (1794), from which Beethoven used the aria *"Ich bin der Schneider Kakadu."*

P.E.M.

Varnhagen von Ense, Karl August

b. Düsseldorf 1785, d. Berlin 1858. Diplomat and writer; studied medicine, philosophy, and literature. He joined the Austrian army in 1809, was wounded in the battle of Wagram and went to Paris in 1810 as aide to Prince Bentheim. In 1814 Varnhagen was aide to Count Hardenberg, Prussian ambassador at the Vienna Congress; he went to Paris in 1815. Later Varnhagen became Prime Minister in Karlsruhe, but was released in 1819 for his democratic ideas. He settled in Berlin in 1824. Varnhagen was the author of many important works; among them the *Biographische Denkmale und Denkwürdigkeiten des eigenen Lebens* is best known. Together with Chamisso and other poets he contributed to Romantic poetry and represented a rare combination of hero and romantic poet. His love for Rahel Levin, whom he married in 1814, is perpetuated in his book *Rahel, ein Buch des Andenkens* (1833). Varnhagen had met Beethoven in Prague and Teplitz in 1811. "At that time the Master was already hard of hearing and not easy to approach. On his lonely strolls in Clari's garden, Beethoven had seen Rahel many times. The unusual expression of her face impressed him, reminding him of somebody close to his heart. He was accompanied by a friendly young man, named Oliva, who introduced us to him. Beethoven could easily be persuaded to play for the couple." Varnhagen became a close friend of Oliva and through him also of Beethoven; Oliva suggested that Varnhagen write a libretto for the Master. On September 4, 1811, Varnhagen wrote to Bentheim: "I made the acquaintance of Beethoven. The wild man acted quite friendly. He is ready to play for Robert (Rahel), but it must be kept a secret. He is just now composing an opera for the theater in Ofen (Budapest), for which Kotzebue wrote the text. On account of Rahel I am doubly pleased." In a letter by Varnhagen to the poet Uhland, Beethoven's name was mentioned again. He called the Master the greatest, most profound, and most resourceful German composer. In his letter to Uhland, Varnhagen is overflowing with admiration for Beethoven, who helped him to overcome his grief about Rahel's departure. In 1812 the two met only briefly in Teplitz. At that time Varnhagen acted as an intermediary between Beethoven and Prince Kinsky on behalf of the Master's pension. In 1814 Varnhagen met Beethoven again in Vienna but felt somewhat less enthusiastic. He did not even care to have Rahel meet Beethoven. Kaznelson tried to prove in his book that Beethoven was in love with Rahel, whom he considered the Distant Beloved. (Cf. Kaznelson: *Beethovens ferne und unsterbliche Geliebte;* Th.-R. III; M. Unger: *Beethovens Badereisen;* Entries: Teplitz, and Oliva; Otto Berdrow: *Rahel Varnhagen.)*

Vering, Gerhard von

b. Ösede (Westphalia) 1755, d. Vienna 1823. Famous physician. In 1775 he came to Vienna to continue his medical studies, which he had started in Münster. He belonged to that group of physicians (like Hunczovsky) whom Emperor Joseph II sent to Germany, France and England for study. Vering was not only famous as a dermatologist and otologist, but also for his "human mind." On June 29, 1801, Beethoven wrote to Wegeler: "I spent a very bad winter. I suffered from terrible colics which threw me back to my former state of health. But when I consulted Vering . . . [here comes the description of his disease], he managed to check my troubles." Vering's successor was Dr. J. A. Schmidt. The circles of the Drs. Vering and Hunczovsky were very interested in music. The latter had been Mozart's doctor. Dr. Vering's daughter Julie was a pupil of Schenk, and became the wife of Stephan von Breuning (1808). (Cf. Wurzbach; Wegeler; Ries; Entry: Physicians.)

Vermin

Everybody who knows about Beethoven's irregular living habits will not be amazed that noxious insects were his frequent guests. This nuisance is mentioned now and then in the Conversation-books. Bedbugs were an additional trouble for the sick Master during his last years. In December 1819, his nephew Karl jotted down: "I am wondering where the many lice are coming from? However, it is healthy to have lice." (Cf. Schünemann: *Konversationshefte,* vol. I, p. 112.)

Vestas Feuer

Play by Schikaneder, performed August 10, 1805 with music by Joseph Weigl. in 1803 Beethoven worked on this libretto (the last one by the author of the *Magic Flute).* The *Zeitung für die elegante Welt* reported on August 2, 1803: "Beethoven is working on an opera by Schikaneder." The original score of this fragment is in possession of the Gesellschaft der Musikfreunde and was printed and completed by Willy Hess, Bruckner Verlag Wiesbaden. Previously Nottebohm (*Beethoveniana* I) had printed the sketch. Raoul Biberhofer had found the libretto in the Viennese National Library. The contents of the play seems to be related to Sporschill's libretto *Die Apotheose im Tempel des Jupiter Ammon.* In this fragment we find a duet between Volivia and Sartagones, *"Nie war ich so froh wie heute,"* the music of which is identical to *"O namenlose Freude"* from *Fidelio.* Komorzynski states that Schikaneder's play consists only of decorations and magic absurdities. The opera by Weigl was a failure. We can understand that Beethoven dropped the subject but his fragment is worth reviving anyway. (Cf. Entry: Sporschill; Komorzynski: *Emanuel Schikaneder* and *Einfuehrung und Revisionsbericht zu "Vestas Feuer,"* Bruckner Verlag Wiesbaden.)

Vigano, Salvatore

b. Naples 1769, d. 1821. Dancer, choreographer, musician and painter. Married the dancer Maria Medina (1783). In 1793 he came to Vienna where he remained until 1795. Stendhal in his *De l'amour,* tells how the Viennese ladies wore maternity dresses à la Vigano. In 1801 Vigano wrote the ballet *Gli uomini di Prometeo,* in two acts, with music by Beethoven, and later expanded into six acts (Milan, 1803). For this new version he used only four numbers of Beethoven's *Prometheus* music and added other music by Beethoven, Weigl, and other composers. His biography was written by Carlo Ritorni under the title: *Commentarii della vita e delle opere coreodrammatiche di Salvatore Vigano,* Milan, 1838. This work was supplemented by Robert Haas in his article "Zur Wiener Balletpantomime um den Prometheus," *Neues Beethoven-Jahrbuch II.* Vigano applied the dramatic principle of Noverre to his own pantomime-dramas. His father, Onorato (1739-1811), whose name originally had been Braglia, later assumed his mother's maiden name, Vigano. Luigi Boccherini, the composer of the ballet *Die Tochter der Luft (Semiramis),* was the brother of Maria Esther Boccherini, Onorato's wife. (Cf. Entries: Prometheus; Dance music.)

Violin-playing

The young Beethoven played violin and viola. The Fischer Manuscript tells that Beethoven's father did not like free improvisations on the violin. In 1789 Beethoven was viola player in the Electoral Orchestra in Bonn. Unlike Mozart, who all his life continued to be an excellent violinist, Beethoven's string playing gradually deteriorated. As Ries related in his *Notizen,* Beethoven took violin instruction in Vienna with Krumpholz and played his own violin sonatas with Ries. "However, this was terrible music" said Ries. "In his enthusiasm Beethoven overlooked the correct fingering." His violin concertos, his violin sonatas and chamber music proved his knowledge of string playing.

Violin Sonatas

Beethoven's ten violin sonatas appear to be works which were called into being by extraneous circumstances. Two of them were actually written for specific persons, and only the last was dedicated to one of the more familiar dedicatees. The first eight were written in a space of four years, 1798-1802, after which Beethoven appears to have turned his back on the medium, returning to the combination only when it was demanded of him, first for Bridgetower and then for Rode. The sonatas show a slight advance over the violin sonatas of Haydn and Mozart, but nothing so radical as in the symphonies. There is perhaps a greater equality among the instruments in Beethoven's sonatas, as well as a greater sonority, but by and large the ten sonatas follow the traditional concept of the medium.

The first sonatas to appear were the three of Op. 12, in D major, A major and E flat. They were first advertised by Artaria in Jan. 1799, indicating that they were probably composed in 1798. These sonatas were dedicated to Salieri with whom Beethoven had some informal instruction at this time. There are sketches preserved for two of the sonatas; those for the third in E flat are found among sketches for the "Pathetique" Sonata while sketches for the A major are found among sketches for the B flat Piano Concerto and the Op. 14 No. 1 Piano Sonata. Nottebohm places the latter group in 1795.

The Op. 12 sonatas reveal a certain 18th century grace and freshness and are completely entertaining works. The third is possibly the least satisfying of the three because of the predominance of the piano and some ungraceful passages for the violin. All three of the sonatas contain only three movements.

The Sonatas Op. 23 and Op. 24 appeared in 1801-02 and were dedicated to Count Moritz von Fries; they were undoubtedly written in the previous year. There is evidence that the Op. 24 Sonata was originally intended as the second of Op. 23; they were advertised in this arrangement by Mollo in October of 1801, and there is a copy of the Op. 24 which is labeled number two. Just why the second later received a separate opus number cannot be ascertained.

Sketches of the first two movements of the Op. 23 are found mingled with sketches of the Piano Sonata Op. 22 and the Op. 24 Violin Sonata. The sketch book was published by Nottebohm in 1865.

In musical inventiveness and expressive string writing Op. 23 shows a great advance over the Op. 12 sonatas, although it still retains the three movement form. Op. 24 is one of the easier sonatas and contains an unruffled calm throughout. Op. 24 is the first of the violin sonatas to appear in four movements, the new movement being a *scherzo*. The title "Spring" Sonata was not applied by Beethoven.

The three sonatas in Op. 30, A major, C minor and G major, belong to the fateful year 1802, although they were probably written before going to Heiligenstadt and therefore before the formulation of the famed *Testament*. The sonatas were published by the Bureau des Arts et d'Industrie in 1803 and dedicated to Emperor Alexander I of Russia. Alexander was supposed to have sent Beethoven a diamond ring in acknowledgment, but according to Lenz no such transaction appears in the Imperial archives. In 1815, when Beethoven had an audience with the Empress for the dedication of the Piano Polonaise Op. 89, he was given 100 ducats for the Violin Sonatas Op. 30.

Sketches for these three sonatas are to be found in the sketch book published by Nottebohm in 1865 among sketches for the "Kreutzer" Sonata and the last movement of the D major Symphony as well as other works. Material for the first two movements of the A major, the C minor, and the G major can be found here. The original finale of the A major is now the finale of the "Kreutzer," it was replaced by a new finale which was less brilliant. According to the sketch book the slow movement of the C minor was first contemplated in G major.

Of the three sonatas in Op. 30, it is the C minor which appears to be the most important. The four movements are planned along almost symphonic lines, and much of the material seems conceived almost for orchestral instruments rather than piano. The customary seriousness of the C minor key is evident throughout. The A major and G major sonatas both follow the three movement plan, the G major omitting the slow movement.

Undoubtedly, the best known, most brilliant and most difficult of the violin sonatas is the "Kreutzer," Op. 47. Sketches for the work date from the years 1801-02. The sonata was originally composed for the mulatto violinist, Bridgetower, for a performance at the Augarten on May 24, 1802. The work itself was not completed until the day of the first performance, Beethoven having to summon the copyist at 4:30 in the morning to copy the violin part of the *allegro* movement. Even so, the difficult variation movement was played from Beethoven's MS and had an immediate success. The piano part, played by Beethoven, was only sketched here and there, most of it being improvised.

The sonata, published in 1805 by Simrock, appeared with a dedication to Rudolph Kreutzer in spite of the fact that it was written for Bridgetower. Many years later Bridgetower remembered that during the composition of the sonata he and Beethoven were constant companions and the first copy bore a dedication to himself; however, he and Beethoven quarreled over a woman and Beethoven changed the dedication. In connection with the question of the dedication, Czerny claims that the concluding theme of the exposition section of the first movement was taken from a published work by Kreutzer.

On the last sheet of the 1803 sketch book appears a title for the "Kreutzer" Sonata, *Sonata per il Pianoforte ed un violino obligato in uno stilo* (sic) *molto concertante quasi come d'un Concerto.* The word *brillante* has been written after *stilo* but scratched out. After reading the title we can have little doubt that Beethoven conceived the sonata in large dimensions. The customary three movement concerto form, the use of sonata *allegro* form for the outer movements and the slow introduction (the only one in the violin sonatas) all point to the concertante character of the music. The composition is indeed a tribute to the virtuosity of Bridgetower and is the only virtuoso piece among the ten sonatas.

The last of the violin sonatas owes its existence to outward circumstances rather than a desire to create for the medium. In 1812 Pierre Rode visited Vienna and the occasion called forth the Op. 96 Sonata in G major. By 1812 Rode was well past his prime and brilliant rushing passages would not have shown him to the best advantage, an observation which Beethoven made in a letter to the Archduke Rudolph. The work is most marked by a simplicity and light heartedness, in spite of the fact that it is probably the most carefully constructed and most homogeneous of the ten sonatas.

On this occasion the five cello sonatas should be mentioned. The first two, Op. 5, were written in 1796 for Pierre Duport (1741-1808), first cellist of the Prussian court orchestra. This opus containing the sonata in F major and the one in G minor was published by Artaria in 1797 and dedicated to Frederick William II of Prussia, himself an excellent cellist.

The third sonata Op. 69 in A-major written in 1807 and published by Breitkopf und Härtel in 1809 was dedicated to Gleichenstein. The sonatas Op. 102 were composed in 1815 as the only important instrumental work of that year. They were published by Simrock in 1817 and dedicated to Countess Erdödy. It was Joseph Linke, the excellent cellist, for whom Beethoven had composed these important works.

The five cello sonatas rank highly among Beethoven's instrumental works and belong to the standard repertory of every cellist. It may be worthwhile mentioning that the beautiful third sonata, Op. 69 reveals, according to tradition, the master's love affair to Therese Malfatti.

F. T. W.

Vogler, Georg Joseph

b. Würzburg 1749, d. Darmstadt 1814. Famous composer and theoretician, widely known as Abbé Vogler. As son of a violin maker, he had early training in music. He came to Mannheim in 1771, where he found a generous sponsor in Elector Karl Theodor, who sent him to Padre Martini in Bologna. In Italy he studied with Vallotti, whose theory of harmony, based on Rameau, appealed to him. In Rome he was ordained as a priest and Protonotarius. Returning to Mannheim, he founded the famous Mannheim Tonschule, and became court chaplain and second Kapellmeister. With his famous "Orchestrion" he toured in Denmark, England, and Holland with sensational success, reproducing on this instrument the sounds of battles and ocean storms. Many of his reforms in organ building are still in use in our time. When he went to Vienna in 1803, Schikaneder engaged him as House Composer for the Theater an der Wien, at the same time that Beethoven was engaged. Vogler composed the opera *Samori,* which was performed May 7, 1804. According to a diary of Gänsbacher, student of Abbé Vogler, recorded by E. Fröhlich in his Vogler biography, a contest between Vogler and Beethoven took place in Sonnleithner's house. Vogler improvised on a theme given him by Beethoven, first *adagio,* then *fugato.* Vogler gave Beethoven a theme of three measures, the E major scale in *alla breve*. Gänsbacher was more impressed by Vogler than by Beethoven. (Cf. E. Fröhlich: *Biographie des grossen Tonkünstlers Abt Georg Joseph Vogler,* Würzburg 1845; Th.-R. II, p. 404: A Swedish Vogler biography is being prepared.)

Vöslau

Resort in the neighborhood of Baden. Beethoven visited there at the same time as Marie Pachler-Koschak (1823) and there wrote the canon *Das Schöne zum Guten* for her.

W

Wähner, Friedrich

b. Raguhn (near Dessau) 1786; d. Vienna 1839. Writer and contemporary of Beethoven, who published his reminiscences of the Master in *Zeitschrift für Kunst-und Literatur* (1837). He came to Vienna in 1818, where he criticized the Vienna men of letters. Wähner was considered a problematic and extremely witty man. In 1825 he was forced by the police to leave Vienna, but returned in 1835. As a result of his addiction to drinking, he deteriorated and lived under miserable conditions until his death. Gräffer, in his *Kleine Wiener Memoiren,* edited by Schlosser and Gugitz, said his character was "gigantic" (*mammuthisch*), his ink was "nitric acid." Wähner's biography is imbued in darkness and was partly brought to light by Gugitz in his comments on Gräffer's above-mentioned work. Wähner's articles are found in Jeitteles: *Aestetisches Lexikon,* in the magazine *Janus,* etc. His reminiscences of Beethoven correspond to his character, as described by his contemporaries, and emphasized the extravagant and sensational in Beethoven's life. Many aphorisms of Beethoven are handed down to us by Wähner, e.g., the statement: *"Bach ist kein Bach, sondern ein Meer."* (Bach is not a brook, but an ocean.) (Cf. Frimmel: *Handbuch,* where a large section of Wähner's reminiscences is reprinted; Wurzbach; L. A. Frankl: *Sonntagsblätter* II, 1843, with an article by Gräffer.)

Waldstein, Count Ferdinand Ernst

b. Dux (Bohemia) 1762, d. Vienna 1823. British Colonel. Entered the Teutonic Order, whose Grand Master was Maximilian Franz, Elector of Cologne, Archduke of Austria. In this capacity he met Beethoven in Bonn (1787). Waldstein was knighted June 17, 1788. For this occasion Beethoven's *Ritterballet* might have been composed, which was performed only on March 6, 1791. Waldstein was credited with being the composer, Beethoven acting as ghostwriter, a fact which explains the definite weakness of the composition. It may have been Waldstein who suggested Beethoven's trips to Vienna in 1787 and in 1792. About Waldstein's relations with Beethoven in Bonn, see Entries: Bonn; Koch. It is well known that Count Waldstein autographed Beethoven's Stammbuch, Oct. 29, 1792, in which he referred to Beethoven's imminent trip to Vienna: "If you continue to strive, you will receive Mozart's spirit from the hands of Haydn. Your true friend Waldstein." The Count had originally been deeply attached to the Elector, but their good relations were severed later. When political conditions in Bonn became unbearable because of the French invasion, both left Bonn at the same time (1793) for Münster, later for Vienna. It was Count Waldstein's desire to enter the British service, and Count Thugut served as an intermediary. Waldstein had planned to go to the colonies as a pioneer, in case his request should be denied. He recruited an army in Germany which he shipped to England in 1795. Archduke Maximilian believed that Waldstein's position as a British Colonel was incompatible with his rank as Knight of the Teutonic Order, and they broke off relations. In 1809 Waldstein served as a British Colonel in the Austrian Headquarters and participated in the battle of Aspern. In 1812 he resigned from the Teutonic Order and married Countess Isabella Rzewuska. She was evidently the same lady who was instrumental in stimulating Beethoven to compose *In questa tomba oscura.* There is little known about the further relations of the Count with Beethoven, who dedicated to Waldstein his famous Piano Sonata Op. 53. Waldstein was described by his contemporaries as an extremely witty man. According to Countess Lulu Thürheim, he became involved in unfortunate financial matters and was completely impoverished. His wife died in 1828. She had been the heiress to a large fortune, from which her husband no longer profited. According to Countess Thürheim, their marriage was a very happy one, but he died in such poverty that the doctor bills could not be paid and Baron Goess paid for Waldstein's funeral. Four days later Waldstein received a big inheritance from his brother. Baroness du Montet, in her memoirs of 1813, described the Count as an extremely educated man, who not only spoke all the European languages, but could tackle all French dialects. "He entertained us with his pâtois Limousin, Auvergnal, Bas-breton, and spoke all dialects so perfectly that he could disguise himself as a horse dealer who brought his own horses to the market." In addition Waldstein met Beethoven in the house of Razumovsky, whose second wife was sister to Lulu Thürheim. In one of the Conversation-books Oliva wrote the following note: "Don't speak too loud (in this tavern), Count Waldstein just left. Does he live here?" Beethoven's answer to this question has not been recorded. (Cf. Schiedermair: *Der junge Beethoven;* Th.-R. I; Entries: Sonatas, Variations, Dance Music.)

Wawruch, Andreas Johann

b. Moravia 1782, d. Vienna 1842. Physician. Studied in Prague, where he was a professor at the University (1812-1819). From 1819 he practiced in Vienna where he had the reputation of an excellent scientist in addition to his skill as a surgeon. After Dr. Malfatti had broken with Beethoven, Dr. Staudenheim and Braunhofer were Beethoven's physicians. Both hesitated for different reasons to treat the Master. According to Schindler, Dr. Wawruch became his last physician quite by accident, because the nephew Karl had asked a waiter in a coffee house to provide a doctor for his uncle. After Beethoven's death Wawruch wrote a report about the disease. (Cf. Entries: Disease, Last Days; Schindler II, p. 110, 132; Breuning: *Aus dem Schwarzspanierhaus;* Wurzbach; Th.-R. V.)

Way of Living

Characteristic of Beethoven's way of living is a certain irregularity. Only in his youth did he enjoy the benefits of a regular life, due to the fact that he followed a rigid schedule in his duties as an organist, a member of the orchestra and a teacher. In Vienna he was free lancing. His frequent moving from one apartment to another, from the countryside to the city and vice versa, the lack of order in his household, and the continuous changing of his household staff had a definite bad effect on his health. Meals were taken at odd times and he did not pay any attention to regular sleeping hours, though he needed a considerable amount of sleep. Beethoven was by no means a total abstainer and frequently ate and drank excessively. Much may be attributed to his being a bachelor; more to his own genius, which placed him outside of human laws (cf. Entries: Eating and Drinking, Servants). His increasing deafness should also be blamed for these deficiencies which doubtless caused his early death.

Weber, Carl Maria von

b. Eutin 1786, d. London 1826. Composer, and celebrated German romanticist; he was the first cousin of Mozart's wife Konstanze. Weber came from a highly gifted family, but their family's questionable reputation was the source of Leopold Mozart's animosity. Weber spent a restless youth traveling with his father and step-brother, Fridolin, who became his first teacher. Later Weber studied with Michael Haydn in Salzburg, and in 1803, after Joseph Haydn had refused to accept him as a student, with Abbé Vogler in Vienna. In Darmstadt he continued his studies with Vogler; Meyerbeer and Gänsbacher were his fellow-students. After having had jobs as Kapellmeister in Breslau, Mannheim, Munich, Leipzig, Berlin, Gotha, and Weimar, Weber became musical director of the opera in Prague (1813). His close association with Vogler resulted at first in an animosity toward Beethoven. As late as 1810 he was opposed to Beethoven's art, as seen in a letter from Weber to Nägeli in Zürich, dated May 21, 1810, first published in *Niederrheinische Musikzeitung,* 1852. Nägeli had called Weber an imitator of Beethoven, a remark challenged by Weber: "In the first place I hate every imitation and secondly my ideas differ entirely from those of Beethoven." Weber felt himself attracted at that time only by Beethoven's early compositions and considered the recent ones a confused chaos, and an incomprehensible struggling for new expression. In Weber's *Fragment einer musikalischen Reise* (1809) the following sentence is worth quoting: "Listen to the newest recipe for a symphony, just received from Vienna: 'Slow tempo, short abrupt ideas sounding completely incoherent. Every fifteen minutes, three to four notes, producing tension. Next a muffled roll of kettledrum, mysterious passages on the viola, then the "general pause" and holes. Finally, after the tension of the listener has reached its highest peak, a *furioso,* but by no means a main theme. The listener should look for himself . . ."

Some years later Weber changed his attitude completely. It was he who brought *Fidelio* to Prague on November 26, 1814. The performance was a failure. On December 2, Weber wrote to Gänsbacher: "*Fidelio* was performed, there are certainly great moments in this opera, but they don't understand it. To hell with the public! The jester is good enough for them." (Cf. Teuber: *Geschichte des Prager Theaters II,* p. 452, with interesting and little known details.) In 1816 Weber performed Beethoven's "Battle" Symphony twice, and in 1823 he performed *Fidelio* in Dresden. When Weber's *Freischütz* was presented in Vienna he came personally to the Austrian capital. Beethoven invited Weber to visit him in Baden. Thereupon Weber wrote to his wife:

"I was very tired, but yesterday evening had to go out again at six o'clock because the excursion to Baden had been agreed upon for seven-thirty. It took place, the party including Haslinger, Piringer and Benedict; unfortunately, however, it rained vilely. The main thing was to see Beethoven. The latter received me with the most touching affection; he embraced me at least six or seven times in the heartiest fashion and finally, full of enthusiasm, cried: 'Yes, you are a devil of a fellow, a fine fellow!' We spent the noon-hour together, very merrily and happily, This rough, repellent man actually paid court to me, served me at table as carefully as though I were his lady, etc. In short, this day always will remain a most remarkable one for me, as for all who shared in it. It gave me quite a special exaltation to see myself overwhelmed with such affectionate attention by this great spirit. We saw the baths, drank from the spring and at five o'clock drove back again to Vienna."

Weber's son supplements this after family traditions, in his biography of his father (1864), as follows:

"The three men were excited when they entered the bare, almost poverty-stricken room inhabited by the great Ludwig. The chamber was in the greatest disorder. Music, money, articles of clothing lay on the floor; the wash was piled on the unclean bed, the grand piano, which was open, was thick with dust, there was a chipped coffee set on the table.

Beethoven came forward to meet them. Benedict says that King Lear or the Ossianic bards must have resembled him in appearance. His hair was thick, gray and bristly, here and there altogether white; his forehead and skull had an exceptionally broad curve and were high, like a temple; his nose was foursquare, like that of a lion, the mouth nobly shaped and soft, the chin broad, with those wonderful shell-formed grooves in all his portraits, and formed by two jaw bones which seemed meant to crack the hardest nuts. A dark red overspread his broad, pockmarked face; beneath the bushy, gloomily contracted eyebrows, small radiant eyes beamed mildly upon those entering; his cyclopean, foursquare figure, which towered but slightly above that of Weber, was covered by a shabby house-robe, with torn sleeves.

Beethoven recognized Weber before he had mentioned his name, clasped him in his arms, and cried: 'So there you are, you fellow, you devil of a fellow! God greet you!' And then he at once handed him the famous writing tablet and a conversation ensued, Beethoven in the meantime first of all throwing the music off the sofa and then, quite unconcernedly, dressing in the presence of his guests to go out.

Beethoven complained bitterly about his situation, scolded the management of the theatre, the concert impresarios, the public, the Italians, the popular taste and, in particular, his nephew's ingratitude. Weber, who was greatly moved, advised him to tear himself away from these repulsive, discouraging conditions, and to make an artistic tour of Germany which would give him a chance to see what the world thought of him. 'Too late!' cried Beethoven. He pantomimed playing the piano and shook his head. 'Then go to England, where they admire you,' wrote Weber. 'Too late!' cried Beethoven, caught Weber demonstratively beneath the arm, and drew him along with him to the Sauerhof, where he ate. There Beethoven showed himself full of kindheartedness and warmth toward Weber."

In 1826 the following can be read in a Conversation-book: "C. M. Weber is said to have died," and Holz jotted down: "Once we played your Quartet in E flat major [Harp Quartet]. He (Weber) believed the second movement to be too long. I replied: 'That is of Beethoven's more intense feelings. He has more imagination than all the rest.'" (Cf. Literature on C. M. Weber; Entries: "Battle" Symphony, *Fidelio.*)

Wegeler, Franz Gerhard

b. Bonn 1765, d. Koblenz 1848. Physician, highly honored in his profession. He was a friend of Beethoven's youth, and the author of *Biographische Notizen über Ludwig van Beethoven,* which is considered one of the finest sources for the Master's youth. According to Wegeler's own statement, he became acquainted with Beethoven as early as 1782. Wegeler lived in close contact with Beethoven up to September 1787, when Wegeler went to Vienna for his medical studies. After Wegeler's return to Bonn in 1789, the friendly relations between the men were continued until 1792, when Beethoven left for Vienna. Wegeler followed him to Vienna in 1794 because of the French invasion of Bonn. In 1796 Wegeler returned to Bonn, and from that time the two kept up a most friendly correspondence. Wegeler, together with Ferdinand Ries, published his *Biographische Notizen* in 1838 (Koblenz, Bädecker). An appendix by Wegeler followed in 1845, on the occasion of the unveiling of the Beethoven monument in Bonn. Both books were reprinted in 1906 by Schuster and Löffler, with additions and comments by Kalischer. Robert Schumann, in a letter to Henriette Voigt (1838), characterized this new publication as most fascinating. (Cf. Entries: Ries, Breuning; Schiedermair: *Der junge Beethoven.)*

Weigl, Joseph

b. Eisenstadt (Hungary) 1766, d. Vienna 1846. Composer. His father, Joseph Franz (1740-1820), was first cellist of Prince Esterhazy; his mother, Anna, prima donna at the Imperial theater. In his early youth Joseph Weigl wrote a number of successful operas, among them *L'amor marinaro,* first performed October 15, 1797. From this opera Beethoven took the theme *"Pria ch' io im-*

pegno," which he used for his *allegretto con variazioni* in his Trio Op. 11. It seems strange that Weigl's name was not mentioned in the first edition of Beethoven's Trio, but according to P. C. Potter, the publisher Artaria gave the theme to Beethoven without indicating its origin. The Master was annoyed to learn of the origin of the theme and planned to write a new finale. The whole matter is highly questionable. In 1808 Collin had suggested to Beethoven an operatic project *Bradamante.* Beethoven rejected the idea, because of the similarity with Weigl's ballet *Alcina,* which was performed January 28, 1798. Weigl's name appeared in the Conversation-books of 1820, when Peters reported to Beethoven on Weigl's *Passion,* performed March 25, 1820, and again somewhat later, when Bernard speaks about Weigl's project to write an opera *Die Tochter der Luft* after Calderon's *Semiramis* (Schünemann: *Konversationshefte,* III, p. 254). The relations between Weigl and Beethoven may be called somewhat neutral. In 1825 Weigl became second Hofkapellmeister, and Beethoven sent him a letter of congratulation. Weigl was one of the torch bearers at Beethoven's funeral. Weigl's opera *Die Schweizer Familie,* 1809, may be called one of the most successful of his time. One can understand that the Master looked upon Weigl with some misgivings, as the latter was not the man to have a full understanding for Beethoven. The Master, who was not too popular in court circles, except for Archduke Rudolph, stood in contrast to Weigl, who had a decisive word at the Imperial Court. No doubt Weigl was an obstacle to Beethoven in this respect. (Cf. Wurzbach; A. D. Eisner-Eisenhof: "Joseph Weigl" in R. M. I. 1904; Th.-R. II-V.)

Weiss, Franz

b. Silesia 1778, d. Vienna 1830. Viola player. He was at first a member of Razumovsky's private quartet together with Schuppanzigh, Sina and Linke. Later he joined the independent Schuppanzigh Quartet (1821), which performed all of Beethoven's quartets. In contrast to the stout Schuppanzigh, Weiss was tall and slim. He was, in addition, a composer of chamber music, piano sonatas, overtures, symphonies, etc. In one of the Conversation-books, Holz told Beethoven that Weiss was drinking heavily. (Cf. Th.-R. II-V; Frimmel: *Beethoven Jahrbuch II,* p. 173.)

Weissenbach, Alois

b. Telfs (Tyrol) 1766, d. Salzburg 1821. Physician and writer. Participated in the war against the Turks and the French as a medical officer and became a professor of practical and theoretical surgery in Salzburg (1804). He came to Vienna in 1814 where he met Beethoven, for whom he wrote the text to the cantata *Der glorreiche Augenblick* (cf. Entry: Cantatas).

For a while Beethoven planned to send his nephew Karl to Salzburg under the care of Weissenbach. In an exuberant letter to Beethoven, the physician invited the Master to visit him. Weissenbach's name appeared many times in the Conversation-books.

The physician wrote reminiscences of his trip to Vienna under the title *Meine Reise zum Congress,* published 1816 by Wallishauser in Vienna, wherein Beethoven played a considerable part. He described and characterized the Master in a most interesting way. There is no doubt that the text to the above-mentioned cantata is extremely poor; even Rochlitz, who substituted Weissenbach's text by another one, entitled *Der erste Ton* could not save the work. Gräffer in his *Kleine Wiener Memoiren* wrote an enthusiastic article on Weissenbach, whom he not only called a passionate admirer of Beethoven, but also mentally and physically kin to him (the physician as well was hard of hearing). According to Gräffer, Weissenbach and Beethoven often met in the Römischer Kaiser tavern. (Cf. Wurzbach; Castelli's Memoirs; Th.-R. III, p. 447.)

Weissenthurn, Johanna Franul von

b. Koblenz 1773, d. 1845. Actress, singer and writer. She came to Vienna in 1789. Beethoven dedicated the song: "Man strebt, die Flamme zu verhehlen" (1792) to her, and Napoleon saw her as Phaedra, and rewarded her with the sum of 3000 francs for the performance. Her name appeared in conversations with Bernard. (W o O. 120.)

Wellington's Victory

This work, the so-called "Battle" Symphony, probably did more to popularize Beethoven during his lifetime than any of his other works. The work was written in 1813 to celebrate the victory of the English forces over Napoleon on July 27 of that year.

The composition of a programmatic battle symphony was by no means an original idea with Beethoven; this type of work had a long and honorable tradition, established by such composers as Kuhnau, Kocwara and Fux, and commemorating the battles of Prague, Jena and others.

The story of the "Battle" Symphony is irrevocably tied up with Johann Nepomuk Mälzel (see Entry: Mälzel), the inventor of the chronometer. Mälzel was in Vienna in the year 1813, exhibiting his mechanical trumpeter, a machine which produced music by means of a metal cylinder. When the excitement of Wellington's victory over Napoleon reached Vienna, it must certainly have stimulated Mälzel's commercial sense and he made haste to interest Beethoven in the idea of composing a battle symphony for a new machine which he called a "Panharmonicon," which contained the instrumentation of an entire band. The original plan was to exhibit the machine in Vienna, then to take the machine to England, with Beethoven accompanying Mälzel on the journey. As we shall see, the plan was not realized, but the idea appealed to Beethoven and he set to work on the symphony. According to Moscheles, Mälzel provided Beethoven with the plan for the symphony as well as suggesting the dramatic implications for the use of the three popular themes, the theme of *Rule, Britannia* contesting with, and eventually overpowering, the French tune *Malborough, s'en va-t-en guerre*. The whole was to be climaxed by *God Save the King*, treated as a fugue.

The symphony was written for the Panharmonicon, but when an opportunity arose for a concert performance of the work, Mälzel gave Beethoven permission to arrange the work for orchestra, no doubt with the intention of raising some money, as well as obtaining some publicity for the future Panharmonicon. The work was first performed at a benefit concert on December 8, 1813, and again on December 12. Shortly after the second performance Beethoven and Mälzel quarreled, and the next performance on January 2, a benefit for Beethoven himself, took place without Mälzel's cooperation. On this occasion, the orchestra was essentially the same as the one for the benefit concerts, being composed of amateurs and professionals from Vienna, among them Dragonetti, Meyerbeer, Romberg, Hummel, Mayseder, Moscheles, Salieri and Schuppanzigh. The work itself was an instant success, particularly among the general public, although some of Beethoven's friends felt that he had degraded himself in writing the work.

As a result of the quarrel, Beethoven refused to return the score to Mälzel, whereupon Mälzel managed to procure some of the parts from which he completed his mechanical cylinder, and left Vienna for England, pausing on the way at Munich to exhibit his Panharmonicon playing the Beethoven symphony. Beethoven immediately instigated a lawsuit which dragged on for some time and was eventually settled out of court in 1817. It was during this time that Beethoven sent a copy of the work to the Prince Regent in London, hoping to forestall a performance there of Mälzel's Panharmonicon. However, the Prince ignored the work, even failing to acknowledge the receipt of the score. Beethoven never forgave the slight.

The work was sold to Steiner and Co., who published it in March of 1816 as Op. 91, dedicated to the Prince Regent of England. Later Beethoven offered the work to the English publishers, and it was purchased by Birchall. (Cf. Entry: Mälzel.)

Wetzlar

Jewish banking family, ennobled by Maria Theresia (1777), receiving the title "von Plankenstein." Karl Abraham (d. 1799) was converted to Catholicism. His sons, Raymund and Alexander, were promoters of art and science. Raymund (b. 1752, d. 1810) played a certain role in the history of Mozart's *Figaro,* as seen in Da Ponte's memoirs, and was even godfather of one of Mozart's children. He was the owner of the "Villa Chaire," where the famous contest between Beethoven and Wölfl took place. Alexander (b. 1769, d. 1810) was the addressee of a letter, written by Beethoven May 18, 1803, in which the Master recommended Bridgetower to him. Evidently Beethoven was not personally acquainted with Alexander. (Cf. Wurzbach; *Archiv für judische Familienforschung,* Vienna, 1915.)

Wieck, Friedrich

b. Pretzsch 1785, d. Loschwitz (near Dresden), 1873. Father of Clara Schumann and father-in-law of Robert Schumann. Famous piano teacher who visited Beethoven in May 1826. Wieck's reminiscences of that visit were published in the magazine *Der Klavierlehrer* 1885, Nr. 17, and are partly reproduced in Th.-R. V, p. 341.

Wiener Neustadt

A city south of Vienna, where Beethoven once spent several hours in the city jail in 1822. Coming from Baden in a bad storm, he had lost his way while running after his hat. His unusual appearance made some passers-by suspicious, and into the picture came the police to arrest him. Beethoven was so busy raging at the authorities that it did not occur to him until somewhat later that Anton Herzog, a choir-conductor of the city's cathedral, was among his acquaintances. Herzog and Blasius Höfel, an engraver, identified him, and the police set him free. Beethoven laughingly related the story to Fanny del Rio, and Höfel, who later became a professor in Salzburg, related the same story to Thayer. (Cf. Th.-R. IV, p. 224.)

Wild, Franz

b. Lower Austria 1791 or 1792, d. Döbling 1860. Famous singer. In his early youth he was a chorister in Klosterneuburg where he studied with Prosper von Mosel, a well-known violinist and choir director. In 1804 Wild became a member of the "Convikt" in Vienna and so excelled as a singer that he even won Napoleon's admiration. In 1811 he was a member of the Leopoldstädter Theater and two years later affiliated with the Vienna in 1819. Wild's autobiography and the Netherlands and returned to Vienna in 1819. Wild's authobiography was published under the title *Blätter der Erinnerung* by Friedrich Förster (1860) and contained some reminiscences on Beethoven. One of these reminiscences was that in 1814 Wild performed the "Adelaïde" to such perfection that the Master was willing to accompany him. Furthermore, Beethoven planned to orchestrate the accompaniment for Wild, but the project was not carried out. Instead he composed for Wild the song "An die Hoffnung," which he accompanied at a matinée. For further details: see Wurzbach; Th.-R. III.

Will

Besides Beethoven's *Heiligenstädter Testament* (see Entry: Heiligenstadt), Beethoven wrote another will on March 6, 1823, in a letter to his lawyer, I. B. Bach. He made his nephew Karl his sole heir. According to Schindler and Breuning, a third will was written on January 3, 1827, which confirms his nephew as sole heir. Bach was reconfirmed as "Curator," and Stephan von Breuning as guardian of his nephew. On March 23, three days before his death, he modified his will to allow his nephew only the interest from the capital. The capital was supposed to be preserved for Karl's natural, legal heirs. This modification was added at the suggestion of Stephan von Breuning. (Cf. Th.-R. V, p. 439.)

Willmann, Magdalena

b. Forchtenberg 1775, d. Vienna 1801. Singer. Member of a widespread family of musicians. One of her brothers, Ignaz, was a violinist in the Bonn Orchestra. In 1790 she was a soprano in Bonn. There is no doubt that Beethoven met her at that time and became more attached to her on the trip the Bonn Orchestra made to Mergentheim. In 1794 she sang in Vienna. Castelli mentioned her in his memoirs, characterizing her as a pretty, slim woman with a clear, soft, and easy-going voice. In 1799 she married a certain Galvani (Thayer). When

Magdalena came to Vienna in 1795 she renewed her acquaintance with Beethoven. Her niece, daughter of the violinist Maximilian Willmann, related to Thayer and Nohl that Beethoven proposed to her aunt Magdalena, but she refused his offer, "because the composer was too ugly and half crazy." Wurzbach erroneously called her Karoline. (Cf. Schiedermair: *Der junge Beethoven*; Th.-R. II; Hanslick: *Geschichte des Concertwesens;* Kalischer: *Beethovens Frauenkreis,* I, p. 108.)

Wolanek, Anton

See Entry: Copyists.

Wölfl, Joseph

b. Salzburg 1772, d. London 1812. Pianist, student of Michael Haydn, Leopold and W. A. Mozart. Mozart recommended the 18-year-old pianist to Count Oginski in Warsaw. After the partition of Poland (1795), he went to Vienna, where he composed a number of operas for Schikaneder's theater. He toured in Europe with the greatest success and settled in London in 1805. There he became involved in jugglery and excelled in this trade. Wölfl as a pianist was one of the greatest technicians of his time. His enormous hands were proverbial; his runs of intervals of the tenth and other tricks were world-famous and equalled only by Hummel. His precision playing was inherited from Mozart, and herein he was superior to Beethoven. Ignaz von Seyfried has described the contest between Wölfl and Beethoven which took place in Baron Raymund Wetzlar's "Villa Chaire" (cf. Entry: Wetzlar). The contest ran smoothly and both virtuosos were equally liked by the audience. Tomaschek, in his autobiography, gave an excellent account of Wölfl's piano playing and his character. Tomaschek related that whoever wanted to see Wölfl had to look him up in the Blaue Weintraube tavern, where he played billiards day and night. In spite of his virtuosity in that line (similar to Mozart) he lost all the revenue from his concerts playing this game. Wölfl was six feet tall, slim and bony. Once, when he performed at a soirée, he threw all his rings into the audience. Another time, escorted by two ladies in the Baumgarten in Prague watching Blanchard's balloon performance, he promenaded barefoot. He caused as much of a sensation as Blanchard himself.

Wölfl's piano compositions do not show the way he played them because he improvised all his tricks. This is evident in the three Sonatas Op. 6, dedicated to Beethoven (1798). (Cf. Th.-R. II, p. 68; Wurzbach, with a list of Wölfl's compositions and "Der Bär" with letters of Wölfl to Breitkopf and Härtel.)

Wolfmayer, Johann Nepomuk

Textile manufacturer in Vienna and a great admirer of Beethoven. He was a partner of Johann Wolfmayer and Company from 1814 on, his associate being Aloys Prigl. When in 1818 the rumor was spread that Beethoven planned to compose a requiem, Wolfmayer offered him the sum of 100 ducats, asking in return only a copy of the work. According to Thayer, the requiem project was Wolfmayer's idea. According to Otto Jahn, informed by Aloys Fuchs, Wolfmayer supported Beethoven frequently in the most delicate way. Sometimes he even ordered a new coat to be made for him; he put the new coat discreetly on a chair in Beethoven's apartment and took away the old one. Evidently Wolfmayer acted as a business adviser, and the Master sometimes had his correspondence addressed to Wolfmayer's office. Schindler called Wolfmayer one of Beethoven's most dignified and reserved friends and said that Wolfmayer was in possession of many of Beethoven's manuscripts. Beethoven originally intended to dedicate his Quartet Op. 131 to Wolfmayer, but he changed his mind because of his nephew, who was about to enter military service; instead he dedicated the work to General von Stutterheim (see Entry: Karl van Beethoven). Schindler claimed to have suggested the dedication of Quartet Op. 135 to Wolfmayer and the matter was discussed on the Master's deathbed. A Conversation-book of 1826 revealed that Schuppanzigh invited Beethoven to a party for which Wolfmayer had provided the drinks. He saw the Master during his last days and wept when leaving the room. Wolfmayer was one of the torchbearers. (Cf. Th.-R. V, p. 328; Frimmel: *Neue Beethoven Studien,* Neue deutsche Kunst-und Musikzeitung, 1895.)

Wolf-Metternich, Countess

Wife of Ignaz, Count Wolf-Metternich. Beethoven's Variations on a March of Dressler, published Mannheim 1783, were dedicated to her (cf. Schiedermair: *Der junge Beethoven;* Th.-R. I, p. 154).

Women

In the life of all great composers women have usually played a great part. Among the great composers of more recent times Bach, Gluck, Haydn, Mozart, Schumann and Wagner were married; Handel, Beethoven, Schubert and Brahms remained single. It is difficult to visualize the composer who fumed and raged while creating the *Missa Solemnis* surrounded by children and taking care of a wife. The explosive character of the Master, his exclusive interest in musical creation, his parental background, and many other factors resulted in an unreserved bachelor attitude. However, this did not prevent him from being greatly interested in women. His occasional desire to get married was not in conflict with his basic attitude; it may be compared to his urge to live in foreign countries, which was never realized. Wegeler and Ries stated: "Beethoven was never without love and always deeply involved." "As long as I lived in Vienna," Wegeler reports, "Beethoven was always in love, and sometimes so successfully that many handsome young men might have envied him."

Dr. Bertolini, his physician from 1806 to 1816, who knew more about Beethoven than anyone else, confirmed that statement and it was also upheld by his old friend Doležalek. According to Bertolini, Beethoven had a predilection for graceful and fragile women, a fact which might be explained by his mother's physical type; he describes her as "slender and beautiful" (Fischer Manuscript). According to Doležalek, Beethoven never showed that he was in love. He certainly was not a communicative type and kept his secrets hidden within himself. Wegeler speaks about Beethoven's and Stefan von Breuning's first love, Fräulein Jeannette Honrath from Cologne. She spent several weeks with the Breunings in Bonn. She was a beautiful and vivacious blonde, well educated, of a friendly character with a strong feeling for music. Jeanette married an Austrian officer, Carl Greth, who died in 1827. The Master's next love, according to Wegeler, was Fräulein v. W. (von Westerhold). Whether his feelings for Eleonore von Breuning were more friendship or more love is hard to decide. One of his youthful piano sonatas (Eleonore Sonata) is dedicated to her. Beethoven was less successful with Babette Koch, the daughter of Wittib Koch (Zehrgarten) and Magdalena Willmann, a soprano.

However, he knew how to console himself. Not much is known of his love affairs during his first years in Vienna. In 1800 he wrote to Wegeler about "that dear and enchanting maiden" who had evidently shaken his soul.

It may be assumed that only beautiful women attracted the Master; otherwise he would not have asked his friend Gleichenstein to find him a beautiful woman in Freiburg. "She must be beautiful, nothing else but beautiful," he said, "or else I would have to love myself." It would be a mistake to believe that Beethoven was sexually pure. Wegeler and Ries report the following: "One evening, when I came to Baden for my lesson, I found a beautiful lady with him, sitting on the sofa. As it seemed to me that I was in the way, I proceeded to leave at once, but Beethoven called me back and said: 'Play a while.' He and the lady were sitting behind me. I had played for a while, when the Master suddenly called: 'Ries, play something sentimental.' And shortly thereafter he said: 'Something melancholy.' And then: 'Something passionate.' Beethoven never visited me more often than when I was living in the house of a tailor, where there were three beautiful but irreproachable daughters. This also explains an allusion at the close of a letter, of July 24, 1804, where he said: 'Don't do too much tailoring, and remember me to the most beautiful of all the beautiful. And—send me half a dozen sewing needles.'" (Wegeler and Ries).

His interest in lower class women was only sporadic; he preferred aristocratic women. From the very beginning of his career in Vienna he moved among the nobility, e.g. Princess Odescalchi, née Countess Keglevicz-Buzin, to whom Beethoven dedicated his Piano Sonata Op. 7. It is characteristic that this sonata is nicknamed the "Amorous" Sonata. A nephew of the Countess commented on this work to Nottebohm: "The sonata was composed by Beethoven at the time when he was her piano teacher. As he lived across the street from her, he came over for her lesson dressed in his robe, in slippers and a peaked nightcap." All this happened in 1797 when Beethoven was 27 years old. Two years later Countess Babette received the dedication of Beethoven's 10 Piano Variations on Salieri's duet *"La stessa, la stessissima"* from the opera *Falstaff*. In 1801 he dedicated to her his First Piano Concerto in C major. The concerto was given to her one month after her marriage to Count Odescalchi.

Beethoven's passion for his Immortal Beloved became the subject of a considerable literature. It is treated in a special entry. Whether or not Beethoven was really in love with Bettina Brentano is more than questionable. More essential were his relations with Therese Malfatti, whom he might possibly have married. In many cases it is hard to decide whether Beethoven felt more friendship or more love.

Princess Christina Lichnowsky, née Thun, acted more like a mother than like a lover towards Beethoven. He dedicated to her the Cello Variations on the theme from Handel's *Judas Maccabaeus* and the piano score of the *Prometheus* music. When (1807) in that memorable night session at the house of Prince Lichnowsky, Beethoven's opera *Leonore* (*Fidelio*) had to be shortened, Princess Christina played the piano part. Her mother was Countess Maria Wilhelmine Thun, née Uhlefeld, who was one of the great patrons of Mozart and Haydn and to whom Beethoven dedicated the Clarinet Trio Op. 11. The complex personality of Beethoven makes it understandable that his attitude towards women swings from frivolous jokes to deepest, almost religious, admiration. Many volumes have been written on this subject. (Cf. Kalischer: *Beethovens Frauenkreis;* and the literature on the Immortal Beloved.)

Worzischek, Hugo

b. Vamberg (Bohemia) 1791, d. Vienna 1825, Composer, pupil of his father, Wenzel, and of Tomaschek. In 1813 I. N. Zizius, professor of statistics in Vienna, came to Prague and discovered Woržischek's talent. He persuaded him to come to Vienna, where he studied mainly with Hummel. When Hummel left Vienna, Woržischek took over all of Hummel's students. At that time the Czech composer was recognized as the foremost pianist in Vienna, competing only with Moscheles. Woržischek had studied law for some years and became an official of the Hofkriegsrat (1822). During this time he was a leading figure in Hofrat Kiesewetter's private concerts. Through him he was recommended as conductor of the Gesellschaft der Musikfreunde. Later he was court organist. Like Franz Schubert, he died young. As a composer Woržischek is considered a forerunner of Schubert, especially in his piano compositions. Beethoven esteemed Woržischek highly. According to Tomaschek he had known Beethoven as early as 1814. In a note in one of the Conversation-books Beethoven praised a work by the Czech composer. Woržischek's Piano Sonata in B flat major Op. 20 (1820) shows definite kinship with Beethoven. (Cf. W. Kahl: "Das lyrische Klavierstück Schuberts und seiner Vorgänger," A. M. W. I and II; Nettl: *Forgotten Musicians,* p. 91; and Wurzbach.)

Wranitzky, Paul

b. Neureisch (Moravia) 1756, d. Vienna 1808. Composer, violinist in the Esterhazy orchestra under J. Haydn, and from 1785 until his death Kapellmeister of the Imperial orchestra in Vienna. He composed numerous operas, symphonies, concertos, chamber music, ballets, etc. According to Carl Czerny's memoirs, Wranitzky was one of Beethoven's visitors when young Czerny happened to pay a visit to the Master. One of Wranitzky's best known ballets was *Das Waldmädchen,* performed in 1796. Beethoven used its Russian Dance a year later in the theme of his A major Variations on *"La danse Russe, dansée par Mlle. Cassentini dans le Ballet: Das*

Waldmädchen" (cf. Entry: Browne). Goethe planned to have Wranitzky compose a sequel to the *Magic Flute,* a project that was never realized. (Cf. Nettl: *Goethe und Mozart,* Esslingen, 1949; Wurzbach.)

Würfel, Wilhelm

b. Planian (Bohemia) 1791, d. Vienna 1852. Composer. Professor at the Warsaw Conservatory in 1815. After a short stay in Prague he went to Vienna in 1824 and became Kapellmeister at the Kärntnerthor Theater in 1826. Among his numerous works listed by Wurzbach, *Der Sieg Wellingtons,* Fantasy for four hands, is mentioned, which is nothing else but an arrangement of Beethoven's "Battle" Symphony. Würfel belonged to the gay party of 1825 with Beethoven, Kuhlau, etc., reported by Seyfried in his *Studien.* He might have been the intermediary between Czar Alexander of Russia and Beethoven regarding the Master's three Violin Sonatas Op. 30. (Cf. Th.-R. V; Wurzbach; Entry: Alexander I.)

Wurzer, Johann

b. Bonn 1770. A friend of Beethoven's youth (cf. Schiedermair: *Der junge Beethoven*).

Z

Zizius, Johann Nepomuk

b. Heřmanmestec 1772, d. Vienna 1824. Jurist and Professor of Statistics. He was a great music lover and Beethoven attended many music soirées in his house. A letter from Beethoven to Zmeskall about 1800 states that Zizius held open house for musicians and music lovers. As a successful lawyer, full professor of the Vienna University, and a rich bachelor, he could afford splendid parties with his sister as a hostess. Leopold Sonnleithner in his *Musikalische Skizzen aus Alt-Wien* (1863), described these concerts vividly. Zizius belonged to the founders of the Gesellschaft der Musikfreunde and represented Beethoven in a lawsuit against Artaria for the unlawful reprinting of the Quintet Op. 29. Carl Maria von Weber and Moscheles mention Zizius as a music enthusiast. Beethoven's acquaintance with Woržischek was made in Zizius' house (Cf. Wurzbach.)

Zmeskall, Nikolaus von Domanowitz (Domanowetz)

b. Hungary (?) 1759, d. Vienna 1833. Official of the Hungarian Court Chancellery. One of the first and most faithful friends of Beethoven in Vienna. It is presumed that the Master met him in Lichnowsky's house. Zmeskall was well acquainted with Klüpfeld, the secretary of the Russian Embassy, with whom Beethoven was on friendly terms. Furthermore Zmeskall belonged to the circle of Count Deym (Hofstatuarius Müller), the Brunswicks and Gallenbergs (1800). He was an excellent cellist, in whose house (Bürgerspital) regular Sunday chamber music sessions took place. Reichardt, attending such a performance in 1809, reported the following: "After a difficult quintet by Beethoven was played (Op. 4), we were fortunate to hear a great fantasy by Beethoven, performed by Mme. Ertmann. It is impossible to hear anything more perfect on a more perfect instrument. . . ." After Beethoven's break with Lichnowsky most of Beethoven's chamber music was played for the first time in Zmeskall's house.

There are preserved more than 100 letters, notes, etc., written by Beethoven to Zmeskall, some of them with funny contents. Often he addressed him "Musik-Graf," "Baron Dreckfahrer" (Scavenger); sometimes he called him "Fress-Graf." Another motif of his jokes was the request for quills which had to be cut in the Hungarian Court Chancellery. Characteristic is the following letter to Zmeskall: "Yesterday, through our Zmeskall-Domanovezian chatter I became quite sad. The devil take you. I don't want any of your whole system of ethics. Power is the morality of men who stand out from the rest, and it is also mine." This letter is an example of Beethoven's self-confidence at that time. Zmeskall was one of those who recognized Beethoven's genius early and in this respect he may be compared to Schindler and Wolfmayer. The two friends met most often in the Zum Schwan tavern, near the Bürgerspital. Sometimes the Master had to ask him for minor financial help. Zmeskall provided him with wine, sent him a mirror, a watch, and loaned him his books. In all of Beethoven's household troubles Zmeskall was consulted.

In 1818 the Sunday chamber music was still going on at Zmeskall's but he unfortunately fell sick in the winter of 1819-20. From that time on he suffered from rheumatism, which hampered him considerably in his musical activities. In 1824 the Count had to be carried in a sedan to the Academy. His illness limited Zmeskall's association with Beethoven, but in 1824 he signed the honorary address to the Master. In addition the Count's name appeared again in some of the Conversation-books. After Czerny visited the sick Master, Zmeskall asked him for details. It is well known that Beethoven dedicated to Zmeskall his Quartet Op. 95 in F minor. In a jocund letter of 1802 Beethoven improvised for Zmeskall a sketch for a three-part composition with the ninefold repetition of the word "Graf," evidently referring to an original composition of Zmeskall (Trio from a G minor Quartet). This letter ran: "Dear victorious, but sometimes failing Count." Thus Zmeskall was treated by Beethoven but the Musik-Graf did not mind. His compositions are preserved in the Gesellschaft der Musikfreunde, including two string quartets, a piano rondo and several cello sonatas. Sandberger discussed them in his article, "Beethovens Freund Zmeskall als Komponist." (*Beethoven Aufsätze,* p. 213). The Count follows more the technique of Haydn and Mozart than that of Beethoven. The E-flat Major Duo for Viola and Cello (W o O. 32), composed about 1796, published 1912, with the title "Duett mit zwei obligaten Augengläsern" might have been composed for Zmeskall. In a letter of 1798 to Baron "Dreckfahrer" we read: "Je vous suis bien obligé pour votre faiblesse de vos yeux."

He left a diary which, according to his will, was to be used for a biography, a project never realized. He was also the inventor of a metronome, explained in a manuscript which he entrusted to Joseph Weidlich. Zmeskall's valuable manuscripts of scores of Haydn, Mozart, Beethoven, and others are still preserved in the Gesellschaft der Musikfreunde in Vienna. The name Zmeskall is by no means Hungarian but Czech. The predicate Domanowitz and Lestynie indicate Slavic origin. (Cf. Wurzbach.)

Zulehner, Karl

Publisher in Mainz, who advertised an edition of Beethoven's complete works for piano and strings in 1803. Beethoven in a warning in the *Wiener Zeitung* strongly objected to the advertisement. (Cf. Th.-R. II, p. 407.)

CHRONOLOGY

Year	*Event*	*Work*[1]
1712	Louis van Beethoven, son of a baker, Ludwig's father, baptized in Antwerp	
1733 March	Louis van Beethoven Court musician of the Elector of Cologne in Bonn	
1764	Johann van Beethoven, Ludwig's father, Court musician	
1770	Ludwig van Beethoven, second child, baptized, December 17	
1782	Substitutes for the organ player. Acquaintance with Wegeler, through him with Breuning family	Dressler Variations W o O. 63. First printed work
1783	Substitutes for his teacher as harpsichordist in the orchestras	3 "Electoral Sonatas"
1784	Applies officially for the position of the Court Organ Player's deputy—he is accepted, gets $70 annually	Piano Concerto E-flat Major. W o O. 4.
1787	Goes to Vienna, plays before Mozart, returns soon to Bonn	
1789	Beethoven's father expelled by the Elector for alcoholic excesses. Ludwig viola player at the theater	

[1] The exact dates of the origin of the works are frequently shrouded in darkness.

1791	Trip to Mergentheim	
1792	Haydn on his way back from England hears in Bonn a cantata composed by Beethoven November 10: Arrives in Vienna, where he lives until his death	
1793	Becomes Haydn's pupil	
1794	Has lessons from Albrechtsberger and Salieri. He stays with Prince Karl Lichnowsky	
1795	Proposes to singer Magdalena Willmann. First public appearance, at the Burgtheater, plays Piano Concerto in B, Opus 19 His brothers arrive in Vienna	3 trios in E♭, G, C Minor, Opus 1
1796	Makes concert tour to Prague and Berlin	
1797		*Sonate Pathétique,* in C Minor, Opus 13 Symphony No. 1, in C, Opus 21 3 trios, in G, D, C Minor, Opus 9
1799	Contests with Wölfl	
1800	First performance exclusively of his own works at the Court Theater First performance of the First Symphony, the Septet, and a piano concerto (in C major?) Prince Lichnowsky gives him a pension of $300 annually	Piano Concerto No. 3 in C Minor, Opus 37 Septet E♭ Opus 20 Sonata in F, Opus 17, for piano and French horn 6 Quartets, in F, G, D, C Minor, A, B, for 2 violins, viola, 'cello

Year	Event	Work
1800	Letter to Wegeler about his ear ailment	
1801	His friends, Stephan von Breuning and Ferdinand Ries, come to Vienna Gives piano lessons to Ries and Karl Czerny	
1802	Heiligenstädter Testament	Symphony No. 2, in D, Opus 36 2 Sonatas, in G and D minor, Opus 31 3 Sonatas for piano and violin in A, C minor, G, Opus 30
1803	First performance of the Second Symphony and the Piano Concerto in C minor First performance of the Sonata in A, Opus 47 (Kreutzer Sonata), for piano and violin Beethoven lives with Breuning, breaks with him	Symphony No. 3, in E♭, Opus 55 (*Eroica*) Sonata in A, Opus 47, for piano and violin (Kreutzer Sonata)
1804	Private performance of *Eroica* with Prince Lobkowitz's Orchestra	*Fidelio* (*Leonore*) Opus 72 Overtures: Leonore No. 1, in C, Opus 138; and Leonore No. 2, in C Sonata in C, Opus 53 *Andante favori*, in F Sonata in F, Opus 54 Sonata in F minor, Opus 57
1805	First public performance of the *Eroica* November 13: Napoleon's troops occupy Vienna November 20: *Fidelio* premiere at the Theater an der Wien	

1806	Visits Prince Lichnowsky at his estate in Silesia, breaks with him	Symphony No. 4, in B, Opus 60 Overture, Leonore No. 3, in C Piano Concerto No. 4, in G, Opus 58 Violin Concerto in D, Opus 61
1807	Concerts at Lobkowitz Palace. Performances of First, Second, and Third Symphonies; first performance of the Fourth, *Coriolanus* Overture, and Piano Concerto in G	Symphony No. 5, in C minor, Opus 67 Overture to Collin's *Coriolanus*, Opus 62 Razumovsky Quartets, Opus 59
1808	King Jerôme of Westphalia offers Beethoven a position as Hofkapellmeister First performance of the Fifth and Sixth Symphonies	Symphony No. 6 (*Pastorale*), in F, Opus 68 (finished 1808) 2 Trios, in D and E♭, Opus 70, for piano, violin, and 'cello
1809	Archduke Rudolph and the Princes Lobkowitz and Kinsky sign a contract for a pension for Beethoven of fl. 4000 annually for life Vienna again occupied by the French	Piano Concerto No. 5, in E♭, Opus 73 Sonata, *Les Adieux,* in E♭ Opus 81a Quartet in E♭, Opus 74
1810	Proposes to Therese Malfatti Bettina von Arnim in Vienna	Music for Goethe's *Egmont*, Opus 84 Quartet in F minor, Opus 95
1811	Pension reduced because of inflation Prince Lobkowitz under guardianship. Payments to Beethoven stop. First visit to Teplitz.	Symphony No. 7, in A, Opus 92 Symphony No. 8 in F, Opus 93 Trio in B♭, Opus 97 for piano, violin, 'cello Sonata in G, Opus 96, for piano and violin
1812	Meets Goethe in Teplitz	

Year	*Event*	*Work*
1813	First performance of the Seventh, and of *Wellington's Victory*	
1814	Beethoven's concert in the "Grosser Redoutensaal." Battle Symphony, Seventh Symphony First performance of the Eighth Symphony Plays the piano part of Trio Opus 97. His last appearance as player of chamber music Premiere of *Fidelio* in its third version	
1815	Court concert in the "Knights Hall" of the Hofburg Agreement with Kinsky's heirs and Lobkowitz Brother Karl dies in Vienna The City Council of Vienna makes him a citizen "without payment of a fee"	
1816	Becomes guardian for his nephew Karl, and sends him to the boarding school of Mr. del Rio	
1818	Takes Karl out of Rio's school and has the boy stay with him Karl's mother brings suit against Beethoven, which is dismissed The state court refers the suit to the city court. Beethoven takes the boy home again with him	Sonata in B, Opus 106

1819	The city court deprives Beethoven of the guardianship. He protests Beginning of the Conversation-books. Schindler's closer acquaintance with him	Work started on *Missa Solemnis*
1820	The court of appeals decides in Beethoven's favor	Sonata in E, Opus 109
1821	Sick with jaundice Arrested as vagabond	Sonata in A♭, Opus 110
1822	In negotiations about *Missa Solemnis* with Simrock, Schlesinger, Artaria, Peters, Diabelli, Steiner Rossini comes to see him *Fidelio* performed after a lapse of three years Prince Nikolaus Galitzin orders two or three string quartets	*Missa Solemnis,* in D, Opus 123, completed Symphony No. 9 begun Sonata in C minor, Opus 111
1823	Offers the *Missa Solemnis* to 15 potentates and gets 10 orders of 50 ducats each, equivalent to $1,200 in total In contact with Grillparzer, Weber, Liszt	Symphony No. 9, in D minor, Opus 125
1824	Eye trouble Louis XVIII of France sends a gold medal First performance of the *Missa Solemnis* in Petersburg In Vienna, first performance of three parts from the *Missa Solemnis,* Ninth Symphony, conducted by Umlauf	Quartet in E♭, Opus 127

Year	*Event*	*Work*
1824	Schott acquires *Missa Solemnis*, Ninth Symphony, Quartet Opus 127, all for $800 Invitation from the London Philharmonic Society to come to London for a guaranteed sum of 300 guineas	
1825	First performance of Quartet Opus 127 Seriously ill Karl in bad company. Beethoven therefore several times from Baden to Vienna. Beethoven deeply hurt. His ill health permanent Performance of the Ninth Symphony at the Rhenish Music Festival in Aix-la-Chapelle Private first performance of Quartet Opus 132 for a private circle of musicians and music lovers: Trio Opus 97, Quartet Opus 132. Beethoven conducts from the piano, later improvises on the piano	Quartet in A minor, Opus 132 Quartet in B♭, Opus 130
1825	Beethoven moves to the apartment in the Schwarzspanier Strasse. Sees Stephan v. Breuning often Numerous public performances of works of Beethoven	
1826	Illness. Eye ailment. Gout. Permanent sickness until March Public performance of Quartet Opus 130, with the fugue, through Schuppanzigh	Quartet in C # minor, Opus 131 Quartet in F, Opus 135 Finale of Quartet in B♭ Opus 130 (Opus 133)

Year	Life	Works
	Conferences for the oratorios *The Elements, Saul;* an opera for Berlin	
	Alterations on account of the nephew. His attempted suicide. Recuperates. Resolved: Karl must enter army. Beethoven with Karl goes to Gneixendorf, Johann's place.	
	Symptoms of dropsy	
	Desperately sick, back in Vienna	Sketches for Symphony No. 10
	December 20: First operation	
1827	Karl leaves to join his regiment	
	Three operations	
	Makes his will	
	Writes to the Philharmonic Society in London asking for support	
	March 26: Dies at 5 o'clock in the afternoon during a thunderstorm	

Acknowledgments

I am indebted to my wife Margaret von Gutfeld-Nettl for intensive assistance. Next to her my assistant Dr. F. T. Wessel was extremely helpful. He is also the contributor of several entries (F.T.W.). Other contributors include: Thomas Atchinson, Bloomington, Ind. (T.A.); Dr. Carol MacClintock, Bloomington, Ind. (C. Mac C.); Wyatt Insco, Bloomington, Ind. (W.I.); Dr. Oswald Jonas, Prof. Roosevelt Univ., (O.J.); Dr. Paul E. Mueller, Evanston, Ill., (P.E.M.); Dr. John H. Mueller, Prof., Indiana Univ., (J.H.M.); Albrecht Roeseler, Berlin (A.R.); Dr. W. Schweissheimer, Philadelphia, (W.S.); Dr. Frank Victor, New York, (F.V.); Dr. Serge Zenkowsky, Univ. of Michigan (S.Z.).

Finally the valuable help of Mrs. Eleanor Pelham, Indianapolis, should be gratefully acknowledged.

Works extensively used: Archiv fuer Musikwissenschaft (A.M.W.); Beethoven Gesamtausgabe, 1864-67, (G.A.); Beethoven, Saemtliche Briefe, ed. by Kalischer; Beethoven-Jahrbuch (Neues) ed. by Sandberger (N.B.J.); Bekker, Paul, Beethoven; Denkmaeler der Tonkunst in Oesterreich (D.T.Oe.); Denkmaeler deutscher Tonkunst (D.D.T.); Eitner: Biographisch-Bibliographisches Quellenlexikon (Eitner); Frimmel, Theodor, Beethoven-Handbuch; Frimmel, Theodor, Beethoven-Jahrbuch (B.J.B.); Jahrbuch der Musikbibliothek Peters (J.M.P.); Kinsky-Halm, Das Werk Beethovens, (Kinsky, K.); Musical Quarterly (M.Q.); Musik in Geschichte und Gegenwart (M.G.G.); Nottebohm, Beethoveniana (I) and Neue Beethoveniana (II); Nottebohm, Thematisches Verzeichnis der Werke von Beethoven; Rivista Musicale Italiana (R.M.I.); Sammelbaende der Internationalen Musikgesellschaft (I.M.G.); Schiedermair: Der Junge Beethoven; Wurzbach, Biographisches Lexikon des Kaiserthums Oesterreich (Wurzbach); Zeitschrift fuer Musikwissenschaft (Z.f.M.); Zeitschrift der Internationalen Musikgesellschaft (Z.I.M.G.).

As my manuscript was finished in 1954, the most important book by George Kinsky "Das Werk Beethovens" published in 1955, could not be used as extensively as desired by the author. However, important dates were compared and, if necessary, corrected. Kinsky's term "W o O." ("Werk ohne opus-no," Work without Opus-number) is also used here.

Book Ordering Information

Ask for any of the books listed below at your bookstore. Or to order direct from the publisher, call 1-800-447-BOOK (MasterCard or Visa), or send a check or money order for the books purchased (plus $4.00 shipping and handling for the first book ordered and 75¢ for each additional book) to Carol Publishing Group, 120 Enterprise Avenue, Dept. 1539, Secaucus, NJ 07094.

Broken Record: The Inside Story of the Grammy Awards by Henry Schipper
In this first-ever book about the intriguing, often hilarious and checkered history of the Grammys, it appears that the music industry's most prestigious award still remains its most conservative. Includes 16 pages of photographs.
$17.95 cloth 1-55972-104-9 (CAN $22.95)

The Beethoven Encyclopedia: His Life and Art From A to Z by Paul Nettl
A uniquevolume covering virtually every important date, event and aspect of the great composer's life, whether referring to his music, his patrons, his personal life, or the forces which inspired his genius.
$12.95 paper 0-8065-1539-2 (CAN $17.95)

Culture or Trash?: A Provocative View of Contemporary Painting, Sculpture and Other Costly Commodities by James Gardner
The art critic for The National Review takes a hard, critical look at the multi-billion dollar industry that calls itself contemporary art.
$19.95 cloth 1-55972-208-8 (CAN $24.95)

Evenings With Horowitz: An Intimate Portrait by David Dubal
Provides a revealing look at the triumphs and struggles, agony and ecstasy of the enigmatic pianist, who became a close, personal friend of the author's. Will be cherished by everyone who loves great music or simply loves this great talent. Includes 16 pages of photographs.
$21.95 cloth 1-55972-094-8 (CAN $27.95)
$14.95 paper 0-8065-1513-9 (CAN $18.95)

The Maestro Myth: Great Conductors in Pursuit of Power by Norman Lebrecht
"The liveliest, most penetrating and best-researched book on the nature of the orchestra conductor, and on the best-known past and current practitioners of that arcane art." --*Publishers Weekly*. Includes 16 pages of photographs, prints and drawings.
$22.50 cloth 1-55972-108-1
$14.95 paper 0-8065-1450-7

The Peter Pan Chronicles: The Nearly 100 Year History of the "Boy Who Wouldn't Grow Up" by Bruce K. Hanson
The colorful history of this beloved character—from his beginnings in a 1902 novel, through stage, screen and televison, and his latest incarnation in the Steven Spielberg film *Hook*. Oversized volume, profusely illustrated throughout with photographs and prints.
$21.95 cloth 1-55972-160-X (CAN $26.95)

(Prices subject to change; books subject to availability)

The Popular Guide to Classical Music by Dr. Anne Gray
Traces the evolution of classical music from the first instrument, to the history of the orchestra. Going beyond the usual encyclopedic approach, Dr. Gray offers engaging biographies and inspiring anecdotes from generations of composers, as well as the context in which they wrote their music. Includes 16 pages of photographs.
$24.95 cloth 1-55972-165-0 (CAN $30.95)

Revelations: The Autobiography of Alvin Ailey by Alvin Ailey, with A. Peter Bailey
The true life story of the pioneer African-American choreographer. A carefully private man, Ailey told his story toBailey, a journalist, and the result is his story in his own words, never-before-published until now. Includes 16 pages of photographs.
$19.95 cloth 1-55972-255-X (CAN $24.95)

The Spoils of War: The American Military's Role in Stealing Europe's Treasures by Kenneth D. Alford
What happened to those priceless, celebrated artworks and other valuable treasures procured by the Third Reich during the '30s and '40s. More than 50 years of research and documentation portrays the American military's role as both liberators...and plunderers. Illustrated with photographs.
$19.95 cloth 1-55972-237-1 (CAN $27.95)

Talks With Great Composers: Candid Conversations With Brahms, Puccini, Strauss and Others by Arthur M. Bell
Between 1890 and 1917, the author engaged in lengthy, candid conversations with the greatest composers of the day. The results is this probing and insightful volume that reveals the agony, triumphs and religiosity inherent to the creative mind. Includes 12 pages of photographs.
$9.95 paper 0-8065-1565-1 (CAN $13.95)

Vaslav Nijinsky: A Leap Into Madness by Peter Ostwald
Tells the tragic life story of one of the greatest ballet dancers of all time—a man who spent 30 years as a psychiatric patient, and dominated by a wife sho sought to maintin his image for her own selfish gain. Includes 16 pages of photographs.
$19.95 paper 0-8184-0535-X (CAN $24.95)

What's Your Opera IQ?: A Quiz Book for Opera Lovers by Iris Bass
100+ questions and answers revolving around opera lore and trivia, including • Who wrote what opera when? • Who sang which role in what opera? • and much more.
$8.95 paper 0-8065-1211-3 (CAN $11.95)